The New Entrepreneurial Age

To: Barbara

Best wishes

Larry C. Farrell

Brick Tower Press

Habent Sua Fata Libelli

Brick Tower Press
1230 Park Avenue
New York, New York 10128
Tel: 212-427-7139 • Fax: 212-860-8852
bricktower@aol.com • www.BrickTowerPress.com

Library of Congress Cataloging-in-Publication Data

Farrell, Larry C.
The New Entrepreneurial Age, Awakening the Spirit of Enterprise in People,
Companies, and Countries / Larry C. Farrell
   p.   cm.
   Includes index.
   ISBN-13: 978-1-883283-88-9, Trade Paper
   1. Entrepreneurship.   2. New business enterprises.   3. Industrial promotion.
I. Title.
HB615.F315   2011
658.4'21—dc21

   Library of Congress Control Number: 2011927472
   Business/Economics, Entrepreneurship

April 2011

The *New* Entrepreneurial Age

Awakening The Spirit Of Enterprise

In People, Companies, And Countries

Interviews and lessons from
the world's great entrepreneurs

Includes, for the first time, application exercises from
The Farrell Company's acclaimed seminars
used by over 5 million participants!

Larry C. Farrell

The World's Most Experienced Authority
On Researching And Teaching Entrepreneurship

"Bigger is better turned out to be another 20th century myth. Larry Farrell has eloquently described why."

—Peter Drucker,
The 20th Century's Greatest
Management Thinker

"If you want to learn about international entrepreneurism, Larry Farrell is your man."

—Tom Peters,
The World's All-time
Best Selling Business Author

"Larry Farrell's enthusiasm, grounded in years of working with aspiring and successful entrepreneurs, is contagious. *The New Entrepreneurial Age* will inspire anyone who has ever dreamed of creating a business, as well as corporate CEOs looking to instill an entrepreneurial spirit across their companies, and even government leaders hoping to jump-start economic development."

—Matthew Budman,
Editor-in-Chief,
The Conference Board Review, New York

"No one captures the spirit and passion of the entrepreneur like Larry Farrell! He provides the road map, the wisdom, the vision and the motivation for all of us to act on our entrepreneurial dreams."

—Howard Jung,
Chairman of the Board, Ace Hardware, Inc.

"Larry Farrell's books and ideas on entrepreneurship are very popular in China. *The New Entrepreneurial Age* will also be well received here. Since 2004 we've had a productive collaboration and our joint venture business in China is producing good results for our clients—and for us."
    —Dr. Zheng Li,
            Vice Dean, School of Economics, Jilin University, China
            Author,
            Creating An Entrepreneurial Economy: Theory and Policy

"India has reached an important threshold when it comes to entrepreneurship. Larry Farrell's experience and expertise will be of great help to the aspiring entrepreneurs of India—and around the globe. Having worked with Larry for the past couple of years, and knowing his deep knowledge of the topic, his latest book, *The New Entrepreneurial Age*, has immense relevance for India."

    —Bipin Chandran,
            Chief Editor, *Entrepreneur Magazine*, India

"The global entrepreneurship revolution has great economic and social potential. But for that potential to be fulfilled, entrepreneurship needs practical wisdom. For over thirty years, Larry Farrell has been sharing his abundance of such wisdom with individuals, universities, businesses and governments around the world. *The New Entrepreneurial Age* reflects the breadth of that audience and crystallizes his thinking."

    —Dr. Peter Heslam, Director,
            Transforming Business—Enterprise Solutions to
            Poverty Project
            Cambridge University, UK

"Larry Farrell has done it again! *The New Entrepreneurial Age* offers readers an engaging, thought-provoking, and contemporary perspective on the "economic power of entrepreneurship." At both JA and Laureate I have witnessed first-hand the legacy of Larry's work through its application to middle school, high school, and university students. This book is his most comprehensive and enlightening work to date!"

> —Darrell Luzzo, Ph.D.,
> Vice President, Product Strategy & Development,
> Laureate Education, Inc.
> (Former Senior Vice President of Education,
> Junior Achievement Worldwide)

"Larry Farrell's passion and commitment for entrepreneurial development, as well as his lifetime of real world experience, combine to help organizations achieve the growth and development of entrepreneurs at every level of capability. His expertise and support helped my tribal community members gain the insight and courage to move forward with their own start-up business planning and implementation."

> —Jamie Fullmer, CEO, Blue Stone Strategy Group
> (Former Chairman, Yavapai-Apache Nation, Arizona)

"Larry Farrell's insight and vision have helped ordinary people do extraordinary things. His latest book is an essential toolkit for: students, early stage and established entrepreneurs, investors and policy makers alike. We are delighted to have him partnering with us."

> —Terri Scott, President,
> Institute of Technology Sligo, Ireland
> (Former Managing Director,
> Invest Northern Ireland, Government of UK & NI)

Table of Contents

PART ONE: ENTREPRENEURIAL PEOPLE
Getting Entrepreneurial—Fending For Yourself
In A Downsized And Uncertain World

PART TWO: ENTREPRENEURIAL COMPANIES
Corporate Entrepreneurship—Reviving The
Spirit of Enterprise In Your Organization

APPLICATIONS: Entrepreneurial Companies
—*The Spirit of Enterprise Seminar*

PART THREE: ENTREPRENEURIAL COUNTRIES
Creating An Entrepreneurial Economy—To Win
The 21ˢᵗ Century Global Economic War

Acknowledgments

The New Entrepreneurial Age is my fourth book over the past two decades. One thing I have learned about writing books is that it can be a lonely job. At the same time, rather paradoxically, succeeding at this lonely endeavor requires a large network of active supporters and allies.

For me, the first level of support has always come from family. Certainly with this book, I'm deeply indebted to Sylvia, my beautiful new wife and long ago childhood sweetheart in Arizona. She has endured long, quiet weeks and months while I completed the book. Her sweet, supportive nature actually made the task easy and enjoyable.

Another level of essential supporters and allies is made up of the great entrepreneurs I interviewed and researched for the book. Without their willingness to share their personal stories, for no personal gain I might add, I would not be able to write these books. In this regard, I must also thank several of my business affiliates around the world who helped arrange some of the amazing interviews in the book.

Next, of course, are the publishing pros who make it all possible. Once again I'm indebted to my literary agent, Bob Diforio, who first inspired me to write and has been there for all four of my books. Bob has been a friend since our days together at Harvard Business School and literally changed my professional life when he encouraged me to write my first book. I must also thank John Colby, the innovative Publisher of Brick Tower Press in New York, for taking on the publishing investment and risk in spite of the lingering, deep recession. And as a further sign of the times, John is the first publisher I've had who insisted on acquiring the e-book rights along with the standard print version rights.

Finally, I want to acknowledge and thank, in advance, all the readers of the book. They are all members of that elite crowd who are seeking to better understand and use the great potential of the entrepreneurial spirit—whether as individual enterprisers, corporate executives, or government economic leaders. *The New Entrepreneurial Age* has been written for them and I wish them all great success as they pursue their own entrepreneurial dreams, plans and projects.

Preface

"You can say everything that needs to be said about entrepreneurship in one paragraph."

—Tom Peters
The world's best selling business author

There's nothing like a severe, unexpected, worldwide recession to get one's entrepreneurial juices flowing. After the initial shock and trauma pass, it finally hits home that you can't trust anyone to run the damn economy and save your job: elected politicians—liberal or conservative, big business tycoons (who by the way are *still* making 350 times their average employees pay!), big labor bosses (economic luddites by definition) or even Nobel Prize winning economists—whether right wingers like Friedman or left wingers like Krugman. You're headed for your own special moment of truth when you finally realize that you're going to have to start fending for yourself to survive this economic mess. Well, that moment has come brother (and sister)—because you're truly on your own in this crazy and uncertain 21st century global economy!

The good news is, if you're fed up with the same old hit-or-miss economic theories and political promises—and are looking for new, reliable answers—you've come to the right place. **The New Entrepreneurial Age** answer is very simple: old-fashioned entrepreneurship is still the best and safest tool ever invented to create prosperity for people, companies and entire countries. In fact, the combination of the world's economic crisis, along with the global acceptance of a *new* entrepreneurial age, makes right now the best time in all history to take advantage of the amazing power of the entrepreneurial spirit. The evidence is everywhere. Millions of new individual entrepreneurs, corporate managers, and government leaders all around the world are proving it every day. So why not give it a try yourself?

HOW TIMES HAVE CHANGED!

This hasn't always been the case. A little over a quarter century ago, when my old friend and former business partner Tom Peters heard that I was keen on researching, writing about and teaching entrepreneurship, he warned: "You can say everything that needs to be said about entrepreneurship in one paragraph." The implication was clear: Stick with the still popular big business management stuff he had written about in his all-time best-selling book *In Search of Excellence*—and a dozen more books since.

An even more telling example of the different world we live in today was the memorable, knee-jerk response I got on my very first attempt to sell our new seminar on "corporate entrepreneurship." After making my pitch, Bill Wilson, the picture perfect IBM Vice President who ran the Hong Kong/China Region, leaned back in his chair, rolled his eyes upward and said: "Why would we want to train our managers to be like entrepreneurs . . . We're IBM . . ." To Wilson's everlasting credit, and with my ever-lasting thanks, he did finally agree to give our seminar a try and IBM became our very first client in December, 1984. Of course the handwriting was already on the wall at IBM. Over the next decade Big Blue was forced to do what its great founder, Thomas J. Watson, said would never be done, and ravaged its workforce by downsizing 180,000 employees. Bill Wilson probably saw the early signs and figured why not give this crazy new seminar a try—nothing else seemed to be working.

Looking back to our own start-up time, who could blame Tom Peters, IBM executives, or anyone else for pooh-poohing my newfound obsession with entrepreneurship way back in 1983? It was still all about *management* in those days. Starting a small business was something you did if you couldn't get a "real job" at a *Fortune 500* blue-chip outfit like GM or Citibank or of course IBM.

We now know how shortsighted that was! People simply hadn't yet recognized that entrepreneurship was the greatest economic growth tool ever invented and that entrepreneurial start-ups, not giant corporations, were becoming the *real* engines of prosperity around the world. Indeed, at that time the business press rarely even talked about the entrepreneurial small business sector and the fact that it was creating 80 to 90 percent of all new jobs—even then. And certainly, back in those days, when Communist leaders were still threatening to bury capitalism, no one could predict that by the 21st century, the old Soviet Union countries and The People's Republic of China would become the entrepreneurial hubs of Europe and Asia.

Well, three decades later, after researching thousands of real entrepreneurs and teaching their proven high-growth practices to millions of individual, corporate and government students—plus writing four books of my own on the power of the entrepreneurial spirit—I'd have to say that either the great Tom Peters got it wrong or it's taken me a hell of a long time to get that paragraph just right. And for the record, fostering "corporate entrepreneurs" has become a mainstream competitive strategy for much of big business today—so Bill Wilson was a trail-blazing business pioneer even if he didn't realize it at the time!

> *"Why would we want to train our managers to be like entrepreneurs?*
> *We're IBM."*
>
> —Bill Wilson, Regional V. P.
> IBM Hong Kong & China

ENTREPRENEURIAL PEOPLE, COMPANIES, AND COUNTRIES

The *New* Entrepreneurial Age, my fourth book, brings forward the very best of all our previous research and writing—combined with an up-to-the-minute accounting of everything we've learned in helping people, companies, and governments around the world apply the power of entrepreneurship.* The number and variety of entrepreneurial programs and projects The Farrell Company has been involved in has literally exploded over the past quarter-century. They touch all kinds of people and all types of organizations. They range from teaching middle and high school students, to helping universities develop entrepreneurial curriculum and programs, to training classic individual start-up entrepreneurs, to assisting *Fortune 500* executive teams re-instill high growth entrepreneurial basics in their business, to teaching myriads of social entrepreneurs, to even advising national governments on how to create a more entrepreneurial economy. Today, with affiliates in Asia, Europe, Latin America and Africa, over 5 million students in 40 countries, across 8 languages, have attended our programs. The fact is, we've taught entrepreneurship to more individuals, companies, and governments than any university or training firm in the world! With this book, I want to describe and distill in one place, our global experience with all these applications, new and old, for the benefit of readers everywhere.

The core message is that the entrepreneurial spirit can and should be applied to three broad economic areas: individual achievement, organizational success, and national economic development. The question is, how exactly do we do that? Are there common principles to be followed in unlocking the treasures of "the **new** entrepreneurial age?" Our three decades of researching and teaching entrepreneurial practices says—yes! And that's exactly what this entire book is about.

And in a final salute to the still great Tom Peters, somewhere among all these words and ideas, I hope I've covered that all-important paragraph! Even more importantly, I hope *you* will find a few helpful and inspiring ideas for yourself, your company, and even your country in the book.

Larry C. Farrell
Arizona & Virginia
March, 2011

* For the first time, I've also included in this book all the Application exercises we use in our seminars for individuals, companies and governments around the world. You'll find the appropriate set of Applications at the end of each Part of the book. Enjoy and learn!

Introduction

Welcome To The New Entrepreneurial Age

"Bigger is better turned out to be another20th century myth. Larry Farrell has eloquently described why."

—Peter Drucker

I had just addressed *Business Week's* Asian CEO Conference in Taipei, and was waiting nervously for the grand old man of management to follow me to the podium. I had delivered my standard pitch that big business management theory was mostly nonsense and would never be a match for old-fashioned entrepreneurship—with Peter Drucker, the father of modern management, sitting in the first row staring at me. Drucker was not known for subtlety. After all, this was the same man that called *In Search Of Excellence* "a book for juveniles." So I was preparing myself for public humiliation and probable early retirement as a *Business Week* speaker after he got through with me. However, to my everlasting gratitude, Dr. Drucker's opening comment was: "Bigger is better turned out to be another 20th century myth. Larry Farrell has eloquently described why." Many people at the conference, including the *Business Week* brass, would later shake my hand, give that knowing nod, and congratulate me for "getting it right" according to the master. Of course, Drucker's supportive comment was referring to my depiction of "The Life Cycle Of All Organizations" which underpins all our research on entrepreneurial practices—as shown below.

Drucker later explained to me in private that only recently had it become so clear to him that size, mass, and economy of scale, at some critical point, begin to make companies less competitive, not more. He called them oversized and over managed. He noted that in almost all industries, the best company, certainly the most profitable one, is rarely the biggest. He even confided that he no longer accepted consulting requests from giant companies: "You can give them the best advice in the world, and they just can't implement it. It's so frustrating; I've stopped trying to tell them anything." Most management gurus last century kept telling us in no uncertain terms that bigger is always better. We all bought in and as with most big myths in life, we've learned the hard way it just isn't so.

THE LIFE CYCLE OF ALL ORGANIZATIONS

"Now I see the problem with lifetime employment.
People live longer than their companies."

—Japanese Manager
Texas Instruments, Japan

At a lecture in Tokyo several years ago, I was showing a slide with this rather startling statistic: "Of the hundred largest U.S. companies in 1900, only 16 are still in business." The Japanese manager from Texas Instruments was attempting humor, but his joke actually lays bare a sobering fact of life about organizations. Companies, like people, and countries, and everything else on the planet, exist in a life cycle. There's creation followed by growth. Growth peaks and decline sets in, leading ultimately to death. And of course there's always the possibility of *untimely death* along the way. Beating this cycle is tough indeed.

THE LIFE CYCLE OF ALL ORGANIZATIONS

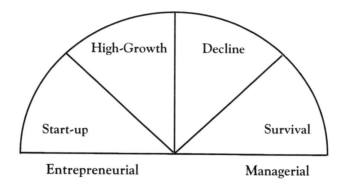

All companies begin with an abundance of the entrepreneurial spirit, inspiring workers as well as owners. Basic entrepreneurial practices fuel the start-up and drive the company well into a phase of high growth. During the start-up and high growth eras, everyone is fixated on a few fundamental notions such as making great products that customers will buy because it's the only way to get paid.

The resultant high growth gets you size. And the passage of time gets you new leaders. The new leaders are almost always professional managers. These subtle shifts in size and leadership produce a new set of objectives. Presto! Planning, streamlining and controlling the enterprise become the new order. Managing this and that become more important than making this and selling that. The highest paid jobs become managing other managers. Meetings, reports and bureaucracy erupt on every front. And slowly but surely, lost in the shuffle are the simple, basic entrepreneurial thrusts that got you going in the first place.

The dominant style of companies on the right hand side of the cycle—the larger and more mature organizations—is "managerial." These companies are typically past their prime and on the down-side of the cycle. Even so, it is the study of these companies, by the business schools and management consultants that serve them, that has produced most of the management theories and fads over the past 50 years.

Conversely, the growth phases on the left-hand side of the cycle are highly "entrepreneurial." The behaviors and practices of the entrepreneurs and their employees during the start-up and high-growth phases of the life cycle have historically been of little interest to the Harvards and McKinseys of the world. This is precisely where we part company with such blue-chip management experts. It seems pretty obvious that it's a lot more valuable to learn how to create and maintain a high-growth enterprise than it is to learn how to manage a declining bureaucracy.

The important questions are why do companies almost always make the shift from high growth to decline and what can be done about it? Indeed, what really caused 84% of America's biggest, richest, most powerful companies to bite the dust in less than a century? It's clear that beating the natural life cycle is tough indeed. It is incredible, even paradoxical, that the high growth that all managers want to achieve produces the mass and weight which in turn produces a growing bureaucracy. To add to the burgeoning problems, the new leaders know next to nothing about the entrepreneurial approach to running a business. This is a deadly combination; too much managing against too little entrepreneuring sets in motion the painful cycle of decline. As the company reaches "mid-life," it's big and bureaucratic and the entrepreneurial spirit becomes buried under an avalanche of bureaucracy and management theory—a classic example of throwing out the baby with the bathwater.

The logical solution is to reverse the organization life cycle, and move back to the high growth phase. To do this, high growth entrepreneurial practices have to be re-instilled in the company. This of course assumes that managers and employees know what they are and how to use them. But that shouldn't be a problem. They're pretty simple actually. After all, this isn't brain surgery or flying to the moon. It's just business.

THE FUNDAMENTAL PRACTICES OF THE WORLD'S GREAT ENTREPRENEURS

"The conduct of successful business merely consists in doing things in a very simple way, doing them regularly and never neglecting to do them."

—William Hesketh Lever
Founder, Lever Brothers (Unilever)

What are those things we must do simply, regularly, and never forget to do? You won't find them on the managerial side of the cycle. They're not the things that business schools teach or management consultants preach. If you want to find the bedrock fundamentals of enterprise, those simple things practiced obsessively, you've got to look at the entrepreneurial phase of business. Here you will find the lessons of the world's greatest enterprisers, from past masters such as Lever, Matsushita and Disney, to more recent icons like Honda, Walton, Roddick, Branson and Jobs. When you think about it, if you're searching for the basics of enterprise, why would you look anywhere else?

• **Sense Of Mission**

"A decrease in profit . . . or a loss of revenue is proof that we have not fulfilled our obligations to society."

—Konosuke Matsushita, Founder
Matsushita Electric

High-minded? You bet. The fact is entrepreneurs believe they are doing something important in the world. They believe they're creating value for customers, employees and of course themselves. We call it having a "sense of mission" about their work. Such high purpose however, gets quickly translated into two very practical questions: *What* to do (essentially what products for what customers) and *How* to go about doing it? To legendary entrepreneurs like Matsushita, Lever and

Watson, these simple words are the two most important questions in business. In modern management lingo, the entrepreneurial "What" and "How" is a no-frills version of corporate strategy and corporate culture. Unfortunately, in many big companies, strategy and culture live in separate universes—one the domain of number-crunching planners, the other the province of touchy-feely culture gurus. In too many big companies, neither have much to do with the real running of the business. In stark contrast, the entrepreneur lives and dies on his answers to what and how—and they're inextricably connected.

"Strategy" isn't a week in Bermuda with the consultants. It's a matter of survival. What products you're going to make and in what markets you're going to sell them is the whole ball-game. And when you get right down to it, it doesn't matter if you do strategy on the back of a napkin, or use ten pound planning books. The part you absolutely have to get right is: what products and what markets. On the other hand, the purpose of creating a company culture is not to make more wall plaques or hold more meetings to bounce around soft, side issues of the business. The only purpose is to get everyone focused on those few values that will give you the competitive advantage to make the business strategy come true. When the values directly support the product/market strategy, watch out! It's the most powerful way known to energize a group of individuals to achieve a common purpose.

Consider a company like 3M where growth from new products is the corporate strategy—and innovation has been the central value since six Minnesota miners ended up owning a worthless gravel pit and invented sandpaper. Today with $23 billion in sales and 60,000 products, this value permeates the entire company. Inventing products is the culture. Every employee knows it. The result? 3M has the highest ratio of new product revenue (30% plus) of any large company in the world. Would 3M achieve this remarkable strategic result, without a powerful and pervasive culture of innovative action? Never in a hundred years.

•Customer/Product Vision

*"The computer is the most remarkable tool we've ever built. . . . but the
most important thing is to get them in the hands
of as many people as possible."*

—Steve Jobs, Founder
Apple Computer, NeXT Inc., Pixar

Steve Jobs wasn't talking about how to manage, or the latest marketing technique, or even how to grow Apple Computer. He was, and still is, obsessed with the two most fundamental ideas in enterprise—customer and product. He said the only thing more important than making computers, was having satisfied customers actually use them. Of course along the way, Apple reached the Fortune 500 roster faster than any company in history.

What was the big secret? Jobs had a big vision. A vision of "the most remarkable tool we've ever built." But then he says: "the most important thing" is to get them used in every office, in every home, and by every child in every classroom. Like no other computer maker, Jobs understood the needs of naive users. That's why Apple made them inexpensive, easy to learn and fun to use. Jobs was an expert on both products and customers. The classic vision of an entrepreneur.

The really important lesson of Jobs and most great entrepreneurs is that at heart they are craftsmen. They have a single, integrated vision of customers and products. They know they need both to survive. They are, in fact, obsessed with making products that customers will buy. But along came the modern functional organization, in its all-out quest for efficiency, and in one fell swoop the craftsman was killed. The functional separation of customer and product is the single most devastating blow to the entrepreneurial spirit ever concocted by management science.

This is not a theoretical problem. Losing the entrepreneur's integrated vision of customer and product can cost you dearly. The classic example is Xerox, which has lost billions over the years by inventing products in California that Marketing, 3,000 miles away in Connecticut, simply never got around to selling. The first personal computer—the first fax machine—the first laser printer—the list goes on and on. Today companies all over the world are trying to put their functionalized organizations back together. They could have saved themselves a lot of trouble by watching Mr. Toyoda at Toyota. In 1947, on his only trip to America, he became fascinated with the supermarkets' daily delivery of milk from the cow to the customer. He saw this as the ultimate customer driven organization. He decided to make cars this way. He organized horizontally, called it *kanban* and the rest is history.

To regain customer/product vision, you can start by tossing out those convoluted five page job descriptions and replace them with three simple questions: Who are my customers? What are my products? And what must I do to satisfy my customers? The message is everyone has a small business to run. This sounds simple but the number of employees who can't answer these basic questions can be shocking. And a final thought—it's not a one year program. It has to be a lifetime obsession, as it was for Charles Forte. From one sweet shop on Oxford Street to the 900 hotels in the Trusthouse Forte empire, he was absolutely consistent on product quality and customer service—and he worked at it for sixty-five years. It may sound monotonous but it has one redeeming virtue; if you do it long enough and hard enough, you get very, very good at it.

•High-speed Innovation

"We Japanese are obsessed with survival."

—Akio Morita, Founder
Sony Corporation

High-speed Innovation is the entrepreneur's ultimate weapon—and it's virtually free. Entrepreneurial Davids like nothing better than competing against muscle-bound Goliaths. So where does high speed innovation come from? For starters you can be sure it's not a genetic trait. And the current fads of setting up innovation departments or hiring consultants to teach creativity miss the point by a mile. It's a natural, human response we all possess, and the bottom line is: "anyone can be innovative and move with the speed of light if their life depends on it." We all know that more gets done in a day of crisis than a month of complacency. The trick then is how to keep this sense of urgency alive in the business—so that innovation becomes a necessity, and everyone has the freedom to act, and act quickly.

While the rest of the world were convincing themselves the Japanese weren't innovators, Akio Morita was crawling around on his hands and knees in a bombed out building in Tokyo, cutting long strips of newsprint and coating it with ferrous oxide to make recording tape. Like everyone else in post-war Japan, the young founder of Sony was "obsessed with survival." With no jobs, money or raw materials, creating something that someone might buy was an absolute necessity to putting rice on the table. This goes to the heart of the matter, proving once again that necessity is the mother of invention. It also helps explain why a too big, too comfortable bureaucracy is the last place you'll find high-speed innovation. But you don't have to wait for disaster to strike to get your innovative juices flowing. You can start today. A daily dose of urgency and an occasional injection of crisis are guaranteed to conquer anyone's complacency.

Just moving quickly could be the greatest innovation of all for big business. But what it takes is the freedom to act, not exactly an abundant resource in procedure-driven companies. Take the race against time to dominate the world's newest super-industry, Bio-tech. An industry promising more change in medicine and agriculture in the next ten years than in the last hundred—and a huge $100 billion market. Actually the race is over and the entrepreneurs have won hands down. While the giant pharmaceuticals researched it to death through layers of management, a thousand scientist-turned-entrepreneur start-ups have exploded on the scene since 1980. As Ed Penhoet, Ph.D. and founder of industry star Chiron, says: "Everyone's smart in the field, but smart doesn't make it. Bio-tech is a horse race. Getting to the finish line first is what counts." High-speed innovation could be anyone's or any organization's ultimate weapon. Why not? All it takes is feeling the necessity to do it better—and the freedom to do it faster.

•Self-inspired Behavior

"I'm looking for people who love to win.
If I run out of those, I want people who hate to lose."

—Ross Perot, Founder
EDS, Perot Systems

Self-inspired behavior is perhaps the sharpest difference of all between entrepreneurs and bureaucrats. But what does it actually mean? What are entrepreneurs self-inspired to do? When I think of legends like Perot, or William Lever, or Soichiro Honda, a couple of images always come to mind. First, they love what they do—they're highly committed to their work. And second, they constantly try to get better at what they do—their performance is high. These two ideas, high commitment and high performance, are the backbone of an entrepreneurial approach to work. When you think about it, it's pretty tough to beat people who love what they do and are damn good at doing it.

The much tougher question is how do we create self-inspired employees? Along-side Lever and Honda, no company leader ever did a better job at this than Ross Perot, the quintessential American entrepreneur. Of course it's also Perot who loves to fire off Texas sized sound-bites like: "people who love to win and hate to lose." This one however, is based on a very solid idea. It's the idea that drives almost all human behavior. Since the beginning of time people have tended to behave in their own self-interest: they do things that bring them positive consequences and they avoid doing things that bring negative consequences. What this really means at work is that everybody wants an answer to the eternal question: "what's in it for me if I do, and what happens to me if I don't?"

Entrepreneurs are mightily self-inspired to win and not lose because they face the consequences, positive or negative, of their behavior every day. This almost never happens in a bureaucracy. In some companies, nothing much good happens to people even when they and the company perform well. In other companies, everyone gets a pat on the back and an annual merit increase even if the enterprise is headed for the trash heap. The most common situation however, is the complete absence of either positives or negatives. Managers and workers just float in perpetual limbo, oblivious to the fortunes or misfortunes of the company and their part in it all. If you boil it down to one thing, the single biggest difference between entrepreneurial and bureaucratic behavior is answering the "what's in it for me" question. Entrepreneurs get their answers powerfully and frequently. Companies must do the same if they're really looking for extreme performance and commitment from workers. You're never going to revive the enterprise if you can't revive the enterprisers.

HISTORICAL PERSPECTIVE

In summary, a little economic history might put all this in perspective. The nineteenth century gave us the Industrial Age, driven by a relative handful of great entrepreneurial tycoons or, as some called them, robber barons. Entrepreneurship was the exclusive domain of the Levers, Carnegies, and Rockefellers. To control the emerging, sprawling empires of the Industrial Age, the twentieth century produced the Managerial Age. An army of consultants and B-school professors began spreading practices and theories worldwide and, in the process, so downgraded entrepreneurship that it practically became a dirty word by the 1960s and '70s.

Building on—but in many important ways rebelling against—this two-hundred- year backdrop, the twenty-first century is clearly shaping up as 'the entrepreneurial age.' This new economic era, which actually began in the late 1980s, is unlike anything we've ever seen in its depth and scope. It is being led by ordinary individuals of all ethnic and political persuasions and is affecting hundreds of millions of people in every corner of the globe. Meanwhile, those same *Fortune 500* companies that gave us the "organization man" are today promoting a culture of "corporate entrepreneurship" as a way to compete and survive in the global economy. Government leaders of all political stripes have also finally discovered that developing a more entrepreneurial economy is the best way to create jobs and achieve sustainable economic development. It's difficult to summarize in a paragraph the importance of entrepreneurship to individual people, companies, and countries, but here's a thumbnail sketch of each:

•Entrepreneurial People

The growing popularity of individual entrepreneurship, propelled by the folk-hero status of the likes of Steve Jobs and Richard Branson, has captured the imagination of people everywhere, especially the young. The fact is, getting entrepreneurial could very well be the best weapon for individuals to prosper in the future world economy. It's no longer an alternative lifestyle for a few go-getters. Preparing yourself to survive by your own wits is an absolute necessity in a downsized and uncertain world. Indeed, it seems everyone these days is thinking about entrepreneurship. And well they should. It is truly everyone's last line of defense.

As a subset of individual entrepreneurism, I'm happy to report that the 'education world' has finally caught up with the 'real world' in terms of preparing young people to consider becoming an entrepreneur as realistic a career option as going to work for a company or the government. At the middle and high school level, I'm very proud to say that Junior Achievement Worldwide, the largest educational institution in the world, reaching some 10 million kids a year, has adopted our *Getting Entrepreneurial!* curriculum for their entrepreneur development programs around the world. This is a massive undertaking. The *JA It's My Business* program for middle school, and the *JA Be Entrepreneurial* program for high school, will teach entrepreneurial skills to more students every year than all the business schools in the world combined! We've also worked with many great universities around the world on their entrepreneurship programs and centers such as: Cambridge in the

UK (where the focus is on using entrepreneurship to alleviate poverty), Ateneo in the Philippines, Jilin in China, KIBS in India and Oklahoma City University and Cal-Tech in the U.S.

A particularly exciting and ground-breaking university project we've just started is in Ireland. The government of Ireland has funded a nation-wide program called "Accelerating Campus Entrepreneurship." The "ACE" initiative mandates that every Irish university student must take at least an introductory course on entrepreneurship. The Farrell Company was selected six months ago as the outside firm to assist the overall effort by providing curriculum development and instructor-training support. It's a big, long-term project to get Ireland on a more entrepreneurial track for the future—all driven by the current difficult economic times in the country. The bottom line is, there is no hotter curriculum today in schools and universities than courses on individual entrepreneurship!

•Entrepreneurial Companies

After decades of trying to manage themselves out of their bureaucratic structures and anemic growth, executives at large organizations are fighting for survival in the super-competitive global economy. 'Corporate entrepreneurship' has become the new organizational mantra for much of big business today. This market segment has always been our largest source of revenue and we're proud to list hundreds of blue-chip companies as clients ranging from: IBM and American Express in the U.S., to Unilever and Finnair in Europe, to Singapore Technologies and Matsushita in Asia, to Banco Itau and Carvajal in Latin America, to numerous clients in emerging markets such as Crescent Petroleum in the Middle East and Sasol in Africa. These and other *Fortune 1000* type companies want divisions full of corporate entrepreneurs, not 'men in gray flannel suits.' The need to re-instill an entrepreneurial spirit of enterprise is great in all organizations—from "Global 1,000" giants trying to compete with smaller, more innovative, and usually cheaper upstarts, to growing mid-sized companies fending off a mushrooming bureaucracy. In a world where 70 percent of the original 1955 *Fortune 500* is gone and where half of all economic growth now comes from industries that didn't exist twenty-five years ago, becoming an entrepreneurial organization is the only way to stay in the game.

And this goes doubly for the exploding new world of 'social entrepreneurship,' which has become the preferred management style in the non-profit sector just as 'corporate entrepreneurship' has in the private sector. Always a tough, competitive business, the U.S. leads the world in the number of non-profits with a staggering 60,000 such organizations in 2010 (up from just 15,000 in 1964) raising and spending some $300 billion each year. The wide-spread acceptance of 'social entrepreneurship' in the non-profit world is a telling example of the near universal appeal of applying entrepreneurial practices in non-traditional areas.

As a cross-over project back to the education world, and illustrative of the growing popularity of social entrepreneurship, we've just developed an on-line 'social entrepreneurship' course for Walden University, the flagship school of Laureate Education Group, which owns some 45 universities around the world. The course is based on my earlier *Getting Entrepreneurial!* book which is also the required text for the students. Happily, Walden's on-line Social Entrepreneurship course is up and running as I write.

• Entrepreneurial Countries

The idea that entrepreneurship is the driving force of national prosperity has become a central theme of politicians and economists all around the world. There is today a high level of investment in entrepreneur development by governments hoping to foster a more entrepreneurial economy to create jobs and spur economic growth. This huge shift in government economic development policy began only about 15 years ago. The old idea of using generous tax incentives to entice big companies to relocate their plants to a particular city or state was never a sound long-term strategy. In our current "race-to-the-bottom" global economy, the day a less expensive labor market appeared on the scene (China, India, Indonesia, etc) the local plant was shuttered forever. The preference today is to create permanent companies and jobs with long-term ties to the locale. The economic development slogan has shifted from "let's beg another *Toyota* to build their next plant in our town" to "lets identify and help our own *Bill Gates* start-up a company in our town."

From China, Northern Ireland and Brazil to New York City and the Yavapai-Apache Nation in Arizona, the governments with which we have worked are re-thinking the basic economic-development theories of the past century. They are all exploring and experimenting with the most important new application of entrepreneurship—transforming their no-growth or declining economies into high growth and job creating countries, states and cities. The end result could be nothing less than unlocking the greatest unsolved mystery in economics: why some nations and societies get rich while others remain poor.

THE NEW ENTREPRENEURIAL AGE

"The inclination of my life—has been to do things and make things which will give pleasure to people in new and amazing ways. By doing that I please and satisfy myself"

—Walt Disney, Founder
The Walt Disney Company

Today, for the first time in history, the entire world is moving in the same economic direction. Both of the 20th century's great experiments, big business and big government, seem to have run their course, at least in the hearts and minds of the public. In their place has come a mighty, global push for searching out and reviving the entrepreneurial spirit in ordinary people, companies and entire countries. The available evidence does point to one simple truth: the entrepreneurial spirit is the best model ever invented for creating growth and prosperity. And in a rare display of agreement, business and government leaders, economists, the press, and even much of academia have bought in. So the operative question becomes, what exactly is the entrepreneurial spirit, and how can we use it in our work and life?

Walt Disney said it best. He described the four fundamental practices of entrepreneurs perfectly: "Inclination" as mission, "making things and giving pleasure to people" is all about customer/product vision, "new and exciting ways"—a perfect description of innovation, and finally, "by doing that I please and satisfy myself" says I am self-inspired by my work. In this book we've short-handed those entrepreneurial basics as follows:

The Four Entrepreneurial Basics

Sense of Mission
The Entrepreneurial Way To Deliver Product/Market Winners

Customer/Product Vision
Entrepreneurial Passion To Produce Continuous Growth

High-speed Innovation
The Entrepreneur's Secret Weapon To Beat The Competition

Self-inspired Behavior
The Power Of Loving What You Do
And Getting Very Good At Doing It

Achieving Disney-like appreciation for, and familiarity with, these common sense business practices is what I hope you will take away from this book. The goal is simple, yet profound: to learn and apply the entrepreneurial basics to create growing prosperity for yourself, your company and your country—in our downsized and uncertain 21st Century global economy.

PART ONE

Entrepreneurial People

Getting Entrepreneurial —Fending For Yourself In A Downsized And Uncertain World

Chapter 1

The New Entrepreneurs

They Are Us

"As I said, everybody here has the ability to do absolutely anything I do and much beyond. Some of you will, and some of you won't. For the ones who won't, it will be because you get in your own way, not because the world doesn't allow you."

—Warren Buffett, Founder
Berkshire Hathaway

Look around you. Seventy out of the next one hundred people you see are thinking about becoming an entrepreneur. Fifteen of the hundred will actually give it a go in the next 12 months. At least five will be successful on their first try. All of them, the dreamers, the do'ers and the dazzling few, are part of the greatest explosion of entrepreneurship the world has ever seen. They all know the rules of survival have changed in a downsized and uncertain world. And more and more they believe the best weapon for winning the economic wars of the 21st century will be themselves—their labor, their knowledge, and their own entrepreneurial spirit. Of course they're right. Whether you work for a giant company, someone else's mid-sized enterprise, or for yourself, getting entrepreneurial has become the name of this game. Like it or not, we're all working and living in "the *new* entrepreneurial age."

In modern industrial history, there have actually been two prior waves of important, but narrow, individual entrepreneurial activity. The first coincided with the rise of the industrial age in the 1860s to 1880s. It produced a few captains of industry and more than a few robber barons. The second, fueled by the promise of unlimited capital, occurred between 1910 and 1929, being cut short by the Great Depression. In fact, these early eras produced relatively few entrepreneurs as a percentage of the workforce. Even more striking, the entrepreneurial activity that did occur was severely limited in geographic scope. The United States and north-western Europe accounted for an overwhelming share of the entrepreneurs. Certainly in terms of historical significance, these earlier entrepreneurial bursts were smothered by much bigger socio-economic waves. In the 19th century, the boom in entrepreneurial activity was just a necessary piece of the "Industrial Age," along with mass-production, organized labor, and the emergence of the first truly, big businesses. All this fed into the 20th century, whose early entrepreneurs became buried in the modern "Managerial Age," and were quietly replaced by "The Organization Man." The entrepreneur was effectively driven into second-class status for much of the century.

While these two earlier entrepreneurial eras produced some famous companies, and an impressive array of new technologies and products, nothing in our history has prepared us for what is occurring today. The current entrepreneurial revolution is simply unprecedented in size and scope. With over 3 million start-ups a year (1.3 million in the U.S. alone), the numbers are staggering. Even more dramatic is the truly global reach of this revolution. India, Brazil, and China are as chock full of entrepreneurial fervor as the United States. Even Japan has joined the trend, proving once again there's nothing like a decade long recession with a lot of American-style downsizing to get the entrepreneurial juices flowing. And money is no problem for the rising entrepreneur class. With $300 billion available from 300 venture capital firms and 250,000 private investors (as in "Silicon Valley angels"), and government "Enterprise Funds" springing up in every country, there's more start-up capital around than entrepreneurs-past dared dream about. The fact is, the average cost of a business start-up in America is only around $14,000, and the two biggest sources of entrepreneurial funding are available to anyone: Personal savings and credit cards. And take my word for it—the list of great companies started for less than $10,000 is very, very long starting with Microsoft and Apple Computer.

All this leads to the most unique characteristic of our 21st century entrepreneurial revolution—which is that very ordinary people are the main players. This is not a revolution being played out by or for the rich and powerful. It is a new page in economic history which welcomes the participation of everyone, from "Welfare-To-Work" graduates starting private day-care centers, to university scientists becoming biotech CEOs, to anyone reading this book who will make a product or deliver a service that someone, somewhere, needs

DRIVING THE ENTREPRENEURIAL BOOM

Some 3 million new entrepreneurs come on the scene each year, from every corner of the world. We've never seen anything like it in history. What's really causing this? Some of the key factors driving this unprecedented entrepreneurial boom, especially in the U.S., are:

• **Seeking Jobs And Prosperity**
In 1985 the three largest employers in the U.S. were General Motors, Sears and IBM. GM was the world's largest producer of cars, Sears led the world in making household appliances and of course IBM dominated the world in computer manufacturing. They all offered high-paying jobs and great benefits. Today the three largest employers in the U.S. are Wal-Mart, UPS and McDonalds. Wal-Mart is selling products made in China and elsewhere, UPS is delivering those products and of course McDonalds is still flipping hamburgers. Is it any wonder that

wages in America are at their lowest percentage of the nation's GDP since 1947! Entrepreneurship has become the last, best option for millions of smart, hard-working Americans who in years past would have gone to work for a big company. It's called "economic entrepreneurship" and it's the main driving force of our new entrepreneurial age.

• The Global Marketplace.

You can be "in business" anywhere in the world for pennies on the dollar of what it used to cost. While the Internet is a factor, it isn't the main reason. It's simply the ease and modest cost of opening up your own shop or finding willing distributors and customers in foreign markets. From Australia to Chile to Ireland, it's a piece of cake. Trust me; I've done it—fast and on the cheap. The total start-up cost in our U.K. office was $5,000, and we opened our Philippine office with the proceeds of our first $12,000 sale to Philippine Airlines—made by phone from the United States—fast and cheap!

• Huge Niche Markets

Most giant companies can't even think about markets as small as $25 to $50 million; they're just not worth it. Therefore, being small and operating on a shoestring can be the entrepreneur's most important competitive advantage in stealing market after market from the big guys.

• Start-up Capital

The world is simply awash in entrepreneurial capital. With the average cost of starting a business in the United States only $14,000, start-up money isn't a problem for most entrepreneurs. Between personal savings (still the number one source of start-up funds,) the $300 billion available from VC firms and angel investors, the Small Business Administration's $45 billion portfolio, and the always-smart idea of lining up your first customer before giving up your day job, all you need is a great idea and you're in business.

• The Ultimate Meritocracy

At the end of the day, this may be the single most important point about entrepreneurship. It doesn't matter what color you are, who your family is, your gender, or where you went to school—if you come up with a great product or service idea you cannot be stopped.

• The Biggest Risk Of All

Most entrepreneurs say the big risk today is working for a big business. The facts are on their side. Over the past 30 years, corporate America has downsized and/or shipped overseas 30 million high-paying jobs—which are never coming back. So not having the confidence and knowledge to fend for yourself and your family's economic well-being—and hoping your future employers will provide lifetime employment, big benefits, and a hefty pension—may indeed be the biggest risk of all.

Of course the question that may still be on your mind is: "What exactly would I do? If I quit my job, or God forbid get fired, or just want to do something when I retire, what would it be? And how would I go about it? What should I really concentrate on, day in and day out, to ensure success?" Well, read on. We've got the answers for you. First, take a minute to review the "great myths and simple truths" about being an entrepreneur and then you'll be ready to digest the "proven lessons of the world's great entrepreneurs." Learning all this may not turn you into the next Warren Buffett, but they are the guaranteed first steps toward making sure you don't "get in your own way."

GREAT MYTHS AND SIMPLE TRUTHS

"When I started Microsoft, I was so excited that I didn't think of it as being all that risky. . . . . The thing that was scary to me was when I started hiring my friends, and they expected to be paid."

—Bill Gates
Co- Founder, Microsoft

In spite of the occasional high profile odd-ball—Ross Perot comes to mind—the fact is entrepreneurs are not much different from you and me. The really good news is that no one, no matter their station in life, is dis-qualified from playing this game. Evidence the fact that a whopping 15% of Americans now work at least part-time from home in a self-employed capacity. The reality is millions of new businesses each year are fueling economies all around the world. The people behind these start-ups come from every walk of life. All the statistics show they're a pretty average lot. Most never planned to be an entrepreneur. It happens because of circumstance. It's usually a circumstance of crisis, like being dirt poor, or full of frustration, or getting fired—the number one reason that people go into business for themselves. Yes, these are ordinary people who simply find themselves in extraordinary situations.

This is important to keep in mind while both business and popular media bombard us with entrepreneurial myths. It's absolutely essential to keep in mind if you're thinking about becoming an entrepreneur yourself. Here are some of the more damaging myths about those people who create and build businesses.

• **Myth Number 1**
Entrepreneurs are born, not made. It's in their genes. This is the most common myth of entrepreneurship.
• **The Truth**
If you really believe it's genetic, you never visited Communist East Germany. Listen to Claus Schroeder, the founder of a container shipping business in Hamburg, describe what 45 years of goose-stepping communism gets you. Claus says Germany's big gift from the end of the cold war was getting 20 million East Germans who wouldn't know a hard day's work if it were injected into their socialist veins. His parents were originally from the east and in the early 90's he eagerly expanded his business to the former communist region. Motivated by both family sentiment and business possibilities, his decision turned into a nightmare: "It's just unbelievable. I can't believe they're Germans. They have no concept of work. If the container ship isn't sitting at the dock when they arrive in the morning, they just go home for the day. The

ship docks thirty minutes later for unloading and there it sits until tomorrow. Nobody thinks, nobody acts, and nobody cares. I'm afraid the whole generation is lost. Maybe their children and grandchildren will be different!" Entrepreneurs are born, not made? Baloney! In western Germany, you had hard working, self-motivated people who transformed their land from total ruin to the world's third richest economy. In eastern Germany, you had lazy, uninspired louts, looking for a government handout—and they all came from the same grandparents! The difference has nothing to do with genes. It has everything to do with their political, social and economic environment.

• Myth Number 2
They all invented something in a garage when they were 15, wear strange clothes to work, and speak in techno-babble. We may have the same grandparents, but they are kind of weird and just different from you and me. I call this the nerd theory of entrepreneurship.
• The Truth
The mundane facts are, the average entrepreneur is 35 to 45 years old, has 10 years plus experience in a large company, has an average education and I.Q., and contrary to popular myth, has a surprisingly normal psychological profile. They dress, talk, and look a lot like you and me—a fairly average bunch.

• Myth Number 3
The overriding goal is to be a millionaire. They do it for the money pure and simple.
• The Truth
Every shred of research denies this myth. Relatively few of them in fact ever earn the kind of bucks paid to CEOs these days. The entrepreneur's real obsession is to pursue his own, personal sense of mission. Money is the necessary fuel to do this. Venture capitalists, shrewd evaluators of the entrepreneurial quotient in people, can spot the get-rich-quick types in a minute and avoid them like the plague.

• Myth Number 4

Entrepreneurs are unscrupulous characters, ready to take legal short-cuts, and are generally on the prowl for suckers to screw. Reading between the lines, this myth really says that big, well-known corporations and their executives are more trust-worthy than entrepreneurs.

• The Truth

This nasty myth gets harder to believe every time another blue-chip corporate executive marches off to jail. And compared to some well known CEOs, raking in their $10 million a year salaries, even as their employees and shareholders are bleeding, entrepreneurs don't seem so greedy after all. With the Enron scandal still etched in our brains, the colossal lapse in ethics, if not outright fraud, of Hedge Fund managers trading derivatives, and the continuing outrage of the same executive teams who got bailed out by taxpayers awarding themselves million dollar bonuses, the Hondas, Bransons, and Waltons of the world look more and more like saintly protectors of old-fashioned virtue. The unhappy fact is that low ethics and illegal tactics seem pretty evenly distributed throughout the population.

• Myth Number 5

They're high risk takers. Real dart throwers.

• The Truth

The sub-title of this chapter says: "Getting entrepreneurial is the best weapon you'll ever have to survive and prosper in a downsized and uncertain world." That sentiment comes on good authority. Every entrepreneur I've ever met believes the greatest risk today is to leave your future in the hands of a series of corporate bosses, all of whom have their own agenda to push. Betting on the corporate lottery for the next 30 years is a risk entrepreneurs aren't willing to take. So the "risk" of leaving a corporate job and starting out on your own has become, as they say, relative. And once they get started, a lot of entrepreneurs turn down-right conservative. They're still innovators but that doesn't make them fools. Remember, it's their money they're risking. The reality is big company executives regularly take greater risks with shareholders' money than entrepreneurs are willing to take with their own.

• **Myth Number 6**
Getting an MBA is the way to go. Business schools will teach you how
to be an entrepreneur.
• **The Truth**
Save your $50,000 and go learn something useful that can help you
create a product the world needs—just as 99.9% of the world's
entrepreneurs still do. This myth is just the latest big lie propagated by
the business education establishment to prop up enrollments. Back in
the eighties, the MBA factories saw that button-down IBM style
management was out and entrepreneurial chaos ala Apple Computer
was in. So they jammed a course on entrepreneurship in between
financial management and long range planning and called themselves
the new breeding ground for the next Steve Jobs. Of course they forgot
how Steve Jobs himself complained about the MBA style managers he
hired at Apple: "So we hired a bunch of managers—sure, they knew
how to *manage*—but they couldn't *do* anything." The moral? Until you
learn how to *do* something, like inventing a great product, don't even
think about becoming an entrepreneur.

START-UP: *THE* MOMENT OF TRUTH

Avoiding these common myths leads us back to the big question posed
earlier. What do you actually do when you start your own business?
What will your priorities be on your first day as an entrepreneur? Here's
a glimpse into how it usually works.

About fifteen minutes into the first morning of your new little business,
it hits you like a ton of bricks. Who's going to pay your salary for the
week? You certainly don't have a payroll department to cut a check. In
fact you don't even have the cash to cover a check. The sweat begins
to break out on your forehead. Then, the moment of truth flashes before
you: The only way you're going to get paid this week, and every week
for the rest of your life, is to make something or do something that
someone in the world will pay you cold, hard cash for. You need a
product and a customer—this week—or your kids won't eat. Welcome
to the world of true believers who know exactly why a clear

customer/product vision is the most fundamental of all entrepreneurial practices.

Next, as you contemplate creating the product and finding a customer, two more insights hit home. First, you realize you have to do this very fast. So you start working at high speed—not because it's your natural bent, but because you have to get this done before you run out of cash. The second insight is, the very best chance you will have of getting someone to buy your product is to make sure they see that it's different and better than other products they could buy. So you know you'll have to be a bit creative and innovative to come up with something that is better, or cheaper, or faster, or easier to use, or something, to give you the competitive edge. You've now learned, early in the game, why high-speed innovation is so important to entrepreneurs.

Fast-forward a few days or even months. You've been able to create and produce a product or a service. And you've also been able to find, sell, and service a few customers. Now your thoughts turn to growing a bit. It's clear that you alone can handle the current product and customer load, but you can't do much more. There just aren't enough hours in the week. You're going to have to take on a partner or an employee to help you grow. So you search around for relatives, friends, or former colleagues who are willing to take a chance and sign on with your fledgling business. After you hire one of them, get him trained, pay him a couple of times, a brand new thought begins to sink in. If this first employee does bring in a few more customers over the next six months, the company will grow and everyone will be happy. If, on the other hand, this first employee doesn't bring in any customers for six months, you're probably facing bankruptcy. You see this as a matter of survival. Your employee sees it as something to cover in his first year performance review. You've just tripped over the single greatest difference between entrepreneurial and employee behavior—having to face every week the real-life consequences, positive and negative, of your job performance. It's what fuels the next fundamental practice of entrepreneurship, which we call self-inspired behavior.

Somehow you survive all these challenges, and complete your first year as an entrepreneur with a nice little business and a bright future. You've become rightfully proud of what you, and your small team, have accomplished. You think that what you're doing is important, and it has the potential to create a lot of value. You even allow yourself to think you may be creating a bit of a legacy for future generations—or at least leaving a few footprints in the sand. You are now deep into that over-arching entrepreneurial practice we've labeled—sense of mission. An entrepreneurial sense of mission usually doesn't form until you begin to believe you're going to survive the start-up phase. You'll know you're getting it when, for the first time, you take a few quiet moments to contemplate what marvelous and profound things the company could achieve over the next several years. In other words, when you actually begin to sense the grand mission of your creation.

So yes, despite all the myths, the truth is the new entrepreneurs are us, and our co-workers, our friends, and even our families. And the things they, and you, will have to do as new entrepreneurs are not so strange or complicated after all. In fact, creating and building a company is sounding more and more like—well—a lot of common sense.

THE FOUR ENTREPRENEURIAL
BASICS APPLIED TO INDIVIDUALS

The Four Entrepreneurial Basics

Sense of Mission
Leaving Footprints In The Sand

Customer/Product Vision
My Customer, My Product, My Self-Respect

High-Speed Innovation
When Your Life Depends On it

Self-Inspired Behavior
Love What You Do And Get Very Good At Doing It

For a complete look at each of the four common sense practices of successful entrepreneurs, read on. And be sure to do the Application exercises in each section. By the time you finish Part One of **The New Entrepreneurial Age**, you will actually have your own personal action plan for starting your own business!

Chapter 2

Sense Of Mission

Leaving Footprints In The Sand

"Tremendously important to me was the feeling that we were doing something that had a significance far beyond building a company or what the financial rewards could be. I was convinced we were doing something that had tremendous importance in the world."

—Benjamin B. Tregoe, Ph.D.
Co-Founder, Kepner-Tregoe, Inc.

Have you ever noticed that entrepreneurs talk a lot about their company and their product? My experience has been (and I should know after interviewing a few thousand of them) if you ask an entrepreneur "how are you," you get several hours of what a great product they invented or company they started. In fact it's gotten so bad, that when I'm on a long flight and I think the person sitting next to me may be an entrepreneur, I put on the head-set and try to avoid all conversation. A couple of years ago I took a flight from San Francisco to Singapore. It takes about 20 hours, so you have to be careful who you sit next to. On this particular flight my seat-mate was a friendly looking fellow from Seattle. I know Seattle is full of entrepreneurs but this guy looked more like an athlete than a business type, so I made the huge mistake of saying those fatal words: "How are you?" Sure enough, he was an entrepreneur—and I got 20 hours on how his fantastic product was going to change the world. And what was this earth-shattering product? Well, hang on to your seat. He and his company had come up with a machine that made perfect sand for golf courses. And since Asians love golf, they were falling all over themselves to get their hands on his wonderful machine—thus his travels across the Pacific. Of course I don't play golf or even watch it on TV, but I heard more about sand and sand traps than I thought anyone could possibly know. Boring? You bet! But the point is, the young entrepreneur from Seattle really believed he had created something of importance and value for the world. Value for his customers, for his employees back in Seattle, and, undoubtedly, for himself.

This is the built-in advantage of all entrepreneurs. They really believe they're doing something important, creating a lot of value, and in some small way at least, leaving a footprint in the sand. They're on a mission—and that "sense of mission" gives them incredible energy, desire, and pride. When is the last time you met government or corporate bureaucrats with a true sense of mission about their work? Or one who talked your ear off for hours on what a fabulously important thing he was doing for the world? Not lately? That's the point. We call it having a Sense Of Mission and it's the first, fundamental practice of entrepreneurship.

THE "WHAT" AND THE "HOW" OF THE MISSION: FOR START-UPS

If you ask an entrepreneur "what's your sense of mission" they may look at you like you're crazy—or at least suspect you're a management consultant. Entrepreneurs aren't typically up on such fancy sounding phrases. But what they are up on, and can articulate with unbelievable clarity—is *what* they're doing and *how* they go about doing it. When you think about it, to succeed at any mission, whether it's a business mission, a military mission, a political mission, or whatever, you absolutely have to know these two things: *what* the mission is, and *how* you're going to accomplish it. We've labeled these two critical aspects of Sense Of Mission: the strategy (the what) of the business, and the culture (the how) of the business. If the words strategy and culture sound a bit grandiose to describe your first time entrepreneurial start-up, just call them your "business plan" and your "business values." Whatever we call them, being very good at both—setting a smart strategy and creating a strong, supportive culture—is a characteristic all great entrepreneurs share. It is also absolutely necessary to the creation of a successful, high-growth enterprise.

One of the most articulate entrepreneurs I've ever come across on this point, was a man named Ben Trego in Princeton, New Jersey. (*Our description of the entrepreneurial approach to strategy is influenced by and in part modified from the original work of my friend and former boss, Dr. Benjamin B. Tregoe who unfortunately passed away a few years ago. We have applied his description of strategy to the entrepreneurial approach for one reason only—it so clearly illustrates why entrepreneurs do what they do.*) Tregoe, a Harvard Ph.D., left the Rand Corporation (the famous think-tank) and founded a company to do one thing: to teach business people around the world how to improve their analytical decision making skills. In 1958 that was kind of a nutty idea. Nobody even thought about how to do that. Forty years later, the firm he co-founded, Kepner-Tregoe, Inc., has taught some 5 million people around the world, in over 20 languages, exactly how to do that. Ben Tregoe was truly a man with a mission.

Just listen to him. You can feel it in his words: "We had this strong sense that we were on to something here that was terribly important. Something that could help improve the quality of the world. We had this feeling, and it sounds very presumptuous to say, but we felt that we could really improve the rationality of the world and it was terribly important to get this out to companies everywhere. We believed we could help improve the communication between organizations and between people. This sense of purpose, this sense of mission, is tremendously important. I mean, I know if we had started the business and just said, 'it looks like we can make some money doing this so let's try it and so on,' we never could have gotten this thing up and running. It was too damn difficult."

Tregoe's sense of mission however wasn't based on hyperbole or theoretical pie-in-the-sky: "When you talk about the strategy of a company, when you talk about the direction that any company is going, it all boils down to your values, your beliefs, and your basic purpose, and then to a real understanding of the product and market. I mean all this stuff about strategy and so on, if it doesn't get down to product/market and your product/market priorities, you really don't have anything. The way you describe any organization, a company or a non-profit, is basically what products and services it offers and to whom does it offer them."

Tregoe also knew what it takes to stay true to your sense of mission over time: "A statement of purpose, the beliefs or values of a company, the product/market statement or strategy statement of a company is essential. But it's only useful if it's guiding what the organization does. If it's guiding the decision making on a day to day basis. And the only way it's going to guide the behavior of a company on a day to day basis, is if it's filed up here in the heads of the people in the business. And that means it's got to be pretty specific and pretty simple."

The bottom line is, entrepreneurs are highly focused on both "what" they are doing (the strategy or plan) and "how" they go about doing it (the culture or values). Whether you're General Electric or a one person start-up, the challenge is to be great at both. It's not good enough to have a smart business plan, but a weak, disconnected set of operating values. Conversely, strong values will never overcome a stupid plan. And of course you won't be around long if you know neither what to do nor how to do it.

New entrepreneurs quickly learn that while both the "what" and the "how" are essential, the plan of the business comes first. You have to know what you're doing before you can determine how to do it. This relationship between your company plan and your company values is often lost as the organization grows big and all manner of management

SENSE OF MISSION

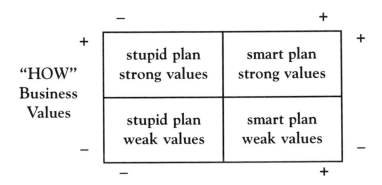

"WHAT" Business Plans

practices are adopted. The reality is, until you set the "what" of the business—what markets, what products, etc., you have no idea what kind of operating values and priorities you need. Indeed the only purpose of developing a set of company values is to get absolutely focused and operationally superb on those few things that will ensure that you achieve your business plan. And the operating factors that are essential for company A may not be important at all for company B. For example, if you're starting a commuter airline, safety had better be at the top of your values list. There's no faster way to bankrupt an airline than having a few headline grabbing crashes. On the other hand, if your entrepreneurial start-up is in the software business, where product life cycles are less than six months, product innovation and speed are probably the values you will need to focus on.

One of the great mistakes young companies make is to read about and then try to copy the culture and values of some big company they admire. The values of Daimler-Benz or Sony or Wal-Mart may have worked wonders for them, but that doesn't mean the same values will make your company plans come true. To keep on track with this fundamentally important point, simply go back to the basic purpose and relationship of the *what* and *how*: First determine what you are going to do—and then get very good at those few things that are crucial to doing it.

CREATING ENTREPRENEURIAL BUSINESS PLANS

There is no more over-hyped and over-used activity of business than corporate strategy and planning. For some never explained reason, this rather passive aspect of enterprise has generated more books, techniques, diagrams, and consultant engagements than anything else. And almost without exception, would-be entrepreneurs at business schools are advised that the most important step in starting up a company is to write a great business plan. Three hundred pages with lots of charts and financial projections are strongly recommended. Of course, no one bothers to remind the eager-beaver MBA students or, for that matter, the millions of cubicle-bound bureaucrats dreaming about striking out on their own, that no great enterpriser from Lorenzo de Medici to Bill Gates ever started a business this way.

Fortunately, there is a simpler way to do a business plan. It's the old-fashioned, entrepreneurial way. First, ask yourself what you really like to do and what you are really good at doing. Make as complete an inventory as possible. Then examine what needs are going un-met or are being poorly met, in markets your familiar with, for which you could possibly produce a superior product or service. And finally, for each possible product/market idea you've come up with; rate your likely competitive position against the very best providers you know of for that particular product or service. By making these assessments, you will find the product/market businesses that carry the highest chance of success for you as an entrepreneur.

Does this sound too simple? Would you feel better with something more sophisticated? Do you want to conduct a full market study, bring in focus groups, and produce reams of financial analysis? Of course you can do all that and more—if you've got all the time in the world and a bucket full of money. Just put this book down and get ready to spend the next year of your life doing research and writing a business plan. But remember—that's not the way great entrepreneurs have ever done it since the beginning of time. If you want to try their way first, read on. Here are the questions you need to ask. Your initial answers may not *guarantee* your entrepreneurial success. But you can be sure that you've asked yourself the right questions. The rock-bottom questions every entrepreneur in the world must ultimately answer are:

- **What Products Or Services Do I have A Passion For?**
What do I really like to do?

- **What Product/Services Could I Provide?**
What am I really good at doing?

- **What Customers/Markets Might I Pursue?**
What is the market need for products or services based on the things I like to do or am good at doing? What un-met, or poorly met, needs do I see in the market—which require products or services I might like to do or might be good at doing?

- **What Competitive Position Would I Have?**
What would my competitive position be, for each possibility, compared to the best providers of similar products and services to the market?

- **What Capabilities And Cash Must I Have?**
Can I really make the product or deliver the service? Can I really sell it? Can I service It? And can I pay for all this?

That's right; the questions are all about products and markets. They are tough questions intended to keep your feet on the ground. There may be other things to examine, but I will guarantee you this: These questions have to be answered. Disregard them at your peril. Which is another way of saying, if you can't answer them, do yourself—and your family—a huge favor and don't quit your day job just yet!

As Ben Tregoe says: "If it (the plan) doesn't get down to product/market and your product/market priorities, you really don't have anything." To the entrepreneur, the "what" of the enterprise always revolves around "what customers and what products will we pursue?" After all, customer and product are not functions or departments of the business: They *are* the business. Being wrong on either of these two questions puts you on the road to bankruptcy. In this environment, strategy and planning have to be all about picking the right products and markets. The business plan, however it is done, takes on specific meaning and awesome importance. Being close to customers and products is not just a good idea—it's the most valuable weapon the entrepreneur has in making the most critical decisions in business. The more we see, the more an entrepreneurial plan looks like "a blueprint for survival." It sure doesn't look anything like strategic planning a la The Harvard Business School. The entrepreneurial approach may not be so elegant or sophisticated, but it has one redeeming quality: It works wonders for getting new businesses up and running.

PICKING MARKET/PRODUCT WINNERS

Whether your planning process is formal or informal, six months out or ten years, uses discounted cash flows or numbers on a napkin—the part you have to get right is "what customers" and "what products." So how do you do this? First of all, where do you even come up with market and product ideas? Then how do you choose among them? What criteria should be guiding your choices? Are there any rules to follow in picking customers/markets and products/services? You are now face to face with the number one question in enterprise. As Tregoe so simply put it: "What products and services will you offer and to whom will you offer them?" You can read a ton of research and hire a thousand consultants to help you figure this out, but at the end of the day, there are just three things you absolutely, positively, have to do. Here they are:

- **Stay Focused On Customers**

Think of every market you know anything about, either as a customer or just an observer. What needs do you see that are going un-met, or are not being met satisfactorily? Carefully thinking this through can be a rich source of business ideas for entrepreneurs. Thomas Watson, the founder of IBM, used to say that the ideas for 95% of all IBM products— came from customers. This is why staying focused on potential markets and customers is so important.

- **Stay Focused On Products**

What do you like to do? What are you good at doing? Answering these two questions happens to be the number one way successful entrepreneurs identify the kind of business they start. So if you don't want to miss the greatest source of entrepreneurial ideas you'll ever have, you had better stay focused on possible products and services.

- **Know The Criteria That Count**

There are only two make or break criteria in choosing markets and products. They are *Market Need* and *Competitive Position*. Entrepreneurs always want to know the specific needs of the markets they enter—and every possible way they can raise the competitive position of the products they offer.

So in choosing the products and markets for your start-up venture, you have to know the answers to these simple questions: "How good is my market and how good is my product?" The Market Need you may pursue can range from great in every way to downright lousy. And the Competitive Position of your product can be anywhere from the best in the world to absolutely awful. To keep it simple, we'll just use *big* and *small* to rate Market Need and *high* and *low* for Competitive Position.

The best story to illustrate the power of these two criteria actually occurred, believe it or not, on one of those dreaded, long flights sitting next to an entrepreneur. As I mentioned earlier, entrepreneurs will talk you to death about their company—especially when they have you captive on a long flight. But once in a while you hit gold and learn something really valuable. This was one of those times. It was the

Stockholm to New York run, and the Swedish scientist in the next seat was already giving me his life story: ". . . so I now live in Florida. . . . I used to be an R&D director for Squibb Pharmaceutical. . . . . I worked at their headquarters in Lawrenceville, New Jersey . . . . . after years of seeing Squibb reject so many good products because the market need was not big enough for them, I left to start my own small medical products business. . . . ." Whoa! This was getting interesting. I turned ever so slightly toward him, airplane etiquette for: "OK, you've got my attention, so please make it good." He not only made it good, he provided a terrific entrepreneurial application of the Market Need/Competitive Position idea, as illustrated by the matrix on page 60.

As he told it, everyone in the industry knows there are hundreds of small, un-met needs in the medical and pharmaceutical markets. Giant companies, like his former employer, can't afford to even think about them. A Tiny $25 million market doesn't get a second look—according to my seatmate. His first product, diapers for elderly people, was a no-brainer. There was a small but real need in the market, and no one was producing diapers specially for aging adults. He leased time at one of the numerous medical research facilities available today, perfected his design, contracted for production and distribution, and had his first successful product. He agreed that it fits squarely in the upper left-hand corner of the Market Need/Competitive Position matrix: Small market need/high competitive position.

This led to a full discussion of his broad perspective on inventing products for different types of markets, first as a small cog in a giant wheel and now as the "big wheel" in his own business. As he described the rich array of market and product possibilities in the industry, he verbally categorized each one. So we can, courtesy of my Swedish seatmate, complete the explanation of the Market Need/Competitive Position matrix with examples from the world of medicine.

- **The "Leprosy Business"**

For starters, as our Swedish entrepreneur explained, there are plenty of limited medical needs in the world for which there are no products, or only inferior products. Take leprosy for example. It's a horrible disease

with a relatively small number of cases—and no cure. And why is there
no cure? Because it's a small market, found mostly in poor countries, and
the Mercks and Glaxos of the world aren't working on it. But suppose
you and your team have a research breakthrough and discover the cure.
You would have a classic example of a small market need/high
competitive position product. The "leprosy business" category is a
common place for entrepreneurs. They can do extremely well in these
niche type businesses. (There's probably a lesson here for consumers
too. If you're going to get a bad disease, hope and pray it's something
popular—so maybe there'll be a cure!)

• The "Headache Business"
How about the flip-side of the "leprosy business?" Think of the biggest
display section of every drugstore in America. That's right, it's the
painkiller section. It seems that all 300 million Americans are suffering
from headaches, the flu, and allergies. There are dozens of brands, and
hundreds of variations. They all make the same claims and have similar
sounding ingredients—resulting in important medical "innovations"
like "regular aspirin, extra-strength aspirin, aspirin PM, coated aspirin,
non-aspirin aspirin"—well, you get the point. I recently noticed in fact
that the ingredients are exactly the same for two separate products from
the same company. Check it out. Extra Strength Excedrin and Migraine
Excedrin are identical, right down to the 65 milligrams of caffeine in
each. Why all this marketing madness? Because the market is so damn
big. It's the humongous "headache business" and it perfectly fits the big
market need/low competitive position quadrant of the matrix.
Entrepreneurs can prosper here also, if they're ready to compete on price
at the low end of the market.

• The "Polio Business"
The place no entrepreneur wants to be is in the small market need /low
competitive position quadrant. There are plenty of recognizable medical
needs here—mostly diseases that have been virtually wiped out years
ago like polio, smallpox, and scarlet fever. These are markets that are
dead or dying, and even if they weren't, the old product patents have
expired and everyone could be in the market tomorrow with a me-too,
low cost cure. The "polio business" arena is no place for fast moving,

entrepreneurial start-ups. There's little money to be made here by entrepreneurs, pure and simple. Interestingly, some old, big companies, not necessarily pharmaceuticals, do seem to keep plugging away in this quadrant. Instead of hanging on with commodity products in dying markets, they should probably kill these businesses and move on to something with a future. If you're working for a company like that, it's enough to make you want to—well, become an entrepreneur!

• The "Heart Disease Business"

And finally we come to the place where most big companies and entrepreneurs dream about—the big market need/high competitive position quadrant. Think about this. The number one killer in the world, for both men and women, is still heart disease. There have been advances in treating all manner of heart problems, but there's still no cure in sight. What if—and here comes the dream—you and your band of entrepreneur/scientists come up with the absolutely perfect, rejection-free, artificial heart? You could give a lifetime guarantee for your perfect heart to your customers. That's a better deal than they get when they're born! So your "heart disease business" would rank right up there with the wheel, electricity, cars, computers—and penicillin, as one of history's true blockbuster products. Can entrepreneurs be successful here? Absolutely. Success is virtually guaranteed—with one caveat. You may become too successful. Getting too successful here will ultimately guarantee hordes of envious competitors, and open the door to government busy-bodies, all of whom will do almost anything to take you down several pegs. Ask AT&T, IBM, and Microsoft how it works once you're deemed a monopoly. So go for it by all means—and get ready to take the heat of intense competition and the heavy hand of government regulation.

* * *

The illustration shows how the four medical examples would be positioned using the criteria of market need and competitive position:

Beyond helping you pick market/product winners and getting your entrepreneurial venture off the ground, the two criteria—Market Need

PICKING WINNERS

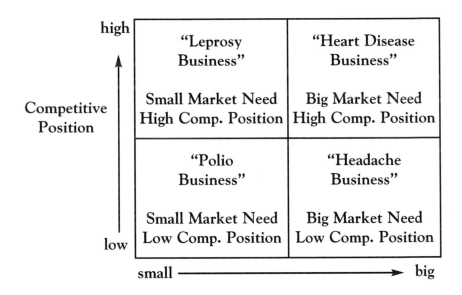

and Competitive Position—will continue to be important as you grow. They will always tell you what kind of actions you need to take to improve each of your market/product businesses. For example, if you're in the small market need/high competitive position quadrant, you need to find more customers for your great product. So focus on marketing, distribution, exporting, etc., would be essential to growing your business. Conversely, if you're in the big market need/low competitive position quadrant, you need to raise the competitiveness of your product. This means that improving product innovation, quality, and costs would be key to generating more growth. The bottom-line is, these criteria will help you grow your business—which is exactly what entrepreneurs do best.

CREATING ENTREPRENEURIAL BUSINESS VALUES

If planning is the most over-used management practice in business, creating and maintaining values is surely the most mis-used. A couple of decades ago the whole subject of corporate culture and values burst on the scene. It was quickly co-opted by industrial psychologists, wild-eyed motivational speakers, HR gurus and various other corporate do-gooders. It also became a new, lucrative area for management consultants to make another buck. Every big corporation worth its salt had to have a mission statement and color posters of holier-than-thou core values began popping up on office and factory walls everywhere. Being good to customers, employees, shareholders, communities, and anyone else the values task force could think of, passed as evidence that you were an enlightened and presumably successful company. This was clearly the route to take to get on one of those annual lists of *best companies*. A lot of otherwise good managers actually began to believe that business values were things you dreamed up in a staff meeting, plastered on every available wall, and then went back to your real job. Of course all this was, and is, down-right ridiculous.

Such shenanigans are not only silly, they are also quite damaging. Creating cleverly worded value statements became a goal unto itself. Wall plaques displaying the corporate mission statement and core values evolved into an official statement of *how* to operate, with virtually no connection to the *what* or the product/market strategy of the business. As discussed a few pages earlier, the purpose—the only purpose—of creating and maintaining business values is to make sure you focus on and get very good at those few operating factors critical to the accomplishment of your business plan. Exhorting everyone to pursue a company culture that is unrelated to the company strategy is a fundamental disconnect for any business.

Entrepreneurs clearly have to get this right. Concentrating your energies on becoming the best in the world at one or two key things produces powerful, competitive advantages. This is why focusing on a few performance defining values that directly support your market/product plan is so important. Nowhere is this more true than with the young start-up venture. In the do-or-die world of the entrepreneur, it almost seems to come naturally with the territory. But be fore-warned, Your entrepreneurial *values* won't sound anything like the beautifully crafted platitudes of the *Fortune 500*. For example, if you're a small player in a very competitive, low-margin business, you quickly learn that letting up on cost control, from salaries to paper-clips, is a one-way ticket to bankruptcy. But cost control rarely makes it onto a big company's list of values. The reasons are clear: The value statement has nothing to do with the product/market plan and anyway, cost control doesn't have that warm fuzzy ring big business PR departments like to promote. Fortunately, the start-up entrepreneur doesn't carry any of that big business baggage, and the question of "what should our business values be?" can be answered directly and simply.

First, the question has to be answered by you, the entrepreneur of the business. It can't be delegated. It's essentially your answer to "How am I going to go about my business?" Your answers will determine what's important to do and not to do in the enterprise—and ultimately how all employees should behave toward customers and products, and ultimately the company's overall mission. The values you choose must be tested against no-nonsense criteria such as: "What actions will give us the most competitive advantage and what behavior must we be personally committed to—without compromise?" So here are the two most critical criteria you have to use in creating your entrepreneurial business values:

• How Can I Raise My Competitive Advantage?

What values, behaviors, or practices will most powerfully raise your competitive position? Which of those practices are absolutely critical to the successful accomplishment of your market/product plan? Product quality? Innovation? Employee relations? Customer service? Cost efficiency? Fast action? Etc.? Whatever those few items are, they must become the operating values of your business.

• How Can I Get Everyone Committed?

Becoming the very best in the world at those few practices most critical to your competitiveness, requires an uncompromising, emotional commitment from you as the leader. Ultimately it will also require the personal commitment of your entire workforce. For you as the leader there can be no wavering on the commitment issue. You absolutely must lead by example. This means your own day-in-and-day-out behavior, the organization rituals and practices you instill, and most certainly the personnel reward/punishment systems you create, must all support and reinforce the business values. This process is the entrepreneurial way to bring business values to life in an organization—and the best way ever invented to get groups of disparate people to focus on and achieve a common goal.

So fostering an entrepreneurial business culture, underpinned by the specific values which will give you the most competitive advantage, has little to do with those feel-good platitudes you've seen decorating the walls of big business—and big government. Entrepreneurial business values are, instead, the most powerful weapons ever invented to beat your competitors and ensure the accomplishment of your market/product business plan.

KEEPING THEM ALIVE

Sure, you have to get the business going before you start worrying about keeping it alive. But in the spirit of "an ounce of prevention," a final thought on business values may be worth its weight in gold. Obviously, those things you determine should be the core values of your business, have to keep working day in and day out, year after year, to do you any good. If your values are indeed: ". . . those few operating factors critical to the accomplishment of your business plan," letting them die is exactly what you can't afford to do.

So for your future reference at least, following are the three greatest influences on keeping values alive. If these all-important cultural influencers support your company values, you can be sure the values will stay alive. If they don't support your values, or even worse subvert them, your values will be quickly lost—and with them, the best insurance you could ever have for achieving your entrepreneurial dreams.

• Your Daily Behavior

It's not a fair world. The founder is "on stage" every minute of every day. Your personal, daily behavior will set the standard for your entire company. You're most insignificant behavior is of intense interest to employees, customers, suppliers, and shareholders. It seems today you can't fool anyone any of the time. So, surprise everyone and actually behave, all the time, as the best example of your company's values. It may not be a fair world but it's a price most entrepreneurs gladly pay. And as the company grows, this same factor, will apply to the future senior management team you put in place. So add it right now into your future hiring criteria!

• The Rituals And Practices You Follow

Everyone knows the written policy manual is not what the culture is all about. Your company's true values only reveal themselves in the mundane rituals and practices of daily operations. How do you actually treat workers on the line? How much service is really given after the sale? Do you take the first pay cut in bad years? Do your employees take extra care to make sure the product is perfect? Does such behavior get rewarded, or even noticed? And what's the reaction to losing a customer: Does everyone just shrug their shoulders or does all hell break loose to regain the client? It's at this level that the culture of any company lives or dies. Not reinforcing your values in the daily rhythm of the business is a damaging oversight. You are absolutely sabotaging your future. You are actively destroying, day in and day out, the very things that you say will give you enormous competitive advantage in the marketplace.

• What You Reward And What You Penalize

How do I get promoted around here? And what does it take to get fired? Your answers to those eternal employee questions will directly and powerfully set the true values of the company—for all employees. The maintenance of a set of values ultimately depends on what actions get rewarded and what actions get penalized. Unfortunately this is the most frequently violated practice in keeping values alive. Most companies simply forget to make them a part of the organization's reward and penalty systems.

It should be clear by now that having an entrepreneurial sense of mission isn't rocket science. It's all straightforward, simple stuff: Creating simple plans, picking markets and products you really care about and know about, determining the few critical values needed to support your market/product plan, and then keeping those values alive and well year after year. It's simple stuff but it's also powerful stuff. So whether you're an entrepreneurial dreamer, or do'er just starting up, or one of the dazzling few already on your way, it's absolutely critical to remember that having a powerful sense of mission about your business is *entrepreneurial practice number one!*

And speaking of rocket scientists, it should also be clear that it doesn't take one to have a powerful Sense Of Mission about your work. It is indeed simple—but powerful stuff. If you want to know how simple and powerful it can really be, the closing story of this chapter will do it. Welcome to "The Mission Of Buel Messer"—and one of the truly unforgettable characters I've ever known.

* * *

THE MISSION OF BUEL MESSER

"How can a blind man rustle cattle? Not very well.
That's why I got caught."

—Buel Messer, Founder
Messer Landscape, Inc.

On a snowy Friday in 1980, Buel Messer was home. He didn't have work. There weren't a lot of career possibilities for a convicted felon, a cattle rustler. Out of boredom and frustration, he grabbed his two young sons and a shovel. "Let's go shovel some snow for the neighbors." He needed the boys to be his "eyes." Buel Messer is also blind.

Hardly the stuff of a great story of enterprise? Think again. It's just a little more earthy than you'll find in the Harvard Business Review. From shoveling snow and mowing lawns, always with his boys, Messer has created a multi-million dollar landscaping empire. Today, Messer Landscape has thriving retail operations, a booming wholesale tree business and large commercial projects are taken in stride. Not bad for a blind ex-con turned entrepreneur. Buel Messer's story has a lot of lessons. The one we're interested in here is all about building a business . . . to feed your family and regain your name . . . and doing it without resources, without theories, with absolutely nothing but a driving sense of mission.

Messer was born dirt poor in the impoverished hills of eastern Kentucky. He was also born with Optic Atrophy, leaving him with only a tiny sliver of sight, about 5%, in one eye. He struggled through grammar school and was finally admitted to a state supported high school for the blind in Ohio. School didn't interest him a whole lot, but competitive athletics did. On a sports scholarship, he went on to college. To see if he could do it, he made the Dean's List his first and last semesters in college. In between he was an inter-collegiate wrestling champion, and set the state record for the mile in Ohio. In a moment of glory, he ran in Madison Square Garden on national TV, against the world record holder, Jim Ryan. Ryan blew the field off with one of the first "under four minute" miles on an indoor track. Still, a pretty good day's work for a poor, blind kid from Kentucky.

Because of his boundless energy and personal example in overcoming his handicap, Messer was a natural as a role model for handicapped students. He threw himself into his first job at The School For The Visually Handicapped in Wisconsin. There he became interested in helping the multiple-handicapped and started graduate study at night. In Wisconsin, he met and married his wife of thirty-five years, also a sightless person. From there, Messer transferred to the Virginia School For the Deaf And Blind. He completed his Masters Degree at the University Of Virginia and enrolled in the doctoral program.

Being an academic, in the challenging but specialized world of teaching the handicapped, wasn't the only thing Messer thought he could do. Along the way, he dabbled in other things that he knew, like farming. He started a small cattle and hog operation. For several years he taught by day and worked the farm all night. Being a farmer entrepreneur became more and more the passion of his life. He expanded the business. In the early days, financing was relatively easy to come by. His reputation was excellent. He expanded again, and again. But at the same time he was getting in deeper and deeper financially. With the first hint of trouble the lenders cut off his credit. Everything was at risk. He didn't know where to turn—until one black night, he signed on with a group of desperadoes to make a few easy bucks and his world fell apart. In one fell swoop, a single act of desperate dishonesty, Buel Messer's hard-earned accomplishments and his family's modest but honorable way of life, came crashing down.

When I first learned about his earlier criminal activity, and that he had been sent to prison for cattle rustling, I was overcome by curiosity. So I asked Messer: "How could you do that? How could it be?" In his always up-beat and honest manner, he gave this classic answer: "How can a blind man rustle cattle? Not very well. That's why I got caught." Despite the novelty, judges and peers weren't amused. In rural Virginia, stealing livestock is as much a sin as a crime. Not only do first offenders do hard time in prison, they can do hard time forever back in their community. This was the bleak outlook on that snowy Friday in 1980. The family was wiped out financially. Messer was "persona non grata" in the academic world. And decent jobs didn't go to ex-cons. An eventual full pardon by the Governor restored his voting rights, but not his dignity.

Never one to feel sorry for himself or blame others, Messer says of that period: "I didn't hold it against anybody. I was the one who created it, and I recognized that. I think the fact that I had, through my own bad judgment, committed the criminal acts way back then, has forced me to do things honestly and forthright ever since. I vowed that if I did anything the rest of my life, I was going to prove—not to everybody, I know that I'll never convince everybody—that I'm honest at what I do. It's been a challenge and a driving force for me. . . "

Let's take Buel Messer at his word. The overarching mission of his life became the redemption of his honor. He had few options but to reach for it through his own enterprise. How has he done it? What exactly is his Sense Of Mission? To get in sync with Messer's approach to business, it's necessary to re-learn plain, blunt English. You'll find no "corporate-ese" here. Backward integration becomes: "we had to have our own trees to sell" and market segmentation gets translated to "little old lady types versus fussy lawyer and doctor types." Once you get the language down, you begin to understand that Messer speaks with a passion and focus rare in business. He knows his markets, he knows his products, and he knows exactly what it takes to beat his competitors. This is the "no frills" version of sense of mission. It's creating business plans and business values—entrepreneurial style.

Starting with the snow shovel back in 1980, Buel's description of the start-up is pure passion: "I had to completely liquidate . . . while I was in prison, which was real depressing and demoralizing. . . It really was rock bottom for me. I'm thinking all the time that there's got to be some way back to something. I've always had a lot of plans and thoughts, but my mind is fatigued. . . So my two young sons, who were about nine and eleven years at that point, and I went around the neighborhood shoveling snow for people. It began to look pretty lucrative. That gave me the idea that snow shoveling was really needed and was almost a public service oriented type thing. So that week I stuck an ad in the paper, hoping to get something for the two kids and me that we could do together in the summer. We ran the ad: 'Wanted, In The North-End, Lawns To Mow For The Season.' This was in the first week of March. So we get about twenty-five or thirty responses to an ad that ran two or three weeks. We selected fifteen—well, between selecting and people deciding whether they wanted us—about fifteen lawns in our neighborhood. They had to be where we could ride a small riding lawn mower to and pull a small cart behind since I didn't drive and the boys weren't old enough. So that's the way Messer Landscape began. And that was twenty years ago this past season.

"I thought it'd be just a little something really to keep the boys occupied and out of trouble. That's what I thought. But I got tired of cooking and cleaning house pretty quickly. And I didn't know there were so many related things to doing those lawns that summer—that one we did just led to another. And I had more time now to think about things. You know, to really let some creative imagination take place. At any rate, we began to do some sidelines. A lot of them were retired people or little old ladies that we were working for. Those were the types we thought would be best, rather than work for doctors and lawyers and people who had lots of money. We felt they might be a problem for us. They'd be too fussy, and we didn't know what we were doing anyway. We thought that little old ladies would better put up with what we had. I should really say, only I thought that, because the boys didn't have any input at that point. It was hard enough keeping them working at it. Mainly they were my eyesight of course, early on, since I didn't see well enough to do what we were doing. With them I was able to actually mow the lawns myself and so forth. So anyway, there was the thing of: 'Would you prune my shrubbery?' And I would say sure, we'll try it. We'd never pruned a bush of our own before but got to doing it and got to reading articles and things about how to do it. It just seemed pretty natural, after that. That first year we had a gross income of $5,400.

"I guess the next kind of major step was a realtor/builder type person that I knew, had two spec houses that he'd built. . . . He wanted to know if we'd be interested in taking some rakes and trying to rake that rough ground out and put in some grass for him. This was our second year. We'd expanded to the point where we had this one part-time guy with his own truck. Think he might have had his own wheelbarrow too. Anyway that's how we got back and forth to the job to do those houses. We did rake those out and put in seven or eight shrubs in front of them, mulched them, and miraculously the grass grew and everything did well. So right away, we're landscapers! My mind starts going kind of wild at that point."

Enterprise doesn't get any more basic. What's behind it? Doing something of value, something worthwhile, pursuing an honorable mission. This is what drives people to create miracles in all walks of life. It's what enables groups of people to do the impossible. Value driven missions are personal. They don't come out of the mouths of consultant's. Yours will be uniquely yours. Buel Messer's meant overcoming incredible odds to redeem his dignity: "It gave me an opportunity to prove that I was not altogether dishonest. Probably I've bent over backwards trying to prove my honesty all along the line. I will say this quite frankly, I've not knowingly or intentionally done one other dishonest thing since. I think I was trying to prove something. I was trying to prove that despite the terrible reputation that I had developed, I still could be a success and a viable entity in the business world and this community . . . which I feel like I have."

I asked Messer to describe how he goes about setting his company plans and whether or not he tries to create company values. As you might guess, his description of company plans and values is unadulterated common sense. It has none of the management consultant's conceptual elegance. It's not "big picture" stuff. Buel Messer's business plan comes straight from the marketplace. Where he's headed with customers and products, underscores his knowledge of and respect for the market. He turns almost reverential when talking about it: ". . . the plan is not from me . . . it's from the need in the marketplace. There's strong need out there. I've been able to see areas where there's a strong need, or will be in the future, that I can capitalize on." His sense of gratitude toward customers borders on the Japanese: "I just feel really fortunate that we were able to convince the public that we would give them their money's worth and if something went wrong we'd make it right."

The key Messer Landscape value is a direct reflection of Buel Messer's eternally, optimistic view of human potential. He sees his employees as great contributors to a great cause. His greatest responsibility is to make it all happen: "I love taking people that have not maybe had a good opportunity or something of that sort and motivating them, seeing them grow. And through their growth, the business is going to grow. I've always had the theory that you don't necessarily need to hire all the highly trained personnel that some people might see a need for. I feel like I'm a good teacher. I thrive on being able to develop people to help them to be better than they were. You've got to make people feel strong about themselves and be motivated. I would say being able to motivate and inspire people might be the secret to everything."

Our story wouldn't be complete without one real life example of how Buel Messer keeps his mission alive. Clearly, personal integrity, honesty and rising above your circumstance are important values to Messer. But how does he instill these values in his company—stuck in an industry notorious for high turnover, low wages and temporary help? By chance I came across a small but telling illustration of the extent to which Messer Landscape tries to communicate its values.

A Dartmouth College student needed a summer job. This "Ivy Leaguer" found himself interviewing for a lowly pick and shovel job at Messer Landscape. It turns out that even part-time laborers are hired primarily on the basis of their "character." The interview was full of questions about honesty and integrity. Here's a sampling: "If the essence of law were defined as protection against insult and slander, would you consider yourself to be a law-breaker? . . . When was the last time you cheated on something? . . . How do you feel about cheating? . . . What do you feel to be your most important personal right? . . . Talk about the last time your personal rights were violated." Messer's Personnel Manager went on to explain the purpose of these questions to the startled Dartmouth man: "The thing you can add to Messer Landscape, aside from doing the necessary work—the real thing, is going to come from your character. So we want to see what kind of character is inside of you. This helps us figure out whether or not you and Messer Landscape can work and grow together."

Such questions might not raise eyebrows at the Philosophy Department at Dartmouth, but they're a little surprising coming from a landscaping company in rural Virginia. What's not surprising is that they got the Ivy Leaguer's attention. And that's the point. If your Sense Of Mission isn't getting your employees' attention, you're headed down the wrong track. Your entrepreneurial mission has to have high purpose and set high standards—like Buel Messer's. It has to be profound and simple at the same time—like Buel Messer's. And the good news is, do it right and your results will be great—like Buel Messer's. The incredible start-up and astonishing growth of Messer Landscape, has truly come from its founder's profound need to survive and redeem him—backed up by his simple, Tennessee common sense."

There's a lot of Buel Messer in all of us. Everyone is missionary about something. The trick is to direct it into your entrepreneurial start-up. This really isn't so difficult—especially if you're doing something you love as most entrepreneurs do. It's probably easier than spending two years of your life getting an MBA. It may even be easier than slogging through another dozen books on how to manage. All you have to do is get your entrepreneurial juices flowing about—what you want to do and how you're going to do it. If it can work miracles for a blind landscaper in Virginia, just imagine what it could do for you! *(Buel Messer recently retired and sold his company for a very nice sum of money. I called him in the summer of 2010 to see how he was enjoying retirement. His answer is classic: "Retire? I'm just getting started in life. Honestly Larry, I've got so many different things going on, I don't know how I ever managed to work 50 to 60 hours a week at a job all those years!")*

Chapter 3

Customer/Product Vision

My Customer, My Product, My Self-Respect

"Managing is the easy part. Inventing the world's next great product is what's hard."

—Steve Jobs, Founder
Apple Computer, NeXT Inc., Pixar

Every book ever written about entrepreneurs says they have vision. But vision of what? The simple answer is; all entrepreneurs are blessed and obsessed with a clear vision of a set of customers who need and will pay for a set of products or services. Think about it. Imagine you're starting your own small business tomorrow. What will you be thinking about?

What do you absolutely, positively have to be racking your brain over? If you're going to get to day two of the enterprise, you'd better be thinking about: "What can I make or do that someone will pay me cold, hard cash for?" Nothing could be more basic to the entrepreneur. This is the *sine qua non* of enterprise. The vision is precise. It is intense. All else revolves around it. It's not really so surprising when you think about it. What else could you be thinking about? Business can take many forms, but there's never been a business, or at least a business that survived, without a product or service of some sort and a customer somewhere willing to pay for it. If you really want to get back to basics, this is where you start.

Now here's the underlying truth that so often gets lost in the shuffle: Great entrepreneurs are not product inventors alone. Nor are they just great promoters. Is Steve Jobs a great scientist or a great salesman? Was Walt Disney a product genius or a marketing genius? How about Soichiro Honda? Did he just love cars or did he understand that the world really wanted smaller, more efficient, and more reliable automobiles? Did Ray Kroc, at McDonalds have a great product concept—or a great customer concept? The truth is, all great entrepreneurs are both—product experts *and* customer experts! Jobs, for example, certainly had a powerful vision. A vision of "the most remarkable tool we've ever built." A computer techie from the word go. Sounds like a product guy doesn't he? But then he says: "the most important thing" is to get them used in every office, in every home, and by every child in every classroom. Now he sounds like a customer guy. What's going on here? The obvious answer—he's a product person *and* a customer person all wrapped up in one. He's an expert on both—a make and sell craftsman—with the classic customer/product vision of an entrepreneur. The really valuable thing about this most important entrepreneurial characteristic is, it produces great competitive advantage against those who don't have it!

Speaking of Steve Jobs, he was recently name "CEO of the Decade" (the first decade of the 21st century) by *Fortune* magazine. This would be an awkward management award to deliver in person, in public, to Jobs. His acceptance speech would almost certainly be laced with more of the anti-managerial comments he's become famous for. My personal favorite came early on when he said he learned something important about managers when he first started hiring MBA types at Apple: "Sure, they knew how to *manage*—but they didn't know how to *do* anything."

Another of my favorite Jobs' barbs against professional management, which gets straight to the heart of this chapter is: "Managing is the easy part—inventing the world's next great product is what's hard." The fact is Steve Jobs has become the greatest modern symbol of entrepreneurial customer/product vision. He's the most pure, and most successful, example of an entrepreneur who loves his product—but loves seeing them used by customers (especially young people) even more.

After founding three great companies, Apple, NeXT, and Pixar (which he sold to Disney for a cool $7.5 billion—not a bad piece of work while waiting to return to his first love—Apple!) with the same obsession, do you really need any more proof of the almighty power of customer/product vision? I'm sure you don't, but here it is anyway. When Jobs returned to Apple as Chairman, after being forced out by his own hand-picked board and management team, it had become a shell of the great company it once was, and had been written off as dead by all the pundits. The company was in disarray, its products had become ho-hum and were losing market share, the company was cash strapped and rumors of bankruptcy were everywhere. The market value of this once great icon of Silicon Valley had fallen to about $5 billion by the end of the 20th century. Jobs was called back to save the sinking ship. Of course you know what happened. Jobs re-instilled the same customer/product passion of by-gone days, re-awakened Apple's dormant spirit of enterprise, energized the depressed employees, and single-handedly brought it back from the dead. Did he ever!

The results are nothing short of amazing! In the last decade, Apples' market value, the real test of any company's worth, has soared from $5 billion to $300 billion—number Two on the *Fortune 500* behind Exxon-Mobil—more valuable than such giants of American business as Wal-Mart, GE, IBM, Bank of America, and Microsoft. A truly amazing feat for a company written off as dead ten years ago.

To drive the point home, here's another handy measure of results. If you had invested $1,000 across the entire S & P 500 a decade ago, your nest-egg would be worth just $844 today—thanks in large measure to the great recession. But that same $1,000 invested in a floundering Apple ten years ago, and passing through the same recession, would have delivered a whopping $7,515! Beyond these gleaming once in a century stats, the even more remarkable story is that Steve Jobs, classic customer/product craftsman, has worked his magic to transform four major industries in his still unfinished career: computers(of course), but also movies, music, and now telecom. Historic entrepreneurs like William Lever, Henry Ford, Andrew Carnegie, Conrad Hilton, Ray Kroc, and Sam Walton all transformed their one industry—but seeing a single person alter four major sectors of worldwide business has simply never happened before.

So what has produced these results? Remember, Steve Jobs never darkened the halls of a business school and I don't imagine he's ever even attended a management seminar—so for starters we can scratch 'management-knowhow.' Maybe it's just all been luck. Well, doing it once, maybe. But coming back a second time, as the comeback kid of enterprise , , , I don't think so. No, it really has to boil down to his being an obsessive master of his chosen product/service scope *and* his chosen customer/market scope. This is wonderful news because it means we can all play this game. To the same heights of Steve Jobs—perhaps not—but believe this if you believe nothing else in this book. Not even Steve Jobs could do what he has done without absolute concentration on and enthusiasm for—making the products his customers want and will buy. There are never absolute guarantees in the world of entrepreneurship, but I firmly believe anyone can reach a good level of entrepreneurial success if they will deliver relentless focus, tremendous knowledge and obsessive passion for being both a product/service expert and a customer/market expert—in their own chosen customer/product fields. There really is no other way to do it. There is no shortcut to becoming the next Steve Jobs, Akio Morita, Richard Branson, or Walt Disney. The one thing you can be absolutely sure of; you're never going to come up with customer/product winners like the Apple computer, the Macintosh, the iPod, iTunes, the iPhone or an iPad studying finance and strategic management at the Harvard Business School.

Jobs' legacy is certainly not complete—but if he went away today I predict the world will still be reading about him at the end of the 21st century. Not because of his specific products or great salesmanship—but more from his general impact on the minds and hearts of people everywhere who are looking for role models to survive and prosper in our crazy, cut-throat world economy. Indeed, one of the unintended consequences of the Steve Jobs story is that he has also become a cultural icon and hero to young people all around the world. Maybe that's not so surprising for the only *Fortune 500* CEO who hangs around with Bono and who's own personal hero is Mahatma Gandhi! But it is still it remarkable—and wonderful in my view—that he has single-handedly (well, with a mighty supporting role by Sir Richard Branson!) made entrepreneurship "cool!" In a 2009 poll of American teenagers he was voted number one, ahead of all rock stars, entertainers, athletes, world leaders, ahead of everyone actually, as the person they most wanted to grow up to be like!

Sometimes you get lucky writing a book. At the very moment I was writing this paragraph praising Steve Jobs and Apple, late in the day on the 20th of April, 2010, CNN delivered the following headline across their newswire:

Apple delivers blowout quarter as iPhone sales surge

April 20, 2010: 5:59 PM ET

NEW YORK (CNNMoney.com)—Buyers just can't get enough of Apple's gadgets. The company sold almost 11 million iPods last quarter and doubled its iPhone sales from this time last year, selling 8.8 million smartphones during the quarter ended March 27. Those sales helped Apple on Tuesday report a profit of $3.1 billion on revenue of $13.5 billion, blowing past Wall Street's expectations. Mac demand is also on the rise. Apple sold 2.9 million computers during the quarter, 33% more than it did a year ago.

"We're thrilled to report our best non-holiday quarter ever," CEO Steve Jobs said. "We've launched our revolutionary new iPad and users are loving it, and we have several more extraordinary products in the pipeline for this year.

The Apple news is all about *products*: iPods, iPhones, Mac computers, iPads—and "several more extraordinary products in the pipeline this year." And it's all about *customers*: "buyers just can't get enough of Apple's gadgets" and "iPad users are loving it!" All told quarterly revenues rose 49% and profits rose 90% over the prior year! This is unheard of for a 34 year old company—and certainly for one at death's door a decade ago. The stock has just hit an all-time high as has the company's total market value—already the third highest on the *Fortune 500.* I rest my case. Instead of calling Steve Jobs the *CEO of the Decade,* I herby nominate him as the *Customer/Product Entrepreneur of the Century* . . . . . at least so far!

Speaking of 'entrepreneurs of the century,' let's turn our attention to the leading candidate for that title for the just passed 20th century—Walter Elias Disney.

THE REAL MAGIC OF DISNEY

Beyond our opening example of Steve Jobs, go down any list of famous entrepreneurs. Think of old-timers like Thomas Watson, Karl Benz and Konosuke Matsushita. Or newer faces such as Richard Branson of Virgin up through internet entrepreneurs like Jeff Bezos at Amazon or Sergey Brin and Larry Page of Google (who are big fans of Jobs by the way.) They all share a finely-tuned passion for producing things exactly the way customers need them and want them. It's a rare skill when you think of the hundreds of businesses you deal with that just don't seem to get this simple concept. And there's never been a better example of 20/20 customer/product vision than Walt Disney.

But have you ever had a management course on Walter Elias Disney? (*Through diligent research, I located the only Disney case study we had at the Harvard*

Business School. It covered the long-range financing for Walt Disney World in Orlando. Of all the rich lessons to be learned from Disney the entrepreneur, long-range financing strategy is hardly the place to start. But of course no one ever accused HBS of being overly practical. For dedicated Disney aficionados, I suggest two fun seminars at Disney University in Orlando: "Management, Disney Style" and "Service, Disney Style." I've attended both and highly recommend them.) Probably not. Why would anyone want to study the business practices of a cartoonist called Uncle Walt? Of course he did create the second most recognized product in the history of the world. Coca Cola is number one and a mouse named Mickey is number two. So on second thought, and since you're starting up your own business, it just might be useful to find out what it actually takes to create the second best known product in the world.

Some observers say Uncle Walt was a lot more than just a cartoonist. And of course they're right. The fact is, he's the greatest product creator in the history of the entertainment business. The list of Disney's technology and product achievements is long: He produced the first talking cartoon, a 1928 black and white cartoon about *Steamboat Willie*, (later renamed Mickey). He also produced the first technicolor cartoon, *Flowers and Trees*, in 1932. Through the use of multiplaned cameras, Disney introduced the earliest version of 3-D movies in 1937. Disney later perfected true three dimensional animation through his Audio-Animatronics electronics system. The year 1937 also marked one of his greatest product achievements and the beginning of a new era in filmmaking. In the face of great Hollywood skepticism, Disney Studios released *Snow White and the Seven Dwarfs*, the first feature length animated cartoon. Sixty-five years later, Snow White still makes millions for the company every time it's rereleased. *Fantasia* in 1940 was the world's first stereophonic movie, and in 1955 Disney unveiled the world's first 360-degree projection at Disneyland.

Moving into television, Disney simply created the longest running (1954-1983) prime time television series ever. *True-Life Adventure's* remarkable 29 year run on TV will probably never be matched and it single-handedly revolutionized the TV documentary. Along the way, in addition to Mickey Mouse, Disney was busy creating an entire family of world famous characters such as Donald Duck, Pluto, Goofy, and of course, Minnie Mouse. From these lovable characters, licensing rights and products like the Mickey Mouse Watch continue to fill the coffers of The Walt Disney Company. The amazing fact is, most of Walt Disney's original products continue to produce profit like timeless pixie dust. The vaults at Disney Studios contain reel after reel of pure platinum. Film classics like *Snow White, Pinocchio Cinderella, Peter Pan, Sleeping Beauty*, and *Alice In Wonderland,* add up to a perpetual profit stream unparalleled in business. These film products alone would earn Disney a place in anyone's business hall of fame, but hold on, the best is yet to come!

The capstone of Disney's product vision came in 1955, with the opening of Disneyland in California. The number one lesson from the instant and incredible success at Disneyland was that it was way too small. Disney determined to insulate future theme parks from the tacky development of motels and fast-food joints that had rapidly engulfed Disneyland. Before he died in 1966, Disney had laid the groundwork for Walt Disney World in Florida. With 27,500 acres, it would be 150 times bigger than the California property. Once underway, Walt Disney World became the largest private construction project in the United States. Under the careful eye of Roy Disney (Walt's brother) it opened on October 1, 1971. Only 10,000 people showed up for opening day. A nervous ripple of doubt went through the company. By Thanksgiving Day, the cars were backed up for miles and the biggest theme park in the world has never looked back. That first year it drew an unprecedented 11 million customers, making it, overnight, the biggest tourist attraction in the world. Today, this 43 square miles of land built on a Florida swamp, draws close to 30 million guests a year. It dwarfs the number of tourists visiting entire countries like Germany and Great Britain. Today, Disney's "dreams come true" theme parks are far and away the top entertainment product in history. The money just pours in from Anaheim, Orlando, Tokyo, and Euro-Disney near Paris. The combined parks entertain over 100 million guests a year. Not bad for a simple cartoonist with no management education! The fact is, Disney's record of product creation and picture perfect implementation are simply unparalleled in business. Surely then, Walt Disney is a great product person—a creative scientist par excellence!

Other Disney watchers, however, call him the greatest customer focused promoter in the history of entertainment—perhaps the greatest in all business. They make a good case. In hindsight, he certainly looks like a marketing genius: A customer person through and through. The cartoons and films show Disney's magic touch in pleasing customers. But it's the theme parks that most dramatically illustrate his extraordinary care and understanding of what customers want. The opening of Disneyland in California was the culmination of a 20 year dream for Disney. In his own words, the idea came straight from a customer-himself: "The idea came along when I was taking my daughters around to those kiddy parks. While they were on the merry-go-round, riding 40 times or something, I'd be sitting there trying to figure out what I could do." (*From Walt Disney World, The Walt Disney Co., 1986, p.6.*) From these simple thoughts of a slightly unsatisfied parent-customer, he eventually came up with the idea for a great outdoor entertainment center for the whole family. He wasn't thinking about an amusement park or another seedy carnival.

Rather, he wanted to create fantasies or themes in which the customers (he called them *guests)* would not be spectators, but would actually participate in the show. The development process was slow: "It took many years. I started with many ideas, threw them away, and started all over again." Disney had no specific business strategy in mind other than creating something fun for everyone.

It was there in Disneyland, that Walt Disney's real magic revealed itself. He loved his *products* for sure, but the one thing he loved even more was seeing the faces of his *customers* using his products. In the early days, Disney spent a lot of time in the park. He could be seen leaning against a fence, watching the children whirl around in the Teacups-with a big smile on his face. He seemed to enjoy it as much as the kids! This passion for making customers happy still works today. Disney's theme parks do exactly what Walt Disney said they should—they really do make people happy! Disney said it best himself, "Give the guests everything you can give them. Keep the place as clean as you can keep it. Keep it friendly, you know. Make it a real fun place to be." Was Uncle

Walt a great customer person? A great marketeer? A super salesman? You better believe it!

Creating themes and fantasies requires perfect products and perfect service to guests. And Walt Disney understood that requires perfect employees-or as he called them, *cast members*. Employees, from janitors to Snow White, aren't service providers-they're performers, members of the cast. When they work, they're on stage. They relax and eat lunch backstage. A cast member's sole reason for being is to make the guests happy. They must treat guests with the same courtesy as they would friends in their own home. Guests with questions are never avoided, they're sought out. All this helps to keep them happy. In this very special relationship between cast members and guests, little is left to chance. Cast members are not sent out into the parks unprepared. Disney training is intense and absolutely explicit on how to make guests happy.

Disney may have been the first person in any business to really understand that caring for the customer and the product is every employee's responsibility. And that it has to permeate every aspect of the business. His attention to detail is legendary. Every inch of the Park had to be perfect. Not just the streets and the attractions, but right down to the details of every cast member's appearance. He certainly had no peer in making this work. In an extraordinarily frank employee pamphlet, *The Disney Look*, appearance and grooming for cast members is covered in excruciating detail. From the length of fingernails to the use of effective deodorants, it's all covered. And the opening message to employees makes it absolutely clear that commitment to Disney's customer/product vision is a condition of employment:

> *"Each guest who makes up our audience is our boss. He or she makes our show possible and pays our wages. If we displease our guests, they might not return, and without an audience, there is no show. For this reason, anything that could be considered offensive, distracting or not in the best interest of our Disney show, even a conspicuous tattoo, will not be permitted."*

Of course the real magic of Disney was simple. He was a product expert *and* a customer expert at the same time. A scientist *and* a salesman. An unbeatable combination and the perfect entrepreneur. It's the beautiful balance between these two basics of business that make the world of Disney what it is. Focus on both is the answer. How could it be otherwise? Well, unfortunately it can, and often is. There are at least three other possibilities. You'll recognize them all. I call them the "*Scientist,*" the "*Salesman*" and the "*Bureaucrat.*"

DISNEY MAGIC

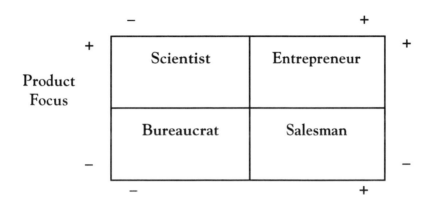

Customer Focus

• The Scientist

Ever come across people, or even whole companies, who are so into their technology or product, they forget they're creating it for someone else to use? We call this the *scientist syndrome*—or loving the product and hating the customer. Think dot-com industry for example. In the world of Disney, it could be the filmmaker who loves to make films but doesn't care if anyone pays to watch them. In the world of Steve Jobs, it's the computer scientist who builds the world's most elaborate machine, but it takes an Einstein to figure out how to use it. This is more common than it at first appears. It ranges from user "un-friendly" products, to simply unusable products, to the adding of so many bells and whistles to a product that no-one can afford it. The scientist often has a peculiar disdain for the need to sell and satisfy customers. He tends to look down a bit on salespeople and even customers. Of course there's nothing wrong with being a scientist for science's sake—if someone else is paying for it. In business however, the trouble occurs when you end up with exotic products that nobody needs or wants. This is the scientist syndrome—or loving products but hating customers—and it isn't exactly the focus you're going to need to grow your new business. The remedy, get re-focused on the customer side of your business and try to remember they are the ones paying your salary.

• The Salesman

Is it possible to love your customer but hate your product? You bet it is. Most of us run into the *salesman syndrome* every day. This is the I-can-sell-anything type. The professional salesman who loves to sell but doesn't give a damn what he's selling. Cars last year, computers this year and Hawaiian time shares next. It has probably never worked and certainly doesn't work today. The fact is most salespeople know how to sell. They're trained *ad nausea* on how to sell. But that's the problem. They know ten times more about selling techniques than they do about their product. The number one customer complaint about salesmen today is not that they don't know how to sell. It's that they can't explain their darn product! Substituting courtesy for competence is a common variation on this theme. It's the ever courteous voice on the phone who never solves your billing problem. Or the smiling baggage attendant at the airport who announces that your luggage just went to Karachi. The bottom line is customers don't want or need more selling and smiling. The harsh fact is, nobody even wants to see a salesman. They want to see real product and service experts—the ones who really care about the product and really know how to make it work. For the entrepreneur about to fall into the salesman trap, forget about more marketing and sales training, and start spending a lot more time making yourself into a product expert.

• The Bureaucrat

If you hate both your product and your customer, consider going to work for the government or at least a really huge company. You'll never make it as an entrepreneur, but you'll be a perfect bureaucrat. The *bureaucrat syndrome* is painfully commonplace. It's so common that some of us believe it must be the driving force of most of the large organizations we deal with. Bureaucrats demonstrate zero excitement about customers or products. They seem to have little interest in even being around the people who make the products and sell the customers. This is a crazy state of affairs—but it may not be entirely their fault. There are plenty of "good employees" who have never seen a customer or touched the company's product. It's hard to get excited about things you never see. Unfortunately, most bureaucrats spend their 40 years in their cubicles passing papers and e-mails back and forth and praying for 5 o'clock to come. In the bargain, they miss out on the joy of working with customers or products—the two, really exciting things about any business. So, maybe they're bored with good reason. As a new entrepreneur, you might think you won't have to worry about the *bureaucrat syndrome* until you are much larger and several years into the business. But be warned, it just ain't so. In my experience any company with three or more employees can become a raging bureaucracy. It's best to stay vigilant on this, and make sure you and *all* your future employees are intimately involved with both customers and products.

• The Entrepreneur: Disney Magic

How about "loving" the customer *and* "loving" the product? Of all the characteristics of entreprencurial behavior, this dual focus on customer and product best illuminates the difference between entrepreneurs and professional managers. Like the craftsman of old, entrepreneurs are intimately involved in both making products and selling customers. This entrepreneurial vision produces appreciation, expertise, and even respect for both customers and products. It also produces great competitive advantage in the marketplace.

Of course entrepreneurs are close to their products. They're intensely interested in the design, manufacture and usage of their product/service. They take it personally. They're ashamed when the quality is bad and they're proud when they get it right. They love their product and make no bones about it. They are clearly product experts.

Entrepreneurs are also very close to their customers. They have to be. They know their paycheck depends on it. They listen carefully to customers, not because someone told them to, but to pick up any new idea to improve their product or service. If a customer is unhappy, it's a major crisis. If the customer is happy, it makes their day. They are clearly customer experts.

THE CUSTOMER/PRODUCT MIND-SET

So what does it take to produce a powerful customer/product vision or mind-set? Even great entrepreneurs don't usually come to the task naturally. Creating a strong customer/product vision is most often the result of necessity. It comes with the territory in a start-up business. As we said at the beginning of this chapter, if you're going to get to day two of your start-up enterprise, you'd better figure out how to make something that someone will pay you for! A few famous examples will illustrate this point.

• Karl Benz

What does it take? It takes some of Karl Benz's fascination with engines, meshed with his belief that customers deserved and wanted real improvements in each new model of his automobile. The notion of turning out a new model every year never occurred to Benz. For him, the rule was to turn out a new model when you had significant improvements to offer the customers. This is quite a different vision of the world from the "planned obsolescence" concept hatched in Detroit many years later.

• Sarah Walker

It certainly requires some personal understanding of what products customers really need. America's first self-made woman millionaire was a poor African American house cleaner who was losing her hair. In an effort to concoct creams and shampoos to specially treat black women's hair and cosmetic needs, she invented and marketed the first line of specialty products for African American women. By the dawn of the twentieth century, Walker Manufacturing Company had 2000 franchisees and Sarah Walker was a millionaire—by inventing and selling products she and her friends desperately needed.

• Soichiro Honda

It may even take some passion, Japanese style. As a young man Soichiro Honda was passionate about driving high-speed racing cars and repairing high performance engines. He was no less passionate in his self-anointed mission of providing post-war Japan with much needed, cheap and reliable transportation. Designed down to the simplest of machines, his first product, the Honda scooter, still stands as a modern symbol of giving customers exactly what they want. Meeting very simple needs, very perfectly, may in fact be the first, passionate lesson of customer/product vision.

• Ray Kroc

Getting passionate about customers and products could also require a bit of the salesman's instincts of Ray Kroc (McDonald's founder,) blended with his personal obsession for delivering quality, service, cleanliness and value, a million times a day. From lowly travelling salesman of milk shake machines to absolute zealot of the clean bathroom, Ray Kroc epitomized the value of keeping your eye on the customer and the product at the same time. His greatest customer/product invention probably wasn't the hamburger: It was the beauty of the clean toilet. Visit the top volume McDonalds in the world on spit-polished Orchard Street in Singapore: Spotless bathrooms. Visit McDonalds in one of the grimiest neighborhoods in America at the entrance to the Lincoln Tunnel in Manhattan: Spotless bathrooms. We'll never know how many billions of Big Macs have been sold just to get at a clean bathroom for the kids—but you and I could retire on it. It all comes from knowing what customers really want and delivering it over and over again. Ray Kroc loved to say: "You gotta see the beauty in a hamburger." And that, it turns out, is the secret to getting millions of others to do the same!

• Estée Lauder

Josephine Esther Mentzer grew up in a poor immigrant family in New York City. As a young girl, she yearned to be one of the beautiful high society women she saw in salons and department stores along Fifth Avenue. She became a sales girl in several of those same stores until she recreated herself as Estee Lauder and started her own small cosmetics business. The company had one overriding mission: to make women beautiful. For years she personally applied her products on customers, honing both her product knowledge and her considerable customer service skills. Eventually she employed 7500 "Beauty Advisors" (not sales girls) and trained them incessantly to give the same personal attention to customers that she did. The one lifelong lesson she learned: "Women really do want to be beautiful—and helping them do that is the way to succeed in the cosmetics industry." Up until her eighties she gave final approval on all new products after testing them on herself and her friends. This intensity on customers and products has paid off. Today Estee Lauder, Inc. is the world leader in fine cosmetics with nearly $4 billion in revenue and over 15,000 employees. It accounts for an amazing 37 percent of all cosmetics and fragrances sold through department stores. Not bad for a poor immigrant girl who only dreamed of being beautiful—and helping other women to do the same!

• Steve Jobs

In conclusion, let's return to the modem American symbol of the customer/product mind-set. That's of course Steve Jobs and his endless string of products that customers love. Jobs is the true example of an entrepreneur who loves his product, but loves seeing it used by customers (especially school children) even more. With all the management drama that occurred in Apple Computer over the past two decades, it's easy to forget that Jobs is the original "user friendly" computer guy. More than any other person, he is responsible for the revolution in computers that took them out of the esoteric mainframe world of corporate IT departments, and moved them into the kitchens and bedrooms of nearly every family in America. Steve Jobs is an American legend who understood the way to get computers used by everyone was to make them easy and fun to use. After founding three great companies, Apple, NeXT, and Pixar, with the same passion, Jobs is living proof of the almighty power of the customer/product mindset.

CREATING A PASSION FOR CUSTOMERS AND PRODUCTS

The most expensive MBA in the world can't give you entrepreneurial passion. The entrepreneur's timeless adage says it all: "My customer, my product, my self-respect." The success of the business is a defining factor in their life. And they really believe customers and products are the heart and soul of the enterprise. It's not an overstatement to say they are obsessed with customers and products. This passion for customers and products will give you enormous competitive advantage against your entrenched competition—particularly those big bureaucracies who think they own your market. So use your passion and instill it in every employee you hire. It's what's going to make you win!

When you have real passion for your customers and products, simple things that a *Fortune* 500 CEO never even thinks about take on monumental importance. For example, customer requests get an immediate response—not "pretty soon" or "I'll get back to you tomorrow," but right now! Old-fashioned courtesy is not a rare event; it's the only way customers are ever treated. Really listening to customer suggestions changes from sloganeering to a daily reality. Individual responsibility for quality is the norm, not a pipe-dream of the corporate quality assurance program. No compromises on quality are suggested, let alone tolerated. Endless product planning is replaced by a true sense of urgency in producing real inventions that meet real needs, real fast. And if you lose a current customer, no one stands around and shrugs their shoulders. All hell breaks loose in a mad scramble to get the customer back. You don't need a Ph.D. in business to figure these things out. They're all common sense ideas—and they're things entrepreneurs do all the time.

Creating a passion for both customers and products is the driving force of great entrepreneurs all around the world. And so it should be for you and your company. There are hundreds of things you can do to create and maintain this passion. Here are several of the most important and common ways entrepreneurs do just that. We call it loving the customer and loving the product.

"LOVING" THE CUSTOMER

The entrepreneurial approach to customers is full of caring, common sense. You'll find no conceptual breakthroughs here. Loving customers is easy when you see them as the only means of putting food on the table. It's hard to hate people who do that for you. It's also easy to appreciate anyone who admires and uses your own creation: your product or service. It's just not normal to dislike folks who think your work is great. So as an up and coming entrepreneur, you will definitely have strong, built-in motivation to love and respect your customers. The really nice thing is that every minute you spend on this is money in the bank. Of all the ways entrepreneurs can show their love of customer, here are four of the most important.

• Knowing Your Product
The driving force of the entrepreneur's relationship with customers is the customer's reaction to his product or service. Loving your customer has everything to do with knowing (and loving) your product. After all, how can you really take care of your customers if you don't know how your product works, how to fix it when it's broken, and how to squeeze more out of it to make life easier for your customer/user?

Behind this broad thought, there's a very practical point to be made. No one really wants to see a salesman. In fact, people go to extraordinary lengths to avoid them. This may come as a big disappointment to the pure salesmen of the world, but it's a fact. And who do potential or actual customers want to see? They are absolutely dying to see people who can really solve their problems. And that takes a product expert, not a salesman with an order form. This little entrepreneurial twist, virtually forgotten by the marketing gurus of the world, could be the most powerful sales tool you will ever have. This is why *knowing your product* is the first step to really showing love for your customer.

• Responding Immediately

The most visible difference between entrepreneurs and big company bureaucrats is the priority they place on responding quickly to customers. Fortunately for you as a start-up entrepreneur, most of your competition will be just plain awful at it. Think of the last five times you made a complaint to a manufacturer. How long did it take them to resolve your complaint? Are you still waiting for an answer? And how about your last visit to a large department store or hotel, or God forbid a government agency? I've come to the conclusion that most of these service people are either deaf, or blind, or have fused spinal cords which keep them from looking up from their desk. Waiting on customers is simply a pain in the neck to most people in most companies. Of course this is good for you as a new entrepreneur—it's a constant reminder of what *not* to do. Responding immediately is never a problem for entrepreneurs. When customers are the only way to feed your kids, you don't need a training seminar on customer service or even a tough boss to get yourself in gear. It simply wouldn't occur to successful entrepreneurs that anything could be more important than responding immediately to customers' requests, questions, and complaints.

• Being Courteous and Competent

Some companies and their employees can be quite friendly, but are technically incompetent. They smile a lot but the steak is still tough as leather. Others may be highly competent but not so courteous. The planes run on time but you're being served by the cabin crew from hell.

Entrepreneurs have a huge advantage in this department. It comes with the territory. Courtesy has a certain ring of sincerity from people who run their own shop. When they thank the customer for making a $200 purchase, you get the feeling they just might really mean it. And if the product doesn't work, they take it personally—and know exactly what to do to get it fixed. This double-barreled behavior, so rare in big companies and government agencies, is just another area where entrepreneurs and their young companies have a built-in advantage over the bureaucracies of the world.

The good news is in the larger companies you will be competing with; it's not easy for employees to be both courteous and competent. There's the old problem of functions and specializing. And there's the even more serious problem that most of these giant companies have downsized to the point they simply can't deliver decent customer service even if they wanted to. It's just not easy in a big bureaucracy these days. I mean how can you remain courteous to customers who are already screaming mad about the abominable service they just got from your colleague over in aisle 8. And if it's not easy, you can be sure such uninspired bureaucrats won't make it happen—especially when they know in their heart of hearts, it's not going to make a lick of difference in their weekly paycheck. So this is the entrepreneurial advantage: Even a little bit of courtesy and competence can give you a huge competitive edge because you will be the only place in town providing both!

• Keeping Current Customers Forever

Your most important prospect for future sales is a current customer, always, always, always! The priorities are clear when your company is young and small. Losing one or two current customers is an unmitigated disaster—to be avoided at all costs. All the annual profit sits in the current customer base.

By far, the most important marketing job in any business is to resell and expand those current customers. This is not an argument against new business—just a common sense look at growing your revenues and profits. Reorders are golden. Repeat business literally keeps you alive. Unfortunately, this idea seems to lose its punch as a company gets bigger. If you allow these things to happen in your growing company, you will have committed the cardinal sin of entrepreneurial enterprise. You will not only be putting at risk the most profitable piece of your business, you will be a sitting duck for every new and hungry entrepreneurial competitor around. Don't let this happen. Make sure "keeping current customers forever" is your first priority, not the last, as you grow your business.

"LOVING" THE PRODUCT

If you have to boil it all down to one thing, the single most critical element in any successful start-up, is the entrepreneur's ability to come up with a better mousetrap. The mousetrap could take the form of a breakthrough product, an innovative new service, or even a new and improved version of an existing mousetrap. But here's the catch: the final judge of the worth of your efforts will be the market, not you. So again, it's the bringing together of the scientist and salesman in yourself and your start-up team, that is required to produce winners. Here, straight from the entrepreneur's handbook, are four of the most basic practices for loving your products—and getting others to love them too.

• **Knowing Your Customer**
There has never been a great product company, such as Apple Computer, Daimler Benz, or Matsushita Electric, that didn't give its customers what they wanted. It's definitional. Can you imagine a great product that no one wanted to buy or use? Knowing exactly what your customers want, and actually delivering it, is the crucial first step in becoming a world-class product company. This is a lesson many entrepreneurs have to quickly learn during start-up. It's especially true if you are starting out from a strong *scientist* mentality.

Any artist, for example, will tell you that no one values their work as much as they, themselves, do. They will also tell you that trying to sell their first work of art can be an ego-smashing exercise. All of a sudden, what matters most is not how beautiful the artist thinks the painting is, but rather how beautiful the customer thinks it is. This gives rise to the most powerful emotion in all enterprise. The anxiety producing, face-to-face trauma of customer judgment. The judgment is aimed right at the ego of the entrepreneur. It can send you to the heights of glory or it can shatter your self-esteem. Successful entrepreneurs learn to accept this, and make it work to their advantage by becoming customer experts as well as product experts. Both of these notions—loving your work and accepting that beauty is always in the eyes of the beholder—are central to creating an entrepreneurial passion for product.

• Feeling Old-fashioned Pride

I've never met an entrepreneur who didn't believe that his product was important and that it was doing great things for customers. Entrepreneurs obviously have a strong sense of personal ownership in the products they make and the services they deliver. This is an entrepreneurial given for creating old-fashioned pride, and it's an enormous advantage you will have over your competition. The important question for new entrepreneurs is how to pass their feelings of old-fashioned pride on to their employees.

We know that employee pride in the product depends on having a sense of ownership of the product, the belief that their inputs to the product are important, and that the product is really satisfying customers. If you want your employees to have old-fashioned pride in your company's product, you simply have to pass on to them some level of your own involvement with the product. At minimum, employees have to have some measure of psychological ownership of the product. They also need to know how and why their work contributes to the success of the product. And they have to believe and actually see that the product is doing great things for customers. This means all employees should meet customers, hear their positive comments about the product, and even listen to their complaints.

A lot of people say that pride in product went the way of most old-fashioned things—down the tube. Well, that just isn't true. What is true is that all people in all jobs need to share to some degree in the entrepreneur's natural pride in the product. This means that one of your most important jobs will be to make sure your employees acquire some entrepreneurial feelings about the company's product. Take these things out of the equation, and you'll be in danger of ripping all pride out of your employee's work—and quite possibly the growth out of your new company.

• Making It Better Than The Next Guy

You can succeed in beating the competition in any one of three ways: Providing products and services of higher quality, or lower costs, or both.

You had better be able to do at least one of the three, or you'll simply be out of the game. But to the entrepreneur, the really important word here is *competition*. Trying to "make it better" means making it better than the competition—not having some infinite standard as the goal. Of course this is another reason why entrepreneurs are so focused on their competitors. Blindly pushing for ever higher quality may get you an ISO 9000 certificate, but it may also drive you into bankruptcy. And you can lower costs a lot if you're willing to make junk that falls apart in a week, but your customer base may also fall apart. But don't despair—the entrepreneurial method works every time—just make sure you're "making it better than the next guy."

• Making It Faster Than The Next Guy

Speed is truly the entrepreneur's secret weapon. And as Akio Morita, the founder of Sony, liked to say: "The best thing about it is it's free." This should be sweet music to your ears. It's no secret that entrepreneur's love to compete with big companies. The reason is simple: getting to the finish line first is practically guaranteed!

In high-tech fields like electronics and software, where product life cycles can be as short as six months, the competitive advantage of *making it faster* is well known. But it may not be so obvious in other twenty-first century industries, especially those with long research and development cycles such as biotech. Ed Penhoet, the co-founder of the hugely successful Chiron Corporation says: "Everyone in biotech is smart. So brains just gets you onto the playing field. Once you're in the race however, speed becomes a bigger competitive advantage than either brains or costs in the biotech field."

In the 21st century global economy, you can be sure that *making it faster* will be a critical competitive advantage, no matter what product or service you offer: From Big Macs, to iPads, to finding the vaccine for Hepatitis B—the entrepreneurial winners will be those who "get to the finish line first!"

It almost doesn't matter which actions you take in "Loving The Customer" and "Loving The Product." It's virtually impossible to go wrong spending time on customers and products. To get you started, the upcoming Application can be used to record your first brainstorming session on loving the customer and loving the product. But just before you do that, let's take a look at a company that thinks of little else other than customers and products. Welcome to the beautiful sights and sounds of Taylor & Boody!

THE SIGHTS AND SOUNDS OF TAYLOR & BOODY

"When you buy an organ from us. . . . .
you can be sure we've never built that same organ before."

—John Boody, Co-Founder
Taylor & Boody Organbuilders

You'll find a Taylor & Boody pipe organ in the chapel at the Harvard Business School. You'll also find one at majestic St. Paul's Cathedral on Fifth Avenue in New York City. You'll even find five of them installed in Japan. And at their wood mill and workshop in Virginia, you'll find young apprentices from Germany, the center of the universe for hand crafted organs for hundreds of years, learning their trade from two Americans, George Taylor and John Boody. This is an industry enjoying a global renaissance, and Taylor & Boody is leading the revival in the USA. There are about 50 Taylor & Boody pipe organs around the world, each one custom designed, handmade, and lovingly installed over the past 33 years. That works out to about one and a half a year—and the current backlog of orders stretches out five years.

When I saw their client list, my first thought was about the missed opportunity at Harvard. What a shame the powers-that-be at HBS didn't have the good sense to invite Messrs. Taylor and Boody over to a classroom to give their students a lesson on the art of "loving" customers and products. It's a safe bet that the young MBAs will never hear, at any business school in the world, anything even close to the passion that Taylor and Boody bring to their business.

Listen to John Boody on what it takes to become one of the top companies in the world making and selling large, traditional pipe organs. First, the Taylor & Boody relationship with *customers:* "A big organ is the only musical instrument that's tied to its room. It's not like a harp or a piano that you tote in there and take what you get and then tote it away. So it's very critical that we get good spaces. We can't work with a lot of new churches and music buildings because they're so flimsy, thin walled and just bad acoustically. So we have to work hand in glove with our customers, going out and hammering these projects into line and then servicing the instrument over the years. We always say that when you buy an organ from us, we're going to join your church or join your family. Our customers become our friends. They call us up all the time and we're in constant communication with them. Every year we go around and visit our customers, including those in Japan—and "lay our hands" on the instruments and keep them in good condition. We oversee the constant maintenance and tuning of all our own organs. As the years go by this is getting to be a bigger and bigger activity for us as we have 50 out there now. In any event, we are exceptionally close to our customers. There's no other way to do this work.

"We've developed a motto here of "just say no." This is because our reputation rides on the success of each instrument. If we don't see any possibility for success for the customer, then we shouldn't build the instrument. The first organ we built in Japan was for a university in Yokohama. We were thrilled with this opportunity. They were designing a music auditorium and we went there to consult about the building of the organ. Their building design was so bad that we came back here, and with some acoustical designer friends, conceived of a building, made a cardboard model, and sent it to them. We told them: 'The building you're designing is all wrong. It's not going to be a success at all unless you do it our way—and we won't build the organ unless you do it our way.' There was a very long silence and we were sure we had lost the business. Then, they came back to us and said OK. They changed the whole design of the building, making it very tall and open in the interior, with galleries around three sides, and so on. All things that had never been done in Japan. We built and installed a big three manual organ for them, and today this auditorium is a very influential music room in Japan. The university is delighted and of course this was our entree into the Japanese market. I suppose if we were starving, maybe we'd have to say yes, but we've been really fortunate up to now in that we can say no. The bottom line is people don't just buy our product, they buy Taylor & Boody. Of course the product has to be good but all that aside, when people are looking to purchase a very high dollar item they have to be able to look you straight in the eye and know you can get along. They have to like you and they have to trust you."

Boody is equally passionate when he describes Taylor & Boody's approach to their *product*. Here's a sample: "We're a craft business. We're not a manufacturer in the sense of someone who makes toasters, honing their product and turning it out one after another. George and I, and everyone in our company, are essentially hand-craftsmen which is a very unusual thing in this day and age. We know the music that we have to play on these instruments. And we know what it takes to make the pipes work really well. And we've become very well known for our architectural ability to do the designs, the moldings, the carvings, the very look of the instruments. You have to couple the musical training with the craftsmanship to build a great musical instrument. Of course this is all very labor intensive. Ninety-five per cent of our costs are directly in labor—hand work. There's no production line. Every organ is handmade and custom made. When you buy an organ from us, like the big one you see out on the shop floor now—you can be sure we've never built that same organ before."

The process of organ building is both time-consuming and incredibly demanding. To illustrate, here's Boody's description of just one of the important steps—the preparation of the wood: "We cut all our own timber and saw our own lumber. Because a pipe organ is a big wooden machine, we found early on if we didn't have strict control of our materials we couldn't get the quality we want. So now we control the preparation of the wood from start to finish. The drying is very critical and we have a dry kiln so we can dry our wood to specification. We have our own wood storage warehouse at our mill so we can keep wood over a long period of time, which gives us very good stability and very good quality. We're known now worldwide for the quality of our wood and we actually supply about ten different organbuilders around the country with our surplus, so the wood business has become sort of a sub routine of our organ building business."

After all this tender loving care, it's not surprising that Taylor & Boody's end products are simply awe-inspiring to look at and listen to. As I was leaving the interview with Boody, he handed me a CD titled *Great Organs Of America: Modern Landmarks*. This was obviously something pretty special. He explained: "This is a recording of the largest organ we've built. It's at Holy Cross College in Massachusetts. Listen to it. I think you'll like it." I did listen. Several times. Even to my un-trained ear, it was glorious and powerful. I can only imagine what it must sound like in person. There was a printed message on the CD's inside cover from George Taylor and John Boody:

> *"The Holy Cross Organ represented a pioneering effort to construct a large contemporary organ conceived in the high Renaissance tradition of Dutch organbuilding. The organ's main case is thirty-two feet high and 16 feet wide. Together with its 3,822 pipes, twelve windchests, bellows and Rückpositiv case of solid American white oak, it weighs some nine tons. Building The Holy Cross Organ was a daring adventure. From the outset it has been a challenge to builder and player alike in understanding a great tradition. From a builders perspective this organ presented, above all, an opportunity to enter a world of rarely-heard sounds and practice our craft on an unprecedented scale. The rewards have been great."*

Indeed they have. And that's what makes this such a delightful story to tell. The only hard part interviewing John Boody was finding him. Just over the Blue Ridge Mountains, a half hour down County Highway

254, and then five miles east on Route 708, I found myself in the most beautiful countryside dotted with white farm houses and cows. There were few signs. I drove right past an old two story red brick school building with no markings of any kind. After seeing nothing but more cows for another couple miles, I back-tracked and went to the school building to ask directions. I walked up the main stairs, opened two very large doors, and saw stretching upward through a large opening in the ceiling, the biggest, most magnificent organ I'd ever seen. Behind it was another, about half the size, but equally beautiful. I figured I had found John Boody. The first thing I learned from Boody is that handmade, mechanical pipe organs have a long history—dating back to the fifteenth century in Europe. They are among the oldest surviving technical inventions in the world. Many, built as long as four hundred years ago, are still in regular use and are revered for their superior aesthetics and dependability. But as happens to most treasures of earlier ages, human ingenuity moves on finding "better" ways to meet the same needs. By the dawn of the twentieth century this certainly looked to be the fate of the historic organbuilding industry. But something very different happened. A century later, traditional, hand-made pipe organs are a booming business. Organbuilders call it the "tracker revival" and it's in full swing worldwide. (*Trackers are the thin strips of wood that provide the mechanical connection between the keys and the wind-chest. They're more responsive to the player than the pneumatic or electric actions. The word comes from the Latin—"to pull"— like in tractor*)

Taylor & Boody are very much in the fore-front of this renaissance, so I asked Boody to explain it: "First of all, as happened to a lot of small businesses by the time the twentieth century came along, the old organbuilders got bigger and bigger and they turned out to be big factories. So most pipe organs in this country were made by large companies—not large by some business standards of course—but they weren't small craft companies anymore. And they converted from the traditional mechanical action to both pneumatic and electrically operated systems. They were able to spread the organs all over the churches and music halls from one end to another, because everything was hooked together by electricity. But along the way they kind of lost the point. They lost the handcrafted care that you can put into a product with a small company. A pipe organ, after all, is a musical instrument and it responds really well to the particular attention you can pay when you have a small, craft-oriented company.

"The rebirth started here because so many American servicemen, who were musicians, ended up in Europe at the end second world war. They discovered there were a lot of historically based organs still being used in Germany and Holland and France, and these organs had more musicality and more sensitivity than the big electric action organs that were being built in the USA. They said: 'Well, how can we get back to this music? How can we re-establish this craft in America? Anyway, this started just after the war but it took a while to build. At first it was just imported European instruments, because they had the jump on us. But then shortly we started, in this country, building instruments in the same way. Now it's completely flipped around. There are about five companies, all in this country, who are leading the pack worldwide in the quality of the instruments that are being built."

Since George Taylor and John Boody's company is part of this elite group, an obvious question comes up. What does it take to become one of the top five companies in the world making and selling million dollar handmade pipe organs? Where do you even learn the business of organbuilding? I asked Boody how he and George Taylor got into such an enterprise in the first place: "George and I came at it in slightly different ways. George went to Washington and Lee in Virginia. He was sociology major, but he was an organ student also. So he played the organ and was familiar with organ technology. The school had a Henry Irvin organ built just after the Civil War. The organ was threatened with a modernizing re-working and George went to the President of the University and said 'if you let them change this organ your doing the wrong thing.' The President was impressed and George basically got to oversee the work that was done. That was his introduction to organ building. Actually we've just recently re-restored that same organ. After he graduated, George received a Ford Foundation grant to go to Hamburg, Germany and do a three year apprenticeship with Rudolph Von Beckerath, a very well known organbuilder. He got his German journeyman papers and then went on to get a Master Organbuilder rating. There are very few people who have done that—learning the organ building business in the German way from top to bottom. He came back to U.S. and began working in a partnership in Ohio for an organbuilder named John Brombaugh.

"All through high school and college I sang in choirs, a cappella groups, and even a barbershop quartet. I've also always been interested in making things, particularly in woodworking. I even took Shop class in school which none of the other college track kids were interested in. Of course that was great training for a future organbuilder. I liked working with wood well enough that I went to the University of Maine and entered their forestry program, which is one of the best in the country. It was good training for me, but after a year I decided my heart was really in music and I changed my major from forestry to music. I ended up getting a BA in music—with emphasis on voice and choral conducting. That also turned out to be a great experience for becoming an organbuilder. At the University I worked for the FM radio station and two things happened: First I started a program called Organ Masterpieces and I learned there was a whole genre of European organs that were original, historic instruments. I got interested in that and wondered if anyone in the U.S. was building organs that way. Another thing that happened was I was given a couple of pipe organs that came out of old Maine churches that were getting electronic substitutes. I started putting the organs together and fooling around with the parts. Because of my interest, I even managed to spend my summers apprenticing for Fritz Noack, a great organbuilder in Massachusetts. We have a saying that you can catch the "organ bug" and I really did. There's just something special about pipe organs being mechanical and musical at the same time. I graduated from college in 1968 and was quickly drafted into the Army and went to Vietnam for 13 long months. When I returned home I got a job with John Brombaugh and Company in Ohio. Of course the day I walked in, there was George Taylor."

So there you have it. Business 101 for entrepreneurial organbuilders. It's a far cry from the management pap that business schools serve up. It's George Taylor's love of organs and his years in Germany and the U.S. learning to be one of the world's masters at building them. And it's John Boody combining his love and skills in music and woodworking, to give the business a worldwide reputation for the high quality of its wood and the fine decorative style of its organ cases. In true Disney style, this is how entrepreneurs who love their products and respect their customers prepare themselves for the business world. Yes, not hearing the Taylor & Boody story was a real missed opportunity for the MBA students at The Harvard Business School . . . . .

So then, why and how did Taylor & Boody Organbuilders get started? What was the impetus to take the entrepreneurial plunge and create their own company? Boody continued: "John Brombaugh was part of that group of organbuilders who, after the Second World War, got interested in making historically based organs. They studied the old German organs and learned how to revive a craft that really had been lost for a hundred years in this country. So John was in the first generation of the revival—and George and I are a half generation removed because we worked together with John for seven years. In Ohio we did a lot of pioneering work in metallurgy, metal technology, and pipe making and kind of returned to the historic mechanical action way of building organs. That time was the perfect incubation for us because we were young and inspired and wanted to change the organ world. And we were willing to work for no money—for the opportunity to learn. I think the first year we made 35¢ an hour. We built some really good organs and a number of those organs were very influential to other people.

"We were building a big organ in Eugene, Oregon and while we were working out there Brombaugh fell in love with the West Coast. He just announced one day he was going to move the company to Eugene. John was a little bit on the crazy side, and he didn't worry about how much money he made. George and I decided we didn't want to do that. We had been starving for a number of years so we decided to try starting our own business. In 1977 we took one contract from our partnership with John, with his blessing, as our startup client. When we started we were still young. I was only 31. It took us more than a year to build that first organ. It was very low priced by today's standards, and we took progress payments to survive financially. Of course we had a very slim organization. We actually built that organ in the garage behind my house in Ohio. George and I, with our bare hands, added on to the garage when we needed to set the organ upright. By the time we were through with that organ we already had secured another contract and since that time we've never, ever lacked for work. We've had one contract after another and right now we're running with a five year backlog of contracts."

What? No business plan? No venture capital? No market research? How can you start a company without these things? Easy according to John Boody—if you've just spent ten years becoming very, very good at what you're doing.—and then keep on doing it for customer after customer. Here's Boody's own take on their continued success: "Most importantly, we've lived up to our promises. We tell our customers when the organ will be ready for installation, and what to expect for quality, and we've been able to deliver. They also appreciate that we have our own saw mill and workshop, and that our workplace is attractive, clean and well organized, with good quality equipment, and all that. And we've been very fortunate that we've had some very prestigious jobs. We built the organ for St. Thomas Church on 5th Avenue in New York, which is one of the premier music churches in the country. Now we're going to build a second organ for them, a small portable instrument, so we'll have two organs at St. Thomas! We've also built for Christ Church in Indianapolis, which is very well known for its musical work. The Harvard organ is a small, portable instrument. The business school has a non-sectarian chapel which has three musical instruments—a very fine grand piano, a very good harpsichord, and now a Taylor & Boody organ. Then there is the huge organ we made for Holy Cross College, which has been recorded numerous times. And of course we're very proud of our five organs in Japan."

It was all sounding so uplifting, that I had to remind myself that Taylor & Boody had to compete with some very tough, high quality competitors around the world. I asked Boody to describe the business and competitive climate: "Today we regularly compete with five to ten companies worldwide who are doing a very high level of craft organ building. In this market, the smallest portable organs are around fifty thousand dollars—while the big jobs run over a million dollars. We have a couple of million dollar plus jobs in our backlog right now. By now, we've kind of worked our way to the top of the heap. A lot of our contracts now come to us without any competition. People come to us and say: 'We want to buy a Taylor & Boody. When can you do it for us?' So I guess in business parlance we've developed something of a brand name. We've been able to provide the quality our customers are looking for and also the business structure that people have come to depend on. They know we will deliver the quality and service they expect."

It seems clear that no matter how much business success George Taylor and John Boody attain, they remain craftsmen to the core. Like all craftsmen, they have to both make and sell. And like all successful entrepreneurs, they are very good at both. It's fair to say that they are indeed, masters at "loving" their customers and "loving" their products. My closing question to Boody was on this point. I asked him to describe how Taylor & Boody's powerful customer/product vision is actually implemented in the day to day business. In other words, how does the make and sell process really work at Taylor & Boody: "It's not that we're re-inventing the wheel every time we build an organ for a customer, but they are tailored to fit where they're going to go. The architectural design is different, the stop list is different, and the whole configuration of the instrument can be changed around. We start by going out and examining the customer's building or the drawings, do the acoustical analysis, and begin to design the organ. The mechanical and architectural design is produced on our computers from start to finish. We post the designs in the shop and our people make the parts.

"Everything is made to very strict specifications. For example the facade pipes are constructed of 98% lead and are hammered, planed by hand and lacquered. Lead is used because it gives a more mellow sound. And we've become well known for making instruments with a really wonderful, decorative look to them. So you have to have craft skills like hands-on wood working and wood carving and all those things. The only electric part we use is a small wind blower so the player can inflate the wind bellows electrically or the traditional way of foot pumping. George and I see how the parts are made on a daily basis so we're sure that everything is made just the way we want it. Then we put the whole organ together in our shop, and we test it for performance. So again George and I are working on and responding to how the organ is going together here in the shop. Then we take it all apart, pack it away, and depending on where it's going, put it on trucks or sea containers or air containers. The organ is transported to the site and our people go and put it back together so we're controlling how the re-assembly is done. Then two or three of us go and we listen to every pipe, and we tune it and regulate it so the organ is making the maximum amount of music for the given situation."

Boody neatly summarized it this way: "So from the first sales contact to the finished product, to the last pipe tuned, we pay attention to every step. One thing all this means is that we can't grow too fast. And that's fine with us. We feel where we are right now—about 15 people—is pretty much ideal. We have enough power to keep everything moving forward but George and I can still work with every customer and have our hands on the products from one end to the other."

Taylor & Boody, master organbuilders and new millennium entrepreneurs, provides living proof that a small company can do great things in the world. When you consider the Customer/Product Vision for your own company, remember the Taylor & Boody model. You're going to need the same *absolute focus on customers and products* to survive and succeed in your own entrepreneurial venture. To help keep this in mind, we'll close with one of the most powerful statements of Customer/Product Vision I've ever found. Here are the words of George Taylor and John Boody at the dedication of one of their magnificent products:

> *"In conclusion, one may well ask why we build organs in an age which is ever less interested in objects of lasting worth. Obviously the construction of traditional musical instruments is an anachronism in our time. Not only is a fine organ difficult and time-consuming to build, when compared with machine-made goods, it is costly indeed. Furthermore, learning to play an organ requires years of devoted practice. Given these facts, it is tempting to settle for less expensive*

alternatives to the traditional organ. But the truth remains that there is a value to the work done by human hands which is sacred. The spirit of those who have contributed to this organ will breathe through its music, a message of peace and goodwill. Herein lies the real meaning of this investment. In return may it bring to life the musical treasures of ages past together with the talents of our time. Let it stand as a sign to future generations of our confidence and faith in God who has blessed us so richly.

Chapter 4

High Speed Innovation

When Your Life Depends On It

"We are studying the most sacred information that exists.
The information that goes into designing you."

—Kari Stefansson, Founder
deCODE Genetics

In 1980 there was not one biotech company in the world. Late in that year the United States Supreme Court ruled that genetically engineered organisms are patentable—and one of history's most important, fastest growing entrepreneurial industries was born. Today there are over one thousand biotech firms around the globe. Fortune estimates bio-pharmaceuticals will soon surpass the traditional pharmaceutical industry's total worldwide sales of $250 billion. And that doesn't even include the biggest potential market of all for biotech—agriculture. The only thing quite like it, where venture capital and entrepreneurial start-ups abound, is the twenty year old explosion of the internet industry—except biotech has been at it for thirty years, with arguably much higher tech and infinitely higher touch.

The biotech revolution is now moving from childhood to adolescence, or in our terms from the start-up phase to a phase of sustained high growth. It's been a story of tiny, scientist/entrepreneur led firms literally stealing a $100 billion market from right under the noses of the world's mature, cautious, and slow moving pharmaceutical industry. And there's no end in sight to the growth of the biotech industry. By all rights, the existing giant companies, many of them with very deep pockets and a hundred years of global experience should own this new market. But they don't. The "owners" are companies no one had even heard of twenty years ago. Companies like Genentech, Amgen, Chiron—and now deCODE Genetics, a fabulously interesting and innovative member of today's biotech elite, founded in that far away Viking land called Iceland.

The year 2,000 was the 1,000th anniversary of Leif Eriksson's first voyage from Iceland to the shores of the western hemisphere. There is another exploration taking place in Iceland today, that may have as profound an effect on human-kind as the Vikings' discovery of the new world. And in a very significant way, these two phenomena are inexorably linked. Iceland was and is one of the most homogenous populations in the world. It's made up entirely of the original Vikings from Norway and a few Irish slaves they brought with them in the 9th century. There has been virtually no new migration into Iceland since then. This twist of history is at the heart of Iceland's greatest entrepreneurial company—deCode Genetics—one of the fastest moving and most innovative companies I've ever come across.

Started in 1996, deCODE Genetics and its founder Kari Stefansson, have certainly received great press. The Wall Street Journal headline read: "If This Man Is Right, Medicine's Future Lies In Iceland's Past." The Financial Times in London reported: "Iceland Cashes In On Its Viking Gene Bank." The New Yorker ran a full length feature article titled: "Decoding Iceland" with this lead in: "The next big medical breakthrough may result from one scientist's battle to map the Viking gene pool." What's all this noise about? And just who is Kari Stefansson? And how did this happen in little Iceland—a country with a grand total of 270,000 people.

Well, here's the scoop straight from Reykjavik, Iceland, where Stefansson graciously submitted to a long interview with yours truly on a cold Saturday afternoon. To put the story into some context, it's worth noting that Kari Stefansson had become Iceland's richest person in just the few years since he left his post at Harvard Medical School. He's gone from living on a professors salary to an estimated net worth of $400 million. This was because his start-up firm had become Iceland's most valuable company with a New York Stock Exchange market valuation of approximately $1.5 billion. (*Not even the virtual bankruptcy of the Icelandic government, deCODE's original and principal investor, during the country's economic meltdown in 2008, has stopped Stefansson's biotech juggernaut. In November of 2009, to avoid a hostile takeover at fire-sale prices, deCODE Genetics declared "technical" bankruptcy. But with big, deep-pocketed U.S. venture capital firms such as Saga, Polaris and ARCH lined up at the door, deCODE was fully re-financed and back on track by January 2010—just two months later! As the world's leader in "analyzing and understanding the human genome," backed up by the discovery of key genetic markers for dozens of common diseases such as schizophrenia, breast cancer, type 2 diabetes, glaucoma, prostate cancer, atrial fibrillation and stroke, this is just too valuable an idea and business to be derailed by the worst global economy since the Great Depression! And of course Kari Stefansson, medical/entrepreneurial visionary, still leads the company.*) Not bad for a few years effort! Of course the underlying asset driving deCODE Genetic's amazing success has been a thousand years in the making.

That asset is Iceland's unique, homogeneous population. There are pockets of inbred populations around the world, but there is only one country, Iceland, with an entire population of homogeneous families. As the genealogy is incredibly well documented all the way back to 874 AD and there has been no new migration since, Iceland is a geneticist's dream laboratory. The whole premise that deCODE Genetics is based on is that the only way to discover the genetic basis of complex diseases like cancer, Alzheimer's, schizophrenia, and multiple sclerosis, is by finding the genetic mutations in a homogeneous population, thereby eliminating the wide genetic variability found among different racial and ethnic groups. Only by comparing the DNA of people with the particular disease to very similar people who don't have the disease, can we hope to isolate the disease causing genetic mutations. Iceland is by far the best place in the world to do this. Not only is Iceland's population uniquely homogeneous, the country has also maintained extensive genealogical records dating back to the Viking sagas, has a high quality health care system, and serendipitously has accumulated an extensive bank of human tissues from biopsies and autopsies. On top of this, scientist/entrepreneur Kari Stafansson has assembled 480 top genealogists, geneticists, and DNA researchers in Reykjavik to work for him. They have identified and are currently working on finding the critical genetic mutations for twelve very tough diseases. Stefansson is therefore sitting atop an array of priceless and unique assets for unlocking the secrets of the world's major diseases. They are also assets that make giant pharmaceutical companies drool and bring the international investment community pounding on the door. It's one of those rare and happy intersections in life of doing something really great and being able to make an honest buck at it.

Here's Iceland's most famous "high-speed innovation" entrepreneur in his own words: "Let's take my discipline which is genetics. I mean what is genetics? Genetics is the study of information that goes into the making of man and the flow of this information between generations. It is basically pure bio-informatics. We are studying the most sacred information that exists. The information that goes into designing you. So you could argue that what we are studying is the quintessential "IT." And what we basically do is that we gather very, very large amounts of data on genetics, and we put it into the mechanism of modern informatics. And what we have done is that we have sort of approached our society as a system of data—which we then mine with the use of the informatics technology. It is by far most powerful way of looking for new knowledge in medicine and new knowledge in bio-tech and it has worked wonders for us. And we are convinced that this is going to be the mechanism whereby we institute a new revolution in medicine.

"One of the things that you have read about a lot or seen a lot in the media in your country is the discussion of the Human Genome Project.

This is Francis Collins and Craig Venter and all of those guys. Collins is very bright and he has been a wonderful leader of the Human Genome Project. But that project is focused on sequencing the entire system of the human genome. And once you have done that, how are you going to turn those data into knowledge? And that is where a company such as ours, deCODE Genetics, comes in. We take this human genome data, and look for the correlation between variances in the genome and variances in human nature. Variances like specific diseases, health problems, longevity, etc. So we are in an ideal position once the human genome has been sequenced. We can plough into it and we can begin to deliver knowledge that can be turned into solutions. We have already started doing this in fact."

"The basic approach to what de CODE Genetics is doing is to look at society as sort of a system of information. And the Icelandic society has an advantage when it comes to that. One of the principal advantages is the wealth of knowledge on genealogy here in Iceland. I have the genealogy of the entire nation going 1,100 years back in time on our computer data base. If you think about human genetics as the study of the flow of information, what the genealogy gives you are the avenues by which the information flows. And therefore it allows you to sort out what information goes where, what are the consequences of this variance and that variance. So we have an extraordinary resource in this genealogy data base. Another resource we are beginning to construct these days is a centralized data base on the health care of the entire nation. So you have the genealogy, which basically tells you who is related to whom, and then you will have the health care information on everyone. Then you can begin to figure out exactly what is inherited and what is not, what is transported and what is not. So I think we are in a particularly interesting position in an exciting field and in exciting times—and we have exactly the right data."

By this point in our discussion, it was clear that Kari Stefansson and deCODE Genetics were on to something significant. But the question that started bobbing up in my consciousness was, how did this little miracle of a company get started? I knew that Stefansson's last job was teaching at Harvard, and while prestigious, that seemed a very distant reality from the man I was facing—this world-class entrepreneur and the wealthiest man in the country! So I asked him, how all this happened in just ten years? Stefansson's personal story goes like this: "It happened in the following manner: I was a professor at the Harvard Medical School and was sitting in Boston studying the genetics of multiple sclerosis when I first started to see the confluence of two very important things. One of them was the times—technology was being produced to allow one to study genetics in a systematic manner. And then I began to think about these incredibly important qualities of the Icelandic nation that would be possible to mine once this technology was in Iceland. Secondly, I began to sense the danger that foreign companies and universities would start to come to Iceland and do "helicopter science." By that I mean transporting the material abroad from Iceland for the studies.

"So I started to look at the possibility of setting up a facility in Iceland. And I put together a business plan and it took me a few weeks to raise enough money to start the company. We raised $12 million. We started the company in the fall of 1996 and now the company is valued at about $1.5 billion. So things are going very nicely. When we started our company in the fall of 1996, we had 20 people and now we have almost 500 people. In February of 1998 we signed the largest corporate deal that a biotech company has ever signed in genetics. The deal, with Hoffman La Roche in Switzerland, is valued between $200 and $300 million. This is basically a research alliance where we are working on the discovery of genes that cause twelve common diseases. We share the intellectual property with Hoffman La Roche and they pay us royalties and licensing fees and fund the work. So things have gone very nicely."

It's always interesting, I think, to find out what people think is responsible for their entrepreneurial success, and especially those people who don't really consider themselves entrepreneurs or even businesspeople. Kari Stefansson fits this bill so I asked him: "If a person who didn't know anything about starting a business, let alone a biotech business, came to you and asked the reason for your pretty amazing success, what would you tell them?" The surprising reply: "What I think characterizes the successful entrepreneur, or the successful start-up which is the extension of the entrepreneur, is in addition to having a good idea, and willingness to work extraordinarily hard, is the love of the risk. It's not only that you shouldn't spend an awful lot of time avoiding risks; I think you should actually seek out the risk. It's the quintessential component of this—to thumb your nose at the risk. Sure everyone is a little bit afraid of risk. But what gives you the courage to look the risk in the face—is the fact that you believe in your idea. First you have to put together an idea or a concept. And the concept has to be good and you have to believe in it. Once you believe in your concept, the risk that others perceive is basically irrelevant. It isn't there. Because you believe your idea is so great, you'll be able to go through anything.

"But it is also the willingness to sacrifice everything for what you're doing. And it's not because the amount of contribution you can make is in sort of a linear correlation with the amount of time you spend on it. It isn't. There is an exponential contribution when you begin to live the concept, rather than just work on it. You elevate yourself up to a higher level. You begin to see things in a way that no one else sees. You begin to understand in a way which no one else understands. I think it is the question of being able to put all of this intensity into it. And if you cannot do that, if you don't do that, nothing is going to come from even the best of ideas. Nothing can possibly come out. This is the modern crusades. This is the modern Viking, you know. You go in and sacrifice everything. And if you have a good concept, and you have good people, you come out a winner. If you don't the first time, never mind. If you are still consumed by your work, the following morning you rise out of the ashes like the Phoenix, and begin again anyway."

It was almost time to close off the interview, but I really wanted to get Stefansson's thoughts on our notion of the "organization life cycle." This should be particularly relevant to a company so dependent on maintaining its speed and innovation. So I said to him: "Kari, our research shows that every company has a life cycle. They start, they grow big, they become bureaucratic, and most of them eventually die. What happens mid-way through is that the entrepreneurial genius that got them going in the first place eventually gets smothered by management techniques and bureaucracy. A primary casualty of this phenomenon is the company's ability to maintain its high-speed innovation—which you just happen to live and die by. Perhaps deCODE Genetics is too young to have faced this yet, but you will. How will you handle it?"

Stefansson thought for a moment and answered: "Everyone has to face this. And I will tell you, this is a particularly difficult task in a discovery based company like ours. Because the fact of the matter is, chaos is essential for the creative process. I know this is the opposite of 'good management' but we must find the way to stay creative. It will be difficult to do but we have no choice. I'll tell you a secret, which shows the importance of failing to do this. The only reason the biotech industry exists today, is that the pharmaceutical industry failed terribly at doing this. We exist because the pharmaceutical industry has been incapable of maintaining a creative spirit within their own labs and organizations.

"So I recognize the near inevitability of the failure to do this if you grow beyond a certain size. But these are exciting challenges to deal with. I am absolutely 100% convinced that we can succeed at it, but it's going to keep us up on our toes. With the products we are developing, plus our gene discoveries and intellectual properties, we may, because of this very problem, spin off these things into smaller companies to try to maintain this creative spirit which we know is so much easier to maintain in the smaller organization."

The following Monday I took up Kari Stefansson's offer to visit his offices and the "marvelous lab" he was so proud of. Joining me was my partner in Iceland, Arni Sigurdsson, and his associate, Olli Olafsson. Our tour guide was Laufey Amundadottir, who has a Ph. D. from Georgetown University and was doing research on breast cancer at Harvard before she returned to Iceland to join deCODE. She is currently the Division Head at deCODE for Cancer Genetics and personally runs the sub-projects on lung cancer and prostate cancer. The first stop on the tour was the work station of Thor Kristjansson, deCODE's Senior Programmer and the architect of the firm's genealogical data base. After a few introductory comments, he suggested a simple demonstration might be the best way to understand his job. He turned to Olli Olafsson, a complete stranger to him of course, and said: "Let's see how you and I are related. What's your complete name and date of birth? Olli told him and Thor typed it onto the screen:

"Olafur Thor Olafsson—26, 11, 1953"

Next he typed in his own name and birth date:

"Thordur Jon Kristjansson—03, 04, 1965"

Then he clicked on a few icons and the page began to scroll with separate columns of the names and birthdates of generation after generation of both his and Olli's direct line of ancestors until . . . . . bingo! A single name popped up, centered in a box, above the two lists:

"Jon Thorsteinsson—born 1687 / died 1762"

Just beneath the name and dates were a couple of indecipherable lines of Icelandic, obviously giving some details about great, great, great, great, great, great, great grandfather Thorsteinsson. "There," Thor proudly announced: "is my and Olli's most recent common ancestor!" Olli almost fell over. My partner Arnie was beside himself. And I, who have spent three decades trying to construct my own family tree, back just three or four generations, stared at the screen in stunned silence. The computer had jumped 313 years and eleven generations back in 10 seconds. Laufey, our guide and cancer expert, simply smiled and said, "This is why Iceland is a good place to do genetic research."

High-speed innovation is obviously the name of the game in biotech. Kari Stefansson knows his company is racing against time—with an insatiable need for innovation. He and deCODE Genetics have these two qualities, speed and innovation, in spades. And he's rightly concerned about keeping them alive as his company grows ever larger. And what about you? Well, help is on the way. Listed below are the two key practices to insure that you can create and maintain innovative action in your own business. We call them "the golden rules of high-speed innovation."

THE TWO GOLDEN RULES OF HIGH-SPEED INNOVATION

By now you may be saying, "But I'm not searching for cures to the world's great diseases and I'm not thinking about inventing the world's next blockbuster product. Anyone could be fast moving and innovative with those kinds of goals. My business idea is more normal, perhaps even a bit mundane. Who is going to feel such a great need for speed or innovation in my business? Where's our feeling of necessity and sense of urgency going to come from?" Unfortunately, there's no free lunch on instilling the idea that high-speed innovation is a necessity in business—any business. And the impetus for it has to come from you, the founder. You have to build it into your business. It comes from your own perceptions of the challenges you face and what needs to be done to succeed. Regardless of your circumstance, whatever your business, doing it better and doing it faster has to be made into an exhilarating race against time. Beating your customers' expectations and beating the competition is a noble challenge for any company. Even beating your own personal best can be thrilling—and sometimes even more important than beating the next guy. For sure, you can't just sit around hoping something big and exciting happens to your business. Fortunately, you *can* make it happen. You absolutely *have* to make it happen if you expect your people to respond with great speed and great ideas.

Akio Morita, the great founder of Sony liked to say: "Innovative action is the entrepreneur's secret weapon . . . and the best thing about it is it's free!" He was right. Just consider this: A landmark study of California companies found that the cost of innovation, as measured by new products and patents, is an astounding twenty four times greater at large companies than small companies. If you're the CEO of a giant bureaucracy, this statistic could keep you awake nights. If you're a start-up entrepreneur, it's the best news you'll ever hear. Few people today need statistics to convince them that speed and creativity are major competitive factors in our global economy. And even fewer would disagree that young, entrepreneurial companies, can and regularly do, beat the socks off their larger competitors. The number one reason: They are both faster and more innovative.

The question, then, is: How do you do that? What is it really that makes entrepreneurs and their start-ups so fast moving and innovative? And can you keep it alive as your company moves along its life cycle— getting bigger and more bureaucratic year after year? These are terribly important things to know—we might call them the "genetic mutations" of the entrepreneurial company. Fortunately, unlike decoding the human genome, entrepreneurial practices are not so complicated. At the heart of all high-speed innovation, are just two golden rules: Feeling the necessity to invent and having the freedom to act.

THE NECESSITY TO INVENT

Remember this bit of old-fashioned wisdom: *Mater artium necessitas?* If your Latin is a bit rusty, it says "necessity is the mother of invention." And we've all been saying it since the time of Caesar—because it's absolutely true. History is replete with evidence that anyone can be innovative if their life depends on it. And nowhere will you find better illustrations than in entrepreneurial enterprise.

Inside most bureaucracies however, you can't find anybody who feels much necessity about anything. From the sales clerks who shrug their shoulders all the way up to the executives who haven't talked to a real customer since 1985, absolutely no one seems accountable for anything. This would be unfathomable behavior to an entrepreneur. When it's down to putting food on the table, succeeding with your business is a burning necessity, not a box to be checked off on the Performance Review form. To make sure the spirit of *mater artium necessitas* stays alive in your business, here are three key points to keep in mind:

• Feeling The Heat Of Necessity

It's hard to beat great stories like, for example, the six Minnesota miners who in 1906 faced bankruptcy after putting their life savings into a "worthless" gravel pit. They hoped it would yield valuable minerals but all they could find was sand. Out of desperation they invented sandpaper—the first product of 3M—and the rest is history. Those six miners in Minnesota felt it. They understood that winning is a necessity because your survival is on the line. It's called taking it personally and it's the most powerful force ever concocted to motivate people.

In other cases, feeling the heat of necessity can lead you to a more cerebral—or should we say virtual—result than sandpaper. Take the incredible case of Jerry Wang and David Filo, co-founders of Yahoo. They were Ph.D. students and buddies at Stanford in the early nineties. At the time, they and their friends were all experimenting with a remarkable new research and information source called the World Wide Web. But Wang and Filo could see that the variety and quantity of information on the Web was becoming so immense, it was impossible for anybody to really know what was out there. And there was no categorization of topics which made using it for research a real hit or miss proposition. As users they feared this wonderful new information access system was imploding into a chaotic mess. *Fortune* described their response this way: "So the two went to work building software that could organize Internet sites into categories. Within a few months the site, which initially was called Jerry's Guide to the World Wide Web, was renamed Yahoo and took on a life of its own. Yang and Filo found themselves working round the clock, and Stanford's computer infrastructure began to creak under the traffic. In late 1994 university officials asked them to find a company that was willing to host their service, and Yang and Filo finally admitted they were onto something big." What they were onto, of course, was the fastest growing internet company in the world—all thanks to their finely tuned feeling of the necessity to invent.

Great companies like Sony and 3M and Yahoo, work very hard at keeping this feeling alive and so should you. Whether your organization is in bricks-and-mortar, or cyberspace, you have to keep innovation and creativity alive. You must make the necessity for invention very visible to all your people. The best way to do this is to make sure they know they're an important part of an important competitive mission. Beating the competition is a powerful entrepreneurial motivation, so why not make everyone a part of the contest? Another critical step for many organizations will be to simply tell their employees why invention is a necessity and why it's an important part of their job. Of course you should back this up with performance goals and awards for being innovative. And don't forget the all-important 3M lesson: that failure in the pursuit of improvement is part of the deal and no one gets fired for trying. Making sure everyone in the company personally understands the necessity to be innovative, is in fact the first necessity.

• Create Crisis And Urgency

Akio Morita, the great founder of Sony said: "A little crisis is a good thing." And so it is. Everyone knows that more gets done in a day of crisis than a month of complacency. And few great leaps forward have ever resulted from careful planning. They almost always come on the wings of crisis. But how do you get this notion embedded in the organization—and keep it alive for decades? You obviously can't go around screaming at people at the top of your lungs (well, once in a while probably won't hurt) or threatening to fire everyone in sight. And you can't constantly be creating fake crises—that the sky is falling in on us if we don't get this report out by 5 o'clock.

But here are some things you *can* do. You can start establishing real deadlines, sticking to them, and even trying to beat them. It also means taking it very hard if a good customer is lost. And it certainly means that all your employees know you are dead serious about making the business a success. The trick is to dole out these messages in small, regular doses. Creating tiny tremors, not giant earthquakes, if you will. It still may not please the all-stress-is-bad crowd, but the entrepreneurial message is clear: A little crisis a day keeps complacency away.

• **Do Something, Anything, Better Each Day**

Thomas Edison, still the all-time record holder of American patents and the founder of scores of companies, was famous for this pearl of wisdom: "Invention is 10% inspiration and 90% perspiration." So what can you do to make sure the "perspiration level" in your business is high? For starters, you and every employee you hire have to believe that the most important task you have every day is to find a better way to do something. "Better" means more quantity, more quality, more speed, and less cost. It's called continuous improvement in human performance—and it's one of the most visible differences in behavior between the hungry entrepreneur trying to survive and the complacent bureaucrat counting the days till retirement.

Wouldn't it be wonderful if every employee you ever hire comes to work each day thinking, "What can I do today a little bit better than yesterday?" But of course they won't -- unless you tell them it's the most important part of their job. Finding a way to do something better, faster, and cheaper every day requires continuous innovation. And making sure this philosophy is worked into the daily performance of all employees could be your core competitive advantage

THE FREEDOM TO ACT

Entrepreneurs have well deserved reputations for high-speed innovation, in very large part because they take for themselves, the freedom to act. In fact, most entrepreneurs say action is much more important than innovation. A great idea with no action to implement it doesn't do much for the bottom line. If a person or company is very action oriented, trying this and trying that, going here and going there, most people would say: "Wow, look at all the things they're doing. That's really an innovative group." The fact is, if you try out a lot of new ideas, if you are willing to experiment, and if you make a mistake you come right back and try again, you are an innovative group. The important brand of innovation in business has never been quiet, ivory tower analysis to come up with a blockbuster idea. It has always been, and will continue to be trying ten different things and hoping three of them work.

It's very much the old story about Amoco, which for many years was the top USA company in oil and gas exploration. When the crusty, long-term CEO was asked how Amoco beat all the other bigger oil companies in finding new oil, he replied: "We drill the most holes. You find a lot of oil when you drill a lot of holes." And so it is in all business. Here are three proven approaches to creating a bias for action in your organization.

• Freeing The Genius Of The Average Worker

Entrepreneurs simply don't buy the notion that you have to be a rocket scientist to run a business. It's not the deep intellectual proposition the big name business schools make it out to be. Enterprise runs on common sense and the bulk of the common sense resides in the bulk of the people. In other words, the average worker. Soichiro Honda called it the "genius of the average worker." It's these people who know the product inside and out. They're the ones on first name terms with customers. It's the average worker who has to deal every day with every stupid form and time-wasting procedure in the company. In summary, they have the most intimate knowledge of the workings of the business. None of this is surprising of course. What is surprising is how little we use their genius. We don't expect great ideas or great initiative from this crowd. And if we don't expect it, they ain't going to give it.

So why don't we strip clean this gold mine of good ideas and mass of energy? A big part of the trouble seems to be with the reality of who is average. Average workers come to work on time, go home on time, and in between do their job. They do what we expect them to do. They're not the superstars in the company. They're never going to become a vice president, let alone CEO. The average workers also aren't the bums of the business. They're not drug addicts, thieves, or lazy no-goods. They don't come to work every day determined to wreck the company. Average means average which means most big time corporate executives don't think about them much.

Not only do those larger corporations not tap their genius, they seem absolutely determined to deep-six any ideas or suggestions the average workers have. Putting good human relations aside, what would you lose if the bulk of your people go brain-dead as they walk in through the factory gate? What is the cost of freezing out the action-taking instincts of 90 percent of your people? The answer is obvious. You'll get a company full of "rivetheads"- the half angry, half sad label coined by Ben Hamper, GM assembly line worker turned writer. From his own experience in the factory, Hamper says you get to the place where "Working the line at GM was like being paid to flunk high school the rest of your life."

As an entrepreneur, fighting for your survival, you can't afford to operate this way. You can't afford to silence your richest source of improvement ideas and kill the initiative of the people who know the most about your business. You have to find a better way.

• Action With Customers, Products, And Inside Your Organization
Where should you aim your improvement actions? If everywhere, all the time, sounds too ambitious (or a little nutty) how about focusing on the core of what keeps you competitive? And that, of course, leads us right back to customers and products. We're not talking about silly things like more customer questionnaires that no one bothers to read, or a new advertising slogan about product quality that no one believes. The actions that change your core competitiveness are always the sleeves-rolled-up efforts to make buying, using, and servicing your product a faster and better experience for customers. You'll simply never go wrong by trying things to improve your products and better sell and service your customers. Of course, every single action may not be a home run, but there's no faster, cheaper way to learn and improve.

Actions directed at the key processes and internal workings of the organization are sure-fire winners also. There is one giant caveat, however: They've got to be connected to the business of making great products and keeping customers coming back for more. We're definitely not talking about marginal activities like who gets the comer office or planning the company picnic. Entrepreneurs are often astounded by what they see in this regard when they get acquired by bigger companies. Dozens of committees, a thousand meetings and a million e-mails are expended on ideas and projects that have absolutely nothing to do with the core business. It's as if the really hard thinking and the most determined actions are reserved for feathering the nest of the bureaucracy or providing perks for the executives. Beyond this caveat, there is serious work to do on the internal workings of the company. High on the list of priorities would be actions to improve the key processes of the business such as: personnel procedures, finance and accounting systems, administrative efficiency, cost control, purchasing, legal, etc.

Next, there is also serious work to do on fighting bureaucracy inside the company. Almost all of it involves getting rid of something, not adding something. Actions attacking dysfunctional procedures, out of date forms and out of touch committees are all worth their weight in gold. It's called battling bureaucracy. Read on . . . . .

• Battling Bureaucracy

What should you, as the boss, be doing about bureaucracy? Plenty! Remember, the fundamental purpose of rapid action in business is to beat the competition to market with better products and services. Anything going on in the company that gets in the way of that goal has to go. In this sense, taking a sledgehammer to any emerging bureaucracy in your business may be the single, most heroic act you will ever take as an entrepreneur. You're the only person who can stop bureaucracy from getting started, and you'll be the only person who can clean up the mess if it does get started.

Here's the bottom line in battling bureaucracy: Don't let it get started in the first place. Every time someone suggests a new procedure, a new committee, or another system, ask yourself: "How exactly is this going to contribute to beating the competition?" If you can't come up with a clear, convincing answer, kill the new idea. Don't worry; the company won't implode into a black hole no matter how passionately the champion of the new program pleads the case. The best approach in this crusade is—when in doubt, don't do it. And use your common sense.

Often simple things can be the most effective: five-minute meetings, one-page memos, periodic crusades to cut down on e-mail, and annual bureaucracy audits to weed out unnecessary practices, procedures, and forms. Finally, don't fool yourself into thinking you can hold off on this because it couldn't possibly be a problem in your small enterprise. Take my word for it—it only takes three people to create a raging bureaucracy!

We'll conclude this Chapter on High-Speed Innovation by taking a look at another great entrepreneurial sector, the booming *Green Marketplace*, driven by a seemingly endless demand for environmentally friendly products and services. Like Kari Stefansson and the biotech industry, this new sector operates in a race against time—with an insatiable need for innovation.

CHANGING THE WORLD WITH A GOOD IDEA

"I actually felt guilty wasting that much water."

—Lito Rodriguez, Founder
DryWash

This is the amazing story of Lito Rodriguez, a young Brazilian entrepreneur, who has innovated a technical and business revolution by figuring out how to wash cars without a drop of water. Given current estimates that half of the world will be facing severe fresh water shortages by 2050, washing cars, and anything else, without using water looks like a business with a big future for the coming "green economy." In fact, Rodriguez's company, DryWash, has only been in business a little over a decade but it has already become the largest chain of car-wash facilities in the world with some 500 locations in Brazil alone. And Rodriguez showed me a backlog of 13,000 franchise applications piled up in his offices, from all around the globe, the day I met him. Just 40 years old, Lito Rodriguez is living proof that high-speed innovation is indeed the entrepreneur's secret weapon—and that you can still change the world with a good idea!

I recently had the pleasure of meeting and interviewing Rodriguez in Sao Paulo, Brazil. We met at one of his busy DryWash locations so I could see the magic in action. Heraldo Tino, my company's long-term affiliate for Brazil, set this all up and even acted as the interpreter for the interview. After watching a couple of spectacular demonstrations of DryWash personnel cleaning and polishing cars without water, I was dying to know how Lito got into such a business. His answer, translated from Portuguese, was disarmingly down-to-earth: "As a car owner I saw the need for a professional approach to car washing. At all the places I used to go to wash my car I found dirty, ugly, and unfriendly people-in an unfriendly setting. I imagined that a chain of car washes with precise standards for the setting, the procedures, and the right way to treat consumers would be successful. It would especially be a more appealing place for women to get their cars washed. With standards, you could measure the results and with a chain you could get your brand name in the head of the clients. Two ideas could summarize my initial plan for the car wash business: high, consistent standards and a chain of locations.

I asked him how he actually started up the business. "I didn't start with the DryWash business at first. What I started was a traditional car wash, with water. I made it very plush, with good standards, a nice waiting room with magazines and coffee and all the amenities possible. That was my idea of a good car wash. We invested about $50,000 to get it started. Now that wasn't the amount we invested in the dry wash process. It was much less but I can't say exactly how much since it was money out of my pocket in the course of washing cars the traditional way. By the way, I forgot to tell you that in the beginning I had a partner. The first time the business required more money, he left. At that moment, I had to sell my car, the telephone lines, my wife's car, everything just to keep the first business running."

How Rodriguez got from the traditional car wash business to DryWash is the heart of his story. "Originally, as a customer, I was not satisfied with what I was getting for my money in all the car wash shops I had been. As I said earlier, at first my considerations were simply two:

standards and creating a chain. However, after getting into the business and studying the problem more closely—and I spent a small fortune getting my car washed over and over at other stations for months—I realized that a car washed by hand or by machinery generates a tremendous waste of water and electricity. We all know how precious water is nowadays and in Brazil we also suffer from high energy costs and sometimes have electricity rationing by the government. So I realized that it is almost impossible to have a clean place where so much water is being jettisoned at high speed against cars, spilling all over the place, and taking a large amount of dirty, greasy water down through the drainage systems. It couldn't be a clean place and it was terrible for the ecology. Anyway, the first thing a successful entrepreneur has to do is to know his product. He must be above everybody in his field on product knowledge. In my case, I really wanted to have the best car wash chain in the world. I started a car wash of my own, washing cars the traditional way, using a lot of water and electricity. But if you apply your intelligence, if you feel the need to improve, and you work in the field 16 hours a day, 7 days a week, you will eventually come up with a better way!

"In any event, the dry wash process was invented because I was unhappy with the wasted water I saw going down the drain every day. I actually felt guilty wasting that much water. To give you an idea, washing just one car requires about 316 liters of water. If you multiply that over a million cars per year, you can see that DryWash is saving the country a tremendous amount of fresh water. Our process also reduces the amount of electricity used per vehicle by 99.5 percent! These are important things and that's why we began to experiment to find a better way. When I started the research, I found out I didn't really have to be a chemist to create this product. That was lucky since I failed chemistry in school! But I started asking questions to people who were chemists. And I read a lot about the cleaning process. So I didn't pay anyone to invent the product for me. After gathering all the information I could, I started trying components, materials, mixing this and that. I actually started by using my mother's cake mixer to do the mixing-much against her will I should add. I do have to admit however, we did pay a chemist to sign off on the final formula, because we legally needed a chemist to endorse and verify the product.

"I can't pinpoint exactly the moment when we finally invented the dry wash process. We were experimenting, experimenting, experimenting, and the formula was getting better and better until we could finally say: 'This is it.' In reality, all our research was based on a simple principle: Water does not wash anything. Friction cleans things, not water. You can stand for hours under a shower and your hair will not be cleaned. It's the friction of the soap and your fingers on the hair that actually cleans your hair."

In just a decade DryWash has established a chain of some 500 auto wash units, cleaning 90,000 cars a month, and employing close to 2,000 employees. The company also created a chemical manufacturing division, which produces all the products to supply the franchisees. This division also manufactures DryWash products to sell through retail chains as do-it-yourself cleaning supplies for homes and offices.

The concept behind its main chemical product, called DryWash Neutro, is the transformation of heavy particles of dirt into light particles through a process of crystallization and fragmentation. This cleans the automobile and leaves a fine impermeable protective film that produces more shine and protects the paint against rain, pollution, and ultraviolet rays. This treatment greatly reduces oxidation and premature wear and maintains the original look of the car a lot longer. The application is simple and efficient, using on average only 220 milliliters of the product which is applied and removed by small washcloths.

The driving force of the company is the franchise system, which is growing by leaps and bounds. DryWash has some large, multiple site franchises, a lot of mid-sized sites which they call Express franchises, and has recently introduced the one-person franchise which has become the fastest growing part of the business. These individual, highly mobile franchisees handle between 10 and 50 vehicles per day at locations such as automobile dealerships, small parking facilities, auto body repair shops, and even upscale private residences. Rodriguez believes it's the individual franchisee segment that will continue to give the network its explosive growth in the future. And there's plenty of room to grow. The potential Brazilian market is roughly 40 million car washes a month. DryWash is aiming for a ten-fold increase in volume over the next decade from the current 90,000 car washes per month to one million. And that will still be only 2.5 percent of the domestic market.

Despite the cynicism of most marketing experts, DryWash has succeeded in developing a franchise network that ensures consistent quality and high standards of service in what has always been a low quality, haphazard industry. The DryWash method, with its strong environmentally friendly characteristics, has drawn a lot of favorable press which has also contributed to the company's rapid growth. Rodriguez has patented DryWash's products and its washing process. This is an important differential in a market which is still very informal, operates with virtually no quality standards, and shows little concern for the environment. Rodriguez's knack for innovation has actually given DryWash a tremendous cost advantage over its competitors. Since it uses no water, consumes 99.5 percent less energy than its competitors, and does not require expensive equipment or facilities, DryWash is able to keep the costs of its franchises very low, providing a healthy profit margin of 20 percent in a very price sensitive marketplace.

All these factors are creating a bevy of new growth opportunities for DryWash. Rodriquez's eyes sparkle when he talks about all the interest he's getting from other possible markets such as the cleaning of aircraft, cruise ships, public transport, all manner of public facilities and more recently desert based equipment from the military. And with such an innovative technology, it's not surprising that the Brazilian entrepreneur has also been showered with franchise applications from the Middle East, Japan, Europe, Australia, and of course the United States. In fact, when we met, Rodriguez was up on the latest news from the U.S. pointing out that many states were suffering droughts at that time. He even named several states that were restricting the washing of vehicles. With a smile, he said to be sure and tell the readers of this book that he is ready to sign up new franchises anywhere in the world!

So Rodriguez has invented a great product and has already built a successful company. Where is he headed today? What's the future mission of DryWash? His answer came with an innovative twist, "The future of DryWash is all about creating self-employed entrepreneurs. We have now started selling a one-man franchise. For as little as $1,000 a franchisee can be trained by our company to apply the DryWash product as a mobile independent. He can do this with house calls, in public parking lots, at apartment buildings, at company parking lots-wherever there's a lot of cars parked. And remember, because of the DryWash process, he can do it without the use of water so our system does not make a mess in the parking lot. I am making an uneducated citizen the owner of his own business. He can make a decent living and raise a family all by himself. All the young people you see at the red lights cleaning windshields—they can become legitimate self-employed entrepreneurs using our product. We've just started this approach and we already have close to one hundred people working in this system. Since we introduced this concept, it's become so popular that our biggest problem is handling all the applications. We have more than 13,000 people applying to be a franchisee-with most of them in the one-man-shop category.

"The exciting thing is, we can actually create entrepreneurs. We can create entrepreneurs inside the company—so to speak. Even big companies need entrepreneurs. Of course you have to find a way to keep entrepreneurship alive in any business. I'm trying to do that by keeping DryWash small-in a way. I mean I do not want to see DryWash itself become a giant company. What I do want to see are thousands of small entrepreneurs like myself, owning their own franchised car wash, being face-to-face with their clients every day. I think that's the best route for DryWash in the future."

DryWash's rapid growth and great success is clearly based on Rodriguez's abundant supply of high-speed innovation. I was curious to learn how he prepared himself to create such a radically different vision for such a fragmented and mundane market. This could be very important as there must be hundreds of similar, old-line industries just waiting for an entrepreneur to come along and create a revolution as Lito Rodriguez did. "First, my background is completely devoid of any technical education. As I said, I did not know anything about chemistry. In fact, I could not get into the University of Sao Paulo because I flunked the chemistry examination. I did graduate from another university with a degree in advertising. And I never really studied business administration. I guess the closest I came to studying business was taking two years of economics in college. But if I had to pick just one word it would be *creativity*. We should do our best to teach young people to be creative. I do not claim to know exactly how this can be done, but creativity is absolutely necessary if you hope to be a successful entrepreneur. I have learned, however, that the first step in coming up with a new and better way to do a business is to really identify with what you do. You have to like what you do. If you do not like it, the chances of success are very slim. At first, you may not be sure of what you want. I tried three businesses before DryWash. I did not succeed in any of them because I did not personally identify myself with them. In my view, most people become entrepreneurs because they feel a need. They feel the necessity to create. It's not an economic need. In fact, if you start a company just to make money, probably you will not succeed. I'm talking about the necessity to find better ways of doing the same thing. It's the necessity to create something. I think this need to create is actually what starts most companies."

Lito Rodriguez, modem Brazilian entrepreneur, typifies the principles of entrepreneurship just as faithfully as earlier legends like Walt Disney, Akio Morita, and William Lever. He obviously has a powerful sense of mission about his work. He is absolutely focused on customers and products. He is clearly self-inspired to do what he does. And he is just brimming over with innovative action. It's nice to know that a good idea can still change the world even if it starts in a single car wash in Brazil!

Chapter 5

Self-Inspired Behavior

Love What You Do
And Get Very Good At Doing It

"I promoted myself."

—Sarah Breedlove Walker, Founder,
Walker Manufacturing Co.

Feeling disadvantaged? Try being poor, uneducated, black, and a single mother in 19th century America. You can be sure that Sarah Walker never had an affirmative action promotion, a seminar on motivation, or a stock option—yet somehow she managed to become America's first self-made woman millionaire—of any race or ethnic origin! And back in 1900 a million bucks was still a million bucks.

Born in 1867, the daughter of former slaves and orphaned at 7, Sarah Breedlove never saw the inside of a school room. She was married off at 14, widowed with children by 20, and earned her keep as a washerwoman. In your great-grandmother's America, you couldn't get more "disadvantaged" than Sarah. Yet this ebony dynamo invented, manufactured and sold health and beauty products for black women, had 3,000 employees and created a 20,000 strong sales agent network— and became the most successful (and richest) woman entrepreneur in the country.

Madame Walker, as she liked to be called, set a whole new standard for self-inspired behavior: "I am a woman who came from the cotton fields of the South. I was promoted from there to the washtub and then to the kitchen. From there I promoted myself into the business of manufacturing hair goods, and I built my own factory on my own ground." And promote herself she did. By the time she died in 1919, sales were close to a million dollars a year and Madame Walker had etched herself a place in business history. How do such impossible dreams happen?

Why are some people so self-inspired while others spend their lives waiting for something to happen? Dig a little deeper into Sarah Walker's history and some of her answers begin to emerge. Like many black women of her time, Walker's hair began falling out at an early age. Whether due to poor diet, disease, or whatever, there were certainly no special products to treat such maladies. Indeed, no manufacturers produced any products to meet the hygiene or beauty needs of African-American women. In desperation she began concocting her own shampoo and hair conditioner to save her hair. Once successful, the word spread throughout her community and she couldn't make enough to satisfy the needs of other black women. She began selling door to door, with many of her customers becoming sales agents themselves. She attracted an army of other self-inspired black women, eager to move up from $2 a week as a domestic, to the $20 plus per week Walker agents could earn. Sold as the Walker System, she soon had factories and hair salons across the United States plus sales operations throughout the Caribbean and South America. This is self-inspired entrepreneurship at its finest.

The authoritative biography of Sarah Breedlove Walker comes from A'Lelia Bundles, her great, great granddaughter. Bundles is an author, former TV news producer for both ABC and NBC, and a graduate of Harvard and Columbia School of Journalism. In her meticulously researched biography—*On Her Own Ground*—she summarizes Walker's life as follows: "As a pioneer of the modern cosmetics industry and the founder of the Madam C. J. Walker Manufacturing Company, Madam Walker created marketing schemes, training opportunities and distribution strategies as innovative as those of any entrepreneur of her time. As an early advocate of women's economic independence, she provided lucrative income for thousands of African American women who otherwise would have been consigned to jobs as farm laborers, washerwomen and maids. As a philanthropist, she reconfigured the philosophy of charitable giving in the black community with her unprecedented contributions to the YMCA and the NAACP. As a political activist, she dreamed of organizing her sales agents to use their economic clout to protest lynching and racial injustice. As much as any woman of the twentieth century, Madam Walker paved the way for the profound social changes that altered women's place in American society."

Sarah Walker's life provides a textbook, rags-to-riches example of both working harder and working smarter. We call it "loving what you do" and "getting very good at doing it" the two qualities which underpin all entrepreneurial behavior. Here's a very different kind of entrepreneurial example, but one that also illustrates exactly the same two qualities.

WORKING SMARTER AND HARDER

"We got the hepatitis B vaccine for only one reason—we started working very hard on it way back in 1981, and we never stopped until we got it. I mean it wasn't an accident. It didn't just fall out of the sky one afternoon."

—Ed Penhoet, Co-Founder
Chiron Corporation

It was quite chic a while back to say: "work smarter not harder." That turned out to be bad advice. The people and the companies who get to the top, do both. Working smarter *and* harder is certainly what it takes to be a successful entrepreneur. When people can out-think *and* out-work their competition, they're simply unbeatable. Take the case of this giant of the bio-tech world, Dr. Edward J. Penhoet—scientist/entrepreneur—and co-founder Chiron.

After 25 years Chiron had emerged as one of the big winners in the worldwide biotech race. It was in fact the number three biotech firm in the world—after Genentech and Amgen. Their first mega discovery and blockbuster product was the vaccine for hepatitis B—a huge scientific and commercial success. That breakthrough propelled the company on to hundreds more laboratory and marketplace firsts—culminating in Chiron's acquisition by Swiss pharmaceutical giant Novartis in 2006 for a whopping $5.1 billion. That purchase, for just 58% of the publicly traded stock, actually translated into a total market value of Chiron of some $9 billion! Not a bad result for 25 years of working smarter *and* harder—as Dr. Penhoet liked to say.

Ed Penhoet and his two co-founders, William Rutter and Pablo Valenzuela, scratched out their first business plan on Easter Sunday, 1981, in Penhoet's living room. They were far ahead of the curve. There weren't yet any markets to analyze or competitors to emulate. Indeed, there was no biotech industry at all. It had only been a few short months since the historic Supreme Court ruling (allowing genetically produced hormones to be patented) that would ultimately turn thousands of scientists into entrepreneurs. Since that day, these three scientists-turned-entrepreneurs have turned an abundance of self-inspiration into both a medical and business miracle.

Penhoet recounted the start-up during our interview at Chiron headquarters in California. "So why would anyone move from the academic world to a business environment? In our case there were two main reasons. First of all, the scope of the science was dramatically increasing. It became clear by the end of the seventies that very large sums of investment money were going to be devoted to the practical application of this technology. So if you wanted to stay competitive in the science, it was important to participate in this growth phase. Second, and somewhat related, we had as a group, a strong interest in doing something practical with the technology. In one sense, it was an explosion about to occur because all of this technology had been building up in the academic world, and not much of it had gotten transferred to the traditional drug world. For us the technology was maturing, but people weren't using it aggressively to solve important medical problems. So it was a drive not only to remain competitive in the field, but apply that to doing something really meaningful on the practical side. That's the underlying dynamic of why we started Chiron."

At this point, Penhoet began describing the kind of performance behaviors needed to succeed in biotech. "What's important to understand was that this was a horse race. It was in fact a race between Bill Rutter at the University of California at San Francisco, the co-founder of Chiron, and Wally Gilbert at Harvard who was associated with Biogen and Genentech. They were competing to do the first cloning of a human gene, which happened to be the insulin gene. It's important to understand the essence of the competition between these groups. You see, in order to understand the dynamic of the industry, you also have to understand the dynamic of the academic schools which founded this industry. I think probably the biggest misconception that the American public has about science and scientists is that it is an occupation which is somehow fundamentally different from any others. Different in the sense that most scientists are not viewed as highly competitive people. The typical American view of scientists comes from Saturday morning cartoons with crazy guys in white coats working in a lab, and being isolated from each other off in a corner doing their little bizarre things." At that moment, I have to admit that my mind was reeling back to high school biology class where my teacher was always cutting up toads and did seem a little crazy. A lot had obviously changed since the fifties.

Penhoet continued. "So Larry, before all these biotech companies were started, the scientific enterprise around molecular biology and biochemistry was already tremendously competitive. So the field was, and is, populated by a lot of hard-charging, very smart, very hard working people. San Francisco was probably the epitome of that. The biochemistry lab at UC San Francisco during the seventies was a place where you could find people at work 7 days a week, 24 hours a day. Anytime that you went there, there were people working, competing, and moving the science along. It wasn't entrepreneurial in the classic sense we normally think about because the end result was not profit—but the behavior was there. So for most of the biotech companies, the behavior of the people who were critical to the enterprise didn't change that much when they moved from the university environment to a commercial environment. They competed aggressively, worked very hard, had a strong commitment to the science, and continued to work in the same style as they had before.

"For example, of all the people I know, Bill Rutter is one of the most hard working. He is a guy that enjoys working 7 days a week, 16 hours a day-and he always has. His style of working permeated UC San Francisco because he was head of the department. Many of us in Chiron had worked for Bill at some earlier point in our career. I got my Ph.D. in his laboratory. Pablo Valenzuela, the third founder and our research director here, was a post-doc in Bill's lab. Pablo's another guy with no energy barrier. You can discuss a new line of research one afternoon, and the next morning he's already got experiments going. So in many ways, Chiron is an extension of Rutter's lab at UC San Francisco. It certainly is in terms of people's *work ethic* and people's *commitment* to the cause."

Near the end of the interview, I asked Penhoet what he thought accounted for Chiron's great success compared to the other thousand or so biotech companies, many of whom hadn't yet produced a commercial product and went through their venture capital money hand over fist. His full answers are summarized into what I think were his two key points:

• **Creating High Performance:**
Some call it *working smarter*—but we'll settle here for *creating high performance*: "First of all we wanted to stay close to the sources of innovation in biotechnology. We wanted to stay plugged in to the

138

university. But historically, there was always this big schism between business and academia. And, in our particular field, there was very little need for each other because the traditional pharmaceutical companies were developing drugs based more on serendipity than on knowledge. They screened thousands of chemicals to find ones that would do a certain thing and many drugs got to market, still do in fact, without a deep understanding of how they worked. Therefore, the pharmaceutical companies themselves did not have a great need for the knowledge that was being built up in the universities. Anyway, back in 1981, we thought we could bridge this gap. We had good reputations scientifically and, at the same time, we had personal skills which allowed us to be seen as acceptable partners for commercial organizations."

• Creating High Commitment

There's no substitute for *working harder*, or as we like to say, *creating high commitment*: As Penhoet asserted: "What distinguishes successful biotech entrepreneurs is really the degree to which they focus their energies and apply themselves to their tasks. So it's really hard work that in the end is the absolutely critical factor. As I look around at who has been successful in our field and who hasn't, there is no question in my mind, for example, that the UC San Francisco work ethic was a significant factor in Genentech's success and in our success. And I think the difference is bigger than it seems between people who work extremely hard and people who just put in an average week. The productivity may go up by a higher order factor, not a linear extrapolation. That is, somebody who works 60 hours probably gets more than twice as much done as somebody that works 30. They may get four times as much done, because it's a matter of total focus on what they're doing. In any event, I can tell you this for sure. We got the hepatitis B vaccine for only one reason-we started working very hard on it way back in 1981, and we never stopped until we got it. I mean it wasn't an accident. It didn't just fall out of the sky one afternoon."

HIGH COMMITMENT AND HIGH PERFORMANCE

If entrepreneurs like Sarah Walker and Ed Penhoet are self-inspired, what exactly are they self-inspired to do? Do quite different entrepreneurial personalities such as Bill Gates, Soichiro Honda and Anita Roddick share any common practices as "workers?" Yes they do, but it is a surprisingly short list. One characteristic of all entrepreneurs I've met is they like what they do. They're highly committed to what they're doing. In addition to liking what they do, they're very keen to be good at doing it. At least as good, and hopefully better, than the competition. In personnel jargon, they're out to achieve high performance. So the self-inspired behavior of entrepreneurs rests on two pretty basic qualities—*high commitment* and *high performance*. In plain English, entrepreneurs "love what they do" and they're "very good at doing it."

ENTREPRENEURIAL BEHAVIOR

	Low	High	
High	Hate It & Good At It	Love It & Good At It	High
Performance			
	Hate It & Bad At It	Love It & Bad At It	
Low			Low
	Low	High	

Commitment

You can find managers and workers occupying any of the locations on the graph. You've probably worked with all of them at one time or another. Here's a quick definition of each:

• **High Commitment/High Performance**
The upper right hand corner is entrepreneurial territory. "I love what I do and I'm good at doing it" is the clarion call of all self-inspired entrepreneurs.

• **High Commitment/Low Performance**
In the lower right hand area are those people who love what they do but aren't very good at doing it. It's not unusual to find new employees here. They can be bursting with enthusiasm for their new job, but they just don't have enough knowledge or experience yet to do the job well. You can also find, unfortunately, long-term employees occupying this spot. They're loyal and they do love the company—but they stopped learning and improving a decade ago.

• **Low Commitment/High Performance**
The upper left hand area houses the exact opposite type of worker, and is much more common. This is home to those who may actually hate their job but are very good at doing it. They're usually highly skilled people who don't like the environment in which they have to perform. Commercial airline pilots come to mind. Flying tourists to Orlando has to be pretty dull stuff compared to combat missions over Iraq and Afghanistan. You can see this type everywhere, especially in large bureaucracies which can drive the commitment out of even the highest skilled workers.

• **Low Commitment/Low Performance**
What can we say about workers who hate what they do and are no good at doing it? If you make such a blunder and hire this type in your business, don't compound the problem by wasting months or years trying to "fix" the person. Cut your losses and say sayonara.

Successful entrepreneurs, by definition, are squarely in the high commitment/high performance area of behavior. That's not the problem. Their big challenge is to pass on and instill the same behavior in their employees. The first mistake you can make is to wait ten years to get going on this. The time to start is with your very first employee. And the place to start is to make sure that you, as the founder, are doing everything you can to personally model high commitment and high performance for all your employees.

ENTREPRENEURIAL COMMITMENT: "I LOVE WHAT I DO"

Commitment comes from the belief that your company's mission has purpose and integrity—and that your role in it is both important and acknowledged. Entrepreneurs are extraordinarily committed to what they do. It borders on the obsessive. It comes from the heart and produces an abundance of pride, loyalty and plain old hard work. Here are the four most important practices to foster such entrepreneurial commitment across your company.

• Love What You Do
The number one rule in commitment remains, "you gotta love what you do!" Fortunately 99 percent of all entrepreneurs really do love what they do. It comes with the territory. They're proud of their enterprise, and they see noble purpose in every mundane step they take. They love it so much that they'll work night and day to see it succeed. A little of this will go a long way in any growing company.

It will be your job as the founder to define that noble purpose and pass it on to your employees. Every job will have to be made important. Challenges will need to be built into even the most mundane tasks. Whether you're in landscaping or finding a cure for cancer, the long-term payoff for getting your people to like what they're doing, and be proud of it, is simply enormous.

• Give Autonomy, Demand Accountability
One sure-fire way to build commitment is to give people some autonomy and freedom to do their jobs. But the entrepreneurial approach is a lot more sharply focused than run-of-the-mill empowerment programs at *Fortune* 500 type companies. In an entrepreneurial environment, empowering people, or giving them autonomy, also means they're accountable for results. It's very much a two-way street. Employees not only understand this, they like it. For

some it may be the first time they've ever been treated like a responsible adult at work. The results can truly be astounding.

But too many businesses, even small ones, continue to control the wrong things. Imagine the production line supervisor who's responsible for 10 workers and $2 million worth of equipment, but can't spend $50 of company money to take his team out for a beer to celebrate a good week. This story gets replayed a thousand different ways for factory supervisors and any other employees who don't have the status to be trusted to do the right thing with a few bucks. The message they get is, you're responsible for the productivity of the 10 people and the $2 million worth of equipment, but we don't trust you to spend $50. Believe me, this is no way to build commitment.

• Share Fortune And Misfortune

As an entrepreneur, you will have little choice but to pin your hopes and fears on the future of your company. You will have to share the fortunes as well as the misfortunes of the business. And so it should be for your employees. What's good for the company should be good for the workers. And if it's good for the workers, it should be good for the company. Conversely, if it's bad for the company, there has to be some negative consequence on employees. It's called having a shared destiny, and without it, you can forget about a committed workforce. How in the world could it be otherwise? Nowhere in the world will employees commit to a company that isn't committed to them. It's simple common sense. Unless you and your employees truly get in the same boat, real commitment—accepting the good and the bad—will never exist. So do yourself a huge favor and start developing your plan now for doing just that.

The greatest examples of "sharing fortune and misfortune" actually come from employee owned companies. And the historical record is clear: when employees have an ownership stake in the business, commitment—and performance—go through the roof. The only question on this isn't whether or not it works—but why still today do only about 15% of companies have meaningful employee ownership plans in place.

• **Lead By Example, Never Compromise**

How can you expect your people to care about what they do if you don't seem to care about what you're doing? Fortunately in the entrepreneurial world, leading by example seems to come with the territory. Being the customer/product guru of the business goes a long way in the leading by example arena. It's actually more critical that entrepreneurs do this than their managerial counterparts in larger companies. Everyone can accept having a cynical, uncommitted manager a few times in their career. It's the luck of the draw and you likely won't have to put up with him very long anyway. But if the creator of the company hates his work, or hates his customers, or whatever, who could blame the shipping clerk for some slippage in his commitment to the cause? Remember, your people are watching you like a hawk, so never forget to show them that you love what you do, even on a bad day. You owe it to your people and you owe it to yourself.

There are hundreds of specific policies and programs you can initiate to foster high commitment. Whatever you do, from major steps like employee ownership to the most mundane of personnel practices, remember that the underlying goal is to make people feel so important in their job and so proud of their company, that loving what they do will just come naturally.

ENTREPRENEURIAL PERFORMANCE: "I'M GOOD AT DOING IT"

Entrepreneurial performance is all about doing it better than anyone else. Performance depends on knowledge, skill and working smart. It comes mostly from the head. Entrepreneurs look at performance as a matter of survival—not scoring points for the next merit review. Here are four key practices that define and deliver entrepreneurial performance.

• **Get Better At What You Do**
Continuous improvement in performance becomes a habit with
entrepreneurs. This happens when you know you're in a competitive
battle of survival. Working smarter takes on dramatic new meaning
when it's the only thing standing between you and bankruptcy. If raising
the bar to stay competitive is the life-blood of enterprise, shouldn't it
also be the life-blood of everyone in the enterprise? Of course it should.
And you can make it happen if it's crystal clear to everyone that "getting
better" is every employee's most important job.

One area entrepreneurs have to pay attention to is deciding what kind
of training their people will need to get better at what they do. Big
company training departments have become famous for training
employees in everything under the sun—from sensitivity training to
diversity training—but too often neglect those core skills that actually
grow the business such as: producing better products and selling more
customers. Fortunately most entrepreneurs will not be fooled by the
razzle dazzle of the endless parade of training programs created and
peddled by psychologists, organization development specialists, and
worst of all, business school professors!

• **Winning At Quality, Quantity, Speed and Cost**
The entrepreneur's shorthand for performance comes down to asking:
"How good can we work, how much can we do, how fast can we do it,
and how efficient can we be? High performance is all about excelling in
quality, quantity, speed and costs—the four basic parameters of
employee work. And the performance standard on each must be very
clear. The bar must always be set high enough to beat your best
competitor. These four common-sense parameters of performance are all
you need. And consistently doing them better than your best competitor
is the only standard that counts.

The challenge for you as an entrepreneurial manager is therefore to
make sure your people are better than the competition at these four
things. That will spell the difference between winning and losing the
competitive battle. You don't need to make it any more complicated

than this. Attitude surveys, high priced seminars on managing performance, and fancy performance appraisal systems dreamed up by personnel consultants can be tossed overboard if you will consistently measure, improve and reward these bottom-line performance factors. This may not have the cachet of more sophisticated HR Management systems, but it does have the redeeming value of helping you beat the competition in the marketplace!

• Save Your Best For Customers And Products

Entrepreneurs save their best efforts for making great products and selling real customers. It's called focus. As an entrepreneur, you will undoubtedly have this kind of focus in spades. It's absolutely essential to getting a new enterprise up and running. As always, the trick will be to pass this on to your employees. Time after time, we've seen promising start-ups lose their focus and blow their opportunity to become a great company. This often happens through the "good intentions" of employees who simply don't share the entrepreneur's original laser-point focus around customers and products. You begin to see time, energy and money being spent on all manner of marginal activities and internal battles. The result? Your company get's diverted from its mission and becomes a prime candidate for early demise. You can avoid this by making sure you and your people stay focused on the only performance that builds any enterprise—that which is aimed directly at making great products and serving great customers.

• Lead By Example, Never Compromise

If leading by example is a good way to foster "entrepreneurial commitment," the same message applies here—in spades. As the creator of the company, you have to personally show the way on performance. You can't avoid it. It comes with the territory. This doesn't mean that you have to be, or even should be, the top performer in your company. It does mean you have to be ready, willing and able to roll up your sleeves and give it your all—side by side with your employees. Seeing the founder of the company putting the product together or personally delivering the service can be an inspiring sight to most employees. The biggest challenge will be to keep it up, especially after your company moves beyond the start-up phase. A million things will come up to keep you off the shop floor or prevent your customer visits. If this happens, watch out. You're losing your most powerful tool for fostering high performance in your people.

ENTREPRENEURIAL BEHAVIOR AND THE ALMIGHTY POWER OF CONSEQUENCES

The essence of self-inspired entrepreneurship still rests on an old, simple truth about human behavior. That is, people behave in their own self interest—taking actions that they perceive will result in some positive consequence, and avoiding actions they perceive would result in negative consequences. This bone deep law of behavior of course depends on the positive and negative consequences being accurate, timely, and powerful. The more the consequences fit this bill, the more "self-inspired" the person's performance will be. This is the classic model of entrepreneurship—squarely based on the power of consequences.

If you're looking for the number one difference between entrepreneurs and bureaucrats, here it is. Entrepreneurs feel the consequences of their performance every Friday night when they count the money in the cash box. If it's full they feel on top of the world. If it's empty their kids won't eat. These are powerful, timely, and accurate consequences—which would affect anyone's behavior.

Bureaucrats on the other hand rarely feel any consequences, positive or negative. I learned how this works in my very first job, years ago, at

THE ALMIGHTY POWER OF CONSEQUENCES

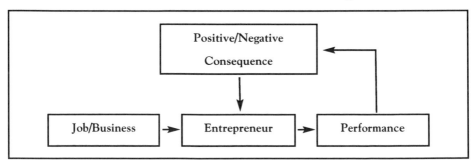

American Express Company in New York. My salary was $1,250 a month, a princely sum to me at the time, and I was very excited to be working in the Big Apple. American Express was and is a great company, but they taught me a very frustrating lesson about consequences—or the lack thereof. It quickly became apparent that if I worked very, very hard for a month and brought in some big customers, I got $1,250. If during the next month I took it a little easier, more of an average month, I again got $1,250. And finally I understood, even if I did nothing for a month, just showed up and stayed awake at all the meetings, I got—you guessed it—$1,250. The message was loud and clear. The company was practically screaming at the employees: "It really doesn't matter what you do!" If this seems a far-fetched example to you—good. Hopefully that means you'll never tolerate such a crazy system in your own company.

In spite of the best efforts of behemoths like American Express, enterprising managers can usually find a way to inspire themselves. The really hard part seems to be inspiring others. Ironically, entrepreneurs aren't much better than professional managers in using the power of consequences to foster commitment and performance in employees. They're usually on auto-pilot in pursuing their mission and don't worry about passing on their own entrepreneurial behavior to future employees. They really expect everyone to behave just as they do. Such optimism (or naiveté) is the reason why entrepreneurs can sometimes be pretty lousy teachers. Unfortunately, by the time they recognize they're leading an entrepreneurial mission that no one is following; the business may be well into its life cycle and is careening down the "managerial" side of the curve. At this point, founders often become brain-washed into thinking that the only way out of this mess will be to create a super-duper personnel department and let them figure out how to motivate the troops. The company reaches into the bottomless pool of available "HRD professionals," and it goes down-hill from there. The power of consequences gets lost in a sea of personnel mumbo-jumbo.

As you grow your company and face the prospect of inspiring hundreds if not thousands of employees, is there another way this story could end?

You bet there is. Meet Jannie Tay, entrepreneurial superwoman and Chinese *mamacita* to a sprawling watch and jewelry empire from Monte Carlo to Tokyo to Sydney.

IT'S ALL IN THE FAMILY

"They become your corporate family and you have unconditional love for each other—you forgive and forget and you share the good and the bad."

—Jannie Tay
Founder, The Hour Glass

Jannie Tay was recently named one of the "The Fifty Leading Women Entrepreneurs Of The World" by The National Foundation For Women Business Owners as part of a global research project, funded by IBM. In the tough, discount crazy Asian retail market for watches and jewelry, you have to be doing a lot right to hit $300 million in revenues after just twenty years in business. Today The Hour Glass has some fifteen retail outlets spread over Singapore, Australia, Malaysia, Indonesia and Hong Kong. Their brands are the world's top names such as Cartier, Rolex, Christian Dior, Patek Phillippe and Mondial Jewelry. They have also integrated backward with two joint-venture watch factories in Switzerland, as well as wholesale operations in Tokyo, Singapore, Hong Kong, Geneva and Monte Carlo.

The Hour Glass has a strong public reputation based on two things: high quality products and exquisite, upscale service. This reputation is backed up by the fact that they were the first watch and jewelry retailer in the world to be awarded the ISO 9000 Quality Certificate. What the outside world doesn't know however, is that both the high quality and the great service are, in truth, driven by Jannie Tay's greatest personal asset: her amazing instincts for inspiring her people. It's her secret formula for making sure all three hundred of her employees truly have that "all in the family" spirit.

Jannie Tay, always in a hurry, was several sentences into her story before I had even turned the tape recorder on: ". . . . . so yes, my father was a very big influence on me. He was a physician by hobby and produced medicated oils as a small business. As a young girl I used to go to trade shows with my father to sell this medicated oil and on the trips I remember stopping in all these little towns where we would visit his customers and have a cup of tea—so maybe early on I got the idea that business could be like a family activity. But you know, back in the 1950s girls didn't have to work. All I really wanted to do was get married, have children, and have a good time, like all the girls in Singapore. But at sixteen I went to Melbourne, Australia to study. The day I entered the university my dad died. It was very sad. In those days young Chinese ladies certainly didn't go off to foreign universities, and I always thank my father for that. My basic degree was in physiology and I got a masters in pharmacology. I also met my future husband in Australia. Henry was a Singaporean medical student.

"At that time in Singapore the big stores began moving out of our traditional retail area, and started opening on the more up-scale and beautiful Orchard Road. I observed that those stores had a very good turn of business and all the tourists wanted to go to Orchard Road. The tourist market in Singapore was beginning to grow rapidly and our little shops in the more traditional Chinese areas were static and not growing. But when I told my mother-in-law we should move to Orchard Road, she didn't want to. So my husband and I decided to sell out of the family business. But it took a lot of money to go to Orchard Road and compete with the big stores. I went to Metro which was the only retailer in town listed on the stock exchange and proposed a joint venture with them. If they would provide the financial backing, we would provide the management for an upscale retail watch business. We were completely surprised when they said OK. It taught me a valuable lesson; you never get anything if you don't ask for it. Anyway they took 51% and we had 49% and we started The Hour Glass in October, 1979. We opened with just one shop in Lucky Plaza, a new, fancy shopping area. After a few years we bought out our financial partners, and owned the entire company—until we went public on the Singapore stock exchange in 1992."

The thing that people remember most after hearing Jannie Tay talk is her passion for Hour Glass front-line employees. See if you agree: "The number one lesson I have learned is that the value of The Hour Glass or any company is in its human resources. Everyone today talks about customer service, and it's true that customers demand good service from the people that work for the retailer. The truth is, if you develop and treat your human resources with respect, and I mean the front-line people as well as the management, you will win the customer's heart. I like the upside down triangle and initially some of my corporate staff were upset because they said I only think of the front-line people. But we have to remember, in a hierarchical situation, the people who are up here in the so called head office are like gods. They are the ones who tell you what to do. They are the ones who pick up your mistakes. And they usually are the ones who get the most benefit from the company. In The Hour Glass, this is reversed. The front line people who are closest to the customers are the ones who will benefit most and I support that. It's a complete culture reversal from most retail companies.

"Managers in a hierarchical system feel they have gone through the doghouse so to speak to get to the top, and now deserve to enjoy their position and their power. In my philosophy, I may have the title of Managing Director, but I'm still that sales girl first, and then I'm the MD. Some of my early managers could not buy this philosophy and they left. They even said it was 'morally de-motivating' to them. I told them that without the front-line people we wouldn't even have jobs. We wouldn't be sitting here. But some people just can't accept that so they have to leave.

"I don't want any anti-entrepreneurial managers because that's the same as anti-growth in my opinion." This is Tay at full stride, describing exactly why and how The Hour Glass has become one of the most entrepreneurial companies in Asia—and I'm sure why she keeps picking up kudos like the "Fifty Leading Women" award. "Entrepreneurship is being challenged and wanting to do innovative things to keep growing—but a manager wants to be safe. You tell them what to do, they do exactly what you tell them, and they deliver the result—but no more. That's managing.

"I think Hour Glass is a very entrepreneurial company because we have developed as an entrepreneurial society in the company. I really believe you can help people change, you can develop them and you can support them. You can do this by letting them make mistakes, by nurturing them along, and giving them a second or third chance. And of course you do push them, you try to break their mind-set, all their limiting beliefs about themselves, and you keep pushing them. At the end of the day, if you do all this, you can bring the entrepreneurship out of anybody. But you have to do it all. People in their 40s and 50s who join Hour Glass, do find it more difficult to be entrepreneurial because for so many years they were so set and structured in their mind. But I've found that they can be very entrepreneurial, once they get rid of their limiting habits. Even the accountants, who have been taught a certain way to do things, to be very responsible, to be careful—even they can be more entrepreneurial in their job.

"You see, when I say entrepreneurship, I mean allowing people to be creative, to be open minded, to test new ground, to be more motivated. Of course you also want them to work as a team, to think first of the customer, to push for sales, but at the end of the day they should enjoy what they are doing, and be very committed to it. If you do all that you will have more entrepreneurial people and you will be a more entrepreneurial and successful company."

The Hour Glass has the highest retention rate of employees of any Asian retail company. It is truly an amazing record. I was hoping to get from Tay, some of the specifics on how this has been achieved. She didn't disappoint: "I realized that if I wanted the ten people who started with me to stay with me, I had to let them be their own bosses and be my business partners. I had to let them run their own businesses or else they would leave me for someone else who would take them away with a higher salary. So today those ten people, plus many after them, have been with me a long time. Now how did we do that?

• "First we develop them. Every Monday we still do training in the offices, particularly personal growth type training. I know these things can help. When I first started I went to a lot of courses on building up my own self-confidence. I even went to an Anthony Robbins course once.

• "We all share our information completely. We share our experiences and how we tackle problems, and we discuss these things like owners of the business, not employees. I tell you, even though many of them haven't gone beyond high school, they have become more knowledgeable than MBAs.

• "All decision making is done by them in their stores and their departments. We support them, even advise them if they need help, but they make the decisions for their own areas of the company.

• "In our culture we want employees to feel like owners, and we do something very important about this. Everyone knows what the profits are and we share 10% of the company profit with all the employees— every month without fail. This monthly distribution is on top of their salary and commission. And at the end of the year, they are also eligible for a one to six month bonus based on their individual performance.

• "All these approaches go right down to our front line people—sales girls and boys just like I used to be. I know what motivates them because I did the same work.

"You know that more than 70% of our people have been with us more than five years which is un-heard of in retail in Asia. And 40% of our people have been here more than ten years. I truly believe this is because they are their own bosses and feel like part owners. At the retail level, we hardly ever have anyone leaving Hour Glass. I guess if someone would offer to double their salary they would leave. But really we have no one leaving us which is very unusual for front-line people in retail."

And then we reached the concept that Jannie Tay is most famous for: an approach to employees that puts her somewhere between Mother Theresa and a Mother Hen, and never ceases to amaze outside observers. I think our own title of "*Chinese Mamacita*" may best describe the flavor of it all: "The key to everything we do is treating ourselves like a family. The employees all know my philosophy—that within a genetic family we love each other unconditionally and we share things with each other. If a member of our family upsets us, we're not political about it. We forgive them and we go on. But when you come to work, if your colleague does something to you, you become political and want to get him out of the company. So I say to our employees: 'Think a minute, and close your eyes. Remember we spend more of our waking hours at work than at home. So what would happen if we feel everyone here is part of our corporate family? Keep your eyes closed and imagine yourself in your home environment, but surrounded by the people you work with. They become your corporate family and you have unconditional love for each other—you forgive and forget and you share the good and the bad.' This is what I say to them—and it's an amazing exercise to go through with your staff.

"I'll tell you one thing that is happening just now, which so touched me. It's about one of our junior staff, a very nice young man really, at one of the outlets. I just found out yesterday morning that he took more than S$100,000 of our stocks, pawned them, and lost the money gambling. He obviously has a serious problem. He was confronted and he voluntarily went to the police and confessed. Now it turns out his wife also works for us and is expecting their first baby. If we could have found this sooner I'm sure we could have stopped him. We could have minimized the loss and counseled him. Of course now this young boy has to go to jail in Singapore. Well today, I was so touched because a movement has started among our employees. They are saying we do not want him to go to jail because he is so young. We will all chip in and try to cover this loss, and hope the courts will not send him to jail and send him back to his wife with some kind of treatment for gambling. His manager even recommended that we hire him back, counsel him and help him. You see, this is how a family would try to deal with a serious problem. Of course this is a difficult example, but my point is that even in such a sad case, we can still try to be a corporate family and not turn our backs on each other.

"At The Hour Glass we do a lot of "internal charity" work, and I insist that every employee must be involved somehow. We have cases where

154 Larry C. Farrell

an employee has died or maybe gotten badly injured in an auto accident, and we keep helping the family. It sets a good standard for the employees, and they see that a company can treat its employees like a caring family."

And finally we got to the bottom-line business woman in Tay. Where the power of consequences always hangs in the air: "Of course employees must understand that in a very dynamic industry like high-end retail, doing business also means cutting expenses, being more productive, and always trying for a better response to customers. From all this effort the profit or loss will come. Our people understand consequences. It's not a difficult concept. They understand that unless everyone in the company focuses on performance, on being a team, on sharing the ups and downs, we all lose. It's that simple."

Then in an almost automatic return to focusing on the positive side of human nature, she ended the interview with these powerful words: "You know, just a few years ago, entrepreneurship was not recognized as something to be proud of. Entrepreneurs were wheelers-dealers. They were people who did not succeed in a job in a company. And they all had to be a little crooked. That was the image in Singapore. After all these years, I now know that being an entrepreneur is about integrity, honesty, truth and credibility. And at the end of the day it's your relationship with people that counts most. It's all about people. It's how you deal with people. How you relate. It's a gut feeling I guess—a common sense feel I have about what's important in my company."

Taking the cue from Jannie Tay's "common sense feel," what about some common sense rules you can depend on to inspire others? Can you really instill entrepreneurial commitment and performance in your employees? Of course you can. Tay cloaks her approach in her "all in the family idea, and others have equally successful ways to get at it. But whatever the slogans or cosmetics, a few central principles run through every successful effort to create "mini-entrepreneurs" in a company. You'll recognize them all from Tay's own story: Individuals must run their piece of your company as their own business, satisfying customers is the bottom-line always, we're all in this together, and the most basic rule of all—making sure that all employees feel the consequences of their behavior. This last one means you have to have rock-solid answers to the eternal question of every employee: "What's in it for me if I do and what will happen to me if I don't?" You have to put powerful, timely, and accurate consequences into the work life of all employees. They have to know there will be positive consequences for good performance and negative consequences for bad performance. Do these things and you'll be well on your way to creating an "entrepreneurial performance system" in the company—using the full power of consequences.

Try these common sense principles and you can forget most of the personnel jargon you ever learned and all those made-in-hell performance evaluation systems dreamed up by consultants. You can trust these basic entrepreneurial ideas, and you can trust Jannie Tay when she says: ". . . if you do all this, you can bring out the entrepreneurial spirit in anybody."

GOOD FOR THE BUSINESS, GOOD FOR THE SOUL

Entrepreneurs like Jannie Tay believe that self-inspiration, the indispensable human quality that underpins the entrepreneurial spirit, carries double-barreled power. Of course it's good for business. That's been true forever. But it may have as much to do with how you live as how you work.

Remember Sarah Walker? She proved this 100 years ago. Driven by her self-inspired entrepreneurial spirit, Walker became an important figure in American business history. She single-handedly exposed the huge economic potential of creating special products for the African-American market. In the process, she literally wrote the book on franchising and multi-level marketing on a national basis. And her indomitable spirit carried over into her personal life. She was the country's first black, woman philanthropist. She was tireless in supporting black social issues of the day. She was especially generous with financial contributions to educational institutions for black women. Through Sarah Walker's generosity and personal example, tens of thousands of similarly dis-advantaged women have found the inspiration and knowledge to rise above their presumed place in society. They are all standing on Sarah Breedlove Walker's shoulders today.

This *is* the mission isn't it—a lifetime of effort to make a difference in the world? I used to think only powerful people like corporate chieftains and government leaders could make a difference. Today I know that's not true. For the real purpose of being inspired is not to move mountains—but to move yourself. To motivate yourself to make your life matter. To believe, when all is said and done, that you did good work and gave it your best. It can make you a great entrepreneur, no doubt about it. But even more importantly, it can make you a great person.

It's the power of self-inspiration that drove Sarah Walker and still today drives people like Buel Messer, John Boody, Kari Stefansson, Ed Penhoet and Jannie Tay—and a hundred others that fill these pages. The truth is, when you go looking for self-inspired people, it's a sure way to get your standards raised. Take Messer for example. It's hard to be too proud of yourself when a blind man out-performs you at every turn. You begin to wonder how your career would have gone if you had no eyes. You discover how much can be achieved with so little—and it makes you wonder at how little is sometimes achieved by those with so much. What does that say about the power of self-inspiration? It says to me we'd better find out how to tap into it.

In the final analysis, why should you want to inspire yourself? Why should you like what you do and be good at doing it? Partly because you're supposed to—a fair day's work for a fair day's reward is still a fair obligation. But mostly because it makes your life worth living. At least the half to three quarters you're going to spend at work. Psychologists call it self-actualization. Entrepreneurs call it doing something great with your life. Whatever you call it, you can be sure that self-inspired behavior is not only good for the business, it's also good for the soul.

Which leads us to perhaps the ultimate in doing work that's good for the business and good for the soul—the new arena of being a social entrepreneur!

USING THE ENTREPRENEURIAL SPIRIT
TO FIX THE WORLD

"The social entrepreneur combines the characteristics represented by
Richard Branson and Mother Teresa."

—Klaus Schwab, Founder
          World Economic Forum—Davos, Switzerland
          The Schwab Foundation For Social Entrepreneurship

Over lunch in his bank's private dining room, I asked Olavo Setubal the most obvious question that comes to mind when visiting Brazil: "With your tremendous economic potential, what's the plan to eradicate Brazil's poverty?" I figured that, as the former Foreign Minister of the country, the ex-Mayor of Sao Paulo, and current Chairman of Banco Itaú, Brazil's second largest bank (which his family owned), he would have a ready answer on what Brazil was doing about its 95 million citizens living in abject poverty. He did, but it wasn't what I expected: "There is no plan. The world has always had, and always will have, poor people. Only you Americans think we can eliminate poverty."

Was he right? Are there unsolvable socio-economic problems in the world that we foolishly keep trying to solve? If so, it would certainly come as a shock to the likes of Curtis Slewa, founder of the rough and tumble Guardian Angels, Millard Fuller, the visionary behind Habitat for Humanity and Bill Gates, the world's richest man. And what does this unlikely trio have in common? They're all trying to solve big social problems—through their own non-profit organizations They're in good company. Slewa, Fuller and Gates are part of a growing worldwide phenomena broadly defined as social entrepreneurship.

Clearly, it's an idea whose time has come. Google "social entrepreneurship" and an amazing three million links pop up! *USA Today* and London's *Financial Times* have recently reported on it, PBS aired a four part series about it last year, and *Fast Company* magazine just announced its third annual "Social Capitalist Awards," an effort to "seek out and evaluate the cream of entrepreneurial organizations in the social sector."

So what exactly is social entrepreneurship? The baseline definition goes something like this: Social entrepreneurship applies classic entrepreneurial practices to create and implement sustainable solutions to important social, economic and environmental problems. Klaus Schwab, who founded the blue-chip World Economic Forum in Davos thirty-five years ago, and it's recent off-shoot The Schwab Foundation for Social Entrepreneurship, probably said it best: "The social entrepreneur combines the characteristics represented by Richard Branson and Mother Teresa." While most social entrepreneurship ventures are formed as not-for-profit organizations, a growing number today actually have a for-profit corporate structure, under the belief the more traditional legal form will produce even more efficiency in carrying out the social mission. Whichever legal form is chosen, the mission remains the same: using entrepreneurial principles to solve social, economic and environmental problems.

When I think about great social crusaders and problem-solvers, certain images come to mind: Clara Barton single-handedly founding the American Red Cross 125 years ago, the multiracial group of six brave citizens creating the NAACP in 1909, Muhammad Yunus of Grameen Bank inventing the revolutionary concept of micro-credit, with no collateral required, for peasant businesses in the 1970s, right up to Jeffrey Sachs, deemed "the most important economist in the world today" by *The New York Times*, who has become a one-man tsunami for ending world poverty.

These are all people and institutions which continue to make huge differences in our world. This is not to say that every non-profit organization, or philanthropic foundation, or socially directed government body is entrepreneurial. Far from it. They can be some of the most bureaucratic and procedure driven institutions in the world. What distinguishes social entrepreneurs is that they actually employ the same behaviors as the world's great business entrepreneurs. The following key practices should have a familiar ring to you by now:

• Having a powerful *sense of mission* about their work.

• Creating world-class *products/services* to meet the market need.

• Maintaining a lot of innovative *action* in the operation.

• Demonstrating extraordinary levels of *self-inspiration*.

And finally, doing it all with the entrepreneurial expectation of being judged by results. Not surprisingly, these are essential ingredients for success in any endeavor—whether it's creating and building a profit seeking private business or a not-for-profit social venture.

While social entrepreneurs come from all walks of life, there's no doubt that famous business entrepreneurs, men and women who originally started for-profit companies, have been largely responsible for propelling the concept onto the national consciousness. After all, it *is* the entrepreneurial age and there are record numbers of successful entrepreneurs who have money to burn and want to see it put to good use. In doing this, they go about spending their fortune with the same entrepreneurial passion they had in making it. Ergo, we're seeing a lot of hands-on, entrepreneurially driven philanthropic organizations guided by master entrepreneurs like Bill Gates, Ted Turner, Tom Monaghan (Domino's Pizza), Oprah Winfrey, Ben Cohen (Ben & Jerry's), Sergey Brin and Larry Page (Google)—not to mention the Oracle of Omaha, Warren Buffet, lurking in the background.

Of course we're not all going to have Bill Gates' billions or Oprah Winfrey's platform to solve the world's problems. But we all *can* identify important social needs in our own community, try to create innovative and sustainable approaches to address the needs, and get started with a small-scale, practical plan. That's exactly how the following successful social entrepreneurs from around the world got their ventures up and running:

Africa: In 1990, Moses Zulu organized a tent shelter to help a few Zambian children orphaned by the AIDS epidemic. Today, Children's Town is a bustling, self-contained community with 22 staff members providing housing, food, and vocational education to over 300 children each year.

South America: Maria Teresa Lea, a school teacher, founded Coopa-Roca in 1981 by starting one sewing cooperative in the largest favela (slum) in Rio de Janeiro. Today the cooperative has 150 seamstress/owners producing and distributing women's apparel across Brazil and last year they began exporting to Europe.

Asia: In 1989, at age 26, Kailash Satyarthi , an electrical engineer by training, mounted his first raid on a bonded child-worker factory. By now he has liberated 40,000 such enslaved children in India and heads up an international movement, Global March Against Child Labor, with affiliates in 140 countries.

North America: Dan West, a young farmer in Indiana, figured out years ago that poor people "don't need a cup of milk, they need a cow." He made his first shipment of donated heifers to poor families in Puerto Rico in 1944. Sixty-two years later, Heifer International is still going strong and has provided food-producing animals to millions of poor families in 115 countries.

A recent, personal encounter certainly made a believer out of me. I was in Ecuador addressing The International Association of Hispanic Women Entrepreneurs. My wife and daughter, who traveled with me, had each been sponsoring a child in Ecuador through Children International. CI, established in 1936 in Kansas City, is helping 300,000 poor children around the world break the cycle of extreme poverty "to become healthy, educated, self-sustaining and contributing members of society." With over 80% of its $110 million annual income going directly to children's programs, CI is recognized as one of the most efficient philanthropic organizations in the world. We visited each child's home, one in Guayaquil and the other in Quito, and saw first-hand both the enormous need and the enormous help that small monthly contributions can make in the health and education of poor children. This personal contact made a profound impact on us—and gave me an everlasting appreciation for the efficient, effective and highly entrepreneurial work of good organizations like Children International.

A second, more work related example is also worth noting. The Murugappa Group, with 32,000 employees and $3 billion in sales is headquartered in Chennai (formerly Madras), India. Murugappa was a wonderful client of ours with a special mission beyond making great products and earning good profits for its shareholders. That special mission was to provide vocational education to teenage slum dwellers in and around Chennai. Suku Subramanian, the VP of Human Resources, headed up the company's considerable investment in the schools, and he was not a bit shy about making sure on my visits that I spent time teaching and counseling "his" young students on how to start their own businesses. If you've ever traveled in the slums of India, you know what depressing sites they can be. But amid all this poverty, the teenagers at the Murugappa schools I've visited, and taught, are so bright and so motivated, and so certain they were being given the chance of a lifetime—it was as if we were in a class at Harvard or Stanford planning out the promising careers of star students. My small investment of time in this example of a "company-driven social entrepreneurship project" was an inspiring and unforgettable experience.

So, should you give it a try someday? If combining the creative power of the entrepreneurial spirit with a passionate desire to solve serious social problems turns you on—you should make a terrific social entrepreneur. You could be a current manager who craves to do something, even part-time, a bit more rewarding than simply selling more widgets to more consumers. Or perhaps you've been a stay-at-home mom who's now ready to do something creative for the whole community. Or you may have already retired but just can't see spending the rest of your life knocking little round balls into little round holes. Once you get involved as a start-up social entrepreneur, it just might be the most satisfying work you ever do.

However, any aspiring social entrepreneur should think about a few serious considerations.

• First, giving Mr. Setubal his due, fixing the world is indeed a daunting challenge. It's not about making a fancier iPod or serving the smoothest caffé lattes in town. Social entrepreneurship is about permanently improving people's lives—and that isn't easy. The startling case of rising unemployment in India is instructive. It's a vivid example of what I call the *"job/baby ratio"* and will discuss more thoroughly in Part Three of this book. This came up when I spoke last year at an economic development conference in Bangalore, India and was followed to the podium by an Indian government economist. The highly regarded economist reported that India must create ten million new jobs a year just to keep up with its population growth—but the most it has ever created in one year is 4.5 million! So, while the conventional wisdom is that India is an up-and-coming economic miracle, in the all-important category of jobs, it's actually getting *poorer* each year. To fix this looming social crisis, India needs to find an "economic Gandhi" right away—or at least a Jeffrey Sachs and a Muhammad Yunus working together!

• Second, the popularized notion of social entrepreneurship is in danger of becoming a "movement" for do-gooders and academics. Burrowed into the 3 million Google references are way too many institutes, business school courses, research grants and award programs naming a "social entrepreneur of the year." In the avalanche of literature being generated, there are huge debates over who has coined the best definition and whether this organization or that really fits the description. I'm sure the definitions and examples I've used in this column will come under fire from some professor of social entrepreneurship somewhere. But don't get side-tracked by all this nonsense. What the world needs are more people like Curtis Slewa, Millard Fuller and Bill Gates actually *doing* social entrepreneurship, not more ivory-tower types *intellectualizing* about it.

• And finally, if you really do want to try your hand as a social entrepreneur, even on a part-time basis, it will definitely be worth keeping in mind that two out of three regular business start-ups end in failure and your odds may be even worse. So the final thought is—don't give up your day job (or your golf club membership!) before you really think through how you're going to "fix the world!"

Of course, all this takes a tremendous amount of self-inspired behavior! Perhaps even more than with founding a profit-seeking venture. With all this in mind, let's move on to *"What's Really Required To Become An Entrepreneur"*—or even a social entrepreneur!

Chapter 6

What's Really Required To Become An Entrepreneur

"Insanity is doing the same thing over and over and expecting different results."

—Alcoholics Anonymous

There must be a lot of insane managers and workers in the labor force these days. Just check the profile of the new American job-seeker: Forty-five years old with a resume that already includes a minimum of four prior jobs. So halfway through your career, you're looking for company number five—at least. Over your entire work life this should work out to eight different corporations, or about seven more than your grandfather worked for.

The response to today's take-no-prisoners era of personnel management is mixed. Older workers dread it and pretty much give up on bettering themselves after their second or third downsizing or merger inspired re-structuring. Most mid-career employees are trying to figure out what it all means and are spending more time honing their job-hunting skills than their actual work skills. Young up and comers, who have never worked any other way, see switching companies the same way the rest of us used to see switching departments or divisions. So one's reaction to the world of diminished company loyalty depends on where you've been. Still, the bulk of employees today (and their families) see all this as pretty bad news—another complication to make life more difficult. The worst reaction you can have is to do nothing and pray it all goes away before you lose another job. Brother, that ain't going to happen! Even so, many loyal corporate soldiers keep trying to find the one big company that will still appreciate their good-soldiering and long-term commitment—a 21st century variation of the AA insanity definition.

CORPORATE CHARLIE FINALLY GETS THE MESSAGE

My old friend, Charlie Bishop, provides an extreme example of this malady. Charlie's first problem was that he had an undergraduate degree in Psychology and a Ph.D. in Organization Behavior. Right off the bat this would make him highly suspect to all the hell-bent corporate downsizers of the world. Here's Charlie's battle record over the past two decades:

- Federal Express (4 years)
- Baxter International (6 years)
- C&S/Sovran Bank (2 years)
- Nations Bank (2 years)
- Quaker Oats Company (3 years)
- ADT Security Services (2 years)
- Belize Holdings Int'l. (1 year)

This is seven companies in 20 years, all at a Director or VP level in human resource positions. It's approximately one traumatic career change every two and a half years. Charlie was never fired for poor performance. Every time he changed jobs it was due to a merger, a restructuring, a downsizing, or some other corporate re-shuffling that left him no options but to move on. I know consultants who work for their clients longer than Charlie has been working for his employers. Maybe he should have seen it long ago, that these giant companies aren't really employers anymore—they're more like clients—and he had actually been in business for himself, as an independent contractor or "free agent" for a long time.

To be fair, I think Charlie knew this all along, but he just didn't say it. Clearly, the reason he was able to keep re-surfacing and surviving, is that he had become very good at selling his product (himself), delivering excellent work, and then moving on to sell another big company. The bottom line is, you will never meet a nicer guy than Charlie. He's smart, hard working, and loyal to whomever he works for. But all this has not been enough to avoid getting him bounced around like a ping pong ball.

Watching all this from afar, I used to wonder: How many more times can this happen to Charlie before he gets the message? Well, I'm happy to report he has gotten the message. A few years ago I received a brochure in the mail from a new firm called Chicago Change Partners. The cover letter was from none other than Charles H. Bishop, PhD, announcing the formation of his own consulting practice.

Like any good entrepreneur, Charlie's offering a product he knows a lot about: "Change." His letter says it best: "After being involved internally in large scale, significant organization changes—Federal Express, Baxter International, Nations Bank, Quaker/Gatorade and ADT—I decided to drop back and assess what it is that I have done in those changes that has made the most significant impact." So Charlie has come up with a couple of consulting services based on his own experience, and I say bravo for Charlie. He truly represents the profile of the new American worker: corporate castoff turned entrepreneur. (*A happy footnote—as of this writing, Charlie has now been working successfully on his own for nine years—the longest running "job" he's ever had So much for the "risks" of becoming an entrepreneur.*)

The good news today is, corporate castoffs don't have to get mad. Like Charlie, they really can get even. There's a large and growing class of big business alumni for whom these changes are creating unplanned wonders. They are rapidly becoming the largest part of the rising entrepreneurial class of the 21st century. They are highly skilled, highly motivated, and see working for themselves as a lot less risky than working for another big company. It's not an overstatement to say that all the turbulence at big business over the past two decades has given the entrepreneurial movement a double-barreled shot in the arm. First, experienced people, at relatively young ages, are being left no option but to fend for themselves. Second, with so many functions downsized, outsourcing has exploded to replace the necessary tasks. And finally we see over and over again the same downsized corporate types, like Charlie, converting the job skills they honed in the corporate world into their new entrepreneurial product/service—and sometimes even selling them back to their former employer as an outside supplier! It's true indeed—in the *new* entrepreneurial age the new entrepreneurs are us!

THE THREE REQUIREMENTS

Becoming an entrepreneur, or a social entrepreneur, may or may not be the right way to spend the rest of your life. But there are no wrong reasons for giving it a try. The days are long gone when, as Jannie Tay said, "Entrepreneurship was not recognized as something to be proud of." And the days are also over when folks talked about Buel Messer's desperate effort to put food on the table by mowing lawns with his sons as the price you pay for making a mistake. So, whether you're a freshly minted Harvard MBA looking for your first billion, or a middle aged mid-manager stuck in a Dilbertesque bureaucracy, or a retiree who just wants to make a few bucks on the side doing something fun—or someone with a burning desire to "fix the world" welcome to the *new and improved* world of entrepreneurial opportunity. If getting entrepreneurial is the way to go for you, what does it take to actually get started? Assuming you're now well armed with the "four fundamental practices" of successful entrepreneurs, the rest is pretty straight-forward. There are essentially three things you have to make sure are in place.

• **A Bit Of Money**

*"I was operating out of a spare bedroom and making only
local calls. There was no capital involved. Zero."*

—Fred Gratzon
Founder, Telegroup

There's something about money that seems to brings out the worst
anxieties in people. Many would-be entrepreneurs suffer a particularly
bad case of this. Some never get beyond the first step because they just
can't imagine themselves raising the money necessary to start their own
business. Making it even more scary, the media hype about IPOs and
young Silicon Valley billionaires has blown the public perception of
start-up financial requirements out of all proportion. A dose of reality
may help.

Our research shows the average cost of starting a business in the USA
today is about $14,000. A pretty good deal when you consider the relative
economic or social cost of some other ways you could spend your time:

• Average business start-up	$14,000
• A year on welfare	$25,000
• A year at Harvard	$35,000
• A year in prison	$45,000

Crazy comparisons aside, the point shouldn't be missed. On average, the
cost of starting up your own business is modest. And of course everyone
knows the smart way is to get your ducks lined up as much as possible
before you give up other sources of incoming cash. This usually means
don't quit your day job before you're ready. Having said that, don't be
afraid if the timing isn't quite so comfortable. There can be, ironically,
great power in having the rug pulled out from under you. Akio Morita,
the venerable founder of Sony says "being obsessed with survival" is the
entrepreneur's secret weapon. As he found out in war-torn Japan in
1945, people can and will do amazing things "when their life depends
on it."

Even if you agree it's not a lot of money, you still have to come up with it. Where are you going to lay your hands on $14,000? According to a survey conducted by Inc. magazine, the multiple sources of start-up financing used by entrepreneurs breaks out as follows: (*The total adds up to more than 100% as some entrepreneurs use more than one source to finance their start-up.*)

	%
• Personal savings	73
• Credit cards	27
• Loans from friends and relatives	14
• All other cash sources	14
• Loans against personal property	7
• Bank loans	5
• Equity investments by friends and relatives	2

One obvious lesson from the above list of start-up financing resources is, don't waste too much time talking to bankers. Banks are "assets lenders"—not "idea lenders" pure and simple.

Regardless of what their "small business ads" say these days, they are not the entrepreneur's friend! However, I believe you should keep your eyes and ears open for potential angel investors and venture capitalists— even though the list shows only 2% of start-up money comes in the form of "equity investments." The fact is, the VC community can be helpful to you at various stages of your company's development: seed money, start-up, mezzanine or scaling up financing, and most certainly "bridge" money to insure a successful IPO if you ever go that way. So for your present or future planning, here is some inside information in what Venture Capital Funds can do for you and what they will expect back from you:

Venture capitalists are typically very selective in deciding what to invest in. Funds are very interested in ventures with high growth potential, as only those kinds of opportunities are likely to be capable of providing the successful exit and financial returns they expect to make, within their typical 3 to 7 year time frame. And it goes without saying; they do expect a good return!

Because their investment will be illiquid, and will require several years to harvest, venture capitalists always carry out detailed due diligence prior to investing in entrepreneurial ventures. They can also be expected to "nurture," the companies in which they invest, in order to increase the likelihood of reaching an IPO stage when valuations are most favorable. Of course "nurturing" can quickly shift to "micro-managing" if things begin to go sour—so be prepared for more help than you will probably ever want if you can't meet your agreed upon growth targets. Having said that, almost all VC people will know a lot more about growing businesses than you do, so they can be very valuable advisors as well as investors. Venture capitalists typically assist at four stages in the company's development: Idea generation, start-up, scaling up and the exit or IPO stage.

Perhaps the most important thing for you to know at this stage is—what the key questions any VC firm will ask you when you seek their money. And of course, how you will answer these make-or-break questions? The great John Doerr, the "king of Silicon Valley" and the funder of many famous companies, says the four fundamental risks he always looks at, and wants clear answers to, are these:

• What's The People Risk: Will the founders stay or move on?

• What's The Technical Risk: Can the product be made—and scaled up?

• What's The Market Risk: Will the "dogs eat the dog food?"

• What's Financial Risk: Can capital be raised again if needed?

Short of entering the arcane world of the venture capitalist, it's reassuring to know, in a pinch, that most people can in fact come up with $14,000 on their various credit cards—so getting entrepreneurial seed money can't be too much of an obstacle. There are in fact, thousands of successful companies started for $10,000 or less. (*Note that the start-up amounts are not adjusted for inflation.*) Here's a diverse list of thirty bootstrapping start-ups over the past century, to illustrate the point, and give you hope:

- Kodak, 1880 $ 5,000
- Coca Cola, 1891   2,300
- UPS, 1907   100
- Black & Decker, 1910   1,200
- Matsushita, 1918   50
- Marriott (A&W Root Beer), 1927   3,000
- Hewlett-Packard, 1938   538
- Sony, 1945   100
- Johnson Publishing, 1946   400
- Lillian Vernon, 1951   2,000
- Kepner-Tregoe, 1958   2,000
- Domino's Pizza, 1960   900
- The Limited, 1963   5,000
- Nike, 1964   1,000
- EDS, 1965   1,000
- Virgin Group, 1970   9**
- DHL, 1972   0
- Body Shop, 1976   6,000
- Apple Computer, 1976   1,350
- PC Connection, 1982   8,000
- White Line Trucking, 1983   300
- Dell Computer, 1984   1,000
- Telegroup, 1989   0
- Horn Group, 1991   0
- EBay, 1995   750
- deCODE Genetics, 1996   5,000
- Google, 1996   0
- Facebook, 2004   0
- YouTube, 2005   0
- Twitter, 2006   0

** *Yes, it's true! Richard Branson's original start-up capital was a £4 loan from his mum (about $9 at the time) to start-up Student, his school magazine, which ultimately morphed into Virgin Mail Order Records in 1970!*

The list above might lure some into thinking that only cyberspace companies can be started on the cheap today. Not so. There are still tons of brick and mortar companies starting up today. There are actually millions of them and a fair share are still being started for under $10,000. Here's a sampling of 21st century companies with all manner of "traditional" type products and services—all taken from *Entrepreneur Magazine's* most recent (covering the first decade of the 21st century) *Hot 100* list of the fastest growing new businesses in America. And these results are coming off the worst recession in the U.S. since the Great Depression in the 1930's! I rest my case. . . . .

2010 *Hot 100* Companies	Start-up Cost	Current Sales
• Motive Advertising	$ 0	$ 4.5 million
• Laminates R Us	900	16.0 million
• WCIT Architecture	1,000	15.2 million
• CIO Partners Staffing Service	2,000	12.0 million
• Ritchey General Contractors	3,000	9.2 million
• Crown Partners	6,000	9.4 million
• Eurostar Cellular	8,000	10.2 million
• Texzon Energy Conservation	10,000	3.3 million
• JUNO Healthcare	10,000	12.4 million
• Endeavor Security Systems	10,000	5.5 million

Just to counter the notion that in the **new** entrepreneurial age, every entrepreneur has to have venture capitalists and investment bankers raising millions, let's highlight one of the more spectacular "zero-based" start-ups on the list above. Telegroup, the brain-child of Fred Gratzon in Fairfield, Iowa (about as far away from Wall Street and Silicon Valley as you can get) was literally started in his spare bedroom without a penny of investment in 1989. As he says: "There was no capital involved. Zero." Gratzon grew the company from nothing to an amazing $300 million in revenues, and 1,200 employees, by re-selling AT&T long distance services. He sold out after just ten years, made millions on the sale, retired, and wrote a very humorous book titled: *The Lazy Way to Success.* To be sure, starting a company with no money at all is rare and you would be well advised to not count on it. Most entrepreneurs do need some start-up money. But how much will you really need? Probably, just a bit.

But, lest we forget, while this list of successful and great companies didn't need or have a lot of money to start, they all did have the one asset that is absolutely essential—a product or service that customers needed and were willing to pay for. This brings us to the second requirement.

• A Bit Of Knowledge

"General graduates of the university are twice as likely to start their own businesses as the MBA graduates of Wharton."

—Professor Ian Macmillan
Wharton School
University of Pennsylvania

The number one reason for new business failure is not a lack of money. It's more basic than that. It is, simply, you haven't come up with a product or service that anyone wants to buy. Or at least not enough people want to buy it to keep the business afloat. So you need to learn how to make a product or provide a service that the world needs. And where are you going to learn that?

Apparently one place you won't learn it is at the leading business schools of the world. Ian MacMillan, the iconoclastic South African innovator, who heads Wharton's highly regarded Entrepreneurial Research Center, developed the first entrepreneurship studies program at a blue-chip business school. And why did Wharton approve his pet project? Because MacMillan's research on how to educate entrepreneurs revealed huge shortcomings in the MBA program, powerfully summarized by his mind-bending statistic quoted above. Predictably, the broader business education establishment hasn't taken this criticism from one of its own lying down.

As an illustration, a few years ago, *The Conference Board Review* published opposing views in a provocatively titled article: "Do Universities Stifle Entrepreneurship?" Arguing *yes* was, ironically enough, another Anglo Professor. Adrian Furnham heads the Business Psychology Unit at University College London. In a wonderful example of the pot calling the kettle black, Furnham claimed that academic universities and their "anti-business, socialist" professors are killing off the entrepreneurial spirit in young people. His solution? Send everyone over to the business school.

The Review invited me to write the rejoinder to Professor Furnham's argument. I pointed out that his case is simply not supported by the evidence. The idea that business schools are in the business of creating entrepreneurs fails both the test of fact and common sense. It certainly failed Ian MacMillan's careful research at Wharton. It's a preposterous claim when you really think about it. It's more of the same B-school nonsense that says management skills are really what entrepreneurs need. . . Nothing could be further from the truth. And it's an absolutely terrible piece of advice for anyone who is thinking about starting their own business—which as noted earlier is about 70% of the workforce today.

Of course it's great sport to blame academia for all manner of fuzzy and mis-guided thinking, but let's be honest. The educational institutions that have done the most damage to the spirit of entrepreneurship over the past 50 years are the business schools—not the broad based universities around them or the "lowly" technical and vocational schools down in the blue collar, working class sections of the community. Universities may be guilty of benign neglect of entrepreneurship but they at least impart knowledge that entrepreneurs need, on everything from molecular biology and hi-tech engineering to the social sciences and even the fine arts. In case the point is missed, these are all fields of study that teach young people about the technologies and needs of some of the greatest economic opportunities and challenges facing the world: bio-genetics, aerospace design, computer architecture, reduction of crime and poverty, and of course America's fastest growing export industry, entertainment. By contrast, business schools and their step-children, corporate universities and training centers, have majored for half a century in teaching theory after discarded theory about how to manage. Ask yourself, how many entrepreneurs have ever been created by studying learning curve theory, matrix management, sensitivity training, re-engineering, six-sigma, or the most current fad—leadership?

So entrepreneurial tip number one is to remember that there has never been a successful enterprise created out of a management technique. If learning management theories won't help, then what kind of education would be helpful? The bedrock essential of entrepreneurship (and all enterprise for that matter) is being able to come up with a great product or service. This is the really tough part of business. Managing is kid-stuff compared to being able to create a better mousetrap. Entrepreneurial tip number two, then, is to become very knowledgeable about something; to become very good at designing and making some product or service that answers a real need in the marketplace. It could be simple or complicated, high or low-tech, but you must become expert at it. And where can you learn this? While not essential for every entrepreneurial possibility, a decent university (schools of engineering, computer science, bio-technology, and even art and music come to mind) can be a terrific place to get started. Certainly technical and vocational institutes and trade schools are also great places to learn how to make something—and in my view are real hotbeds for creating entrepreneurs. And of course, regardless of your formal education, there is always 'on-the-job-training' in existing companies—which just happens to be the number one source of product/service knowledge for today's most common new entrepreneurs—the 'corporate-refugee' or 'corporate-Charlie' types noted above. Let's look at a few real-life examples.

Take the case of Edward Penhoet, co-founder and CEO of Chiron, the hugely successful bio-tech company that discovered the vaccine for Hepatitis B. Where did Penhoet learn his trade? At a business school? Of course not. He learned it by getting a Ph.D. in bio-chemistry at the University of California. None of this is new. Bill Hewlett and David Packard never studied management. They, like a thousand other computer entrepreneurs who followed them, were engineering students.

A prime example: Andy Grove made Intel the "essential company of the digital age" with an engineering degree from tuition-free City College of New York. Or how about Clark Abt? He founded Abt Associates, the largest social/economic research think-tank in the world. With 1,100 scholars and researchers on the payroll, Abt knows a thing or two about the value of intellectual capital in building an organization. His academic inspiration? A Ph.D. in Political Science from MIT. For an even more off-beat example, consider the career of Jodie Foster, arguably the most powerful woman in film-making today. Acting in, then directing, and now producing Hollywood blockbusters is big business by anyone's standard. Yet she's never seen the inside of a business school. She learned her "business" at the Yale Drama School. And on and on it goes—in an ever spiraling coincidence of being highly knowledgeable and skilled at something that people want and need.

An even less recognized source of essential entrepreneurial knowledge can be found far away from a country's institutions of "higher learning." Ray Kroc, the great on-the-job-entrepreneur behind McDonalds and a high school dropout, had the right idea. He was notorious for giving large gifts to good causes (and now after his death, so is his wife Joan— who recently gave the Salvation Army the largest single gift they've ever received!) but he drew the line at giving to most universities and all business schools: ". . . they will not get a cent from me unless they put in a trade school." He held that old-fashioned belief that young people ought to come out of school knowing how to do something practical, like grow a tomato, repair a two-stroke engine or put up a wall that won't fall down. Kroc may have stumbled onto an even bigger socio-economic idea. In America, a "blue collar" education began to lose status in parallel with the rise of the 20th century notion that everyone had to have a full university degree to be socially respectable. Sending your children to a trade or technical school became downright embarrassing. It was somehow more honorable to hold a dead-end, middle management job at AT&T than be a prosperous, self-employed electrician, plumber, or farmer.

This was not only a crazy elitist notion but it obscured a very important fact: vocational and technical schools are a rich breeding ground of small business entrepreneurs—the driving force of every growing economy in the world. Today it's clear that whether you choose landscaping, auto repair, medical testing, construction, or graphic design, you'll be in a trade with great entrepreneurial promise in the 21st century. So don't get hung up on "higher education" being the only path to prosperity. Certainly the list of world-class entrepreneurs who were university no-shows is very long, from Walt Disney and Soichiro Honda to Sam Walton and Richard Branson. There are also plenty of famous college dropouts like Bill Gates and Steve Jobs who tasted academia and decided they didn't need it after all.

The important lesson in all the examples that fill these pages, from self-educated Sarah Walker to Harvard Ph.D. Ben Tregoe, isn't where and how they acquired their knowledge. The one mighty thing they do have in common when it comes to knowledge, is that they all managed to become very good at something. They understood that what's required to produce high growth enterprise is not becoming great at managing, but becoming great at making products or delivering services that a lot of people in the world need and will pay good money for. And that, indeed, takes a bit of knowledge.

• An Entrepreneur-Friendly Culture

> *"I decided to run the big company*
> *the same way I ran the small company."*
>
> —Fraser Morrison, CEO
> Morrison Construction

Beyond acquiring the necessary *bit of money* and *bit of knowledge*, entrepreneurs still have to play with the hand they're dealt in terms of the environment in which they operate. Or do they? Of course you can't, by yourself, change the macro-economics of the day or control the political/social fabric of your country. But you can do a lot about the kind of culture you design for your own company and the immediate environment you choose to work in. Some companies struggle to survive in depressing, anti-entrepreneurial environments while others flourish in supportive, entrepreneur-friendly cultures. Learning how to navigate these tricky waters could mean the difference between entrepreneurial success and failure. Here's a real-live case of doing just that.

It's the story of Fraser Morrison in Edinburgh, Scotland. By the numbers it's an amazing story of selling a profitable $3 million family enterprise and regaining it 15 years later as a money losing, $300 million bureaucracy. To Morrison himself, the human side of the story is more important. He was saving his father's entrepreneurial business from the clutches of a giant, faceless conglomerate. Morrison fits in nicely in a long line of legendary Scottish entrepreneurs from Andrew Carnegie to—well, himself. His great uniqueness however is that he has seen it from all sides: From growing up working in the small family business, to a very long and tough 15 years running the business under the most anti-entrepreneurial conditions imaginable, and then finally bringing it back into the entrepreneurial fold—with the added twist of having to stop the hemorrhaging losses quickly or lose it all forever. And in the process he has become a guiding light for showing what it takes to move your business from the death-grip of an uncaring, bureaucratic world—to the passion of a high-growth, entrepreneurial organization.

When I interviewed Fraser Morrison, it was clear this had been a gut-wrenching experience for him. In his own words, here's how it all started: "In 1948, my father started the business from a cold start with absolutely nothing. It was very small, what we called a jobbing contractor. He slowly built up the business, virtually on his own, within a very small radius of his home-town which was a place called Tain, Scotland. I joined him right out of school. In that kind of situation you get the opportunity to get involved in everything that's going on. So I might have been setting roads or houses one day and go home that evening and help prepare the accounts. It was, very much, an all-hands-on-deck situation. Anyway in 1974, we sold the family business to Mining Finance House, a large public conglomerate in London. We were still small, working only in Scotland, and turning over maybe £2 million. My father retired and I became the MD, reporting to people I didn't even know in London."

From these modest beginnings, Fraser Morrison travelled a long, miserable journey until finally regaining his family's business. Along the way, everything that could go wrong in a big conglomerate went wrong. The holding company changed hands four or five times. The construction group, which Morrison Construction was a small part of, began bleeding huge losses in Asia, the U.S. and even in the UK. Dozens of corporate bosses came and went, each with their own agenda. Meanwhile Morrison Construction was the only profitable piece of its group and was minding its own business in Scotland as best it could. But the losses from the construction group, now being run by finance people, were overwhelming the entire holding company. No one in London seemed to have the foggiest idea of how to fix it. Here's Morrison's description of the environment in which the giant conglomerate in London worked: "We were part of the big holding company, and we watched our parent group just write themselves off. You see it every day—companies who are having constant changes at the top or companies that are in an endless restructuring process. Again and again you see the focus of attention going away from the operation of the business. The senior people had lost touch with what was happening in the real business. They didn't understand what the people thought. They weren't particularly interested in what they were doing. I had always thought, even when you are in a financially difficult situation, if the day to day operations are working well, you'll get back to a strong position. But the more effort the headquarters people put into corporate politics and what was happening at the holding company, the worse the situation became down on the sites and the weaker the overall situation became."

Finally the holding company became very disillusioned with the entire construction business and wanted to chuck it all. Morrison tried to buy back Morrison Construction but was flatly rejected. The holding company wasn't about to "sell the only good part and keep all the dogs." Instead, in a total misjudgment of Morrison's personal ambitions, they "promoted" him to run the entire Construction Group. He hesitantly agreed but asked for an option to buy the whole group if it were put on the block. Another rejection, this time because the Board was testing the market for a spin-off. Not surprisingly there weren't a lot of buyers for a hugely unprofitable construction group. So eventually Morrison was told he could buy "the bit in Scotland but only if he took the bad parts of the dog along with it." He decided to go for it as the only way to regain his company. He went deeply into debt, and to avoid financial collapse he would have to turn around the big losing operations practically overnight: "So we ended up buying back Morrison Construction. I had finally reached my long held ambition to restore family control. But we also had to buy the parent company along with it. So I had a business with overall sales of about US$300 million but losing very big. But we owned 100% and I thought I knew how to turn it around. Thankfully my hunch was right. In our first year we increased sales and actually made a small profit! The next year, 1990, we pushed sales up a bit to and actually made a respectable $11 million profit—and have never looked back."

How exactly did Fraser Morrison change years of losses into profits in just twelve months? He simply transformed the total atmosphere in which the company worked. He started running the big business the same way he'd always run the small business—in a very entrepreneurial environment: "We made an awful lot of changes on day one. We retained only two directors and the rest, eight or ten, went. We structured the company so that it was operating on similar lines to the business that we had in Scotland. One of the great difficulties we found, when we added up all of the contract delays on the sites, was the sites were cumulatively eight years behind contract schedules. When you think of the overheads on our construction sites, they can be anything from £10,000 to £100,000 a month, and we were eight years behind schedule! So, I focused peoples' attention throughout the business on bringing those eight years delay back to zero within twelve months. Everybody said it couldn't be done. Well, giving people impossible targets sometimes works. In fact, we got it back to plus 30 weeks on the 12th month."

Morrison has obviously thought a lot about that critical era of rapid transformation—and exactly how he and his team pulled it off. Today he concludes that he actually changed five key factors in the overall operating environment of the company—which made it all possible. These five factors translate into valuable general principles which anyone, including you in your future business, can apply to create and maintain an entrepreneur-friendly culture in your organization. Here they are, in his own words:

• Keep It Small
"We split the business up into relatively small—I call them family size—units. So a director will have a business between only £5 to £20 million turnover. They have a team of between 30 and 60 staff plus the hourly paid employees. That way they can get to know all of their people quite well. It's worked very well for us. A small operation just works better. The people enjoy it more and take a huge amount of satisfaction from it. You can get the team spirit going which is very important in construction. The same with commitment. I think it's in the small companies that you tend to find it. As we grow, it's a priority to make sure that we create the structure to be able to continually feel like a small company."

• Keep It Personal
"I learned a lot of lessons from seeing them try to run our company because they always gave us the feeling that they knew what to do. We weren't important. We only just dug holes in the ground. It was a huge lesson to me on how to run a business because you have to let the people feel that they are the key element of the business. Hopefully our structure now is such that people have got a strong personal interest in developing the business. A strong sense of feeling important and that they themselves have a strong entrepreneurial input to the business."

• Keep It Honest
"The main factor that contributed to our success is the enormous commitment that I and the people around me have. When we bought the business back, we sold about 18% of it immediately to the key managers. So we have all senior people who have a shareholding in the new company. I told all of them we want to run the business in a way that's in their best, long term interests also. Business needs this kind of personal commitment and honesty at the top and I'm sure we have it today."

• Keep It Simple

"As in life generally, you shouldn't try to make things complicated. You've got to try to make it simple. And the simpler it is the easier it is to understand by everyone. The single most important thing that I've learned throughout this process—and I haven't found a situation yet where it isn't appropriate—is that if you forget about the nuts and bolts of the business, you're lost."

• Start Over With The Basics

"I'd been telling the parent company I knew what needed to be done to sort this business out for a long time, but they decided that they knew better, and weren't interested in our philosophy. They were running it as one big company. So when we got it, we split it up and re-focused the attention of the people away from looking toward the group in London, back to the sites and the operations of the business. We put new directors in who we knew would put all their attention on the sites. We had to very quickly re-focus everyone back to the basics of the business—toward the site, which in the construction business is the only place we make money."

THE AMAZING ODYSSEY OF RON DOGGETT

"The most successful businesses don't do anything new, exotic, or dramatic. They do very simple things—very well."

—Ron Doggett, Founder
GoodMark Foods

I've known Ron Doggett since we were at the Harvard Business School in the late seventies. Since then he has lived the great American entrepreneurial dream: Led the leveraged buyout of a tiny subsidiary of a giant bureaucracy, built that small business into an entrepreneurial powerhouse, and then sold it off to another giant bureaucracy for *five hundred times* more than he originally paid for it! And to top it off, he's just about the nicest, humblest, and most honest man you'll ever meet.

Ron Doggett is living proof that sometimes the good guys in business do finish first!

Ron had toiled for twenty years as a financial manager at General Mills, the third largest food company in the United States. He then led an early example of a leveraged buyout of a small, money losing subsidiary of the giant company. The price on paper was $31 million, but over 99 percent was to be paid out of future revenues. Doggett and his three man team got the deal for just $200,000 in equity—which they borrowed from a local bank—because General Mills couldn't find anyone else to take the bleeding subsidiary off their hands. Eighteen years later, he sold the company to ConAgra, the fourth biggest food company in the United States for a whopping $240 million—while he personally still owned 34 percent of the company. His entrepreneurial career, sandwiched between two giant bureaucracies, made him a very rich man and gave him a unique perspective on the cultural divide between *Fortune 500* companies and an entrepreneurially driven business. In other words—what to do and what not to do—to create and keep alive an *entrepreneur-friendly culture* in your business.

• General Mills' Corporate Culture
   —Conglomerate Merry-Go-Round

Here's his story. "When General Mills acquired the Slim Jim sausage company, they transferred me to become the CFO, and we re-named it GoodMark Foods. At the time, General Mills was also acquiring a lot of other businesses. They were trying to grow a fashion division, a jewelry division, a toy division, all businesses way beyond foods. They even owned some great furniture companies. This was the era of the conglomerate. They were going off into all kinds of different and unique businesses and like usually happens, they lost focus. Of course today, like all of those big conglomerates, they've returned to their core business— they're strictly a food company again. Anyway, General Mills was eager to build the Slim Jim product but they couldn't relate to the business and it wasn't a product that fit well with their main product lines. That's not being critical of General Mills; It's just how it was. At any rate, they wanted to build this business through supermarkets, and give it to the General Mills sales force who were busy selling Wheaties, Cheerios, Bisquick, Gold Medal Flour, and O-cello Sponges. So we were the last one on the sales order form, just below O-cello Sponges! It's interesting, and a little sad, how they operated with our small business. General Mills was just a huge company. They were what I called a company that could only relate to boxcars. To boxcar loads of products like Wheaties and Cheerios—whereas we shipped parcel post. We shipped Slim Jims a case at a time.

"Then, out of the blue, General Mills decided to sell the business. They had decided to get out of all the 'less than boxcar load' kinds of businesses. We were among the first to go in this big change of strategy. This was at the time that all the conglomerates were turning right around and shedding all the acquisitions they had just made. I think General Mills was having a difficult time managing them. They weren't growing. These were small businesses that were taking more time than they wanted to give them, and I really think they realized they had lost focus and they wanted to go back to things that were more mainstream if you will—and easier to manage. Ours was not an easy business to manage. It's fairly unpredictable. Meat costs, our primary ingredient, were highly volatile. You could make a lot of money one year and three years later you could lose a lot of money, and General Mills didn't like that.

"We just didn't fit into a big company picture for all these reasons. There wasn't time to be responsive; there wasn't time to put a personal touch on it. There wasn't time to have one-on-one relationships with small customers. At GoodMark we dealt with one-man wagon jobbers up to distributors with a thousand trucks. It takes a variety of talent to work with these customers. It isn't like calling on headquarters accounts and covering the nation as a result of your single headquarters call.

"In any event, General Mills executives told me although there 'could' be something for me in General Mills, they strongly encouraged me to look elsewhere. That moment was when I became very motivated to try to buy the business. Here was a product, Slim Jim, that I really liked, and which I knew had a great future. So I went to see the President of GoodMark and brought my team in and we announced that we were putting together an offer to acquire the company. It was a big decision and we weren't very sure that we were going to be successful. The President told us that 'us little guys' were not likely to get the company so everybody should relax. Our offer wasn't accepted at first. We were told to hang on, and if nothing better came along they would talk with us. That was the gist of General Mills' response. The fiscal year ended in May and they didn't have a better offer so they agreed to meet with us to talk about our plans. Of course I didn't have any money. We owned a $35,000 home and had only about $ 7, 000 equity in it. That was our biggest asset!"

• **GoodMark Foods' Entrepreneurial Culture—Back To The Basics**
After long and torturous negotiations, which included looking under every rock for a way to finance the purchase, Doggett and his team became the proud owners of a sausage company hemorrhaging cash. As Ron put it: "The financing we came up with was unique for the time. General Mills reluctantly took back a lot of paper and a 10 year stream of royalty payments. So with the combination of General Mills paper, a stream of royalties over 10 years, and the one loan we all signed our lives away for from a local bank, we were able to come up with an offer of approximately $31 million to acquire the business —— but with only $200,000 in equity. Of course the worst case for General Mills was that if we failed they would just get the company back. That was General Mills' worst case really."

I asked Doggett what he did to turn the company around. His answer covered some pretty obvious things—nothing dramatic: "At that time GoodMark was doing about $40 million in revenues and losing a lot of money so we had to move fast. There were several things we did immediately to get the business moving in the right direction:

"The first thing was that we had to restore quality. General Mills had cut quality to increase margins, so fortunately I knew exactly what to do about the quality issue. We immediately restored the Slim Jim to what it originally was. We took out the preservatives. We took out the fillers, the low cost inferior ingredients and restored it to what it was, which was costly to us. It cost us margins on the product. But the first thing we did was we fixed the product—back to what consumers wanted.

"Secondly, we had good people but they didn't have direction, they didn't have focus, and they didn't have respect for the vision of the company. I knew that we had to establish this. We had to give the people a sense of direction, all marching to the same drumbeat, and they had to know how committed we were to them and the new company. So through a lot of face-to-face communications and putting the right people in the right places to do the right things, we got the people motivated and committed and feeling responsible for moving the company ahead.

"One of the ways to go ahead was through marketing. The product was under marketed. One of the reasons for that was, we never had a stable product. It was inconsistent. Quality was up and down. We couldn't deliver the product. So once we straightened out the quality issue, and we straightened out the people issue, we then focused on fixing the marketing and sales support.

"Beyond these things was the service to the customers. Our customer service was deplorable under General Mills. So we set up minimum standards for serving our customers. At that time our turn-around on orders had to be no later than seventy-two hours which was darn good in our business. But we eventually got that down to where we were processing and shipping orders within twenty-four hours. That was a huge success for us—being responsive. We had to be different than the snacks we were matched up against. We had to be better. So we worked hard on being more responsive and faster moving than any of our competition."

I wondered why such obvious things weren't handled long before. If these basics were the kind of things that were needed, why didn't General Mills do them long before? Doggett's response was a knock-out punch to bigger-is-better thinking: "Well, they were the simple things.

Easy things. Little things. Easy to identify but difficult to do on a consistent basis. General Mills' focus was on the large corporate overview with a large structure. We spent most of our time, at General Mills, on developing reports, analyzing results, building plans. Our long range strategic plan each year was about 70 pages. And then we had a program review session which went on for three months of the year. We had program reviews, budget reviews, that sort of thing. We spent more time on management procedures than we did on creating and leading. So I'm talking about little things that weren't working that we really needed to fix and make them work. But you succeed at the things, I believe, that are important to you, that you are committed to, and that commitment was just not there for this business at General Mills. But as owners I can tell you, we were 110% committed to it. We had simple plans and implemented them day by day. We lost a lot of sleep and shed a few tears too. The result was we started making a profit in nine months with the business.

"So Larry, the things we did were very simple things, whether it was customer service related, people related, product related, operationally related, financial, they were all simple things. I'm convinced, and I often told our people this, the most successful businesses don't do anything new, exotic, or dramatic. They do very simple things very well. They're companies that are highly focused on their mission, just as you point out in your seminars, and they consistently do the simple things in their businesses that are most appreciated by their customers. Those are the kinds of things that we did here at GoodMark. They're customer driven kinds of things and very simple: time, relationships, shipping an order, good quality, being responsive to needs, recognizing what stores need for displays or promotions, that sort of thing.

"Two years in, things had really started to turn for us. The business was going well, we were really getting some enthusiasm going for the business, the people were starting to have fun, they were enjoying what they were doing, the quality was restored, capacities were up, we had installed some higher technology equipment, our packaging was better, and the marketing programs were coming together. One of the most important things we did was to establish an incentive reward system for our people. I believe strongly in the risk/reward theory, I think you call it "positive/negative consequences." I promised them if they took the same risk with me, that it would be beneficial to them and they responded to that. Everyone does. Also we pushed the decisions down to the lowest level we could. We took it away from how the large corporate culture operated down to our own culture. You had to have the guy on the manufacturing line, on the shipping dock, or face-to-face with the customer responsible and accountable for what they did—and if they did it well they got rewarded for it. It was getting to be fun. And we owned the business!

"Well, actually General Mills and the banks owned the business because we owed them a lot of money. That was one of the reason we decided to go public early on. But the main reason for going public, in my heart at least, was I believed this was going to be very successful, and here's a way to share with the people. And it was a successful offering on the Nasdaq exchange. Going public really made it possible for employees to become owners. We used stock to reward people; we had a stock purchase program, and a stock option program. So we have quite a number of people who became—it may stretch the word to say wealthy—but they made an awful lot of money by growing this business and getting options from the company. Our employee stock option program was quite large. Now it's a part of ConAgra's program—but they don't get nearly the amount of incentives and bonuses and stock options that we used to give out. It was a very big part of our success.

"In any event, we worked hard at these simple things. That's *the* thing that made this business successful. We started with a $40 million business, which was losing money, made it profitable in nine months and for the next 18 years that I was CEO, had a compound revenue growth rate of 12 percent and a compound earnings growth rate of 19 percent. Today the company is doing about $250 million in sales and is one of ConAgra's most profitable subsidiaries. And, I should add, GoodMark Foods is number one in the world in the meat snacks category! Even our troops in Afghanistan carry them because of their high protein content!"

• ConAgra's Corporate Culture—Here We Go Again

I visited again with Ron Doggett a couple of year after he had sold GoodMark Foods to ConAgra, the $13 billion food behemoth based in Omaha, Nebraska.(*ConAgra is the 4th largest U.S. food company with revenues of $13 billion and General Mills is number 3 with current revenues of $14.7 billion—so Ron Doggett knows of where he speaks when he contrasts giant bureaucracies with mid-sized entrepreneurial enterprises!*) I asked him to bring me up to date: "You know Larry, I really did not have a plan or a time horizon for myself in the business. I saw it going on indefinitely I guess. I was having too good a time and it was growing every year. I had become the major shareholder of GoodMark Foods and we had been asked by a dozen companies over the years if we would sell the business. I had absolutely no interest in that because it was going so well and I was having the time of my life. But my board began to encourage me to think forward about an exit strategy. And the more I thought about it, the more I realized it was the only fair thing to do for the employees and the shareholders. Selling while we were on top of the world seemed the right way to go. Well, one of the businesses that had been chasing us for years was ConAgra. They told us that they had a philosophy of operating with *Independent Operating Companies*, or IOCs, and that was very appealing to me and my management team. We thought that philosophy would allow us to operate as an autonomous entity which was important to us. We were given every assurance that it would be that way. Of course ConAgra is a giant company—and grows mainly through continuous acquisitions— so they really wanted us and we came to an agreement in a short period of time at a good price for our shareholders. They paid $30 a share— which came out to about $240 million."

I asked Ron how the "IOC" concept was holding up. He diplomatically replied: "Well, ConAgra is struggling with that. They've changed the concept of IOCs from when they acquired us. They've consolidate them into seven or eight large divisions versus eighty separate IOCs. They said they found that was too many IOCs. They could not get their arms around them so they've consolidated." Hmmmm. . . . . my good friend didn't sound so convinced that this was turning out exactly the way he'd been promised. This tightening of control sounded to me like the first ConAgra shoe had already been dropped on Ron's former entrepreneurial enterprise.

Then, shortly after that talk with Ron, I read in the *Wall Street Journal* that a second, very heavy, ConAgra shoe had just been dropped. ConAgra announced it would be terminating 8,000 jobs and closing 15 plants. It was termed a "restructuring and consolidation plan," with across the board expense reductions to keep up its twenty year record of earnings growth. Does this sound vaguely familiar? Could this be some of that same old corporate-speak that Doggett happily left behind three decades earlier at General Mills? With GoodMark's sales booming and growing at 29%, it hardly seemed the right time to go into a cost cutting mode in the Slim Jim business. But the cuts were to be companywide as almost always happens in giant companies. It certainly doesn't seem to be the kind of entrepreneur-friendly culture Ron Doggett worked so hard to create. In fact, things have gone from bad to worse on the autonomy front. The name GoodMark can't even be found on ConAgra's website today. And just this month I read, again in the *WSJ*, that the old headquarters and the main plant in Raleigh, NC, where the bulk of Ron Doggett's people always worked, is being relocated to Ohio. Ron recently confided to me that, with all the turmoil at GoodMark Foods, he had actually tried to buy the company back from ConAgra. As you might imagine—he was turned down flat.

So, hello centrally controlled bureaucracy! Goodbye entrepreneurially driven enterprise! The fact is, there are always tradeoffs to be made in giant companies like ConAgra. Big business has "corporate needs," and those corporate needs will always be more important than the needs of each small part of the organization. That's the way it's always been and that's the way it's always going to be—or so it seems.

To move off that sour note, let's close with Ron Doggett's super positive and uplifting thought from our very first interview—which I pass along for any entrepreneurial dreamers still sitting on the fence: "I thought it was the opportunity of a lifetime, and it was. So my message to others is to seize your opportunities. Seize your opportunity and leverage yourself to get it if you have to. Too many people pass their opportunities by in this life." At the end of the day, what do you actually have to do to pursue your entrepreneurial dream—as Ron Doggett did? To be sure, you need to learn and apply the practices of the world's great entrepreneurs as covered earlier: *Sense Of Mission, Customer/Product Vision, High-speed Innovation,* and *Self-inspired Behavior.* And then, as Ron's story illustrates, you'll need to acquire *A Bit Of Money* and *A Bit Of Knowledge* and create the most *Entrepreneur-Friendly Culture* you can.

However . . . . . if you're still not quite ready or convinced that you should try to become the next great entrepreneur, that's fine. A lot of very smart and happy people prefer to be part of a team in an organization. If this is you, read on to *Part Two—Entrepreneurial Companies.* It's all about getting entrepreneurial inside your company— and developing those same skills in your employees. The good news is a large and growing number of organizations are encouraging, and rewarding, exactly this type of behavior. We call it *corporate entrepreneurship,* and it may be a perfect fit for you.

APPLICATIONS

Entrepreneurial People

From The Farrell Company's Getting Entrepreneurial! Seminar

Editor's note: The following Applications are used in The Farrell Company's individual entrepreneurship seminars. They are included here with the hope they may be of interest and practical value to all aspiring entrepreneurs—as well as school and university teachers of entrepreneurship.

APPLICATION 1

YOU'RE AN ENTREPRENEUR! WHAT NEXT?

Imagine you've just started your own business. It's the first day in your new role as an entrepreneur. You want to be successful and grow. You sure don't want to go bankrupt. You've mortgaged your family house to raise the money to get started. Everything you have is on the line, including the welfare of your children.

You have an idea of a product and market that excites you. You think it has potential. But with your limited financial resources, you have to get started fast! What will you concentrate on? How should you spend your time? What will your priorities be as an entrepreneur?

There are no "right" or "wrong" answers for this first Application. It's simply intended to get your "entrepreneurial juices" flowing—by seriously thinking through what you would really have to focus on as a start-up entrepreneur.

MY ENTREPRENEURIAL PRIORITIES

1.

2.

3.

4.

5.

APPLICATION 2—A
CREATING ENTREPRENEURIAL BUSINESS PLANS

What do you love to do and what are you good at doing? What needs do you see that are going unmet, or not being met adequately? Within these questions you will find the market/product business(es) that will carry the highest chance of success for you as an entrepreneur. Obviously, starting a business in something you hate doing, and are no good at, and for which there is no market need, is a recipe for disaster. Completing this four-part application won't guarantee your entrepreneurial success, but it will ensure that you have asked the right questions, which is the starting point for every successful entrepreneur. Review the *Creating Entrepreneurial Business Plans* section for more background.

Finish the first column and then translate your answers into a potential business activity in the second. "I like computers" could become "computer repair" or, "I'm good at gardening" could become "landscaping service." Some of your interests and skills may require creative thinking to redefine them as a business. A few might not work at all. Just set those aside and move on.

WHAT DO I REALLY LIKE TO DO?   **MARKET/PRODUCT WINNERS**

-
-
-

WHAT AM I REALLY GOOD AT DOING?   **MARKET/PRODUCT WINNERS**

-
-
-

WHAT MARKET NEED DO I SEE?   **MARKET/PRODUCT WINNERS**

-
-
-

APPLICATION 2—B
PICKING MARKET/PRODUCT WINNERS

List your market/product winners (potential businesses) from 2-A. For each of your market/product winners, rate both the market need and your likely competitive position, using a scale of 10 to1. Use your best estimates and your common sense to answer these questions. Be as objective as possible. The generic questions for each rating are:

Market Need: How big is the market in number of customers and in sales volume? Is it growing, declining, or staying the same? How critical is this need to the market? Is it a necessity, a luxury, or a passing fad?

Competitive Position: How much better, cheaper, and faster could you provide this product/service compared to how it's currently being offered by others?

MARKET/PRODUCT WINNERS From Application 2-A	RATINGS (10 High / 1 Low)	
	Market Need*	Competitive Position*
1.		
2.		
3.		
4.		
5.		

* Note any critical information you will need to verify later.

APPLICATION 2—C
PICKING MARKET/PRODUCT WINNERS

Plot the ratings of your market/product winners from 2-B on the matrix. For example a "9 market need" with a "9 competitive position" rating would be very near the upper right hand corner. A "3/7" would be near the center of the upper left hand quadrant, and so on. This matrix will give you a visual overview of the combined market need and competitive position for each of your possible market/product ideas. This analysis will highlight your real "market/product winners."

1. **Small Market/High Competitive Position:** Good possibility of success in this Rolls Royce type business. Work to find more markets for your excellent product.
2. **Big Market/High Competitive Position:** High possibility of success, but once successful, you will likely attract a high level of competition. Be prepared for strong competitors.
3. **Big Market/Low Competitive Position:** Good possibility of success, but you may have to compete on price at the low end of the market. Work to raise your competitive position.
4. **Small Market/Low Competitive Position:** Poor chance of success. Avoid this business like the plague.

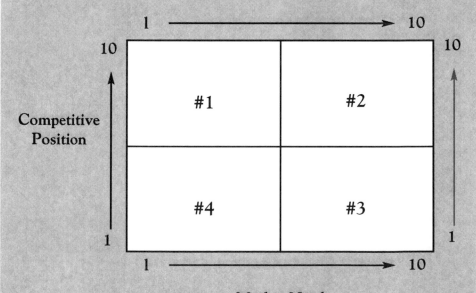

APPLICATION 2—D
IT'S START-UP TIME!

Application 2-C identified your market/product winners with the best possibilities of success. Based on that, what are the most important actions you should take over the next 90 to 180 days to get started? Your actions should be focused on the fundamentals required to get any business up and running. Although described earlier, they are restated here as action questions.

**Actions To Identify And Promote
To Potential Customers/Markets?**   **WHEN**

1.

2.

3.

**Actions To Design And Make The First Version Or Prototype
Of The Product/Service For Testing By A Customer?**   **WHEN**

1.

2.

3.

**Actions To Set Up The Operating Capabilities
Required To "Make, Sell, And Service"
The Products And Customers?**   **WHEN**

1.

2.

3.

**Actions To Identify And Secure The Sources Of Cash
(including customers) To Cover The Start-Up Phase
Of The Business?**   **WHEN**

1.

2.

3.

APPLICATION 3—A
CREATING ENTREPRENEURIAL BUSINESS VALUES

Values determine what you focus on, and become great at, operationally. Therefore, the values you select must be things that give you competitive advantage in products and markets and will have the commitment of the bulk of your employees. The other two columns are check points to reinforce the importance of competitive advantage and employee commitment. Identify below what specific actions you can take to implement your future business values. Review the *Creating Entrepreneurial Business Values* section for more information and examples.

WHAT VALUES DO WE NEED TO ACHIEVE THE PLAN?	WHAT'S THE COMPETITIVE ADVANTAGE?	HOW WILL I GET EVERYONE COMMITTED?
1.		
2.		
3.		
4.		

WHAT ACTIONS CAN I TAKE TO IMPLEMENT THESE VALUES?   **WHEN**

1.

2.

3.

APPLICATION 3—B
KEEPING THEM ALIVE

What can you do to insure that you focus on and maintain your selected values? The three greatest influences on keeping them alive are shown below. For each, jot down one or two ways in which that particular factor could have the greatest impact on supporting each value. Then, identify below what specific actions you can take now, or in the future, to make that happen. The *Keeping Them Alive* section can be reviewed for more information and examples.

VALUES	MANAGEMENT BEHAVIOR	RITUALS & PRACTICES	EMPLOYEE REWARDS & PENALTIES
1.			
2.			
3.			
4.			

WHAT ACTIONS CAN I TAKE TO KEEP THESE
VALUES ALIVE   WHEN

1.

2.

3.

APPLICATION 4
CREATING A PASSION FOR CUSTOMERS AND PRODUCTS

As the leader of your company, creating a passion for customers and products may become the most important job you have. Application 4 is designed to give you a jump start on keeping customer/product vision alive in your entrepreneurial venture. As you tackle the questions, keep in mind the key practices described in the *Loving The Customer* and *Loving The Product* sections. For the future, consider holding monthly brainstorming sessions using Application 4 as the format. This will be a simple way to maintain your customer/product passion and give you a constant source of great ideas.

GREAT IDEAS FOR LOVING THE CUSTOMER   WHEN

1.

2.

3.

4.

GREAT IDEAS FOR LOVING THE PRODUCT   WHEN

1.

2.

3.

4.

APPLICATION 5
GROWING THE OLD-FASHIONED WAY

Application 5 may become the best growth-marketing tool you'll ever have! After all there are only four ways to grow any business—and they're all on this simple chart! So focus on *what products to what markets*, identify the most promising areas, and plan the actions to get you there. You can use this application over and over again, every time you want to find new ways to grow your business! *Growing The Old-Fashioned Way* is fully described later in Chapter 9 but I've included the Application here because start-ups can use it too.

	Current	New	
New	New Products To Current Customers	New Products To New Customers	New
Current	Current Products To Current Customers	Current Products To New Customers	Current
	Current	New	

Products

Customers

ACTIONS   WHEN

1.

2.

3.

4.

APPLICATION 6
CREATING HIGH-SPEED INNOVATION

High-speed innovation is the fastest, cheapest, and surest way to gain competitive advantage in the marketplace. It truly is the entrepreneur's secret weapon. Now is the time to think through the actions you should take to make high-speed innovation a major thrust in your new business. As you tackle Application 6, keep in mind the specific examples of *The Necessity To Invent* and *The Freedom To Act* sections of the chapter. So what are the most important actions you should take?

TO ENCOURAGE INNOVATION:
Improve something, anything, every day.				**WHEN**

1.

2.

3.

TO SPEED UP ACTION:
Create a sense of urgency.					**WHEN**

1.

2.

3.

TO WIPE OUT BUREAUCRACY:
Growing big by staying small.					**WHEN**

1.

2.

3.

APPLICATION 7
SELF INSPIRED BEHAVIOR
RAISING COMMITMENT AND PERFORMANCE

Creating and maintaining a great company ultimately depends on two essential ingredients: the commitment and the performance of the managers and workers. From commitment flow pride, dedication to the mission, and plain old hard work. From performance flow expertise, innovation, and working smarter. If you're looking for competitive advantage, it's hard to beat people who love what they do and are good at doing it. You can start planning now how you're going to instill commitment and performance in yourself, your first few critical hires, and ultimately every employee in the company. What are the most important actions you can take now to create or raise employee commitment and performance in your new venture? Before you do Application 7 you might review the key practices in the *Creating Entrepreneurial Commitment* and *Creating Entrepreneurial Performance* sections of this chapter.

CREATING HIGH COMMITMENT   **WHEN**

1.

2.

3.

CREATING HIGH PERFORMANCE   **WHEN**

1.

2.

3

APPLICATION 8
THE ALMIGHTY POWER OF CONSEQUENCES

Use the *Entrepreneurial Performance System* chart below to raise the commitment and performance of your employees. Before you try it the first time, you might jump ahead to Chapter 11 for a more complete description of the EPS. By going through the following questions, you should discover which of the EPS components needs to be adjusted to change the behavior of the employee or employees. And remember the *power of consequences*! The easiest, cheapest, and surest way to change behavior is to make sure every employee feels positive and negative consequences from their performance. Based on your analysis, take the appropriate action to make the necessary changes.

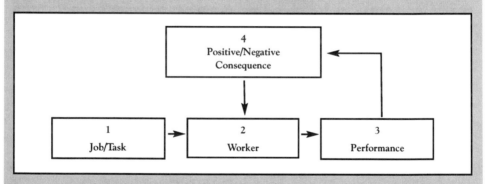

COMPONENT	QUESTION TO ASK	SOLUTION
1. Job/Task	Does the worker know *what* to do?	Set clear job standards.
2. Worker	Does the worker know *how* to do the job?	Provide training.
3. Performance	Does the worker have the resources to do the job?	Provide tools, people, time to do the job.
4. Consequences	Are the positive and negative consequences to the worker in balance?	Reset the positive &. negative consequences.
	Is the worker aware of the consequence?	Give accurate, timely and powerful feedback.

APPLICATION 9
WHAT'S REALLY REQUIRED?

The three broad, but essential, requirements for getting your new venture off the drawing board and into the real world are: operating in as supportive an environment as you can, securing the necessary money for the start-up period, and arming yourself with great product and market knowledge. Application 9 will help you think through how you can manage to meet and surpass these requirements. For each one, what are the most important action steps you can take, and when will you take them?

**ENSURING AN ENTREPRENEUR-FRIENDLY
CULTURE**   **WHEN**

1.

2.

3.

**SECURING THE NECESSARY
BIT OF MONEY**   **WHEN**

1.

2.

3.

**ACQUIRING THE NECESSARY
BIT OF KNOWLEDGE**   **WHEN**

1.

2.

3.

APPLICATION 10
MY 'GETTING ENTREPRENEURIAL' START-UP ACTION PLAN

We started off, in Application 1, asking you to imagine the most important things you would have to do to get a new company up and running. Now that you've completed Part One of the book, and all the other Applications, it's time to ask the same question again—for real! What are the most important actions to take, starting today, to *actually* get your entrepreneurial venture off the ground? And if you've already started your own business, which I suspect many of you have, what are the most important actions you can take now to keep it on a steady course of high growth? In the following spaces, write down the actions you commit to take over the next three to six months, to *really* start getting entrepreneurial!

**WHAT ARE THE MOST IMPORTANT
ACTIONS TO TAKE?**   **WHEN**

1.

2.

3.

4.

5.

6.

PART TWO

Entrepreneurial Companies

Corporate Entrepreneurship
—Reviving The Spirit Of
Enterprise In Your Organization

Chapter 7

Corporate Entrepreneurship

OOPS! WHO'S EXCELLENT NOW?

I still carry the November 5, 1984 issue of *Business Week* in my briefcase. I carry it to keep me humble, and to remind me to never believe

THE LIFE CYCLE OF ALL ORGANIZATIONS

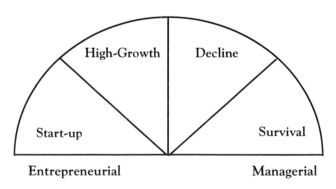

anything management consultants say, even if it's written down in the most famous business book in history. My fledgling company had actually been founded on the strength of having the contract to introduce Tom Peters' *Excellence* seminars internationally. It looked like a sure thing. After all, his book was the best selling management book of all time. We were moving fast. In just 18 months I had set up joint ventures in fifteen countries. Then all hell broke loose. The famous "Oops!" cover of *Business Week* appeared. The feature story rolled out the awful truth that in less than two years since *In Search Of Excellence* had been published, fully one third of the list of "America's best run companies" were on their knees financially. *Business Week* clearly had their facts right—and I had an entrepreneurial disaster on my hands. If so many of the "Excellent" companies were falling apart in less than two years, what company would want to train their managers in the "eight characteristics of excellence" so carefully laid out in the book and our seminar? The answer was damn few!

Clearly something had gone wrong with the conclusions of this famous book. But I had a more immediate problem. It had been tough enough to get the Germans, Japanese, and others in my global territory to buy anything based on American management prowess in the early eighties. Now, thanks to *Business Week* and the sorry facts they reported, *Excellence* was beginning to look like just another American management fad that didn't work. My entrepreneurial start-up was in dire need of a new product.

As often happens, necessity became the mother of invention. I hit upon two simple ideas. First I thought if the most popular business book in history didn't get to the bottom-line truth about what creates growth and prosperity in business, where in the world could we find those answers? It struck me that maybe Tom Peters and his co-author, Bob Waterman (both big-time McKinsey consultants by the way!) and the whole crazy industry of management gurus were asking the wrong questions—or at least looking in the wrong places for the answers. Maybe the place to look isn't the world's famous, giant companies. Maybe by the time they become a famous giant, it's already too late. What if they're already past their prime and their current management practices are the reason for their approaching decline, not the cause of their earlier years of growth? Bingo! The place to look for the true basics of successful enterprise had to be in the business practices of the entrepreneurs who created and propelled all those famous companies in the first place—during their start-up and high growth years.

The second, related idea was the notion that companies do change over time. And the real key is to understand the phases of a company's life cycle, as opposed to taking a snap-shot today and assuming the latest hot management idea is the source of all business success. Understanding the dynamic of the life cycle of organizations turned out to be the single most important discovery we made. Admittedly, these insights came a lot easier because I had just started my own company and I could see that as an entrepreneur, the priorities I felt and what I had to do every day to get my new business up and running was completely different from what I had been doing as a President or senior manager of the larger, more mature organizations where I had formerly worked.

I was getting more and more excited by all this and we began to do serious, hands on research with successful entrepreneurs all around the world, to flush these ideas out. By late 1985 (one year after the Oops! revelations) I knew we were on to something very interesting and very important. Additionally motivated by the on-going need of meeting payrolls in my London, Hong Kong, and USA offices, my associates and I began giving lectures and seminars on the power of entrepreneurial practices to anyone who would listen.

Our premise back then is still valid today. It's the entrepreneurial spirit, not managerial technique, that drives successful, high growth companies everywhere. We said then and say now, that much of big business is drowning under an avalanche of management fads, people theories, financial wizardry, and bureaucratic rules, none of which have anything to do with growing a business. The prescription is blunt: It's high time to dismantle your 20th century corporation and start over by instilling proven, high growth entrepreneurial practices in your managers—and even your rank and file employees.

BEATING THE ORGANIZATION LIFE CYCLE

You will recall, and may want to review, the full description of the life cycle diagram from the Introduction to this book. Certainly companies, like people and countries, and everything else in our world, exist in a cycle. As detailed earlier, there's the start-up followed by growth. Growth peaks and decline sets in, leading ultimately to death. Beating this cycle is tough indeed.

The fact is, the life cycle of companies is alive and well around the world today—causing plenty of big trouble at big business! The statistics are shocking, really. More profound than the high failure rate of the so-called "Excellent" companies, are these facts: Of the hundred largest, richest and most powerful U.S. companies in 1900, only 16 are still in business today. And 75 percent of the first *Fortune 500* list in 1955 are already gone. And perhaps most telling of all, just twenty-five years ago the three biggest employers in the U.S. were IBM, General Motors and Sears. These three great icons of American business all *invented, designed,* and *manufactured* products. IBM was the world's largest maker of computers. GM, the world's large car manufacturer. And Sears, the world's largest maker of home appliances. America's three largest employers today are McDonalds, still flipping hamburgers, Wal-Mart, selling products mostly made in China, and UPS, delivering packages of those products mostly made in China. While McDonalds, Wal-Mart, and UPS are obviously great companies, this huge shift in employment is not a good sign for the American economy, and it's a wake-up call for big business everywhere. Just getting bigger and bigger—Peter Drucker called it becoming oversized and over managed—does appear to end up being a competitive disadvantage. The good news is that any company can, and a few actually do, learn how to beat the dreaded life cycle.

The bottom-line is that downsizing, another re-structuring, hiring more management consultants and sending people off to business school courses won't get you a penny of real, organic growth. To start growing your business again, you've got to reverse your organization's life cycle and move back to the high growth phase. To do this, basic entrepreneurial practices have to be re-instilled across the company—which means you have to re-create a powerful **sense of mission**, maintain absolute focus on **customers and products**, produce a lot of **innovative action**, and re-develop a **self-inspired** workforce. It's called creating a more entrepreneurial organization. Or in today's jargon, we could say instilling "corporate entrepreneurship" as the dominant style of the business. The truth is, developing your "corporate entrepreneurial spirit" will give you the best weapon you'll ever have for growing your business. It's also a lot more interesting and fun, and certainly cheaper, than hiring legions of new Harvard and Stanford MBAs, ever so eager to try out their classroom theories on your faltering company—or paying out millions to get the latest strategic planning model dreamed up by the ever so over-paid consultants at McKinsey or Bain.

The following chapters describe exactly what corporate entrepreneurship is and how you can transform your 20th bureaucracy into a 21st century entrepreneurial organization!

THE NEW CORPORATE ENTREPRENEURS

"Today your career is your business"

—Andy Grove, CEO (retired)
Intel Corporation

Successful entrepreneurs who stay around to lead their companies well after they become big, such as Victor Fung in Hong Kong, Richard Branson in the UK and Michael Dell in the U.S., naturally run the business with a strong entrepreneurial bent. But can professional managers, who have never started a business from scratch, also run a business in an entrepreneurial way? I would say up until the 1980s, it would have been hard to find many so-called "corporate entrepreneurs." Remember, from the Great Depression, through World War Two, continuing right up to the hey-day of the MBA craze of the 1950's, 60's, and 70's, any manager worth his salt, who ever hoped to get a promotion, worked diligently to be the ultimate "organization man."

Rocking the boat, taking risks, doing anything "out of the box," was not the way to get ahead. Being the best and most predictable bureaucrat you could be was the smart career strategy.

Then big business, which had grown to be really big, began to stumble badly in the 70's and 80's. A few very bright, and ambitious, managers began to sense that the time was right to take some radical departures from textbook management practices and business as usual. They had seen first-hand how too much MBA style management and too much bloated bureaucracy were choking off the company's growth. At the same time, rising entrepreneurial mavericks like Akio Morita, Ross Perot, Steve Jobs and Anita Roddick were becoming the new heroes of business and were getting all the good press. These new leaders were doing things in very unorthodox ways and their customers and shareholders loved it. This confluence of trends opened the door for a new breed of corporate executive, what we now call the "corporate entrepreneur."

In my opinion, the watershed event in the legitimizing of corporate entrepreneurship came in 1981 when Jack Welch, an engineer, not an MBA, was handed the job of reversing General Electric Company's awful slide into oblivion. As *Fortune* magazine said at the end of his first decade: ". . . when he took over a moribund, ninety-year-old General Electric in 1981, 'Neutron Jack' wanted to run GE like a small, entrepreneurial business. He flattened GE's nine levels of management, cut the number of pay levels from twenty-nine to five, obliterated the corporate staff, and you guessed it—cut one hundred thousand jobs. He also got rid of all product lines that weren't first or second in their markets. And he took dead aim at the old functional structure and replace it with GE's new, highly entrepreneurial 'salesman/scientist' idea to get more customer friendly products to more market faster. The result: In the past decade, sales and profits have climbed steadily while GE's market value streaked skyward from a paltry $12 billion to $65 billion, making it the most valuable company in the world."

Fortune ended its piece with: "What's happening at GE now . . . is an explicit rejection of many of the old canons of modern management—

which GE largely wrote. In the past decade Welsh has tried to infuse the company with a sense of entrepreneurship, and in doing so has become the country's' most admired CEO."

So in the span of ten years, Welch's corporate entrepreneurship brought GE from death's door to being the most valuable company in the world! Now that's a turn-around equal to any entrepreneurial success story! Of course Welch wasn't burdened with any MBA theories—he was just an engineer. . . . .

All of a sudden, out of nowhere it seemed, the pin-striped, buttoned down, Harvard Business School look was out—and the hands on guys and gals who came up through the factory trenches, and the lowly sales routes were getting the big promotions. These were people who were experts on products and customers, just like real entrepreneurs! They didn't have MBAs and most of them had never attended a management course. A perfect example of this new brand of entrepreneurial manager was Intel's life-long engineer and CEO, Andy Grove. He wanted to instill the entrepreneurial spirit in every employee and the work environment at Grove's Intel was indeed highly entrepreneurial—as long as you were contributing to the overall corporate mission. That mission of course was to make Intel into what *Time* magazine ultimately called it: "The essential firm of the digital age." Achieving that mission was all about creating high purpose and demanding high standards. It's not easy to constantly push the frontiers of technology (Intel passed the unthinkable barrier of 600 million calculations a second out of their Pentium II chip while Grove was still at the helm.) and maintain a 90% world market share—which is exactly what Andy Grove asked his people to do—year after year.

In constantly reaching for the moon, everyone at Intel was encouraged to think like a free agent—not an employee. No one was allowed to rest on last year's laurels. And forget about guaranteed lifetime employment. The company was not a security blanket for slackers—rather a place full of opportunity for the best and the brightest. Get really good at something, work at it with a passion, and you could have ten good jobs waiting for you at Intel. Sit around waiting for a seniority promotion and a pension, and you'll be left in the dust in the do-or-die global competitive war Intel was fighting.

Grove's most famous management dictum was: "Only the paranoid survive." And who could blame him? After all, Andras Grof survived both scarlet fever and Nazi pogroms as a boy. Then, at age 20, with the Red Army approaching, he fled Budapest after the failed 1956 revolution. With no money, little English, and a new American name, young immigrant Andy Grove hit the USA shores running. With a hard-won Ph.D. from Berkeley, he joined Fairchild Semiconductor where the legendary Gordon Moore ("Moore's Law" correctly predicted microchips would double in power and halve in cost every 18 months) became his mentor-for-life. Of course Grove was no scientific slouch himself, running the team that purified silicon, a huge breakthrough that made the digital revolution possible. When Moore founded Intel, Andy Grove was at his side, putting him center stage in one of the most turbulent, unpredictable and entrepreneurial businesses in the world.

Surviving mighty ups and downs, Grove's Intel became number one in the semi-conductor world. For a period it was even ranked as the third biggest company in the U.S. in market value. Today it faces tough Asian competition, but is still the number two semiconductor firm in the world—and in early 2010 introduced a series of technology advances widely acclaimed by analysts. It has of course provided its long-term investors with enormous year over year returns. Even so, this is an industry so fast paced, with such high stakes, that even Intel could be wiped out with a single strategic lapse. The 1994 recall of the Pentium processor, resulting in a massive $475 million write-off, is still a grim reminder. Through it all, obsessed with the ever-present possibility of falling behind, Grove's entrepreneurial management style set the tone. Intel employees knew that when he told them: "your career is your real business," he meant it. Today, as a retired CEO and Chairman, he remains as an advisor to Intel's board—where I'm sure his entrepreneurial influence is still being felt.

On a personal level, it's important to note that some fifteen years ago, Grove achieved a different sort of world-wide acclaim for his amazing personal research into seeking out the best treatments for his battle with pancreatic cancer—which largely through his own efforts he managed to beat and has remained cancer free to this day. Currently he is demonstrating the same engineering and entrepreneurial zeal in his battle to overcome Parkinsons Disease. In this effort he is an advisor, and the largest financial contributor (with a bequest of some $40 million,) to the Michael J. Fox Foundation For Parkinson's Research. He has in fact become a high profile advocate for a "cultural revolution in the bio-medical sciences" to spur research into finding cures for numerous terrible diseases. So Andy Grove's entrepreneurial spirit lives on today—perhaps even more profoundly as a *social entrepreneur* than as a *corporate entrepreneur!*

Managing and marketing one's own career has become the clarion call of 21st century corporate life. For those who bemoan a more entrepreneurial environment in corporations, it's all a matter of perspective. Sure, there are reasons to be sentimental about the good old days when company loyalty and life-time employment were in vogue. But in an age of massive restructuring and downsizing, and a near complete lack of loyalty toward employees from big business, who can blame managers and employees today for getting more entrepreneurial in their approach to their careers? And also, let's not over-romanticize spending forty years in the same company, doing the same job, and fighting the same battles. As Ben Hamper, the former GM assembly line worker turned author says: "In the 'good ole days' working at GM was like being paid to flunk high school the rest of your life."

Like it or not, most of us have to play with the hand we're dealt. Remember, we're living in an age when the biggest "provider of jobs" in America is Manpower, Inc., a temporary help agency. Getting entrepreneurial is not really a choice any more for most of us. But don't despair. We have a great suggestion for you. It's a "don't get mad, get even" suggestion. How about learning to be a "corporate entrepreneur?" It's the new, smart, entrepreneurial age strategy for anyone who really prefers being part of a large, world-class business—versus starting their own operation from scratch. There can be enormous benefits to you and your company. Big business may have had to re-shuffle the deck a few times over the past couple of decades—but giant companies haven't gone away—they've just gotten a lot smarter. The fact is, big business has fallen in love with managers who can run their small part of the big business as if it were their own. Probably all you really need are a few starter ideas and examples on how to become an entrepreneurial manager.

This is the real message from Jack Welch, Andy Grove and hundreds of other modern, entrepreneurial CEOs: Getting entrepreneurial will be good for your company, no doubt about it. But more than that, it will be absolutely great for your career. It's the win-win formula for reviving the spirit of enterprise in yourself and your business!

If you're interested, this section of The **New** Entrepreneurial Age should be especially important for you. A good way to start is to really know that it's possible—that real entrepreneurial managers and real entrepreneurial companies really exist in real places. The story of Lincoln Electric, sitting squarely in the "rust belt" of Ohio, and the world's largest manufacturer of welding equipment, will answer that in spades.

THE MOST ENTREPRENEURIAL BIG COMPANY IN THE WORLD

"When workers are treated like entrepreneurs,
they behave like entrepreneurs."

—Fred Mackenbach, President (Retired)
Lincoln Electric

How many companies do you know that have to keep their gates locked before the morning shift to keep employees from starting to work too early? Welcome to Lincoln Electric, an old economy company, manufacturing heavy industrial equipment in the rust belt of America. They're also the world's largest maker of welding equipment and a company that stands conventional wisdom on its head. When I first saw the story on CBS TV's 60 Minutes, I couldn't believe it. So I checked it

out personally with President Fred Mackenbach in Cleveland, Ohio—
ground zero of the rust belt. Along with the locked gates to keep workers
out, Lincoln Electric also has some very strange ideas about
compensating employees. Mackenbach says: "The company only gets
paid by making good welding equipment, and we don't see any reason
for paying employees for anything other than making that welding
equipment." And they don't. They don't pay anyone for holidays, sick
leave, lunch time, coffee breaks, trips to the toilet, or for poor quality
products that no one will buy.

Then, with a twinkle in his eye, Mackenbach let slip that the employees
don't really seem to mind since they are all earning from $60,000 to over
$100,000 per year, making Lincoln employees the highest paid factory
workers in the world. Mackenbach said they had built the entire
company on the notion that: "Lincoln can pay the highest factory
salaries in the world because our people know that, like entrepreneurs,
the more good welding equipment they produce the more money they
will make. And second, also like entrepreneurs, they know they don't
get paid for downtime or rejects—so they've all become self-managing
which means we don't need to hire 500 supervisors to stand around and
watch them work. Anyway, they all work damn hard and there's a lot
of profit to be shared in that welding equipment."

It's a modem day version of 19th Century piecework pay, with two huge
differences. First, all those savings go back to the workers in profit
bonuses. In a good year, they average more than $20,000 per worker—
an unheard of figure in American factories. Second, the company
guarantees continuous employment to its workers, and hasn't had a
layoff since it was founded in 1895. Over the years, all Lincoln
employees have been asked to temporarily cut their time as much as 25
percent, but everyone in the company agrees this is preferable to the
standard industrial practice of layoffs and outright terminations.

Other unusual things happen when corporate entrepreneurship takes
hold. Mackenbach explains, "Large organizations are usually devoted to
minimizing risks, not seeking them out. We're fortunate at Lincoln
because our strong pay-for-performance system forces us to take risks on

a daily basis. We take a risk every time we make a new hire. We look for a strong work ethic and a burning desire to succeed. Evidence of that desire is the best predictor of success in the Lincoln culture. If we are wrong about a new hire, that person's substandard performance will adversely affect the productivity of everyone in that department. Since we are exactly staffed, the other employees will have to pick up the slack. So at Lincoln, we consider each new hire to be a risky business decision.

"We also constantly take risks in our effort to better serve the customer; because of course the customer ultimately is our reason for being. We have a program called 'Guaranteed Cost Reduction' in which our sales representatives guarantee our customer, in writing, that by using Lincoln products and recommended procedures, they will save a specific amount of money within a certain time frame, or we will pay them the difference. As President of the company, I personally sign those guarantees. Is it risky? Sure. A couple of times the savings have failed to materialize and we had to cut checks for those customers. Has it been worth the risk? Absolutely. We've generated millions and millions of dollars of business by being willing to take this risk.

"We also take many risks by encouraging our employees to be self managing. This means that we are willing to relinquish a high degree of control, in exchange for the tremendous energy and initiative highly motivated people bring to our enterprise. Of course the big benefit of having 6,400 self-managing employees is that we don't have to pay people to watch other people work. Our customers couldn't care less about is how much time and money we spend micro-managing our workforce. But the nonproductive cost of supervision could have a devastating impact on the prices we charge our customers—and *that*, they care about!

"And of course our formal policy of guaranteed continuous employment entails an almost unheard-of risk. It is a risk we have continued to take, day by day, month by month, year by year, through recessions and very hard times in our industry. But we believe the upside in all this is worth it. An example is the remarkable performance of our people last summer, when a sudden spike in demand for our products forced us to sharply increase production. Lincoln employees voluntarily deferred 614 weeks of vacation in order to meet that challenge. Their efforts broke all of our production and sales records. And I must tell you, our records were already high."

The most current financial results say Lincoln Electric's entrepreneurial approach is still working. On the *Fortune 1000* list, they are once again a star within their industrial grouping. You'll find them in the "Industrial and Farm Equipment" category—about as "old economy" as it gets. Industry stalwarts like John Deere, Detroit Diesel, and Timken are bigger and better known—but the Ohio manufacturer of welding equipment really shines when it comes to key financial ratios. With $2.48 billion in revenue it ranks just 18th in overall size in the category—but here's the entrepreneurial payoff: As a percentage of revenue it's number two in profitability and number three in total return to investors!

Even more impressive is its ability to continue growing in tough times: Operating in the most basic of old line industries, located at ground-zero of the rust belt, and facing the worst recession since the 1930s, Lincoln Electric still manages to grow! While half the companies in its industrial category suffered declines last year, Lincoln's revenues were up an impressive 8.7% and its profits grew 4.7%. And of course they still do it as they've always done it; with no work stoppages and no layoffs. As a 41 year old plant foreman was quoted in Time magazine: "I never have to wake up in the morning wondering if I still have a job." That means a lot in this day and age. And to an employee working in a U.S. manufacturing company, trying to keep his home and feed his family, it means everything.

Of course Lincoln Electric isn't Ford Motor with half a million people to worry about. But it could very well be a Ford billion-dollar division— and that's the best part of the Lincoln story. Any big business in the world can operate like Lincoln Electric if they want to. There's nothing holding you back. As Fred Mackenbach concluded: "It's all pretty simple really. When workers are treated like entrepreneurs, they behave like entrepreneurs. Lincoln employees will do anything it takes to produce more welding equipment. It's just amazing." Then he chuckled: "That's why we have to lock the gates sometimes!

THE FOUR ENTREPRENEURIAL BASICS APPLIED TO COMPANIES

The fundamental business practices of great entrepreneurs, as applied to companies, are:

The Four Entrepreneurial Basics

Sense of Mission
Keeping The Sense Of Mission Alive As You Grow

Customer/Product Vision
Re-Instilling Customer/Product Vision In Every Employee

High-speed Innovation
Fostering High-Speed Innovation Across the Company

Self-inspired Behavior
Making Self-Inspired Behavior The Organization Standard

Chapter 8

Keeping The Sense Of Mission Alive As You Grow

Creating An Entrepreneurial Strategy & Culture

"When it comes to setting up new companies, one of my advantages is that I don't have a highly complicated view of business."

—Richard Branson, Founder
Virgin Group

Richard Branson is Great Britain's most successful and famous entrepreneur since the days of William Lever, George Cadbury and Jesse Boots. And he deserves every bit of his fame and his fortune. He's made

Virgin a household name the world over with Virgin Music, Virgin Records, Virgin Atlantic Airways, Virgin Films, Virgin Direct, Virgin Megastores, Virgin Cola, and dozens more Virgin businesses.

But as terrific as he is, I'd hate to have to learn how to be an entrepreneur by listening to him explain how he did it: ". . . to be successful, you have to be out there, you have to hit the ground running, and if you have a good team around you and more than a fair share of luck, you might make something happen." This is classic (and entertaining) "entrepreneur-speak." But you still don't know how in the world he became a billionaire entrepreneur, or more to the point, what you should do to become one yourself! Maybe in some deep psychological way that I don't comprehend, leaving it pretty fuzzy may be just fine with Richard Branson. Regardless, this is a common characteristic of most great entrepreneurs: They're obsessed with creating and building businesses, not teaching others how to do the same.

Still it's impossible to not admire Branson and be motivated by his persona. And along the way, we can at least try to make sense of some of the pearls of wisdom he imparts. For example, it's just plain refreshing to hear him describe his approach to market research: "When I think about which services I want to offer on Virgin Atlantic, I try to imagine whether my family and I would like to buy them for ourselves. Quite often it's as simple as that." And some of his comments do at least sound like ideas any company could try: "Convention dictates that 'big is beautiful,' but every time one of our ventures gets too big, we divide it up into smaller units. By the time we sold Virgin Music, we had as many as fifty different subsidiary record companies, and not one of them had more than sixty employees." Finally, who wouldn't be inspired at least a little by this description of the core reason for The Virgin Group's meteoric rise: "More than any other element, fun is the secret of Virgin's success."

But just as you're beginning to think that maybe Richard Branson is a teacher after all, he comes up with this "description" when asked about the future mission of Virgin: "I tend to either avoid this question or answer it at great length, safe in the knowledge that I will give a different version the next time I'm asked." Come again? How are you going to teach your people to be corporate entrepreneurs with that? You're not of course—and that's why our mission has become to distill what these great people do—not what they say they do.

Now for the easy part with Branson. There is one, absolutely clear behavior that he's demonstrated over the past four decades: Richard Branson has an all-consuming "sense of mission" about his work. He believes that what he is doing is important—and he is incredibly committed to doing it. So we thank you, Richard Branson, for giving us an exciting, modern example of that old truth about entrepreneurs. And now we can move on to the business of figuring out how to put your brand of business, your sense of mission if you will, into some simple, practical steps which any employee, in any company, can actually follow!

Sense of Mission is the starting point for all entrepreneurs. They do truly believe they are doing something important. They see genuine value in their work: For their customers, for their employees, and certainly for themselves. They are convinced their products produce needed benefits for customers. And without exception, they know the only way to stay alive is to produce products and services that someone, somewhere, will pay for. In this sense at least, all organizations start off reflecting the goals, the philosophy, and the sense of mission of their founders. This is true in spades, of course, at Richard Branson's Virgin Group.

Perhaps, none of this is terribly surprising. What can be surprising is the degree to which start-up employees also share in this sense of mission. In the young, entrepreneurial company, feeling some excitement, some team spirit, or as we say, a sense of mission, seems to come with the territory and is very infectious. But when you think about it, maybe it isn't so unusual. Consider your own career history: Most employees say the most exciting times in their working careers have been when they were involved with something new: Launching a new product, opening a new market, fighting off a new competitor, etc. In the final analysis, however it comes about; we know that having a sense of mission is a gift of enormous competitive value.

While it comes somewhat naturally for the original entrepreneur and his start-up team, it's going to be trickier to instill this powerful competitive advantage in an existing company with long-term employees and fixed attitudes about things. The first step is to have a clear understanding of exactly what Sense Of Mission is all about. And the best way to do this, given the kinds of explanations offered up by most of the great entrepreneurs of the world—such as Sir Richard—we have to look beyond their words, to their deeds.

THE "WHAT" AND THE "HOW" OF THE MISSION: FOR BIG BUSINESS

If most entrepreneurs are not terribly clear in verbalizing their mission, they are exquisitely articulate in their behavior; that is, in *what* they do and *how* they do it—day in and day out. These are the two essential elements of any mission. A person, a company, or even a country, has to be know *what* its mission is, and be absolutely clear on *how* to achieve it. All entrepreneurs' behavior is, in fact, highly focused on what they are doing and how they go about doing it—which we've translated into business language as corporate strategy (the *what* of the business) and "corporate culture" (the *how* of the business.)

For entrepreneurs, the strategy really comes down to picking the right products and markets. And the culture has the specific role of making sure the strategy is achieved. The entrepreneurial ideal is to be great at both. It's not good enough to have a strong strategy, but a weak, non-supportive culture. Conversely a strong culture will never overcome a weak strategy. And of course you won't be around long if you know neither *what* you're doing nor *how* to do it!

The lesson that is so often lost in the bureaucracy of larger companies is that corporate strategy and corporate culture must be connected. You set the strategy, and then you determine those operating activities and

SENSE OF MISSION

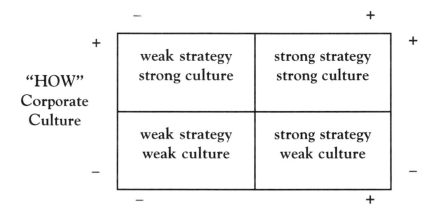

"WHAT" Corporate Strategy

skills that are most critical to achieving the strategy. One of the great modern examples of the power of that connection is 3M. Everyone knows 3M's reputation for product innovation. It has, in fact, the highest ratio of new product revenue to total revenue of any big company around. First, 3M sets as its corporate strategy—and, on average, achieves—an incredible 30% ratio of new product revenue. Their definition has always been that any product invented within the past five years is classified as "new." So, how does 3M achieve this remarkable performance? First, by planning to do it—making new product revenue the core of their corporate strategy. And second—and here's the part so often missed by others—3M has built its entire corporate culture around product innovation. It has made innovation the number-one, in fact the only, corporate value of the worldwide company. This is both very smart and very effective. Would 3M hit their strategic goal year after year if, for example, they simply copied the values of say, Wal-Mart, or Singapore Airlines, or Mercedes Benz—all great companies in their own right? Of course not! It's called connecting your culture to your strategy. The question is: To achieve our specific product and market strategy, what specific culture must we create. Not making this connection is the most common mistake that managements make in trying to instill an entrepreneurial Sense Of Mission in their companies.

The challenge for you is to make sure your and your employees' behavior is also "obsessively focused" on these two fundamentals of successful enterprise. To do that, let's look at one of the great role models for creating an entrepreneurial strategy—Japan's greatest entrepreneur of the 20th century.

CORPORATE STRATEGY À LA MATSUSHITA

"Our duty as industrialists is to provide conveniences for the public, and to enrich and make happier all those who use them."

—Konosuke Matsushita, Founder
Matsushita Electric

Konosuke Matsushita was a young salesman in Osaka. In 1918, he invested his life savings of 100 yen (about $50) in imported electric sockets from Great Britain. He was excited and very focused on getting the first batch sold and ordering more. He was certain this type of product would sell very well in the new, miracle age of electricity! He was wrong. None of the shops he called on were interested in stocking his electric socket. It was so bad, in fact, he went bankrupt. So the great Matsushita's first entrepreneurial venture was a bust. And in Japan, at that time, failing in business was about as shameful an act one could commit. Then he did something that few salesmen ever do—and changed his life forever.

He went back to all the shopkeepers who wouldn't buy his product, and for the first time, asked them: "Is there anything I could do to change this socket so that you would want to buy a few for your shop?" Many of the shopkeepers gave him suggestions like 'make it bigger, make it smaller, change the color, do this or do that.' He took all their suggestions and began tinkering with his sockets at home. He even fashioned a few proto-types of his own from scratch. He went back to the market with the customized versions and tried again. And again. And again. He kept repeating his routine of asking the potential customers how he could change the product so they would want to buy it. It was this process of back and forth customer/product strategizing that produced Konosuke Matsushita's marvelous invention; the world's first two-way electric socket. With it he began winning customers and the fledgling Matsushita Electric played a small, but critical, role in exploding the electrical appliance industry in Japan. Now, a single electric line to a house could connect two appliances at once—an electric fan and a radio, or a cooker, etc. And as we know today, it gave birth to the world's largest producer of electric and electronic products. It also was a lesson in corporate strategy that Matsushita Electric never forgot.

By his own later account, Matsushita was unsuccessful at first because he was thinking too much about selling and not enough about what customers really wanted. So what was his successful "strategic process?" Simply this: "Ask the customers what they want, and then do that rare and unexpected thing: Give it to them!" When you're looking for simple, practical steps to follow—the no frills customer-product strategy of Matsushita would be hard to beat!

In 1932, some fourteen years after start-up, Konosuke Matsushita again did something that most salesmen (and great entrepreneurs) never do. He started thinking about and putting on paper, the principles of enterprise as he had lived them. It took him five years to get it down. The result was a very thin, twenty-three page booklet titled: Matsushita Management Philosophy. These twenty-three pages contain as much wisdom about enterprise as some entire business school libraries. It provides a philosophical and strategic framework for any company, which not surprisingly, all boils down to making products that markets actually need. It should be required reading at every MBA program in the world.

For ninety plus years, the *what* of the business at Matsushita has been driven by knowing very specifically, *what customers* want *what products*. Doing this better and more consistently than their competitors has always been the ultimate competitive advantage of Matsushita Electric, and its famous brands like Panasonic and National. In so doing, Konosuke Matsushita raised customer/product strategy from black magic to near certainty, and it all comes from those unsold electric sockets way back in 1918.

WHAT'S IN *WHAT*

Is there, then, an entrepreneurial strategy setting approach you and your people can use? Well, it may not qualify as a full-blown (and incredibly expensive,) strategic planning process a la McKinsey or Bain Consulting, but there are definitely some basics to keep in mind– whether your creating a top-down corporate strategy or simply your own business unit plans. (Again, *our description of the entrepreneurial approach to strategy is influenced by and in part modified from the original work of my friend and former boss, Dr. Benjamin B. Tregoe who unfortunately passed away a few years ago. These descriptions and modifications appear in Part One and more significantly in Part Two of the book. We have applied his description of strategy to the entrepreneurial approach for one reason only— it so clearly illustrates why entrepreneurs do what they do. I highly recommend Ben Tregoe's own books or Kepner-Tregoe, Inc.'s advisory services on the broader subject of corporate strategy.*)

For starters, if the strategy is supposed to tell us what we are doing, we need to be crystal clear on what's included in the "what." And this doesn't take three hundred pages to figure out. It only requires answering four straight-forward questions. Listed below are the *"what"* questions that matter most. If you know the answers cold, you're on top of your business. If you can't answer these basic questions, you not only don't have a useful plan, you may not have a business to worry about much longer.

- **What Customers/Markets Will We Pursue?**
Are we really clear on what markets we will and won't tackle? What's the criteria for choosing? What do they really need? What will they really pay for?

- **What Products/Services Will We Provide?**
What's the scope of products and services we can and will provide? What's the criteria for picking winners? Will our products and services be better and cheaper than our competitors? Will they be only better? Will they be at least cheaper?

- **What Capabilities Are Required?**
What operating capabilities and resources are required to make, sell, and service our products and customers?

- **What Cash Will We Have?**
Where will the cash come from and where will it go? Even if your company doesn't require it, thinking and planning in cash keeps your feet on the ground, right where they have to be in an entrepreneurial world.

CREATING AN ENTREPRENEURIAL STRATEGY

The best way to get a handle on creating an entrepreneurial corporate strategy is to recall the last big company, strategic planning session you attended—and then do everything as differently as possible. If your planning and presentation experience is anything like most of us have had, it probably went something like this:

You're in an exclusive resort or the even more exclusive, corporate board room. All-powerful executives sit as judge and jury, while scores of nervous underlings parade to the front making the projections they think the board wants to hear. Your soft estimates become hard facts as they get cemented into the overall corporate plan. The usual assortment of pin-striped consultants come and go, pitching their own version of your future. And of course there are the reams of research and planning books, piled high on the table that nobody ever reads. Somehow out of this surreal, big business ritual comes the big black book called "The Strategic Plan," and everyone goes back to doing real work for another twelve months. If it doesn't ring a bell, be thankful. Because this is no way to pick products and markets.

I may have an even more jaundiced view of strategic planning presentations than most. When I was just 28, I had the chance of a lifetime to impress the big brass of my Fortune 100 employer, American Express Company, at their headquarters in New York City. I was the Marketing Vice President for a small, new acquisition that offered language training and translation services. Like all Amexco divisions and companies, we had to present our five year strategic plan to the board, and I was asked by my President to accompany him. A couple of years earlier, American Express had embarked upon an aggressive acquisition strategy, hoping to grow faster by moving beyond their core products, which was all the rage at the time. The high-flying Amexco acquisition team had apparently thought that since American Express was the "company for people who travel," why not also teach them foreign languages? We all found out later that language training was a real mom and pop type business—and even the world leader, Berlitz, had taken eighty years to get to only about $25 million in revenue from some 100 schools. (*For the record, a year after this story I was recruited away from American Express (where I had worked for 5 exciting years) by Berlitz to become their marketing chief. I left after only two years to become the Marketing VP and eventually President of Kepner-Tregoe, Inc. where I stayed 10 delightful years—before starting-up The Farrell Company. Twenty-seven years later I'm still here doing things I really love to do like writing this book—and the best part is I haven't had to make another strategy presentation in all these years!*)

Our subsidiary, which had begun trading under the name American Express Language Centers, had only three schools in the whole world: New York, Washington, D. C. and Mexico City. To make us look as good as possible, we had really pumped up our projections for the Board presentation. We all knew, short of a miracle, we weren't likely to meet them—but we had convinced ourselves we should present as aggressive a plan as we could to the Board. American Express had hired McKinsey Consulting to install a Strategic Planning System and I spent weeks with some of their young consultants putting our plans into the right format and so on. Overall, our personnel had put months into the planning process which we all believed was state of the art stuff.

On the big day, I entered the old American Express headquarters at 65 Broadway in lower Manhattan and made my way up to the executive floor, which I had never even seen before. We were second or third on the list of presentations that day but I was ushered into the boardroom through a side door while the preceding presentation was wrapping up. Upon entering, the first thing I saw was the giant mahogany board table—the biggest table I had ever seen in my life. The carpet seemed about two inches thick, and everything was beautifully polished. The room was huge, and everybody was there. The Board members were all sitting around the enormous table of course. Seated around the edge of the cavernous room were various minions: The advertising agency folks, several of the strategic planning consultants, the PR people, lots of upper-middle looking executives with thick binders, and a dozen gophers racing in and out of the boardroom! The group presenting before us was the Travelers Checques Division, a hugely profitable business. The highlight of that presentation was their prediction that by summer of the next year, the "float" on Travelers Checques (amount sold but not yet redeemed) would hit a cool $1 billion for the first time in history. I'm sure it's many billions more today, but from my seat at the side of the room I quickly calculated the interest per year on a billion dollars and winced. With this closing piece of good news there was much guffawing and self-congratulation around the Board Room and then—my President and I were up.

My boss had the somewhat redundant name of Jeffrey Jeffries. Jeffrey Jeffries was a long-term American Express guy, who was desperate to retire with his pension intact. After a brief introduction full of corporate platitudes, he turned to me, and as if he had just thought of it said: "Larry, why don't you give the board your projections." Even though I was extremely nervous with anticipation, I do remember thinking: "Why is Jeffrey Jeffries acting like we haven't been rehearsing this for days, and much more troubling, when did these become *my* projections?" So by showing my charts, and forcing as upbeat a voice as I could muster, I somehow got through the show and ended with the big number: the five year out revenue projection—which I knew we couldn't hit without an act of God—of $4 million. I sat down. It turned completely silent. Nobody said anything. I peered up and scanned the Board members who were all just staring at my $4 million figure on the chart, saying absolutely nothing. It was as if no one had ever seen such a small number at an American Express board presentation! After the long silence, the great and powerful Chairman, Howard Clark (who's signature was on every one of those billions of dollars worth of Travelers Checks) turned to Executive V. P. Hap Miller, my boss's boss's boss, and said: "I'm sure this young man you've got presenting here is a fine salesman Hap, but I gotta tell ya, the salesman I'd like to meet is the one who sold us this damn company in the first place! He must be one hell of a salesman!"

I looked straight at the Chairman, but all I saw was my career flashing before my eyes—until that is, Jeffrey Jeffries, the guy with one foot in retirement and a veteran of "CYA" corporate maneuvering, sprang into the breach with: "It would be interesting to take a second look at the acquisition team's original projections and contrast them to the reality we now know we face." A masterstroke! There was a consensus grunt of approval and in the twinkling of an eye, Jeffrey Jeffries had shifted the blame from us to the guys who bought "this damn company in the first place." He leaned over to me and whispered: "Close call, but don't worry, you made a good impression on the board so you'll probably get a spot in corporate marketing which will be better exposure for you anyway." I gathered up my charts and walked out of the boardroom, having learned an important lesson in strategic planning and career development at giant corporations: Successfully delivering your plan at the end of the year may not be nearly as important as successfully delivering the presentation of your plan at the beginning of the year!

Of course all this flies in the face of entrepreneurial common sense. While the entrepreneur's strategy focuses on the survival of the business, traditional, big company strategy is often focused on creating financial projections to please the board and excite Wall Street. It's not so exciting, but creating an entrepreneurial strategy is still based on that old-fashioned business of picking the right products and markets. Trying to figure out how to survive is, after all, a pretty down-to-earth business. Here's how entrepreneurs approach it.

• It's A Matter Of Survival

The goal is survival, not an affirmative nod from the board. And today it's career as well as business survival that we're talking about. If you get the plan right, you stay in business and you have a job. If you've picked the wrong products and markets, you don't get to try it again next year—you're history! At least that's the way it works for entrepreneurs.

• Don't Make It A Big, Complicated Project

Doing the plan is not the objective. Growing the business is. To the entrepreneur, creating the company strategy isn't a six month project, or a conference in Bermuda, or an excuse for consultants to get rich. Their method: keep it simple, do it quickly, and get back to the real work.

• Stay Focused On Customers

The best partners you'll ever have in business are your customers. They know more and cost less than any market researchers and consultants you could ever hire. They'll tell you exactly what they need, what they're willing to pay for it, and how they'd like it delivered—if you'll only ask them. To create an entrepreneurial style strategy, your plans have to be designed *with* your customers, not *at* your customers.

• Stay Focused On Products

The best product consultants you'll ever have are free. They're your customers and your competitors. In fact there are three possible sources of great product and service ideas: You, your customers and your competitors. Mining all three sources, all the time, is the entrepreneurial way to create a product strategy. And remember—while it's true that entrepreneurs "love their product," what keeps them in business is making sure their customers love their product.

- **Know The Criteria That Count**

Choosing products and markets is the name of the game. The information entrepreneurs want most is intimate knowledge about market need and their competitive position against the best competitors in the field. These are the two criteria that always count most!

THE CRITERIA THAT COUNT

As Matsushita told his managers, you can write your plan in a 200 page book or on the back of a napkin—but always remember, the two things you must know are what do customers really need, and do you have the best product for that need? So we think Konosuke Matsushita would agree when we say the criteria that really count are market need and competitive position. To make the best choices about markets, you will have to practically live with your prospects and customers. And to make the best choices about your competitive position, you have to know everything you can possibly (and legally) find out about your best competitors. In short, you need to become an absolute expert on the "what, when, where, and how much" on both your customers and your competitors.

Here's a final word about "picking winners"—and the traditional planning cycle: Choosing products and markets has to go on all the time. It happens when ideas and opportunities present themselves. Most great market ideas aren't going to pop up in October just because you've started your planning cycle. And damn few great products have ever been conceived at a planning conference in Bermuda. So stay flexible and don't get locked into the notion that picking products and markets is a once a year job.

The chart below can be used to rate and then combine the ratings of the two criteria for all your markets and products. While entrepreneurs aren't big fans of matrices and charts, this one will give you a simple, easy-to-see method of evaluating any market/product business you are considering. In other words, it will help you determine if you have picked a "Market/Product Winner" or not. As you may recall from Part One of this book, each quadrant in the matrix represents a unique market/product position. (*To review the complete descriptions of the four market/product positions, see Chapter 2 in Part One.*) And the actions required to improve your market/product position will differ greatly for each quadrant. The overall objective is to take those actions that will move your product or business in an upper-right direction—toward bigger markets and a higher competitive position.

THE CRITERIA THAT COUNT

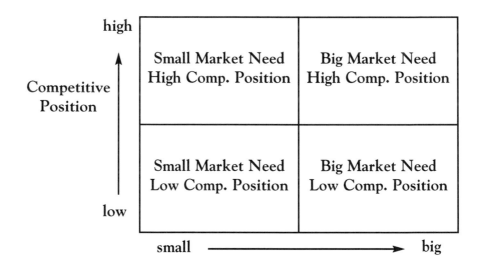

Market Need

So now you and your organization have a clear strategy for what markets and what products. And everyone should have a clear picture of what to do. The only thing standing between you and success is how well you can do it. This is where corporate culture, and the specific values that drive it, must get plugged into the business mission.

CORPORATE CULTURE À LA WATSON

*"The beliefs that mold great organizations frequently grow
out of the character, the experiences, and the convictions of a
single person. More than most companies, IBM is the reflection of one
individual—my father, T. J. Watson."*

—Thomas J. Watson Jr., Chairman
IBM

This could only happen to IBM: Your 20th in sales and 4th in profits on the current *Fortune 500* list, but everyone keeps saying you're over the hill. In an odd sort of way, it's actually a tribute to the awesome power and reputation that Big Blue carried for most of the 20th century. In fact, with the benefit of some perspective, one could make a strong case that IBM was the greatest and most profitable corporation for the whole of last century, if not in the entire history of business. If you have to pick a single factor at the core of IBM's long run at greatness, it was that they were the best in the world at doing those few critical things that were absolutely essential to the achievement of their business strategy. Tom Watson, Jr., called it the "power of IBM's beliefs."

Thomas J. Watson Sr. founded IBM in 1914, and immediately went about instilling in all IBMers his now famous set of beliefs: Outstanding customer service, respect for every employee, and superior performance in even the smallest of tasks. History shows these beliefs, or as we call them—the values, served IBM well for at least seventy-five years. Where did they come from? Did Mr. Watson take a vote among his employees or hire consultants to tell him what the IBM values should be? No, they came from Watson himself, as he figured out what IBM had to focus on to achieve its strategy.

T. J. Watson was an eternally optimistic salesman, and he didn't see IBM's strategy as a product leader and innovator—like 3M, for example. In fact, in the early days, IBM's products were fairly humdrum: Butcher scales, meat slicers, coffee grinders, time clocks, and a primitive assortment of punched card tabulating machines. Watson saw IBM's essential competitive advantage in providing outstanding customer service, whatever the product. This value was verbalized as a flat-out, un-compromising promise to the world: "IBM will give the best customer service of any company, in any industry, anywhere in the world."

Watson set out on a life-time mission to make that promise come true. For years, IBM corporate advertising simply declared: "IBM Means Service." IBM salesmen were trained like no sales-force ever before. They spent as long as eighteen months in IBM schools before seeing their first customer. Early on the company began recruiting sales trainees from college campuses, an unheard of practice at the time. And Watson invented the idea of "customer engineers" being assigned to all sales teams—to ensure that customers had face to face contact with IBM's highest level of technical expertise. IBM schools were opened to customer personnel, further fostering interaction and good relations between IBMers and the people who paid their salaries. IBM sales and service teams were legendary for working weekends and round-the-clock to get client systems up and running on schedule or back in service after repairs. In a brilliant master-stroke to strengthen respect for customers, IBM publicly declared that 95% of all IBM product ideas came from customers. And perhaps most powerful of all, everyone in IBM knew the absolutely, guaranteed way to get fired was to be rude to customers. These and a thousand other means were used to instill the "customer service belief" in IBM—as the primary competitive advantage of the company.

Next, Watson strongly believed that giving the best customer service in the world required having the best employees in the world. Watson's belief was transformed into the second IBM value: "IBM will respect the dignity of every employee." This straight-forward value has probably created more IBM folklore than any other single facet of the company's history. It generated the trim "IBM look": White shirt, dark blue tie, and close cropped haircuts. Women employees also had to toe the company line with white blouses and blue scarves. From this belief also came IBM's unique policy of subordinates formally rating their managers, their famous open-door policy as a "deterrent to the possible abuse of managerial power," an incredible amount of training for all employees, a strong promote-from-within policy, and yes, even some company hoopla. Sixty-five years of the no-layoff policy, followed even during the darkest days of the Great Depression (yet inconceivable in today's IBM,) didn't hurt company loyalty and morale either. And, of course, IBM's consistent record of paying top dollar and top benefits was the cement for all the above.

Some of this "people stuff" may sound quaint—in an entrepreneurial age—but the principles behind these policies are important. Take the IBM dress code for example. Thomas Watson Jr. explained it this way: "Our management has long believed that sharp contrasts between blue collar and white collar people in a business have to be avoided." And of course in those early days at least, employees in all companies wore uniforms; they were just different uniforms. It was easy to tell who the first class corporate citizens were: all the managers with their suits, ties, and starched collars. And it was obvious who the second class people were: the factory workers with blue collars and dirty coveralls. T. J. Watson said in IBM: "There will be no second class citizens" and that's why IBM made everyone, including factory workers, wear a white shirt and dark blue tie. That's not a bad principle even for today's entrepreneurial style organization.

Value number three was where the rubber hit the road, so to speak. It was stated as: "IBM expects and demands superior performance from its people in whatever they do." T. J. Watson was an unabashed believer in striving for perfection, telling his people: "We believe an organization will stand out only if it is willing to take on seemingly impossible tasks. The people who set out to do what others say cannot be done are the ones who make the discoveries, produce the inventions, and move the world ahead." Reading between the lines, it's a safe bet that T. J., like many other great entrepreneurs, wasn't the easiest guy in the world to please! But this striving for perfection did feed into his natural optimism and can-do attitude. During the Great Depression for example, Watson was asked how in the world IBM could still be hiring salesmen while the rest of the industry was cutting back. His answer: "Well, you know, when a man gets to my age, he always does something foolish. Some men play too much poker, and others bet on horse races, and one thing and another. My vice is hiring salesmen."

On the bottom-line message of why it's important to create and instill an entrepreneurial style culture, the early IBM was crystal clear. The rationale for their belief about people is a good example. While recognizing his father as a compassionate person, Thomas Watson Jr. once bluntly described the business purpose of the IBM value on respecting people: "Our early emphasis on human relations was not actually motivated by altruism, but by the simple belief that if we respected our people and helped them to respect themselves, the company would profit."

And finally, compared to some of the nonsense today (beautifully framed mission statements et al) that gets passed off as corporate culture, the most unique thing about how the values at IBM were implemented is the amazing fact that nobody even bothered to write them down for fifty years! The first written description of IBM's values came from Thomas Watson Jr., in 1963, half a century after his father founded the company! As a matter of company history, Watson Jr. produced a marvelous thirty-three page booklet titled: A Business And Its Beliefs—The Ideas That Helped Build IBM. (This, by the way, makes a great companion piece to Matsushita's twenty-three page booklet! I'm fortunate to possess copies of both of these out-of-print masterpieces.)

The fact is, the IBM values were instilled and kept alive by T. J. Watson's unremitting personal commitment and example. He had no culture consultants telling him how to do it. He had no Corporate Culture Department producing long lists of motherhood and apple pie slogans. And for sure, no one was racing around the IBM offices plastering framed copies of his beliefs on every wall. We call it "corporate culture à la Watson"—and it's the best advice you'll ever get on how to create and instill a powerful and competitive set of operating values in your organization.

CREATING AN ENTREPRENEURIAL CULTURE

The primary value at 3M is product innovation. At Singapore Airlines it's safety, then customer service. At Mercedes Benz, it's making the highest quality machine in the world year after year. And the plaques on the walls at McDonalds still say their values are quality, service, cleanliness, and value for money—but in their increasingly global marketplace, the over-riding company value may have become "world-wide consistency" in delivering those four fine virtues—which would seem to be just fine with Big Mac fans everywhere.

So whatever your values should be, and however they may evolve over the years, remember that their real purpose, as with Mr. Watson's beliefs at IBM, is to focus your effort on those few things that will make your strategy come true. This is the crucial connection between the *what* and the *how* of the business so casually missed by many big companies. You can't afford to miss it—if you want to give your people and your business a more entrepreneurial sense of mission.

Creating an "entrepreneurial corporate culture" isn't a completely unstructured task. All cultures are based upon a discreet set of core beliefs or values—that the bulk of the society agrees with and commits to. Doing this successfully in large, modern organizations depends on a few basic ingredients being in place. Whatever you do and however you do it, you must focus on "Competitive Advantage" and "Personal Commitment" These are the only musts on the list. The overarching reason for fostering change in the company culture is to improve your competitive position. And the change must have the binding, personal commitment of management. To create the culture that maximizes your competitive prowess, consider the following:

• Competitive Advantage
To the entrepreneur, this is not another drill in dreaming up slogans and banners to paste on the office and factory walls. This is the deadly serious business of identifying those things you absolutely, positively have to be great at in order to achieve your strategy. The objective is to

get very, very good at those few operating factors that are most directly related to the success of your customer/product business strategy. And once you've determine what those two, three or four critical factors are, they must become the operating *values* of your business. This is not a one-size-fits-all exercise. The values can come from a wide variety of possibilities: innovation, cost control, global distribution, product quality, employee relations, etc. The values that would make an automobile company successful, for example, may have little impact on a biotech firm, and so on. The test is, if they don't maximize your competitive advantage, they may sound nice but they aren't entrepreneurial business values.

• Personal Commitment

If the values you choose are indeed, those few things that will make or break your business, you'd better find a way to get people committed to them. Allowing people to shrug off the company's declared values is worse than not having them in the first place. This clearly will require the full and active commitment of all top managers—no exceptions. This is buy-in-or-get-out time for the executives. For the rank and file, you at least need a critical mass who are committed to the values. The fact is, employee commitment to the company's values is one of the few things that really does need to be "controlled" at the top of the business.

• Behavior, Not Words, At The Top

Your behavior is more eloquent than your words—always. Believe this if you believe nothing else in this book. The moral for management: Don't announce the *new culture* until and unless you are living it yourself. There is nothing more devastating to employee commitment that the CEO who preaches that "the customer is king" and hasn't seen one for thirty years.

• It's Not A Big, New Project

As with setting strategy, the entrepreneurial approach to creating culture is not about setting up a *culture staff*, hiring consultants or packing the executives off on a corporate retreat to create new wall plaque slogans. Remember, nobody at IBM even bothered to write the company's beliefs on a piece of paper for fifty years. This is truly a day-in-day-out, on-the-job task.

• **Few And Simple**

How many things can you be best at? Two or three? Well, if you're lucky, maybe one! But the good news is, that's all it takes. 3M doesn't try to be all things to all people. They try to be great at one thing. And you can do the same. OK, try for four if you want, but be absolute certain you hit the bull's-eye with one or two. There's another important and related reason to keep the list short. The culture of the company has to be carried around in the minds and hearts of employees. It can't be a list of twenty-five different things they have to look up in the policy manual to just remember.

• **Never Compromised**

Here's the really hard part. You just can't go around changing your principles because you're having a bad day, or even a bad quarter. Unfortunately, compromises are often more habit-forming than principles. One well placed compromise can reverse years of principled effort. So, never means never. This doesn't mean however, you can never change your values. You can and should change them if your strategy changes or the conditions for achieving the strategy change. Sticking to the same values and culture too long may well have been what IBM did wrong back in the seventies and eighties. What we're talking about here is shipping junk to make your numbers—while all the wall plaques say "Quality Is Number One."

KEEPING IT ALIVE

> " . . . a philosophy is not only preached but also practiced at the very top of a company . . . sound principles vigorously applied."

—Lord Charles Forte, Founder
Trusthouse Forte Hotels

Creating an entrepreneurial culture and values is not so tough. The hard part is keeping them alive for decades. In too many companies, slogans and shifting priorities begin to replace the original culture. The deeply held convictions and inspiring personal examples of the founding group just disappear over time. The unhappy fact is, corporate culture can, and often is, trivialized beyond recognition. This all flies in the face of the entrepreneur's hands-on, lead-by-example style. Great entrepreneurs like Watson, Matsushita and yes, Richard Branson, maintained their corporate cultures for decades by being the best example of the values themselves.

Of course it's easier to say than do. I learned from first-hand observations of eighty-five year old Lord Charles Forte, just how tough and frustrating it is to be the last entrepreneurial role model in the company. The energy he and other great entrepreneurs have to put into keeping their corporate cultures alive is awesome. The good news is, if you do it hard enough and long enough, you do get very good at it.

To keep your values alive for decades, which means keeping your competitive advantages alive, here are the three most important practices to follow:

• **Daily Behavior Of Senior Management**
Lord Charles Forte, the founder of Europe's largest hotel chain, Trusthouse Forte, was right. Maybe it's not a fair world after all. The top management of any company is "on stage" every minute of every day. In this regard it's very important to remember that to the lowly clerk on the shipping dock, his supervisor is "management." So whatever your level, the people below you are watching you like a hawk. Your most insignificant behavior is of intense interest to employees—as well as to other interested observers like customers, suppliers, and share-holders. While this may give you a feeling of great power, it also carries serious responsibilities. For example, if customer service is a core value of the company, you had better be first in line to show love for customers. If product quality is the value, you have to be the one who never, ever, allows junk to go out the door. The fact is, the single most powerful factor in keeping any company's values alive, is management's daily behavior. So if you violate the company's values, you may as well pack up your tent. The culture is already dead.

• Organization Rituals And Practices

Suppose you decide that innovation has to be value number one in your company. You announce it in your annual message to the staff, and it's even noted in the Mission Statement posters hung around the premises. The initial hurrahs are all good. But for the next five years the rank and file don't hear about it again. Innovation isn't a line item in their annual plan or budget. It's certainly not written into anyone's job description or annual performance review. It's not discussed in meetings. The company newsletter has never had an article about innovation. There's never been a training program on *creativity*. There's not even an active suggestion program in the company.

These are important things—because any company's values reveal themselves, not in the policy manual, but in the mundane rituals and practices that get woven into the fabric of the business. If the values are not part of the daily life of the company, and don't impact the on-going routine of employees, they will be as dead as yesterday's newspaper.

• Reward And Penalty Systems

The most frequently violated practice in keeping values alive, is whether or not they are part of the reward and penalty system of the company. What do people really get rewarded for around here? And what do they really get penalized for? To employees, the answers to these two questions absolutely define what the company values really are. Say for example, "loving the customer" is the big value in your company. Employee "X" is widely recognized as "Mr. Customer Service" who will do anything to satisfy the customer. Employee "Y" hates customers and everyone knows it. At the end of the year, X and Y both get a slap on the back and the across-the-board 8% raise. Good-bye "loving the customer" as a corporate value.

Dramatic changes in a company's strategy and culture can and do occur. The effect on customers, employees and shareholders can be extraordinary. This is the important, final point about re-instilling a sense of mission in your organization. As you've seen, doing it the entrepreneurial way—the Matsushita and Watson way—requires a lot of hard work and old-fashioned common sense. This approach doesn't have the cachet of going off to Bermuda or Hawaii with the consultants to do strategy, or floating sets of freshly minted *corporate values* posters down through twenty layers of management. But it has one redeeming quality: It does indeed re-awaken your and your company's—sense of mission!

Chapter 9

Re-Instilling Customer/Product Vision
Growing the Old-Fashioned Way

"The inclination of my life—has been to do things and make things
which will give pleasure to people. . . . ."

—Walt Disney. Founder
The Walt Disney Company

Walt Disney had it right in his famous quote above. When he said:
"...do things and make things which will give pleasure to people" he
wasn't talking about the latest management theory or granting more
stock options. He was talking about the two most important ideas in
enterprise—products and customers.

At the core of Disney's philosophy, was his belief that he had to be good at both making the product, and selling/servicing the customer. Remember the "scientist-salesman-bureaucrat-entrepreneur" classifications from Chapter 3 in Part One of this book? Disney, like all great entrepreneurs, was squarely in the entrepreneur's box on the chart. Focusing on, caring about, and being an expert on customers and products simultaneously is the essential entrepreneurial practice. It's the art of the craftsman—the original make and sell enterpriser. After nearly thirty years of looking, I haven't found one great entrepreneur who didn't have this integrated customer/product vision.

THE FUNCTIONAL ORGANIZATION
—DEATH OF THE CRAFTSMAN

However, it hasn't been easy to remain a craftsman in modern times. Along the way, we got the industrial revolution in the 19th century, which produced companies of a size and scope never before seen in history. And then, in response, the 20th century managerial age began inventing all manner of tools and rules for dealing with the increasing size and presumed complexity of corporations. The result? Enter the 20th century answer to growing bigger and more complex—the modern, functional organization.

The aim was noble enough. As companies grew bigger and bigger, it just wouldn't do for everyone to do everything like in the good old days. That sounded like chaos, the one thing, above all, that both the industrial and managerial revolutions couldn't tolerate. The solution was to specialize across the company, and create a command and control hierarchy up and down the company. It was at this apocryphal moment in business that the organization chart was born. The beauty of the org chart, as everyone soon found out, was that it showed everyone exactly where they fit: in which company silo they belonged—and how many rungs up and down the corporate ladder they could climb—or fall. It all looked terribly rational and efficient, as our fathers and grandfathers were all herded into the wonderful world of *The Organization Man*.

Aside from whatever else the modern functional organization achieved, it was quite literally, the death knell of the craftsman. The entrepreneur's integrated vision of customer and product was simply organized out of existence in the functionalized corporation. The quest for organizational control and efficiency created un-natural barriers in companies. Some employees: sales people, service personnel, market researchers—those more or less focused on customers—were put on one side of the company. Others: scientists, product designers, assembly line workers—those more or less focused on products—were put on another side. And rather amazingly, the huge numbers of workers who weren't focused on either—the folks who cut the payroll, write the leases, handle personnel—were all lumped together at headquarters and called the administration. So today's large, rationally designed organization, ends up with more or less three super-functions. And in the process, employees have been transformed from entrepreneurial business people to *product people*, or *customer people* or *administrative people*.

THE MODERN (DYS)FUNCTIONAL ORGANIZATION

Product   Administrative   Customer
People   People   People

The "supremely efficient" (most highly functionalized) companies find themselves in the absurd situation of having product people who have never seen a customer, customer people who know nothing about the product, and administrative people hopelessly out of touch with both customers and products.

Breaking up real business units into functional silos and then centralizing everything from R&D to market research may look like a good idea in theory. However, the hierarchical and specialized organization has given us instead a very large, very rigid and clearly *dysfunctional* form of enterprise. In the real world, it's a proven prescription for creating boredom and bureaucracy for average employees. And for our purposes here, it has dealt the single, most devastating blow ever concocted to the entrepreneurial spirit in even the best of employees. It killed the craftsman.

• Xerox

The most famous case in all business of the disastrous effects of functionalizing and separating product people and customer people belongs to Xerox. Its Palo Alto Research Center (PARC), founded in 1970, virtually paved the golden road to the modern computer industry. The only trouble was, none of the gold ended up in Xerox hands. You may recall that in the seventies PARC invented the Alto, the world's first personal computer, but never marketed it. Not so well remembered is the fact that Xerox had earlier invented the world's first fax machine, called the Telecopier, and let it die also. In fact, the long list of digital age technologies created by PARC, but commercialized by others, is truly astonishing: From computer animation, to laser printing to the ubiquitous "mouse' we all use today. *The New York Times* (*October 6, 1991, Sec. 3, p. 6*) sampling below is enough to make any Xerox shareholder cry:

A SAMPLING OF TECHNOLOGIES CONCEIVED AT XEROX PARC

Technology Invented	Later Marketed By
Personal computers	Apple / IBM
Facsimile machines	Canon / Panasonic
Modern chip-making technology	VLSI Technology
Silicon compilers for chip design	Silicon Compilers
Portable Computing	Grid Systems
Bit-mapped screen displays	I.B.M. / Apple
Mouse and icon-based computing	Apple

Laser printers	Hewlett-Packard / Apple
Drawing tables	Koala
Graphics computing	
and computer animation	Pixar
Ethernet office network	3Com
Data-base retrieval systems	Metaphor Computer
"What you see is what you get"	
word processing	Microsoft
Smalltalk language,	
object-oriented program	Park Place Systems/Digitalk
Postscript language used	
in high-end printers	Adobe Systems

How could this possibly happen? Easy—if you completely separate your product development and marketing functions. It didn't start off that way of course. Back in 1946 in Rochester, New York, Chester Carlson made and sold the world's first photo-copier and founded Xerox. By the 1960s, Xerox produced only two major products, but dominated the world in both: photo copiers and electronic typewriters. Being dependant on just two products, albeit the market leader in both, seemed risky. So Xerox came up with a smart strategy on *what* to do instead. The company would embark on an all-out attack on developing new technologies and new products. Unfortunately the management team wasn't quite as smart in determining *how* to go about it.

Xerox like most other blue-chip companies at the time (RCA, GE, IBM, AT&T) got caught up in the "lab in the woods" theory of doing product research and development. That was to set up large research facilities in remote, serene places, far from the annoying interruptions of people like company salesmen and customers. They were also caught up in the wonders of functionalization—and couldn't imagine that the great and mighty Xerox couldn't gather together the great scientist and researchers to come up with block-buster products.

They were right of course. They create PARC, located it in sunny Palo Alto, and stuffed it full of young, bright and very hip California scientists. They only forgot one thing: they left all their young, bright, and very pin-striped marketing people in their Stamford, Connecticut headquarters. These two groups were not exactly made for each other. The *product people* were the brilliant, hippy scientists with long hair and gold chains in California. The *customer people* were the high-flying, two-martini, marketing and sales chiefs with their Ivy League MBAs— sitting 3,000 miles away. The two groups not only didn't share the same company culture, they didn't seem to come from the same universe. The result: the Palo Alto scientists came up with one great idea after another—which the marketing people in Stamford mistrusted and just never got around to selling. If R&D and marketing couldn't get together on personal computers, the hottest electronic product since TV, the outcome for the rest of the sorry list is easy to understand.

Tens of billions of lost sales later, Xerox has been making a huge effort to put Humpty Dumpty back together again by creating cross-functional teams between marketing and R&D. Stay tuned. They're trying to catch up for lost time and get everyone marching to a new drumbeat. Or should we say old drumbeat? Today you will find marketing people on all product development teams at PARC and R&D people assigned to follow through with marketing groups introducing PARC's 21st century product ideas. We call it "re-instilling customer/product vision."

• Toyota
Xerox could have hired Eiji Toyoda as a consultant and saved itself a lot of grief. Toyoda (with a "d") was the founder of Toyota (with a "t") Motor, arguably the best all-around car maker in the world—in spite of its out-of-character recall problems over the past year. It's certainly become the most valuable in the auto industry. The current *Forbes Global 2000* ranks Toyota number one by a mile in market value at $127 billion. Trailing far behind in second and third place are Honda at $63 billion and Ford at $42 billion. In revenue, in even the worst auto market since World War Two, Toyota is the fifth largest company in the world with an astounding $211 billion in sales last year. Only Wal-Mart and the three oil giants, ExxonMobil, Shell and BP are bigger. Clearly, they remain the number one car maker of the 21st century, and they're going to be damn hard to knock off that lofty perch. Their operating margins are the highest. They can assemble a car in 13 hours versus

about 20 for Honda, Nissan and Ford—GM is farther behind. They regularly match or beat Mercedes quality using one sixth the labor of their luxury class German competitor. And a completely built-to-order car can be in the hands of the customer in an amazing week to ten days. Nobody else even comes close.

What's the secret of their success? It can all be laid to the customer/product vision of founder Eiji Toyoda. He started making cars in 1933 and assumed the car business, like any other enterprise, had to be built around customers. From design to after sale service, the customer called the shots at his company. But he still didn't have the right framework or organization to be as responsive to customers as he thought the company should and could be. That would soon change.

In 1947 Toyoda and his legendary production boss, Taiichi Ohno, visited America for the first time. They went to Detroit to learn how the Americans made cars, but they didn't see much there that they didn't already know. What they did happen to see, that just amazed them, were American supermarkets. At that time, and still today in some sectors, distribution methods in Japan were archaic and agonizingly slow. By comparison, Toyoda saw in the U.S. supermarkets a distribution system that operated with lightening fast speed, especially with perishable foods. He described the rapid re-supply of fresh milk at the dairy counter for example, as a system where customers literally pulled products through the company. He saw this delivery of fresh milk from the cow to the supermarket to the customer, often two and three times in twenty-four hours, as a great idea for the car manufacturing business. Toyoda and Ohno went back to Japan and designed their own *customer driven production* system for making cars. They established complete business units, putting design, production, marketing and sales together under the same boss. They called it *kanban* or *just-in-time* production and started a counter-revolution in the auto industry against the slow, un-responsive, functional method of organizing.

Their famous *chief engineer system* became the organizational method of choice. This method dictates that all new car models have a chief from start to finish. Thus, the chief engineer has enormous authority from design to production through marketing for a specific model. Once in place, it's practically impossible for design people to disregard production people, and for production people to disregard marketing people, and so on. Obviously Toyota is "organized." People and groups of people have specific tasks to perform. But the kanban culture, constantly tracking the customer, overrides the entire organization. Sure, kanban is just a technique, but it's a technique driven by an integrated customer/product vision. It's a vision that says we all jump together when the customer speaks. The point is, nothing could be further from the coast to coast mess Xerox found itself in.

• Dell

Kanban has been brought to a new level in the 21st century by companies like Dell Computer, Amazon and EBay. For example, let's take a look at entrepreneur Michael Dell's amazing company, which he started in his dorm room while still a student at the University of Texas (which he had to vacate because the university wouldn't allow *commercial* activity in the dorms—so much for UT's spirit of enterprise!) Even a cursory look shows that Dell Computer is driven by maintaining an integrated customer/product vision. Of course Michael Dell is the guy who eliminated the middlemen and put his entire company into direct contact with their customers—who originally were primarily more sophisticated, corporate buyers. He literally invented selling computers direct to customers and enabling them to custom design their purchase—over the phone and now via the internet. Talk about bringing your product and customer functions together: It doesn't get any more integrated than this. You can't be just a *salesman* and still expertly assist every customer to custom design their computer. Conversely you can't be just a *scientist* and spend eight hours a day talking to customers. Michael Dell himself says the company's mission was, and remains, to bring to bear all its human and technology resources to better serve customers: "We're always looking to see what we can do to make our customers' lives easier or save them money. It pervades every part of the company."

Like kanban before it, Dell's approach, which the world now knows as the "Dell direct model," is revolutionizing how business operates in many key areas—particularly in business to business selling. The internet, which Michael Dell calls the "ultimate direct model," accounts for 30% of Dell's sales and is rapidly growing. Dell predicts it won't level off until it hits at least 50%. Dell's model of selling custom-made machines directly to buyers, gives it some hard-to-believe competitive advantages. Aside from obvious things like tons of direct customer feedback and no re-sellers to deal with, it also means Dell carries no finished goods inventory. Dell's total inventory costs run less than 2% of sales! What old-line manufacturer wouldn't die for that kind of inventory management? Dell has not just taken Toyota's *just-in-time* game to a new level; they've created a totally new ballpark in which to play the game. When you hear Dell people say "our only religion is the direct model," you can believe they mean it!

All of this is pretty radical stuff when you think about it. Even *Fortune* magazine, not prone to hyperbole, called Dell the most "customer obsessed" computer maker. The results of Dell's innovativeness around re-connecting traditional customer and product functions does appear to be good for Dell's clients—and very good for Dell. To start out in a university dorm room and become the number one PC computer company in the world in just two decades is a big order—even by Texas standards!

• Disney
And finally, we end up back with our old friend Walt Disney—who also could have helped Xerox—had they asked. In the theme parks at least, The Walt Disney Company still today tries to follow Mr. Disney's customer/product vision. The Disney training manual at Disney World in Orlando says: "While a department may not deal directly with the public, it is imperative that each department within an organization view its customer or 'public' as the person/people who actually benefit from the service of that department. For example, at the WALT DISNEY WORLD Vacation Kingdom, the wardrobe department's actual 'client' is not the guest, but the host and hostess who will be interacting with that guest. Or, the accounting department can view their 'clients' as a variety of internal departments. The people in any department might be three or four layers removed from the guest who

purchases a MAGIC KINGDOM Park passport. Nonetheless, their attitudes toward service will ultimately affect the quality of service the guest receives—a real domino effect!" (*Service Disney Style, Walt Disney Company, (undated), p. 5.*)

You know that every employee in your company *could* pay more attention to the quality of their own product and the needs of their own customers. An increase of just 10% in their efforts could have enormous impact against your competition. Fortunately, there is one very helpful step any company can take, anytime. It's a step practically guaranteed to produce that first 10% change in attitude. It will require treating employees as businesspeople—not salesmen or scientists or clerks. It's straight talk, designed to get managers and workers out of their functional pigeon-holes and back to the business of enterprise. Here's how it works:

Start by axing all those convoluted, five page job descriptions. They just confuse the issue. Replace them with our *Entrepreneurial Job Description* which contains just three questions. They are the questions entrepreneurs live and die by: "Who are my customers/users? What are my products/services? And what exactly do I have to do to satisfy my customers?"

Every employee in your company should be able to answer these three, simple questions. In some organizations, however, the number of employees who can't answer them can be shocking. For many managers and workers, defining their positions in terms of their customers and their products can create a totally new mind-set of what their job is all about. Of course this is the point. This first, modest step may not instill the customer/product obsession of Eiji Toyoda, or Michael Dell, or Walt Disney in your organization, but it could be a giant leap forward away from the choke-hold of the anti-entrepreneurial functional organization. For sure, this is an effective start to developing mini-entrepreneurs in any company. The *Entrepreneurial Job Description form* follows as *Application 5.*

CREATING AN OBSESSION FOR CUSTOMERS AND PRODUCTS

What bureaucracies desperately need, and entrepreneurs have in spades, is passion for the firm's products and customers. Entrepreneurs go to sleep at night thinking about customers and products. They dream about them. They wake up thinking about them. They are truly obsessed about customers and products.

Instilling this obsession in the average worker and making it stick, is the key. This usually requires a big change in organizational priorities. And since it's you, not your workers, who determines what's important, the changes have to start at the top. When senior management really gets serious about customer and product priorities, things do start to happen. Simple things, that everyone talked about for years and didn't do, will take on monumental importance. For example, providing an immediate response to all customer requests. Not tomorrow, or I'll get back to you soon, but right now! And old-fashioned courtesy will no longer be a rare event—it will be the only way customers are ever treated. Really listening and really doing something about customer suggestions will change from a slogan to a daily reality. Individual worker responsibility for quality will become the norm, not more wishful thinking by the Quality Assurance department. Compromises on quality won't even be suggested, let alone tolerated. Endless product planning will be replaced by a sense of urgency in producing innovative new products that meet markets needs. And ultimately, losing a current customer will become the one, unforgivable, cardinal sin in the business.

You don't need a Ph.D. to figure out that these are the kinds of behaviors you must inspire in your people to become a company with entrepreneurial zeal for customers and products. They're all common sense ideas. They're things entrepreneurs do all the time. Large companies do some of these things some of the time. In the entrepreneurial organization, employees do all these things all the time. There are literally hundreds of great ideas you could implement to re-instill customer/product vision in your company. If you're serious about creating a more entrepreneurial company, getting everyone to *love their customers* and *love their products* is the place to start. Here are some simple, common sense basics for doing just that.

"LOVING" THE CUSTOMER

"I solemnly promise and declare that every customer that comes within ten feet of me, I will smile, look them in the eye, and greet them, so help me Sam."

—Sam Walton, Founder
(Employee Pledge)
Wal-Mart Stores

One day during 2001, a recession year, Wal-Mart Stores, that down home retailer from tiny Bentonville, Arkansas, became the biggest company in the history of the world—in less than forty years since their start-up!

With sales of $219 billion, the amazing customer-friendly discount chain literally galloped past its rivals for the top spot. Ten years later we're in another, much worse, recession and they're still on top of the world! Unlike most businesses, Wal-Mart seems to thrive in good and bad times. Some pundits claim recessions actually raise Wal-Mart's market share as bargain hunters abandon higher end stores and storm their aisles! Regardless, their current revenues are a staggering $408 billion, and their profits of $14.3 billion are second only to ExxonMobil. But there's more: Wal-Mart, not yet 50 years old, still covers less than half of the U.S. market, and only a fraction of the global retail market. It's gone from one store in 1962 to nearly 8,500 today, and they're just getting started. As amazing as it sounds, this is a company with a lot of room to grow.

How did all this happen? How could a five-and-dime retailer from Arkansas become the biggest business ever? We've all heard about Wal-Mart's super-duper information systems and its hard-nosed purchasing. But those are not the reasons I go to Wal-Mart. And they're not the reasons millions of others go either. After all, Target, K-Mart, Costco, and a dozen more discount chains have about the same information and purchasing systems. What I, and I suspect the millions of other customers, really like about Wal-Mart is: It's the one big company that really and truly makes you feel welcome. Like the famous Wal-Mart employee pledge quoted earlier, everyone and everything at Wal-Mart says: "We love our customers!"

Take the official Wal-Mart job of "People Greeter." The idea, which came from an employee, is that when you visit a Wal-Mart store, it should be like visiting a friend's home. So there's a People Greeter to greet every visitor, at every door, of every store. Essentially what they do is smile, say hello, give you a cart and wish you a good visit. Each of the 8,500 big stores must have seven to eight People Greeters to cover all the doors and all the shifts. So that's about 68,000 employees standing around, doing nothing much but saying hello to customers who enter the stores. They don't sell, stock the shelves, check out customers, or even sweep up. They just say *hello*. There's no doubt the first thing any efficiency consultant or cost-cutter would do at Wal-Mart would be to get rid of all these "nonproductive" employees. And in one fell swoop, they would cut the legs out from under Wal-Mart's number one competitive advantage.

Loving the customer, along with loving the product, is the sine qua non of entrepreneurial behavior. But it becomes a cliché in so many companies. Imagine what it would be like if all your employees actually did behave as if they loved, and respected, customers. It would be like ... well ... it would be like Wal-Mart! To create this highly entrepreneurial approach to customers in your business, here are some simple but powerful lessons your people will have to start following.

• Knowing Your Product
The number one complaint in the world today about sales people is they don't understand their products. What's the message you're giving to customers when you can't even explain how and why your product will solve their problem? This opens up an enormous competitive opportunity for those organizations willing to inject their marketing,

sales, and service people with a strong dose of entrepreneurial customer/product vision.

Think of the last time you chose a doctor. Or wanted to buy a car. Or needed to acquire outside help to solve a business problem. Who did you want to see? An expert of course. Someone who really knew the ins and outs of solving your problem. Certainly not a salesman—no matter how friendly he might be, or how many lunches he might buy you.

The truth is, most people will clear their calendar in a second to get their hands on a real product expert. This is pure entrepreneurial territory. It gives the entrepreneur—or the entrepreneur team—an enormous opportunity to out-shine the competition. Of course it all goes back to that integrated vision of customer and product exemplified by Disney, Benz, Matsushita, et al. The opportunity to do what the highly functionalized and specialized corporate types could never do, is the best reason why *knowing your product* is the first step to really loving your customer. So toss out all those business cards with titles like "salesman" or "marketing rep" and replace them with cards that say "Product Genius." And then cancel the sales training courses for the next five years and put every sales and service person in the company into intensive, on-going product training.

• Responding Immediately
The number one complaint in the world about service people is they are always so busy with other things, you have to wait, and wait, and wait some more . . . . Think of the last couple of times you time you were in a department store, or standing in the "customer service" line at the airport, or checked into a big, busy hotel. Did it seem the staff behind the counter knew every trick in the book to avoid making eye contact and getting sucked into waiting on you? If you had a dollar for every minute you've waited at airline counters, hotels, department stores, gas stations, on the phone with parts or service departments, not to mention renewing your driver's license, you probably wouldn't be reading this book. You'd already be sitting on the Riviera! I've come to the conclusion that most of these "service" people must have broken necks or fused spinal cords. They actually seem physically incapable of raising

their heads too quickly. Maybe this is what keeps them frozen in place staring down at their desks and computer terminals. Whatever the reason, what's the message the customer gets? "I've got something a lot more important to do than wait on you."

Of course response time to customers is a standard part of all customer service training. It's taught over and over again and nothing changes. Why? Because giving customers an immediate response is not a training problem or a systems problem. It's a deep seated problem with the priorities of the service giver. Waiting on customers is simply a pain in the neck to most people in most companies.

But, what wonderful news all this is for the entrepreneurial style company. To entrepreneurs, responding immediately to customers is one of the greatest weapons ever invented to beat the competition. This is why Sam Walton insisted that every employee take the Wal-Mart pledge. It's also why he put Wal-Mart "People Greeters" in every store. It's not very scientific, but this is the kind of immediate customer response "stuff" that's made Wal-Mart the fastest growing retailer in history. And it can do wonders for you too—if for no other reason than you'll be all alone—the only place in town doing it.

• Being Courteous and Competent
"When we answer the phone, we're very courteous. That's the good news. The bad news is we don't answer the phone." Famous last words from Ramon Cruz, former CEO of Philippine Airlines, lamenting the lousy telephone system in Manila. What he was really saying was that courtesy without competence will get you nowhere. The most courteous airline in the world (which PAL may well be) can't overcome chronic lost baggage problems and reservation systems that don't work. The opposite is also true. Competence without courtesy isn't going to get you in the winner's circle either. Lufthansa will get you and your luggage where you're going on time, every time. In fact they usually have the best on-time performance of any airline. But, oh those concrete-hard leather seats. They seem to actually tilt forward slightly, forcing passengers to do perpetual isometrics to keep from slipping onto the floor. And while we're on the subject, an occasional smile, perhaps just

one per flight to break the ice, would be a welcome add-on to this airline's unrivaled reputation for technical competence.

Bigger companies often have sterling intentions around courtesy and competence, but it's tough. Employees are shifted from department to department, with no regard for their core product knowledge. The folks who made this little machine that doesn't work are never the ones you see. The young sales clerk may smile, but he doesn't know diddly about the gas-powered garden tiller you need—or what software is really best for the kind of graphics you produce. It's just not humanly possible to be an expert in computers this month and garden equipment next.

At another level it's just not easy to always be courteous to thousands of people you don't know and will probably never see again. And it's really tough if you know in your heart of hearts it makes damn little difference to your boss and your company—and no difference at all to your next performance review. This is the real nub of the entrepreneurial advantage: believing a lack of courtesy and a lack of competence can drive you out of business—and out of a job. And where coming to work means you have to do more than just show up.

• Keeping Current Customers Forever

Thomas Watson, the founder of IBM, liked to say: "The most important customer we'll ever have is the one we already have." The message was clear. Don't lose current customers. And in the early days he put his money where his mouth was. IBM had a sales commission system that actually penalized salespeople for losing existing clients. Now that's a powerful way to get the "current customer" message across.

Today, everyone still says that current customers are important. That repeat business is what we want. And that we know with the sky-high marketing costs of acquiring new business, all of the profit for the year sits in the current customer re-order base. However, all these entrepreneurial notions seem to get lost in the shuffle as the company grows larger.

If current customers are so important to us, why does everyone scream and cheer over every new customer but just shrug their shoulders when one of the current customers quietly slips away? Why do 99.9% of all sales compensation systems pay a premium for new business but à la Watson, nobody gets penalized for losing old business? Why are the best people thrown at new clients and the ten year-old client ends up with the "B Team?" And why, in so many companies, is new business marketing the champagne and caviar side of the business while spare parts, repairs and on-going service feeds on a diet of warm beer and grits? None of this is an argument against new business. It's just a common sense reminder that the best and most profitable way to grow most businesses is—"keeping current customers forever!"

"LOVING" THE PRODUCT

"Her name is Mercedes."

—Gottlieb Daimler, Co-Founder
Daimler Benz Company

Karl Benz was the "product man" of one of the greatest teams in the history of business. He was in fact the inventor and product genius behind the first commercially viable automobile. Historians rank his contribution alongside electricity, antibiotics, computers and space travel as one of the most profound scientific and technological advances of the 20th century. We can say that Karl Benz was one businessman who truly knew and loved his product.

He would likely be shocked to see himself identified as a seminal thinker or inventor. He was at heart, a relentless tinkerer, totally dedicated to making his engines the best in the world. He believed customers deserved real improvements in the automobile products he and Daimler produced. He felt this so strongly that the notion of turning out a new model every year never occurred to him. For him the rule was to produce a new model if and when you had significant improvements to offer the customers. He would have been confounded by the concept of "planned obsolescence," that nifty marketing plot hatched in Detroit many years later. Benz was essentially a car maker who could sell if he had to. This made him the perfect partner for Daimler, the first of the great car salesmen and tire kickers.

Which leads to the following set of entrepreneurial practices for loving the product. To awaken the entrepreneurial spirit in your organization, loving the product, along with loving the customer, is the place you really do have to start:

• Knowing Your Customer
Gottlieb Daimler is usually hailed as a great maker of engines and cars. It's true that the Daimler automobile set the world standard at the beginning of the 20th century. But in reality, he was a near-fanatic on knowing exactly what his customers wanted. It was Daimler, more than his partner and technical genius Karl Benz, who understood that knowing your customer is the essential first step in producing great products. He was technically competent to be sure: He produced the first fire engines, motorcycles, motorboats, engines for rail vehicles, and motorized airships. But he was first and foremost, a salesman who loved his product. Indeed, Fritz Nallinger, the German biographer of both Daimler and Benz wrote: "Daimler was completely possessed with the idea of equipping every conceivable vehicle with Benz's engines."

For Daimler, the whole point of making cars was to please and even astonish the customer. Everywhere Daimler went he saw a great market for his wonderful machines. He went to Paris and licensed his engines to a young man by the name of Peugeot. He went to Coventry and made his engines the envy of Britain. He personally opened the branch in St. Petersburg where he enthusiastically, and a bit optimistically it turned out, judged the sales prospects to be enormous. Even the great brand name Mercedes came about to please a customer. In the early 1900s the largest distributor for the Daimler automobile was in Vienna, Austria. This dealer threatened to switch to another car maker in France so Daimler rushed to Vienna and promised him the company would do *anything* to keep his business. As a joke the dealer told him he'd only stay with the Daimler car if the company put his 11 year old daughter's name on the hood. And what was her name? You guessed it: "Her name's Mercedes . . ." and the rest is history.

Probably no customers will ever ask you to put their names on your product, but then again, maybe you should. If not that, you'd better at least find another dozen ways to show you really care about what your customers want and need—and be prepared to deliver it.

• Feeling Old-Fashioned Pride

I like to tell the true story of the retired Honda worker in Tokyo who shined the chrome on any Honda he saw parked on the street "because I can't stand to see a dirty Honda." Now that's taking real pride in your product, as much as any entrepreneur would. Which just goes to prove that some big companies can instill old-fashioned pride in their people. It's easy for entrepreneurs to have pride in their own product, but how many people in today's giant bureaucracies really feel that kind of enthusiasm and love for the products their companies make? Entrepreneurial pride is clearly based on believing that what you're doing is important, and that your particular job is an essential part of making the enterprise successful.

So how many of your employees feel that what they're doing is important? That their job is essential to the company? How many even know how their job affects anything at all? These are the things that rip the pride out of work, and these are the things the aspiring entrepreneurial organization has to guard against. A lot of techniques have been invented to put pride back into employees' work: job autonomy, quality of work life, psychological ownership, etc. These are not wrong ideas; they're just not central ideas. Having autonomy, quality and ownership in a dead-end, un-important job won't make a bit of difference.

In my experience the best way to keep old-fashioned pride alive and well is to make sure everyone knows how and why their role in the business is important—from helping to make the product better right up to the moment-of-truth in business, having face-to-face interaction with customers. As any entrepreneur will tell you, there is really no substitute

for getting praise from happy customers—and getting yelled at
occasionally by unhappy ones.

• Making It Better Than The Next Guy

Lord Charles Forte grew Trusthouse Forte from one sweet shop on
Oxford Street in central London to over 900 hotels and 93,000
employees worldwide. (*Forte died in 2007 at the age of 98—a decade after he lost
control of his company in a bitter and hostile $6 billion takeover by the British media
conglomerate, Granada. Proving once again that professional managers can destroy fifty
years of great entrepreneurial growth in a single decade, the company is unrecognizable today
and headed for the trash heap of history. Apparently the "life cycle of all companies" as
described in the Introduction is alive and well in the United Kingdom.*) He knew
something about entrepreneuring and how to make it better than the
competition. When I first met him several years ago, he gave me the
best definition of "making it better" that I've ever heard. Forte said that
when his managers proposed opening a hotel in a new city or country,
which they did all the time, he asked them just three simple questions:

• Can we make the hotel cheaper and better than the competition?

• If not cheaper and better, at least better?

• If not better, at least cheaper?

If he didn't get a strong "yes" to at least one of those three questions,
the conversation was over.

That simple system seemed to work rather well over the years for
Europe's largest hotel chain. The underlying point is, most
entrepreneurs, like Charles Forte, don't get all caught up in academic
and consultants' definitions of quality. They typically see popular
concepts such as Six Sigma, TQM, and the ISO 9000 certification as a
lot of bureaucratic poppycock. The missing link in many theories and
techniques on quality is the word *competitive*. The entrepreneur makes
his living by beating the competition. And, as Charles Forte said, you
can beat the competition three ways: higher quality, or lower costs, or
both. And lower costs can be just as good a way as higher quality. This
very competitive approach explains why Trusthouse Forte was equally

comfortable with owning low cost chains like Travelodge in America alongside some of the ritziest properties in the world such as the glamorous Savoy in London.

In an age when the life cycle of products and services can be six months or less, we may have to add one more question to Lord Forte's simple list: Can we make it faster? And that leads us to the next entrepreneurial practice for loving the product.

• Making It Faster Than The Next Guy

Ed Penhoet, the founder of Chiron, is one of the super-stars of the bio-technology industry—and a man in a hurry. He says the entire biotech industry has been a horse race: "Everyone in the industry is smart so you don't get much of a competitive edge with just brains. . . The winners are the ones who get to the finish line first with FDA approved products. So it may be that speed is even more important than cost. . ." So even here, in the super hi-tech field of bio-genetics, speed looks like a bigger competitive advantage than brains or costs. This is a lesson no 21st century company can afford to forget.

Naturally "making it faster" is just as important for big, mature companies as it was for start-up Chiron getting there first with the Hepatitis B vaccine. Ross Perot, that quintessential entrepreneur from Texas, really hit the nail on the head on this point. After selling Electronic Data Systems (EDs) to General Motors for $2 billion and becoming their largest stockholder, he was stunned and dismayed at how slowly everything seemed to happen in what was at the time the biggest company in the world. He went public with this famous complaint: "I just don't understand it. It took us four years to win World War Two—but it takes these people seven years to produce a new Buick." Touché!

The real lesson here from the world's great entrepreneurs: It's simply impossible to go wrong spending time on customers and products. So before we leave the topic, here's a final thought on growing your business the old-fashioned way.

A FINAL THOUGHT:
GROWING THE OLD-FASHIONED WAY

"My mind started going kind of wild at that point with all the possibilities."

—Buel Messer, Founder
Messer Landscaping

Providing more products to sell to more customers used to be the way all companies grew. But a lot has happened since we all went to business school and got our MBAs. Today, there seems to be a lot of ways to grow. Mergers and acquisitions, credit default swaps, pushing accounting rules to the limits, getting bailed out by the government and outright fraud (think Enron, Bernie Madoff, et al) are some of the current day favorites. So yes, we have lots of ways to grow a business today. On the other hand, some big companies have simply given up on growth altogether. The strategy here is to make a virtue out of not growing. With great fanfare, companies announce they are returning to their core business, which is really a corporate euphemism for admitting that their current strategy has run into a brick wall. Have you noticed that companies that are growing by leaps and bounds never announce they're returning to their core business? And in a classic "same clowns, new circus" routine, it's never quite explained why mergers and acquisitions were such smart strategies last decade -- but now it's even smarter to do the opposite.

The old-fashioned way of growing is easier to understand. All you have to do is make more products and sell more customers. To do this, you don't need M&A specialists, investment bankers, lawyers, or accountants. You do, however, have to know the answer to a very important question: Where exactly are our opportunities for growth?

Fortunately we have the answer, which was inspired by that all-time master of keeping-it-simple, Buel Messer. You'll recall that he is the blind cattle rustler turned landscaping entrepreneur back in Chapter 2. It struck him one day that the most important reason to focus on customers and products is that they hold the key to all future growth of the business. Here is Buel Messer's commonsense analysis of how to grow any business.

• Current Products to Current Customers

Messer actually started out shoveling snow with his two small boys in the winter of 1980. He had a small group of customers lined up for the entire season. He quickly realized that in his existing business, his income was going to be determined by how many times he could provide this same service to the same group of customers. It didn't take a genius to figure out that the more it snowed, the more money he would make. Messer discovered the first way to grow any business: selling current products to current customers more often. Creating growth this way, which may eventually hit some natural limits, requires a tremendous amount of attention to the ongoing servicing and selling of your existing customers.

• New Products to Current Customers

By March of 1981, the snow shoveling business was finished and Messer wondered how he would make a living during the summer. Since he had developed a good relationship with his snow removal customers, he asked a few of them if he could mow their lawns during the summer. They liked his work and quickly agreed to employ him for the summer. So, Messer discovered that another way to grow his business was to sell a new service to his satisfied, current customers. Growing this way, constantly producing new and improved products for your current customers, typically requires focus on, and investment in, new product research and development.

• Current Products to New Customers

Once he was up and running with year-round work, he got the expansionist bug. He began to look around for new market areas in which to offer his existing services of snow shoveling and lawn maintenance. He advertised and behold, he acquired several new customers in other parts of town and even in nearby communities. Messer was now pursuing the most common method of growing any business: offering current products to new customers. Growing this way typically involves geographic expansion, new distribution channels, exporting, and so on. It requires a heavy dose of solid marketing and selling.

• New Products to New Customers

Finally, Messer hit his stride and became a full service landscaper. What it meant was developing completely new products and services for completely new customers. Managing tree farms, creating large tracts of shrubs, buying land-moving equipment and dozens of trucks, was a far cry from owning a snow shovel and a lawnmower. Likewise, bidding for multimillion dollar landscaping projects for government offices and corporate headquarters is hardly the same as becoming friends with a few homeowners in your end of town. What Messer did of course, was to use the fourth way of growing his business: offering new products to new customers. This avenue to growth, similar in most respects to actually starting a new business, requires intense focus on both new product development and new customer marketing and selling.

In pursuing all the possible ways to grow his business, did Messer once think about mergers, acquisitions, strategic alliances, or fancy accounting techniques? Of course not. Messer and virtually all entrepreneurs grow their businesses the old-fashioned way: making more products and selling more customers. Since we now know there are only four possible ways to do that, it isn't all that complicated. Graphically displayed on the next page for you to ponder, are the (only) four options for growing your business.

Of course realizing bottom-line payoff from "Growing The Old-Fashioned Way" will require that you and your people get very focused on the two most critical elements in any business: "Loving Customers" and "Loving Products." Such passion and concentration is exactly what's needed to re-instill customer/product vision in your people and across your entire organization.

Growing The Old-Fashioned Way

	Current	New	
New	New Products To Current Customers	New Products To New Customers	**New**
Products			
Current	Current Products To Current Customers	Current Products To New Customers	**Current**
	Current	New	

Customers

Chapter 10

Fostering High-Speed Innovation

The Necessity To Invent, The Freedom to Act

"Anybody can be innovative if his life depends on it."

—Akio Morita, Founder
Sony Corporation

Akio Morita was the right person to ask about action and innovation. The company he founded, Sony is still recognized today as Japan's most innovative large company. Morita learned firsthand in post-war Japan that anyone can move quickly and creatively if their life depends on it. It's a lesson he never forgot. And it's the central lesson to learn in transforming any bureaucracy into a fast moving, innovative, 21st century competitor.

Most people probably think that Sony's first product was the transistor radio. Hardly. In Japan in 1945, products had to be much more practical. Akio Morita was a young Japanese Navy lieutenant returning from the war. He obviously had to start looking for a new career. What he and everyone else discovered upon returning home was shocking. Tokyo was a devastated, burned out city after four hundred straight days of allied bombing. There were no jobs, no money, no raw materials to make anything, and little food. Surviving was a day to day challenge. In this chaos, Morita thought that making something for sale or barter might be the best thing he could do. He and a small band of friends asked themselves: "What can we possibly make that the Japanese people still need and will be able to buy?" Everyone ate rice. But they weren't farmers. They were unemployed engineers. They eventually came up with the idea that if everyone was still eating rice, maybe people would have a need for something to cook the rice in—like an electric rice cooker. But they faced an immediate problem. There was no finished metal available. And they couldn't afford to go to the black market which was the only possibility they knew of—until they remembered all those American B-29 Superfortress bombers that had flown thousands of missions over Japan. The B-29s had American fighter escorts which, because of the great distances, had to carry extra fuel tanks under their wings. Before returning to the American bases, the fighter pilots would release the empty, extra tanks, which fell to the ground. So in fact, there was a lot of available metal all over Japan. The group scavenged the hills around Tokyo and brought back all the fuel tanks they needed. They heated, cut, and re-formed them. So by early 1946, Sony had its first product which was—you guessed it—a Japanese rice cooker made from the fuel tank of an American fighter!

Sony's first "hi-tech" product came in 1950. Morita wanted to make a giant leap forward and get into more sophisticated products. He was keen to try magnetic tape which he reasoned he could at least sell to the Ministry of Education for classroom use. Again he encountered a major roadblock in raw materials. There was no plastic available in Japan and making recording tape without plastic seemed impossible. Morita and his colleagues tried cellophane but it didn't work. They then tried standard newsprint and found it was more stable. On their hands and knees, Morita and his team cut long strips of the paper. They coated them with ferric oxide, a compound they found at a local chemist—and lo and behold—it recorded sound. By 1965, just fifteen hectic years later, this little known firm in Japan had gone from making recording tape from newsprint to becoming the great IBM's biggest supplier of magnetic computer tape!

Morita always chafed at the criticism that Japan is a nation of imitators, not innovators. He said in fact there are three types of creativity that must be pursued: ". . . . . creativity in technology, in product development, and in marketing. To have any one of these without the others is self-defeating in business." There is no doubt that just after WW II, all Japanese companies—Sony, Honda, Matsushita, etc., concentrated their creativity on simple product development, out of market and economic necessity. They couldn't worry about researching future technologies or implementing global marketing strategies while they were still using American fighter plane fuel tanks for raw material. Over time however, Sony's record of high-speed innovation expanded to encompass the other two areas. A quick glance over some of their early achievements illustrates tremendous innovative action covering all three areas of creativity cited by Morita:

- 1950—First recording tape in Japan.

- 1953—Founder Morita works in the USA for four years as a Sony company salesman to learn the market.

- 1955—First transistor radio in the world.

- 1957—Discovery of the "electron tunnel effect" by Sony employee Esaki, for which he became the first scientist in Japan to receive the Nobel Prize.

- 1959—First transistorized TV in the world.

- 1960—First VCR in the world.

- 1964—First desktop calculator in the world.

- 1970—First Japanese company to be listed on the New York Stock Exchange.

Of course there are hundreds of other great innovations by Sony over the years. Perhaps the most unusual innovative action at Sony had nothing at all to do with technology or product development. It had everything to do with Morita's third area of creativity -- marketing. How many founder/CEOs have you ever heard of who left the executive suite to spend four long years pounding the beat as a store-to-store salesman? My guess is none. Yet that is exactly what Morita did in the early years. When he realized that the U.S. was going to be the biggest market in the world for the kind of electronic products he was creating, he wanted to know everything he could about that giant market. After all, the future of the company was at stake. So he simply packed his bags, and with his family, moved to the U.S. and sold Sony products door to door, one retailer at a time for four straight years. He later claimed: "There's no better way to learn what your biggest market really wants, than selling the buyers face to face."

One of the most famous Sony products, the Walkman, was personally invented by Masaru Ibuka, Sony's great technical genius. He designed it in his spare time simply because he loved to listen to music while he worked, and his old phonograph and tape recorder were too heavy to carry to the office. So much for sophisticated market research and focus groups. And to be sure, they've made mistakes—like pushing their technically superior Betamax VCR far too long when the competing VHS technology was capturing the market instead. But this happens when you're innovating like crazy. Morita was happy to take the occasional mistake to keep up the torrid pace of innovation.

In any event, I'm sure you get the message. Morita and his company knew a thing or two about high-speed innovation. Sony was born out of necessity and required fast, creative action to survive. And in the sixty-five years since, Morita learned how difficult it can be to keep that competitive advantage alive. As he said in his later years as Chairman: "Sony has become too big, too rich, too secure and too complacent. Our greatest threat today is not from our competitors—it comes from our own internal complacency." He fought this complacency for his entire career, trying to keep the entrepreneurial spirit alive in the company: "It is said the creativity of the entrepreneur in Japan no longer exists. I disagree. Big companies like Sony must, and are, doing all they can to think small. From a management standpoint, it's very important to know how to unleash people's inborn creativity. My concept is that everybody has creative ability, but very few people know how to use it. We try to promote entrepreneurship right within our own large company by the way we manage. For example, as an idea progresses through the Sony system, the original presenter continues to have the responsibility of selling his idea to technical, design, production, and marketing staffs, seeing it to its logical conclusion whether it's an inside process or a new product going to market. Sony has even funded former employees' businesses, who originally presented their idea to Sony but for one reason or another it was not taken up. As an aside, this is quite opposite actually from the Western practice of tying corporate researchers up in knots with non-compete agreements."

Which brings us back to the powerful, most basic lesson of Morita: Innovative action is not a mark of genius. It's not a skill you learn in management school. It is a normal human reaction to crisis and challenge—and it can disappear in a hurry if people and organizations lose their sense of urgency and crisis. In your own organization, just as in Morita's Sony, your gravest threat may not even be coming from your competition—it may be coming from your own growing bureaucracy and self-satisfied complacency. Recognizing these internal threats, and knowing how to beat them off has to be your first line of defense in keeping high-speed innovation alive in the company.

THE SEVEN DEADLY SINS
AGAINST HIGH SPEED INNOVATION

"Everything that can be invented has been invented."

—Charles H. Duell, Director
U.S.A. Patent Office, 1899

Short of hiring Mr. Duell to run R&D, what are the biggest roadblocks you'll face in creating new ideas and employing rapid fire action? With all good intentions, bureaucracies commit numerous "deadly sins" against speed and innovation. There will always be a "good reason" for another procedure, another committee, or another control point. All such rational-sounding arguments underlie the very different purposes of managing and entrepreneuring.

The reasons why growing organizations keep shooting themselves in the foot over high-speed innovation go to the heart of modern management theory about how to handle size and complexity. The scientific method say we can manage anything if we analyze it enough, plan it enough, and implement the plan like clockwork. Five seconds into pursuing this fantasy, you're knee deep in planning, controlling, systemizing, and generally smoothing out any bumps and covering any potholes in the road ahead. Man conquering chaos may be a noble pursuit but it misses the innovation point by a mile. Fast-moving and creative enterprise is not about removing rough edges and eliminating surprises. With rare exception, in fact, it's the bumps and the potholes that contain most of the real gold.

This, then, is the dilemma: Laudable efforts by your managers to run a tight ship will have the perverse effect of sinking the ship. Following are some specific illustrations of well-intentioned efforts to streamline and run a tight ship. We call them "deadly sins" and growing entrepreneurial companies have to avoid them like the plague.

• I'm OK, You're OK

Mr. Duell's "I'm OK, You're OK" complacency is at the top of the list. Insisting we're all OK, another gift to business from the psychologists, produces terminal inaction for companies in the heat of competitive wars. The entrepreneurial point is, we're not OK, we're never OK! Crisis and stress may have become politically incorrect in business, but they do at least scream out we're probably not OK, and we'd better fix it in a hurry! Everyone knows that more gets done in an hour of crisis than a month of feeling good.

Eliminating stress has become a corporate obsession at big business. One has to wonder how many stress-management courses does an already lifeless bureaucracy really need? Granted, unchecked stress may be tough on the arteries, but on the other hand, when was the last time you did something really great with no stress at all? I'm okay, you're okay" is the first sure step to killing innovation and action. Believe it long enough and your business fails—not an okay result for anyone!

• One Best Way—Silencing Workers Forever

If you really want to silence workers, there's no better way than to instill a "one best way to do the job" mentality in your company. This ranks as the original sin of "scientific management" and comes straight from the granddaddy of all industrial consultants, Frederick Taylor. Way back in the 1890s, this Philadelphia cost cutter popularized the idea that there is one best, optimum way to perform every task. Whether it's turning a screw on a motor mount or timing the toilet trips of assembly line workers, everything could and should be optimized.

This could be great news for mass-production fanatics but it's the death knell of worker innovation. The bottom line? "One Best Way" managing can do wonders for uniformity, but it's not much help in inventing products, beating deadlines, hitting new levels of quality or fostering employee commitment.

• Out Of Touch With Customers And Competitors

There are three proven sources of innovative customer/product ideas in any business. The most obvious would be within your own organization. Tapping the collective genius of all your people has to be an on-going internal process. The next two sources however are outside the company. In fact the odds are very high that the next great idea for a new product or service will come either from a customer or a competitor. Thomas Watson, the founder of IBM, used to say that the idea for 95% of all IBM products came from customers and competitors—not from inside IBM. This is why being out of touch customers and losing sight of competitors is so damning to successful product and service innovation.

Whatever the ratio for your particular business, you can't afford to miss any sources of new, good ideas. This means you have to virtually live with your customers and know your competitors like the back of your hand. Being close to customers and competitors comes with the territory for the entrepreneur, and you have to create the same behavior in your company if you hope to stay ahead of the "great idea" learning curve.

• Centralized Everything

The argument for centralization rests on two shaky assumptions. First, centralizing will give us the economy of scale to do things cheaper. This is the usual argument for centralizing purchasing, personnel, R & D, and even production facilities. The second assumption is that centralizing authority will ensure that things are done right.

What about centralizing to achieve economies of scale? Are big factories really more productive than small factories? Does central purchasing really get things cheaper? Is the big R & D center the most efficient (or effective) way to invent products? And what does a headquarters personnel department really contribute to the bottom line? Every company has to make these judgments for itself, but be careful. The evidence to date says, bigger is rarely cheaper and centralized is almost never more efficient.

"Making sure it's done right," is a heavy statement about who knows best and who performs more responsibly. At its core, it's about who trusts who to do what. But controlling is not actually the problem: it's what's getting controlled that causes concern. Too often the wrong things are being centralized and the things that truly need some corporate control are left to the discretion of any employee. Being true to the values of the company is an obvious example of this. We may have elaborate systems for financial reporting, but nobody tracks commitment to the core values of the company.

Whatever the merits of centralization, you can be sure fostering high-speed innovation is not one of them. Remember that wherever and whatever you centralize, the trade-off will be innovation and fast action. Therefore, for companies trying to operate in an entrepreneurial mode, the wise rule of thumb is: When in doubt, de-centralize!

• Lab In The Woods

This is the big bang theory of product innovation. It's the story of Xerox's infamous Palo Alto Research Center, RCA's Sarnoff Center in Princeton, GE's 600 acre R&D facility in upstate New York, and a hundred other corporate research facilities hidden away in the woods—far from the hustle and bustle of the marketplace. The idea that corporations would need such idyllic spots to do research and invent products came shortly after World War Two. Big business was impressed with war era achievements like the Manhattan Project, the U.S. effort to manufacture and deliver the Atomic bomb. Since this work was being done in great secrecy in the middle of the New Mexico desert, building your own Research Center in the middle of nowhere became all the rage in corporate America.

It turned out that building an atomic bomb in the middle of a war to drop on your enemy wasn't really the same as building products that customers will buy. Over the decades it became painfully apparent that a lot was going into these labs in the woods, but not much was coming out. At least not much that could be manufactured and sold. And virtually nothing that would qualify as a "first mover" innovation, to borrow the in-phrase for blockbuster ideas. The big bang theory of R & D was launched on a false premise.

Maybe all those stories about inventors in garages are true after all. For sure you don't need a giant research center in the woods to be innovative. Some of the best product and service innovations in the world have come out on the floor of a noisy, dirty factory, or in a brainstorming session with a bunch of salesman, or face to face with complaining customers. At least give all these more entrepreneurial approaches a try before you sink untold millions into your own lab in the woods.

• Marketing Takes Over
The antidote to the "Lab In The Woods" mess is not to go to the opposite extreme and expect your customer folks, all by themselves, to come up with the next great product innovation. But this is exactly what often happens. The marketing argument goes: "If our scientists and engineers can't come up with the new products our customers want, why not give us a crack at it?" Some CEOs, particularly those who genetically distrust R&D anyway, buy this offer hook, line, and sinker. After all, it's marketing and sales who know what the market really wants. They do all the market research. They hold the focus group sessions. They're "in touch with the customer." In the past, this approach gave the world such memorable, and cosmetic, product "improvements" like striped toothpaste for white toothpaste, giant fins on already over-sized cars, and a hundred ring-tone choices on your already too complicated cell phone.

Marketing's product innovation role really picked up steam when customer service began to be recognized as an integral part of the product. With this new opening, marketing departments everywhere went into overdrive on coming up with product/service "improvements." They were typically little more than cosmetic embellishments, often with a distinct "California feel." Take for example, the near obsessive insistence in some companies that all customers get called by their first name. What's the point here? Is it really more courteous to use first names for people you don't know and who are twice your age? In the same vein, how about the mandatory script followed by your perky waitress in many "marketing driven" restaurant chains? You've heard it many times. The memorized cant, delivered with the frozen smile, turns out to be a sales pitch for exotic drinks and dishes you know you don't want. And very recently, some marketing innovations have taken a decidedly tricky turn, especially on the telemarketing front. Here, half-truths and outright lies are replacing direct, straight-forward product offers. It's as if they know you'd never buy their product in a hundred years, so the marketing ploy is to get you to buy it without really knowing you've bought it.

What's wrong with this picture? Plenty. It seemed to be working until consumers discovered that striped toothpaste doesn't clean teeth any better than the old white stuff. And the waiter's hip courtesy and memorized script don't make the tough T-Bone taste any better. No, giving marketing full rein on product innovation is a great concept— until your customers begin demanding real product improvements.

So why don't marketing inspired innovations go right to the core of the matter and make fundamental improvements in products and services? *Because marketing people are not product experts!* Conversely, why doesn't R & D, toiling in their idyllic research centers in the woods, come up with the product innovations that customers want and need? *Because product people are not customer experts!* There's no one to blame for this dysfunctional mess. Marketing and R&D are both prisoners of the artificial functionalizing of business. A lifetime of separating product/customer innovation, has given us too many specialized exerts and too few Disney style craftsmen. This doesn't have to happen in your company. Simply resist over-functionalizing and put your best "scientists" and "salesmen" back together on the same team. You will significantly raise your odds of coming up with the new products and services the world wants and will pay for.

• Senior Management Dis-Connected
A recent survey of CEOs asked: "What functions in your company do you trust the most and the least?" Dead last on this list was R&D. Show me a company where upper management distrusts or dis-connects itself

from the innovative processes of the company, and I'll show you a company where nothing new is going to happen for a very long time. Of course moving at the speed of light and living with uncertainty rests very uneasily with rank and file executives. Yet encouraging rapid experimentation and even tolerating some chaos are central to fostering action and creativity. But who can blame the executives, really? For one hundred years the business schools where they all got their MBAs have been teaching nothing about chaos and unpredictability except they must be stamped out.

The irony here is that most senior managers got to be senior managers precisely because they were able to "beat the system" throughout their career. The play-it-by-the-rules type rarely does anything spectacular. Much more often, it's the guy (or gal) that turned several divisions upside down, broke some rules along the way and carries battle scars from hand to hand corporate combat. They most definitely are not wallflowers. They *are* human however—and once at the top, the last thing they want is a lot of unpredictable chaos roiling beneath them. It's as if they decide they will be the last rule bending innovator in the company! Whatever the reason, when the top of the company stops practicing and fostering high speed innovation, bureaucracy and slow motion can't be far behind. The solution? Make sure your senior managers are the most dedicated practitioners and biggest cheerleaders of high-speed innovation in the entire company.

Now that you know the "seven deadly sins" against High-speed Innovation, let's turn to the Golden Rules. You'll be happy to see there are only two you have to follow.

THE GOLDEN RULES OF HIGH-SPEED INNOVATION

Akio Morita said that high-speed innovation is the entrepreneur's secret weapon. So as a corporate entrepreneur, the key question becomes how can you make sure that high-speed innovation is working in your company? What is it really that creates and drives such behavior? And if you have it yourself, can you pass it on to your employees? These are critically important things to know. Fortunately, unlike decoding the human genome, or inventing the first transistor radio, entrepreneurial practices are not so complicated. At the heart of all high-speed innovation, are just two golden rules: feeling the necessity to invent and having the freedom to act.

Sony may be Japan's most innovative big company, but the world champion in this category has to be the Minnesota Mining and Manufacturing Company, known around the world as 3M. This great company has shown the world that entrepreneurial speed and innovation can be maintained—even as a *Fortune 500* company. From the beginning in 1906, when six miners invented sandpaper to avoid going bankrupt with their investment in a worthless gravel pit, this has been a business built on a single-minded strategy—to grow by inventing new products year after year. And do they ever! 3M has the highest percentage (around 30%) of new product revenue of any large company in the world. They define *new products* as those invented within the past five years. With $23 billion in revenue and some 60,000 different products, this is a tremendous record. How does 3M do it?

It's important to note, up front, it isn't from throwing massive amounts of money around. 3M's R&D budget as a percentage of its revenue is only average for its industry. They do it, first and foremost, by *aiming* to do it. Their most important strategic goal each year is in fact hitting the 30 percent new product revenue target. Next, they have created an incredibly focused corporate culture, in direct support of that strategy. Their corporate culture has only one value: *product innovation.* Everyone in the company understands the most important thing to do at 3M is to invent something. It's the way to get big bonuses, big kudos, and most importantly it's the way to get promoted to the top. So after a hundred years, the culture of innovation at 3M is pervasive. Indeed, the company is run by people who love science and products, not MBAs. This means that all senior executives push like crazy to get new products in their divisions. And if you invent a product, you get first crack at running that product business, a highly unusual and motivating factor for company scientists. In other areas of the business, you can't miss the importance of innovation. Every 3M ad for years has talked about innovation or used the tag line "Borne of Innovation." Inventing a product is the basis of the most important employee awards, including being invited to present your ideas at the prestigious 3M Inventors' Forums held around the company. And day-dreaming is an official activity. Engineers and scientists are given 15 percent of their time to day-dream about new and different products, away from their official projects. And perhaps the most important thing of all is the company mantra that "failure is a good thing." At 3M you don't get demoted or fired for making honest mistakes in your efforts to invent new technologies and products. Of course, 3M learned this lesson long ago since it was founded on a mistake—that worthless gravel pit—that forced them to invent sandpaper as the company's very first product.

If you ask 3M people for the secret of their success in inventing new products, they're likely to come up with some vague answer like: "Accidents, or failures, or mistakes." They'll tell you about the laboratory accident that led to the discovery of Scotch Guard for example. Or you'll hear about the repeated, failed attempts to make a super light glue that failed to stick permanently-and ended up as one of 3M's great all-time products, Post-it Notes. But, of course, all companies have accidents and failures. What makes 3M so different is that after their accidents, mistakes, or failures, they ask a naive question: "Have I come up with something here that anyone in the world might need!" They then put together a make-shift marketing team and go find out if anyone wants to buy this unplanned concoction from the 3M lab. The beauty of it is, the answer comes back yes often enough to give 3M the greatest record in the history of business for inventing new products and racing them to the market.

When you look at the speed and innovation of entrepreneurs, and the few highly innovative big companies such as 3M and Sony, you will see that it's not a system, or a process, or a management technique that is producing these super competitive practices. If you look very closely, and peer a little below the surface, it's clear that they are being propelled by a couple of basic, powerful forces. First, they all have a passion for, and belief in *the necessity to invent*. For them, innovation is not icing on the cake. It's the cake. And second, they are simply brimming over with *the freedom to act.* From the CEO to frontline workers, experimenting and trying new things is part of the job. It's expected of everyone. These two common sense practices, the necessity to invent and the freedom to act, are the entrepreneur's golden rules of high-speed innovation.

THE NECESSITY TO INVENT

"We did it because we believed we had to."

—Larry Hillblom, Co-Founder
DHL

A great way to describe invention as a necessity is the amazing story of Larry Hillblom. He was a young law student in northern California who worked as a free-lance courier on weekends. At the time there were no courier companies. Hand delivering time sensitive documents, cash, and travelers' checks around the world was an individual and disorganized business. It had been done that way for decades. For Hillblom, it was also a great way to spend a weekend. He got a lot of studying done and pocketed a few bucks. On his long flights across the Pacific, he began to wonder why no company provided this valuable service. On one of his 20 hour trips he scratched out an idea to create an international courier company. He got two of his law school buddies, who were also freelance couriers, to join him. They called it DHL (for Dalsey, Hillblom, and Lynn), and they literally invented an industry. (*Larry Hillblom was killed several ago while flying his own plane. It disappeared without a trace into the Pacific Ocean near his home on the island of Saipan. Larry shunned publicity all his life and became a virtual recluse by the time he was 40. He died as he lived—doing his own thing in his own way. I only met him twice, but like everyone who knew him, I was fascinated by this rebellious business innovator.*)

There was certainly a need. Everywhere Hillblom went he found interested prospects. After all, he was offering something revolutionary. Business documents from Tokyo to Milan could take 10 days. From Lagos to Mexico City forever. In a world where postal delivery times between Philadelphia and New York had gone from three days by Pony Express to five days by the U.S. Post Office, overnight delivery anywhere in the world had a terrific appeal. But the three young entrepreneurs quickly learned that big banks and shipping firms weren't about to contract out all their worldwide courier needs to three students who didn't have business cards, let alone a single overseas office to serve them. Hillblom saw that creating a DHL global network was an absolute necessity to getting the business up and running. In fact, they had to have most of the network in place *before* they could get the big clients they desperately needed. A half-built network wouldn't be very interesting to the Deutschebanks and Toyotas and IBMs of the world. DHL had to be everywhere they were. This meant that DHL would have to create a worldwide network of offices overnight. But how could three students with no business experience and no money possibly do this?

Hillblom told me that they pulled it off for one reason only: "We did it because we believed we had to. No network, no business. And we didn't know there was any other way than bootstrapping it, which was lucky for us. If we had spent our time writing business plans, lining up bank financing and venture capital, and using headhunters in 50 countries, there would be no DHL today." And what a network they built! They opened an amazing 120 country offices in the first 10 years (1972 to 1982) of DHL's existence—still the fastest international expansion of any company in history!

Their method was pure *mater artium necessitas*. They started in Asia, built the company on the run, and never looked back. On every courier trip each of them took, they signed up anybody they could find to be their local partner. They weren't too discriminating. They got a taxi driver at the Sydney airport, the manager of an A&W Root Beer stand in Malaysia, a toy salesman in Hong Kong, and so on. They offered generous terms, up to 50 percent ownership, and in return the local partner had to ante up an address, a phone and fax number, and a promise to pick up and deliver the DHL pouch every day at the airport. Using this seat-of-the-pants approach, the DHL network began to grow country by country, gaining momentum with each new location. By the late seventies it was like a thunderbolt roaring across the globe. There were no plans or systems or procedures, and zero external financing. Handshakes sealed all the deals. The partner or manager in each DHL outpost was, by default, king of his territory. Each fiefdom had one overriding obligation: "Whatever comes in, and whatever goes out, handle it with the speed of light." Most importantly, Hillblom was able to show the big banks and other prospects an impressive, rapidly growing list of worldwide DHL locations. It worked. The business exploded and the rest is history.

Thus was born the worldwide network of DHL partners and mini-entrepreneurs—all based on a level of high-speed innovation bordering on the unbelievable. Larry Hillblom (Dalsey and Lynn opted out early) did indeed create quite a network, without resources or experience, because he had to. In the process he also created a $3 billion company with 40,000 jobs. These things can happen when you truly feel the necessity to invent. The following tips, from the masters, will get you and your company on the right path.

• Feeling The Heat Of Necessity
Feeling the heat has to start at the top. Visits to the headquarters of companies can sometimes provide contrasting, if symbolic, examples of this. I first met Fredy Dellis when he was President of Hertz International. He had done a magnificent job of keeping Hertz number one in the wildly competitive international car rental business. Dellis was right for the job and the place he worked, Hertz International's headquarters in London, was right for the business. For starters, the Hertz headquarters was physically located on heavily trafficked Bath Road, right at the entrance to Heathrow Airport. Heathrow is the busiest airport and the number one car rental location in the world. This is ground zero for the international auto rental business. The Hertz building itself was one of those ghastly, plastic looking, 1960s British office structures and the noise and fumes of the Heathrow traffic overwhelmed the reception room. Hertz cars were jammed into the side and back parking lots of the building. It looked more like a rental location in a bad part of town than a corporate headquarters—the upside of which was that real customers were forever dropping in with problems or questions. The constant roar of planes taking off and landing at Heathrow replaced the quiet pitter patter of other, more stately corporate headquarters. There was no carpeting to soften the

sounds and busy looking staff in Hertz uniforms were coming and going. All the big name competitors -- Avis, Budget, National—were just a stone's throw away at the airport and everyone knew exactly what their competition was up to. From President to clerk, no one could miss the daily reminders that Hertz has a ton of tough competition. All in all, these were down and dirty digs, but they delivered a strong message. As Dellis himself put it, "We're in the thick of the battle here. Everyone in this headquarters knows what customers and competitors look like, smell like, and what they think of Hertz."

The last time I saw Dellis, he had a bigger job and a bigger challenge. As the new President of Burger King International, his mandate was to close the gap in the chain's eternal, and losing, market share battle with McDonald's. He certainly had a bigger and fancier headquarters to do it from. A first visit to Burger King's headquarters is indeed a stunning experience. Located somewhere outside of Miami, through what seems like miles of orange groves, an enormous pink coliseum takes shape in the distance. Driving closer you get the feeling you're approaching the Acropolis or some grand fortress. Eventually the structures square off, revealing wide drives and a beautiful man-made lake at the rear. There are actually three or four large pink buildings in a gigantic clearing ringed by citrus orchards. It's a breathtaking sight. The design style is somewhere between Mormon Tabernacle and early CIA. The interior is more of the same—a spacious mausoleum look with thick carpeting. Everything is picture perfect right down to the manicured gardens in the multi-storied lobby. It's large, elegant and way too quiet. Perhaps as a sign of the times, few people are in sight. The staff cafeteria, the only place to eat for miles around, is sort of the Russian Tea Room version of a fast food joint. Eating there is definitely a different experience from the Burger King you and I know. As I said, a stunning experience—and a stunning sense of isolation from the real world of Whoppers and Big Macs.

The contrast between Hertz on Bath Road and Burger King in the Florida orange grove is striking. My first thought was how could anyone working in this idyllic paradise have the foggiest idea of what it will take to steal market share from McDonald's and Wendy's? What in the world does this place have to do with serving thousands of impatient customers and cleaning dirty toilets at a Burger King in downtown Chicago or on Orchard Road in Singapore? When a headquarters appears completely untouched by the marketplace—by customers or competitors—you have to wonder where the innovative ideas for great new products and radically improved services will come from. Maybe we've stumbled across the reason why Hertz remains number one in its industry and Burger King remains mired in the number 2 spot—or is it 3 now—in its industry.

It doesn't have to be this way. It can't be this way if you expect to have a company full of fast-moving innovators. The best way to instill the idea that innovation is a necessity for your business is to make sure that everyone from your headquarters staff to the frontline, feels some personal heat from the marketplace. Dealing with customers face-to-face, and obsessively benchmarking competitors, is the surest way to start this process. At the end of the day, your employees have to understand that their own economic survival, as well as the company's, is on the line every day. When your people begin to lose this feeling, you'll know it's time to move on to the next point—and re-instill a sense of crisis and urgency in the business.

• Create Crisis And Urgency

I've got good news for you. Creating a sense of urgency can be done most powerfully—by that simple, old-fashioned technique of setting high standards and then leading by personal example. The best I've ever met on this score—keeping a sense of crisis and urgency alive in a big company—is my friend up north, Jimmy Pattison. He's the founder and sole owner of The Jim Pattison Group. With over US $4 billion in revenues and 25,000 employees, it's Canada's largest company owned by a single individual. As you might guess, Jimmy Pattison has a knack for getting people's attention. I've addressed his company conferences several times, but the first time was the most memorable. He personally called my office (from Frank Sinatra's former house in Palm Springs by the way—which he had just purchased) to invite me to address his annual company conference which was to be held at a beautiful site in British Columbia. Naturally, I agreed.

Several months later, upon arrival at the conference site, I noticed the printed schedule showed that I was to open the conference the next morning with my talk—at the bewitching hour of 7 A.M. At dinner that night, to make sure it wasn't a misprint (which I secretly hoped it was); I asked Jimmy if 7 A.M. was really the starting time. He said matter of factly, "Yes we like to start all our meetings by 7. And by the way, would you mind showing up a little early because I really don't like to start late." I said, "Of course," went to my room and set the alarm for 5 A.M. to be safe. I got to the large meeting room about 6:40 the next morning and noticed everyone was already seated waiting for the conference to begin. I'd never seen that before. Jimmy grabbed my arm and started walking me toward the stage saying, "I think everyone's here so let's just start now." I cleared my throat, took a quick gulp of water, and started presenting to the 300 managers in the audience. I glanced at my watch. It was 6:41 A.M. and The Jim Pattison Group annual conference was rolling! Jimmy was center aisle, front row, taking notes. I'll never forget it as long as I live.

And that's the point of course. What I later learned that makes this little tale worth telling is that Jimmy Pattison never starts a meeting on time. He always starts them early. He's sending a powerful message. One of his VPs told me, "It's Jimmy's way of getting our attention, of telling everyone we have to keep moving—that we all have a lot to do and we can't sit around wasting time! I can tell you one thing, nobody in this company ever shows up late for anything." Why don't you give this a try in your organization? It's guaranteed to get your peoples' attention. Jimmy certainly had the attention of his top 300 managers—and brother, I promise you, he had mine too!

• Do Something, Anything, Better Each Day

Imagine the entrepreneurial dream of every employee you ever hire coming to work each day thinking: "What can I do today a little bit better than yesterday?" But of course that will never happen—unless you tell them it's the most important part of their job. Most corporate managers don't tell their people to do this because they don't think about doing it themselves. In the typical bureaucracy, everyone comes to work ready to do the job exactly as they did it yesterday, and last

week, and last year. The entrepreneur can't afford this. Finding a way
to do something better, faster, and cheaper every day is the core
competitive advantage of any entrepreneur. And making sure this
philosophy is worked into the daily performance of all employees is the
only way to keep this advantage alive. The once-a-decade grand
strategic stroke is always welcome, but it's day-in-and-day-out
improvements by everyone that will really keep you ahead of the pack.

To get this idea across in your organization, there are a dozen common
sense things you can do. Probably the first thing is to get this notion
into every job description. You might then put real teeth into it and
make it part of everyone's performance goals and evaluations. I would
even be so old-fashioned as to run a half-day meeting or a workshop on
why it's critical and provide simple examples of exactly what you want
people to do. It's much too important to just announce along with the
daily blizzard of e-mails, so try it face to face. Remember, if every single
employee truly came to work every day and actually improved
something in their job or area, you are talking about a miracle in
company-wide improvements. It just may be worth a try!

It certainly was worth trying for our old friend, Larry Hillblom, at DHL.
Of course continuous improvement doesn't just happen. People like
Hillblom make it happen. He consciously set out to make a mundane
sounding business an exciting, heroic enterprise. Hillblom's real genius
was to involve lowly couriers in the heroic battle. To see a DHL courier
racing through the streets of Hong Kong, sweat flying from his brow and
a grim determination on his face, is to see living proof that companies
can instill in their employees a passion to do their job better and faster
each day.

The first time I met Larry Hillblom I got to see this same impact on his
senior management. I was delivering a mini-seminar in London to
DHL's Board and top 50 executives. I assumed Hillblom didn't attend
such meetings. His reputation as something of an international Howard
Hughes, living on the Pacific island of Saipan, was well known. He
never granted interviews or made public appearances. However, about
two minutes into my presentation, a youngish looking, red-headed

American with a beard strode purposefully to the one empty seat at the front. He was dressed in tennis shoes, levis, and a red plaid lumberman's shirt. I'd never seen such a figure at a board level meeting, especially in London. I carried on assuming this wandering lumberjack was crazy or lost. It wasn't long before I found out that Larry Hillblom is far from crazy and is never lost. He took the seminar very seriously. In the breakout teams, he had more questions and more ideas than anyone else in the room. He got emotionally involved in every point. And when it was over he vanished into thin air. No fanfare or goodbyes. I later learned this was classic Hillblom: He periodically showed up at company meetings, got everyone passionately involved in improving the business, and then disappeared back to Saipan. I must say it seemed to work that day. He had a bigger-than-life impact on his top team— not by issuing new edicts and demanding more revenue—but by personally demonstrating his own passion for doing something, anything, better each day.

THE FREEDOM TO ACT

"The trick is to get to the finish line first."

—Ed Penhoet, Co-Founder
Chiron Corporation

If you can only follow one golden rule at a time, you'd better make it the freedom to act. Innovation without action might get you a Nobel prize, but it won't get you a customer. Most entrepreneurs agree that fast action is more important than innovation. The fact is, if you try out a lot of new ideas, if you are willing to experiment, and if you make a mistake you come· right back to try again, you *will* be an innovative group. The important brand of innovation for business has never been quiet, ivory tower, analysis to eventually come up with a blockbuster idea. It has always been, and will continue to be, trying ten different things and hoping three of them work.

Creating a fast moving, action-oriented company requires a high level of freedom within the organization to take action, to continuously experiment, and to make an honest mistake or two. The biotech industry is a perfect place to learn how to do this. And Chiron Corporation is the perfect company to investigate. As mentioned earlier in this book, some 25 years after its founding it had grown to be one of the big winners in the biotech race. By 2005 it was the number three biotech firm in the world—after Genentech and Amgen—with about $2 billion in revenues and healthy profits. Some years earlier, Swiss pharmaceutical giant Novartis had purchased a substantial stake in the company and in 2006 it acquired the remaining 58% of Chiron's stock for a whopping $5.1 billion. So the total market value of the little bio-tech business dreamed up in Ed Penhoet's living room had grown to some $9 billion. Chiron's first blockbuster product, which really put them on the map, was the hepatitis B vaccine—now estimated to have prevented millions of cases of hepatitis and hundreds of thousands of deaths. They also have products for the treatment of kidney cancer and melanoma, pediatric vaccines, and blood tests for HIV and hepatitis. Ed Penhoet, the co-founder and CEO, raised half a billion dollars in capital, acquired Cetus, another big industry star, and signed product distribution agreements with the likes of Merck, Johnson & Johnson, and Novartis. Chiron was a charter member of that elite family of biotech firms that produced big products and big profits.

My first encounter with Ed Penhoet was pure luck. We were both speakers at a conference in San Diego. I listened to this articulate scientist/entrepreneur deliver a dazzling talk about the future of the biotech industry and I knew I had to interview him. A couple of months later, I went to Emeryville, California, Chiron's headquarters, for a tour of their famous labs and a long interview in Penhoet's office. I didn't know quite what to expect. I had never discussed business with a world-class scientist with a Ph.D. in both biology and chemistry. I knew I couldn't speak his language. I hoped he could speak mine. It turns out he can speak both quite well. I shouldn't have been surprised. The first thing you notice about Penhoet, and others from his industry, is that they're very smart. And I had assumed, given the incredibly high-tech nature of the industry, that success primarily depends on how smart your scientists are. It turned out that I was in for a big surprise: "We're all smart. In our field we've already been preselected, in the sense that by the time you get to people who have PhDs from major institutions like Harvard, UC Berkeley, or UCSF, it's a given that they're smart. They've gotten 99 percentile on their SAT scores and all the rest. In this group there are very few people who are really very much smarter than the rest—damn few. In the beginning it was just a race. We all knew what had to be done. We had to be able to hit the ground running and stick with it. Everyone is now talking all about speed, right? Well, it's particularly true for biotechnology. It's always been a race. I suspect in today's environment, with the world moving as fast as it is everything is a race to some degree. So I think every company has to come to grips with how to move more quickly and how to cut out the blockages. Certainly in biotech ... the trick is to get to the finish line first."

Who would have imagined that speed is a more critical competitive advantage than IQ in the ultimate high-tech business of biogenetics? After all, this is an industry where even junior staffers have PhDs. Penhoet went on, "It may be that speed is even more important than cost in the end, because really—you can't save your way into success in this business. Do you know what I mean? The real value comes when you get some very valuable products in the marketplace. That creates the margin so that you can keep the other ones flowing through the pipeline. If our history has taught us anything—after all these years of being in a horse race—it is that you have to focus on speed as the key element in building any organization. I could go through our product portfolio with you, tell you who the other players were, and what we knew about where they were at various points of time. I wouldn't want to leave you with the impression that this is a theoretical race—this is a very real race. I mean, we knew who the other entrants in the race were. We knew when the starting gun was fired. We tried to keep track of where they were, where we were, and whether they were ahead or we were ahead. Take a number of these projects we were working on like Factor VIII, the antihemophilic factor, or hepatitis B, or IGF, it wasn't, oh gee, we're racing against the world. No, we were racing against Genentech and Genetics Institute on Factor VIII. So, it's a very personal kind of race really, and I think as a company gets larger, the

issue is to keep that sort of personal competition inculcated in the group.
You know, it's you and me running to the finish line against each other.
I think that has been tremendously valuable to us. Probably it was good
for both Genentech and Chiron, for example, that we were competing
against each other in several products, because it became very direct and
very personal."

It would be impossible to make up a more compelling argument for the
competitive value of speed and action than Ed Penhoet's own words
provide. That is why Penhoet is one entrepreneur you really must listen
to. Unlike many others, he's really thought through *how* he did, *what* he
did. His summary on the success of Chiron completes the circle. It's all
about having the freedom to act and act quickly—and how that
translates into the entrepreneur's most powerful competitive advantage:
"The overall competitive advantage Chiron has is speed. I'm measuring
speed from the point where somebody conceives of a new piece of
biology and it gets commercialized at the other end. It's one thing to
move an opportunity which is obvious, but it's another to recognize a
new opportunity. So I think where we have special skills is first of all,
recognizing new opportunities very early on, grabbing those, and then
running with them in a very aggressive manner. The large companies
have difficulty competing in a rapidly moving field like biotech. In large
part, it's because their bureaucracy requires too many levels of review.
By the time you've educated everybody in a large organization about the
advantages or disadvantages of a new program, somebody else who has
a more light-footed organization has already moved the product so far
along that the large company is no longer in a position to compete.
Whenever people have visited Chiron over the last 20 years, the
number one impression they've left with is a feeling of energy. When
you walk by the lab you feel the energy. People are busy. Things are
happening. So energy is an extremely important part of our success
without question. So it's that sense of urgency, feeling of energy,
knowing the competition is there—it's our whole culture if you will."

This is what you want to be able to say about your own company no
matter how long you've been in business. If high-speed action is a
defining advantage even in biotech, what are the odds that it will also

be a critical competitive factor in your business? If you're thinking about a thousand to one, you're probably right on the mark. So your challenge is to figure out, up front, how you're going to make that happen. Remember, entrepreneurs (even the ones in biotech) aren't action-oriented because their genes are different. They move fast because they personally feel the need to act and they don't have to ask six layers of management before they move off the dime. To create such a bias for action, and keep it alive in your company, your people have to have the freedom to act, the freedom to experiment, and the freedom to make mistakes. It's not any more complicated than that. Here are three proven ways to get you started.

• Freeing The Genius Of The Average Worker

Who should be free to take action in your company? Who has the good ideas? How about the average worker? Enter Soichiro Honda, Japan's most interesting, and perhaps most important, entrepreneur of the twentieth century. Honda was never part of the blue-blood establishment in Japanese industry. Indeed he was the "working man's man." I got the inside scoop on this great entrepreneur when I met and interviewed Tetsuo Chino at Honda's headquarters in Tokyo. Chino was the former President of Honda (USA) and a life-long friend of Mr. Honda.

Chino told me a wonderful story of how Honda got on with the rank and file: "The workers idolized him. For example, several years ago when Tadashi Kume was introduced as the new President, the first to replace the founder, we had a big party. Thousands of employees came. Mr. Honda stood up to introduce Mr. Kume. It was emotional and a little tense because the great founder was stepping down. Mr. Honda started this way, 'This company, Honda, we always seem to have a kind of sloppy person for President. A person just like me. Have you noticed? Well, here we go again. Tadashi Kume is a very sloppy person and that is why he now becomes the President.' Then he turned straight to the audience of several thousand employees and said: 'So I'm sorry to tell you, but because you have such a sloppy President, you will have to work harder or the company will collapse.' And you know, the employees just cheered and cheered. They loved it." Chino covered many other Honda actions that endeared him to the average workers, "You know he built three Honda plants in Japan just for handicapped workers. The rest of the employees really appreciated that. And also, he had a very unusual rule for a Japanese company—neither he nor any top executives could have any of their relatives working in the company. He said he didn't want a dynasty because it would be unfair to the rest of the employees." Chino concluded right on the point of who in a company should be trusted to make decisions and take action: "Mr. Honda really thought the genius of the company was in the workers. And they knew that he trusted them. This was very much appreciated by the employees and it was very unusual in big Japanese companies." I would say Mr. Honda's practices would be unusual in big companies, period.

So who will be the geniuses of your company? Who will have the good ideas and should be encouraged to try out new ideas? Who in your company will have the freedom to act? Honda often said that in any group of one hundred workers, 5 percent will be superstars, 5 percent will be bums, and 90 percent will be average. And he really did believe the average workers were the geniuses of the company. They were the ones that built the cars and literally made the company go. The only problem, as Mr. Honda saw it, was that some managers spent all their time with the superstars and the bums. They were always doing things to try to keep the superstars happy and they expended a tremendous amount of time and energy trying to fix the bums. They simply forgot about the average workers. They never even talked to them. Honda's idea was if you got just one good improvement action a month from each of the 90 percent of the workers, company performance would go through the ceiling. The moral of the story: Free the genius of your average worker and you can create a miracle in your company—a miracle of good ideas and innovative actions that no competitor will ever match.

• **Action With Customers, Products, And Inside The Organization**
Where should you aim your high-speed innovation? The entrepreneurial answer of course would be, on the core of what keeps you competitive. In other words on your customers and products. You can never go wrong on taking actions to improve your customer service

and making your products better. The other area that's a sure-fire winner is actions directed at improving the internal workings of the company. I'm not talking about trivial things, but improving the core processes of the company such as employee development, product innovation, purchasing and market research.

Welcome to the world of Sabrina Horn, wunderkind of the high-tech public relations industry. Horn was still in her twenties when she founded Horn Group, Inc. (HGI). Over the past two decades, HGI became one of the fastest growing PR agencies in the country. With offices in San Francisco, Boston, New York and Washington D.C., plus agency partnerships in Europe and Asia, HGI became a high-speed, innovative example of a new kind of PR firm; one totally dedicated to the high-tech industry.

HGI has always been on a super-fast track. It was an "Inc. 500 Company," making *Inc. Magazine's* list of America's fastest growing companies. It was also named "Best U.S. Employer" by *Working Woman* magazine, an unheard of accolade in an industry famous for its high pressure, burn-out rate. The firm has received numerous awards and tributes, but its most interesting attribute for our purposes here, is that HGI is on the cutting edge of reinventing the PR industry. Everybody knows that high-tech companies move at the speed of light and live or die on relentless innovation. But the very specialized, high-tech PR firms that present them to the world actually have to stay one step ahead of the hurricane that cyberspace has become. Whether it's the unending string of new product launches, or new strategic alliances being signed, or make-or-break initial public offerings (IPOs), the PR agencies have to be ahead of the e-commerce industry curve every day in every way. From the simultaneous distribution of thousands of virtual press releases, to using hyperlinks for streaming video and audio trailers, to online press conferences, HGI's high-tech PR services have become a largely paperless business mirroring the cyberspace style of the clients they serve. This is a different Public Relations world from anything ever seen in the old economy.

I visited the Horn Group in their totally wired, but warm and inviting, San Francisco headquarters. Since HGI had been recognized as one of the fastest growing new companies in the United States, I began by asking her: "How have you done that? What are the key things you do to grow HGI?" She didn't hesitate a second: "Three big things come to mind. First, in this industry you have to be looking at where the technology is going and where you need to go, but at the same time you absolutely need to have a core expertise. PeopleSoft was our first client and I think it's important for entrepreneurs to focus on an area of competence, and not get distracted by opportunities and by too much of a good thing. So I initially built a franchise of clients around PeopleSoft's technology, and that was a key thing in our growth. I think that was really good for us in the early days because we built a reputation for ourselves as being really good in one market segment of software. Everybody knew we did it and they all called us and we had our choice of the companies we wanted to work with.

"Secondly, in the service business your *product* is your people. If we were manufacturing TVs for example, we'd have engineering support, manufacturing standards, quality assurance—we'd have all this infrastructure to support making that product. And what service companies don't do enough of is to support their *product*, which is of course their people. So that's what we do. That's certainly our reputation and we've even won awards for it. We won this award last year for *Best Employer in the U.S.* I have to say that for a PR agency to get that kind of recognition is big stuff because they're usually terrible places to work that burn-out people in a hurry. So the second thing is, if you're an entrepreneur in a service business, it all starts with your people. They are the product you have to offer. So if your creative, willing to try new things, and do everything you can to make your people happy, then you have a much better chance of having a growing, happy business.

"Finally we've always tried to be on top of, or one step ahead of, new ways of doing PR so that our firm and our services are never just another cookie cutter type business. I'm always trying to reinvent the way we do things. And it's not just from using better technology in PR, but also in our internal processes and procedures. Always trying to get more effective and more efficient inside the company. Whether the client sees it or not, we are always kind of re-tooling what we do and how we operate as a company."

Those three key things are exactly what we're talking about in this section. Aim your best improvement actions at the areas that will really make a difference: Your customers, your products (or your people as Horn defines it), and the key processes inside your company. Sabrina Horn has it down pat—and look where it's got her—on the list of the fastest growing entrepreneurial companies in America. Try her advice and we'll look for your name on the same kind of list for big business!

• Bureaucracy Bashing Bosses
At most big organizations, the real battle is to wipe out fifty years of bad habits and mis-placed priorities. Only bosses can handle this job. Mid-level task forces just don't get the job done. For openers, getting everyone's attention is a very necessary ingredient in successful bureaucracy bashing. The most insidious thing about bureaucracy is, it's almost always well intentioned. Bureaucratic practices, rules and procedures are never introduced to destroy the business. They're put in place to solve some earlier glitch, or to make sure things are done correctly in the future, or to ensure equal treatment of all employees, etc. Unfortunately, after several years of implementing all these good intentions, the place starts feeling more like a police station than the innovative, fast moving company it used to be. The best solution to rampaging bureaucracy is to never let it get that far.

To learn how the day in and day out battle against bureaucracy can be won, even in a giant company, there's no better role model than Norman Brinker, who single-handedly invented the full service, chain restaurant business in America, including his flagship brand, Chili's Grill & Bar. I had the great pleasure of meeting and talking at length with him when he unexpectedly showed up at one of my seminars in, of all places, Singapore. I had written about his great exploits in an earlier book and he just dropped by to introduce himself and say thanks. It was a memorable meeting. (*Brinker, small town boy, Olympic athlete, entrepreneurial visionary and the god-father of America's full service restaurant industry, passed away in July of 2009. I was honored to have met him and hear his thoughts firsthand.)*

I first learned about Chili's Grill & Bar (Brinker International today) when I visited their headquarters in Dallas, Texas some 20 years ago when it was still on *Forbes'* list of "The 200 Best Small Companies in America." As an indication of their amazing growth, Brinker has now been on *Fortune's* list of "America's Most Admired Companies" every year from 2001 right up through 2009. The numbers confirm the accolades: In the quarter century since its start-up under Brinker, the company's revenues today stand at about $4 billion—with 1,700 restaurants in 27 countries and 125,000 *BrinkerHeads* as employees affectionately call themselves. Brinker International has been one of the fastest growing companies in the United States for the past quarter century, and in the process, Norm Brinker rewrote the book for high-speed innovation and beating bureaucracy in the food service industry.

Norm Brinker was a farm boy from Roswell, New Mexico, whose first brush with a much bigger world came when he rode for the U.S. equestrian team at the 1952 Olympics in Helsinki. Professionally he did it all: worked an entry level job at Jack-In-The-Box, owned a single coffee shop, was chairman of both Burger King and Pillsbury's massive restaurant group, and created one big brand after another such as Steak And Ale (his first in 1966,) Bennigan's, Chili's Grill & Bar, Romano's Macaroni Grill, and On the Border Mexican Grill & Cantina. Along the way he became a living legend in the restaurant business.

If the best way to combat bureaucracy is to not let it get started in the first place, here's a front-line warning from experienced bureaucracy basher Brinker, "The larger you get, there tends to be a rigidity that sets in—over time. When you're small you're scrambling and flexible—quicker on your feet—partly because there just aren't that many things to change.

The larger you get, the harder it becomes. Take McDonald's with thirty thousand locations. You change one thing, you've got to change thirty thousand restaurants. You have to change thousands of procedures, hundreds of thousands of employees, whatever. So well-intentioned bureaucracy sets in to control all this as the company grows larger."

To battle this ever growing bureaucracy, decentralized action taking became an article of faith for Brinker: "At most companies it's red tape, or levels of approval you have to work your way through to get something through all the doomsayers. A big company has a lot more people saying how you *can't* do something than how you *can* do it. We don't like to fail at Chili's, but we're not afraid of running hard and hitting the wall and bouncing off and then getting up to run again. We tried a lot of things that didn't work very well; we retreated and attacked again from a different direction. That's hard to do in a big bureaucracy."

Brinker was also not a fan of sophisticated market research and analyzing reams of data. He was famous for going straight to customers and employees to tell him what needed to be done: "Before I walk into one of our restaurants or a competitor's restaurant, I wait for a group of people to come out, and I ask them, 'How was it? Is this place any good?'" At company headquarters he almost never called meetings, but spent a big part of his time just talking to people. He liked to wander into someone's office and explore any new idea on their mind. He told new managers to look around and point out anything they thought could be done better before they became "Chilized." Brinker knew the importance of taking advice from the people in touch with the customer and the dangers of the bureaucracy stifling employee creativity and action: "People either grow or shrivel. It all depends on the company's attitude. There's the attitude that says, 'Boy, I've got a great idea, let's go try it.' Or there's the attitude that says, 'That's not the way we've ever done things—and besides you need six approvals to try that.' Say that enough and all the employees get the message."

So there you have it, Brinker International's proven recipe for battling bureaucracy: Implementing continuous improvements, keeping employees involved, decentralized action taking, permitting some failure along the way, and perhaps most important, top executives who make it a priority to never let it get started in the first place!

Just as it's so important in this last section on "Bureaucracy Bashing Bosses," it will take top-down action to instill all aspects of High-Speed Innovation in any large, mature organization. Keeping your company creative, flexible, and fast moving, as you grow bigger and bigger, are challenging goals and areas where top management must take the lead. Whether it's fostering innovation, speeding up action, or wiping out bureaucracy, leading by example is the necessary, first action.

Chapter 11

Making Self-Inspired Behavior The Standard

The Almighty Power Of Consequences

"Get rid of the committees and consultants and MBAs. Stop showing contempt for your dealers, your employees, and your customers. Give up the corporate dining room, the chauffeured limousines, the hefty bonuses. Get back to the trenches. Listen to the troops. Take care of them first, and they'll take care of you."

—H. Ross Perot, Founder
EDS, Perot Systems

I first became intrigued by Ross Perot way back in 1979. But it wasn't because of this Texas entrepreneur's business exploits—even though he had already made a name for himself as the founder of Electronic Data Systems. I had a more personal reason. Like many other Americans working in Iran around that time, I had gotten trapped in the wild and woolly Iranian revolution. Yes, that would be the same revolution that brought down America's pal, the Shah of Iran, declared America the "Great Satan," and produced our most intractable foreign foe ever since.

I was in Teheran to close down an office I had myself opened just three years earlier. On my arrival I saw a very different Teheran from the one I thought I knew. The ride in from Mehrabad Airport had been an eye-opener. It looked like a war-zone. We were stopped and searched every few blocks. Tanks, nervous soldiers and sandbags clogged the streets while a million demonstrators screamed anti-Shah and anti-American slogans. It was an angry and eerie sight in a country where such behavior had been unthinkable for decades. Everyone in the country seemed on strike save the troops loyal to the Shah and of course the Ayatollah's demonstrators. At the Sheraton Hotel where I was staying the windows were all broken, the staff was gone, and we few remaining "guests" helped ourselves to what food was in the kitchen.

Over the next week the situation went from bad to worse. I won't bore you with the details but it evolved into a surreal mixture of "house arrest" in the Sheraton lobby and being guarded 24/7 by wild-eyed Iranians with AK47s, all swept up in the revolutionary fervor. One thing seemed certain—there was no way to get out. That is, until a young Frenchman, an employee of Air France, came to my rescue. Because the revolution's leader, Ayatollah Khomeni, had been given political refuge in France for many years, the French were still free to come and go as they liked. So Air France was allowed to bring us one meal a day. Anyway this brave young man offered to help me escape in his Air France jeep if I was game to try. I was—and he did. I'll never forget our back street ride to the airport, trying to avoid both the nervous government soldiers and the frenzied demonstrators. What was normally a thirty minute drive took about five hours. It didn't really make much difference as the airport was closed and everyone was on strike. No planes were allowed to land or take off. I did have lots of company however. There must have been 10,000 Iranians and all sorts of foreigners at the airport trying to leave the country.

Once inside the airport my French host and helper seemed particularly encouraged with my chances when I told him I had no preferred destination. "This means you will go any direction?" he asked. "Yes, any direction, any country" I responded. "This is good. Just sit or sleep on the floor near the Air France counter, and I will find you when the right time comes." So I took up my spot on the floor just like any other refugee. Over the next 36 hours I waited.

In the middle of my second night on the floor, like a shining knight in blue, the Air France agent leaned over and whispered: "Come with me. There's an Air France 747 out at the end of the runway. She's been allowed to re-fuel but cannot discharge or take on any passengers. But I think I can get you on-board." He shoved an Air France jacket toward me: "Put this on, it's safer." In a bit of a daze I followed him behind the counter, through the office area, down several corridors and presto, we were on the tarmac. There was no ticketing, no passport control, no customs, nothing. We got in an Air France jeep and shot across the runway heading for a beautiful, blue and white bird with Air France emblazoned across its side. The agent was yelling as we drove: "I can give you no ticket. Everything is broken. I will tell the Purser you have to buy your ticket when you arrive." Just then it dawned on me that I didn't have the foggiest idea where I would be arriving!

At the plane, the agent directed the mechanic's ramp ladder to the front cabin door. Up we went, the door opened, and a rapid fire exchange in French took place between the agent and the purser. The agent turned to me, stuck out his hand and said those wonderful words in French that even I could understand: "Bon voyage." The purser led me to a seat and asked: "Monsieur, where do you want to go?" I replied: "I want to go where ever you're going" "We're going to Bangkok, is that OK?" was the polite response. Without thinking I sputtered: "That's wonderful. I've never seen Bangkok before. Let's go to Bangkok." Air France never charged me for the flight and to this day, unlike some Americans, I have a very soft spot in my heart for the French.

After I returned home, one evening I happened to be watching the news on TV when Perot's face popped up on the screen with the incredible story of how he had just rescued two EDS executives from Evin Prison in central Teheran. The news story reported how Perot had

308 Larry C. Farrell

organized and paid for a commando team of ex-Green Berets, a couple of planes and helicopters, and plenty of guns to bring his two employees home. It seems that when Perot became convinced that President Carter couldn't or wouldn't rescue his people, he decided to do it himself. I was of course fascinated by this daring exploit in a place I had just escaped from on my own. And I was stunned that a company CEO would put so much on the line to save a couple of employees. I remember turning to my wife and musing: "Do you think my company was going to send commandos to rescue me?" We both knew the answer of course. Perot's heroic mission seared into my consciousness a question I still ponder, which you might want to ponder also—*if you ever get thrown into a foreign prison, who do you want to be working for?*

All of this made great headlines and even a great book and movie: *On Wings of Eagles.* Perot has in fact become a bigger-than-life character with his brand of example setting. Over twenty-five years ago he personally went into Laos trying to get supplies to American POWs in North Vietnam. He bought the Magna Charta for $1.5 million and promptly lent it to the U. S National Archives to be a national reminder that individual liberties only come from individual action. Amid great controversy, he headed a commission to get Texas education out of last place in the country; his thanks was the eternal resentment of the education establishment. And no matter what your politics, his 1992 run at the Presidency, against both Bill Clinton and George Bush, produced one amazing result. He forced Republicans and Democrats alike to take the out-of-control U.S. budget deficit seriously, something neither party had done for decades. And along the way, he garnered nearly 20% of the popular vote—more than any third party candidate since Theodore Roosevelt in 1912!

Like most people willing to take strong stands on controversial issues, he has ended up in the love-him-or-hate-him category of opinion polls. But in the opinion poll that counts most with Perot, there's no ambivalence. There's no CEO in the world who has had more respect and loyalty from employees than Perot enjoys. The commitment of some of his people borders on the unbelievable. One executive gave up $900,000 in GM stock to go back and work for Perot Systems. Recently in Brazil, two of his company managers choked up in describing to me how Perot had inspired them early in their careers. The corporate motto at Perot Systems is "One For All And All For One." It may sound corny to some, but if history is any guide, this slogan really means something when you work for Ross Perot.

Yes, Perot's style makes great headlines. It also makes great people management, if you're looking for extreme commitment and performance from your people. His personal history as a high performer is well documented. In his first job—after graduating from the Naval Academy at Annapolis and serving in the U.S. Navy—as an IBM salesman, he met his annual sales quota by the end of January. When he discovered he had maxed out on the commission system and would receive no additional sales commissions for the next 11 months, he quit and started up EDS with $1,000 borrowed from his wife's savings account. On the commitment side, his deeds are legendary. Imagine what it would be like to work for a CEO who built a company worth billions, but set his salary at $68,000 in 1965 and never gave himself a raise? Having a boss like that would be a unique experience for anyone. Or, if you were a GM "rivethead" working the assembly line, how would you feel when the largest shareholder went public with the very things you'd been saying all your life? Odds are you'd be cheering when Perot unleashed his public, take-no-prisoners attack on the entire GM Board. (As in his very public and, by most accounts, very well deserved attack on the General Motors Board quoted above, Perot became their biggest shareholder and loudest critic after he sold EDS to GM. They eventually paid him another $750 million to get him off the board and shut up about their "contempt" for customers and employees.) And perhaps most dramatically of all, what would you do in return for the CEO who hires commandos to rescue you from a foreign prison?

Here's a closing reminder that Perot isn't finished yet. He may never become President of the U.S., but his entrepreneuring days are hardly over. After selling EDS to General Motors, he founded and grew Perot Systems to $2.8 billion in revenue, with 23,000 employees—over the past twenty years. In so doing he became the first entrepreneur in history to have two companies end up on the *Fortune 1,000* list. In 1999 he took Perot Systems public and added another cool billion to his personal war chest. And just recently, in September of 2009, *The Wall Street Journal* announced: "Dell Inc. agreed to buy Perot Systems Corp. for $3.9 billion, paying a fat premium to play catch-up with big tech rivals (like IBM and HP which now owns EDS) . . . to expand beyond their traditional businesses."

So at 80 years young, this Texas billionaire, the quintessential American entrepreneur, may still have an entrepreneurial dream or two up his sleeve. This final quote perhaps best summarizes the Ross Perot approach to business and to life: "I'm always looking for people who love to win. If I run out of those, I want people who hate to lose." This goes to the heart of what Perot always looks for, and tries to inspire, in people. He wants employees who really care about what they're doing— and are damn good at doing it. We call it "Creating High Commitment and High Performance."

CREATING HIGH COMMITMENT AND HIGH PERFORMANCE

Remember this chart? Pretty simple stuff, right? High commitment and high performance are easy to describe, but they can be hard to achieve. How many people in a typical company really love what they do—and are really good at doing it? How many work as hard as they can and as smart as they can, all the time? Certainly some, but probably not most. Yet high commitment and high performance are the fundamental behaviors that produce successful enterprise. Think about it— competing against a band of people who absolutely love what they do and are very good at doing it—well, that's going to be one tough competitor!

SELF-INSPIRED BEHAVIOR OF ENTREPRENEURS

	Low	High	
High	Low Comm. & High Perf.	High Comm. & High Perf.	High
Performance			
Low	Low Comm. & Low Perf.	High Comm. & Low Perf.	Low
	Low	High	

Commitment

So how do you create and maintain both these highly entrepreneurial qualities in your company? While carrying overlapping effects, the distinctions are important. Training for instance, is an action to improve performance. It presumes a lack of knowledge or experience. If people hate their jobs, training them till hell freezes over won't raise their commitment.

To create inspired employees, you don't have to become a larger-than-life character like—*public figure, Ross Perot*. But in your own world, and in your own way, you do have to do some things like—*company manager, Ross Perot*. You have to personally demonstrate self-inspiration in whatever you do. You have to show you really love what you do. And you have to work darn hard at doing it well. Being a corporate entrepreneur *yourself* may be the easy part. Getting 10,000 workers to do the same is the real trick. Creating a company full of highly committed, high performers may the toughest challenge facing entrepreneurs and managers alike.

HIGH COMMITMENT:
GETTING EMPLOYEES TO LOVE WHAT THEY DO

"No employer-capitalist with a true feeling of brotherhood can be happy in the enjoyment of wealth without feeling a strong sense of dissatisfaction with present industrial conditions and a strong desire to improve them so that employee-workmen may be raised to a much higher level in social well-being."

—William Hesketh Lever, Founder
Lever Brothers (Unilever)

To set the record straight, employee stock ownership wasn't invented in Silicon Valley in 1990. Way back in 1909 William Lever announced the Lever Co-Partnership Trust, the world's first employee stock ownership program. By 1925 an amazing 18,000 employees were members of the Trust. Was Lever a man ahead of his times? Probably. If nothing else, he put his money where his mouth was in urging workers to cast their lot with his company.

Lever was an early believer in entrepreneurial "tough love"—doubly inspired by entrepreneurial passion and the belief that workers should get their fair share of the pie. In 1900, Lever Brothers was the largest company in the world. (*Unilever was formed in 1929 through the merger of Lever Brothers and several smaller Dutch companies. It operates today as a Dutch/UK group, with headquarters in both countries.*) Today, the *Fortune Global 500* ranks Unilever 53rd in world-wide market value, 121st in revenues, and 35th in profits. This amazing 110 year performance makes Unilever—hands down—the most consistently successful big company in the world over the past century! No other company even comes close. They are the shining example of how to beat the deadly *Life Cycle Of Organizations*. They must have been doing something right all these decades. And most people who have researched the company, including yours truly, agree that the single most important reason for their astounding long term record is that Unilever has always been, and continues to be, an absolutely great company to work for.

Here's how it started. When it came to business, Lever was a very tough competitor indeed. Aggressive and expansive, he literally overwhelmed traditional competitors. He traumatized the gentlemanly world of London commerce with massive and outlandish American style advertising. He literally invented brand recognition, the concept of market niches, and the production of multiple brands to compete against each other. By 1888 he dominated the British market and by 1910 Lever Brothers had 60,000 employees in 282 operating companies spread across five continents. He also demonstrated an autocratic model of leadership, demanding hard work and high morals from employees, insisting they were the root of all success in business and in life.

But we also find caring words and radical deeds in his commitment to employees. Creating the first employee stock and profit sharing program was truly revolutionary for the times. Taking this giant step toward the creation of mini-entrepreneurs within the organization was among his proudest achievements. Beyond the Co-Partnership Trust, Lever instituted many employee benefit programs we all take for granted today. Unilever was the first company on record to provide company training, sick leave, annual paid holidays, and pension plans. These were all radical steps.

The most famous example of Lever's commitment to employees is Port Sunlight, the model community Lever Brothers built for its employees in 1889. Working class Britain at that time endured living conditions equivalent to the worst, modern day slum. Port Sunlight eventually housed 3,500 people and became a model of company sponsored living unequalled to this day. A less famous example, but in some ways more telling, was Lever's battle with the trade unions over the length of the work day. No, management wasn't pushing for more and the union less. Quite the opposite. Lever proposed to reduce the standard work day to six hours and provide two hours of "self-improvement" classes for workers. His fellow industrialists thought he had lost his mind. But the real surprise came when the union leadership opposed the idea of "compulsory education" and that was that. Talk about being ahead of your time!

Perhaps the cap-stone of Lever's efforts to honor the dignity of the common man, came late in his life while serving in the House of Commons. In 1907 he was the author of Britain's very first legislation to provide old age pensions for its working class citizens. Not exactly the act we'd expect from a soap tycoon.

So what are we to make of this self-inspired entrepreneur and his life-long commitment to workers? The legacy of Lever's "tough love" approach to employees is clear: The company has enjoyed a high commitment/high performance work force for well over a century—and is still overwhelming the competition! The bottom line may be, like most things in life, commitment is a two way street. The underpinnings of creating high commitment may seem obvious, but they are worth reciting. Here are four of the most important:

• **Love What You Do**
Remember Ray Kroc, the great founder of McDonalds who said: "You gotta see the beauty in a hamburger!" OK, it's not a fair world. Everyone can't "love" every job they will ever have. I haven't and you haven't. But that doesn't change the principle. People aren't going to get committed to jobs they hate and companies they're not proud of. It starts with hiring people who are interested in what you do, trying hard to enrich the jobs that perhaps aren't so exciting, and really letting people "own" their piece of the business. Generously rewarding those who are highly committed to the mission doesn't hurt either. Those rewards, monetary or otherwise, should be a great investment in your future. And in some cases, it may have to come down to saying goodbye to those who just aren't ever going to give a damn about their job or your company.

At the end of the day, why should people love what they do? We know it's good for the business. That's obvious. And a fair day's effort for a fair day's wage is still a fair obligation. But there may be an even more important reason. Think about it. If you have to work for a living, which virtually everyone does, you're going to spend more time in your life at work than with your family. You'll spend more time at work than with your friends, or enjoying a hobby, or just taking it easy. In fact you're going to spend more time at work than on any other activity in your entire life. This is why it's important to love what you do. It's your *life* we're talking about! And it's the *lives* of your employees. And God help you and your employees if you spend your lives doing something you hate. So taking a little extra effort to ensure that everyone loves what they're doing is a bargain you shouldn't pass up. Remember, it will be great for the business *and* great for you and your people.

• Give Autonomy, Demand Accountability

Remember the illustration in Part One on this point; about the plant supervisor who's responsible for ten workers and millions of dollars of equipment but isn't allowed to spend $50 of the company's money to take his team out for pizza to celebrate a great week on the production line. This wouldn't be so awful if we didn't also realize that one unnecessary first class airfare by an executive can cost $5,000 and nobody thinks twice about it. The point isn't the $50 or even the $5,000. It is that to get the commitment of people, a little freedom goes a very long way. And everyone understands with freedom comes the responsibility to perform. We call it giving a little autonomy, and getting a lot of accountability in return. That happens when you begin to treat people like mini-entrepreneurs, responsible for their own piece of the business.

Ron McDougall, who was Norm Brinker's President at Brinker International (Chili's Grill & Bar, et al), has this down to a science. He told me: "The restaurants are highly decentralized and spread out into hundreds of little entrepreneurial style businesses. We *really* do delegate, decentralize, and give a lot of autonomy! And the field stays focused on what they're doing because it's in their self interest. Everyone's in profit sharing. Everyone. The wait staff runs their own profit sharing with tips. All the managers in the units get bonuses based on what their one restaurant does in profitability. So they're kind of self-contained little businesses out there. Each restaurant is like a little $2 to $3 million factory. And when they hit their goals, they all get their bonuses. So they're very focused to make it happen." But at Brinker there's also a downside, and it's a big one. In their super-charged growth environment, there is just no room for what McDougall calls the *laggards*. "The laggards? They set bad examples for the people that are working for them and with them. Tough as it sounds—it's bad for morale to keep the laggards around. So you've got to be proactive. You've got to prune the tree. Dead branches just make the whole tree look brown."

Every company must find its own particular way to focus on employee autonomy and accountability. Brinker International's amazing record says it has found a pretty good way: Energetic commitment from the top, a completely decentralized organization with self-managing entrepreneurial units, and every employee, top to bottom, on profit sharing.

• Share Fortune And Misfortune

Nowhere in the world will employees commit to a company that isn't committed to them. This is just simple common sense. In practice this means that your people have to believe: "If it's good for the company it will be good for me. And if it's bad for the company, it's going to be bad for employees." This is the ultimate entrepreneurial mind-set about sharing fortune and misfortune.

Of course it's easier to share the good times than the bad. But for sure, no employee will be ready to share any company misfortune if they haven't experienced along the way a fair share of the company's good fortune. Unfortunately, at too many companies, large and small, the first real sharing employees are asked to participate in has been a cost reduction program, a downsizing, or some other equally unpleasant edict from headquarters. And in many other organizations, government bureaucracies come to mind, neither fortune nor misfortune have ever been shared with employees.

All these examples illustrate why handing out million dollar executive bonuses while lowly employees are being downsized is guaranteed to destroy commitment. Such actions may not be immoral—but they're certainly stupid. These are all bad habits that need to be broken, fast. The absolute, a priori, requirement for creating entrepreneurial commitment to the cause is a full sharing of both the good and tough times with your people.

• Lead By Example, Never Compromise

Leading by example is a given for most entrepreneurs. Many of them believe it's also their most powerful people management tool. It can and should be the same for every manager in a company. To not lead by example will, of course, deal a fatal blow to employee commitment. To put it squarely on the line—it's the height of arrogance to expect more of subordinates than you can personally give. This doesn't mean you have to be the best salesman or the greatest product developer in the company. But you cannot take a second seat to anyone in terms of commitment to the mission—if you hope to create entrepreneurial high commitment in your own staff. It just won't work any other way.

So never be shy in showing that you love what you do. Openly demonstrate your pride in the company's products. And never, ever, forget that the customers pay your salary also. Leading by example, and never compromising, could be your most powerful people management tool too.

HIGH PERFORMANCE:
GETTING EMPLOYEES TO BE GOOD AT WHAT THEY DO

*"If I can't sell better than anybody in the company,
I don't deserve to be President."*

—John Johnson, Founder
Johnson Publishing (Jet, Ebony, etc)

Would the Harvard Business School hire a professor who said he believed the most important management principle of all is—hard work? You doubt it? Well, that means they wouldn't hire the entrepreneur who founded and ran for many years, America's largest black owned and operated company. Meet John Johnson, whose mother, back in 1946, hocked her furniture to loan him $500 to start a magazine

in Chicago. Against great odds he created Jet magazine, and then
Ebony, and ultimately built the great media and cosmetics empire we
know today as Johnson Publishing.

Johnson said he only had two important jobs in the company: First was
to know exactly what his employees thought of their jobs and the
company, so he personally interviewed every new employee and every
departing employee. His second job was to sell a lot of advertising space,
which he learned on day one was the only way to stay alive in the
magazine business. He actually believed CEOs and Presidents of
companies are supposed to be able to sell their product. What a novel
idea that would be to most *Fortune 500* CEOs today—as well as to the
hordes of young MBAs coming out of business schools these days who
see themselves as headed straight for the executive suite. Johnson took
it even further with his motto that if he couldn't sell the product better
than anyone else he didn't deserve to be President. This is performance
aimed squarely at the heart of the enterprise—the kind that really
interests entrepreneurs.

John Johnson's high performance career—his never ending effort to be
good as what he did—brought him fame and fortune. Johnson
Publishing has become the world's largest African-American owned and
operated publishing company. And Fashion Fair Cosmetics is the world's
largest black owned cosmetics firm. Ebony, the publishing firm's flagship
product, has been the largest circulation black owned magazine every
year since its founding in the 1940s. And on a personal level, Johnson
was the first African-American to land a spot of the *Forbes 400*, the
listing of America's wealthiest people. And most important of all to
Johnson himself, was President Clinton's bestowal upon him in 1995,
the Presidential Medal Of Freedom, the country's highest civilian
award!

Recently, due to the double-whammy of the digital age and the deep
recession, the Johnson Publishing empire has had to face the same
problem as the rest of the print-media world—sharply declining
advertising revenue. Even so, CEO Linda Johnson Rice, (John
Johnson's daughter by the way) has vowed to not sell the company and

tough out these new challenges under the same motto her father made famous years ago: "Failure is a word I don't accept." As of this writing, she's succeeding as the business is weathering the storm in reasonably good shape. Under her leadership, the company has completely re-designed both Ebony and Jet magazines to appeal to younger readers, gone heavily into digital publishing, and installed a new high-powered team of senior managers and editors.

The fact remains, the brands built by John Johnson are so much a part of the heritage of African-American entrepreneurship, and are so commercially valuable, that if the company were ever put on the block there will be buyers aplenty. Interestingly, one who has tried in the past to buy the business is none other than Earvin "Magic" Johnson, the former basketball hero turned successful entrepreneur. At least that ownership change would keep the family name on the door! One thing that will never change however is that John Johnson, who died in 2005 at the age of 87, has left an indelible mark on entrepreneurship, business and the value of hard work in America.

As everyone knows, all manner of managerial techniques and training programs have been invented to improve the performance of your employees. Some of them may even be useful, if your people first understand the entrepreneurial mandate that says making more products and selling more customers is the goal—not writing long e-mails that nobody reads, or looking good at staff meetings, or attending another management conference. In other words, you want your people to perform like entrepreneurs—and actually move the business forward.

To the entrepreneur, high performance is an on-the-job fight to the finish—not scoring points for their next performance review. And their performance is highly focused on what matters most—making more products and selling more customers. In this arena, your employees' existing job descriptions and performance reviews are probably pretty useless. They rarely focus on customers and products and almost never help you "get better at what you do." Here are four key steps to getting your people started on the road to entrepreneurial high performance:

• Get Better At What You Do

Seeking continuous improvement in product quality has been used for decades. How about applying the same idea to people? We need to tell employees that their most important job is to improve something every day. This may or may not require working harder, but it surely means working smarter. Show me an employee who on his or her own, is seeking out new ideas and methods to improve their performance, and I'll show you a high potential mini-entrepreneur for your company.

Examples of entrepreneurs who continuously seek to get better at what they do are legion. For starters, there is Akio Morita, founder of Sony, who spent four years of his life knocking on doors in the U.S. to learn how to make and sell electronic products for the American market. And what about Karl Benz, who spent his entire life designing and engineering improvements for his beautiful cars? And right up to today, we have the wonderful example of Steve Jobs still coming to work every day at Apple to work with his teams to find the next great product! On and on it goes—as it should for you and the employees at your own company.

And one important caveat for corporate entrepreneurs—watch out for your own corporate HR and Training departments. Your biggest challenge may be keeping them out of your way as they try to put your people through every cockamamie seminar dreamed up by the endless stream of industrial psychologists, motivation gurus, and business school professors hawking their programs. To entrepreneurs, "getting better at what you do" doesn't include New Age retreats at Indian Sweat Lodges, being screamed at by Tony Robbins clones, or even talked down to by Harvard Business School professors who have never in their life had to meet a payroll.

• Winning At Quality, Quantity, Speed and Cost

Quality, quantity, speed, and cost are the entrepreneur's four fundamental parameters of high performance. How good can I work? How much can I do? How fast can I do it? And how efficiently? The answers to these four commonsense questions will define the competitiveness of your employees and your company. Instilling these fundamentals in your people, constantly getting better at them, and measuring every employee by them will give you the employee performance standards you'll need to end up in the winner's circle. To help make these fundamentals easier to remember, the following is an entrepreneurial dream team that illustrates extreme achievement in each of the four parameters of high performance.

- Quality—How Good: Gottlieb Daimler and Karl Benz set out to make the highest quality car in the world every year. One hundred years later, their great company is still doing it.

- Quantity—How Much: Ray Kroc started a hamburger empire that has grown to 30,000 locations around the world and each day sells enough food to feed 50 million people. How much did he accomplish? A lot!

- Speed—How Fast: Think about Larry Hillblom and DHL's expansion to 120 countries in a decade, which is still an all-time record.

- Cost—How Efficient: Lito Rodriguez' DryWash technology in Brazil uses not a drop of water, saving 316 liters of fresh water per car and uses 99.5 percent less electricity per car than its traditional competitors. Now that's efficient!

Such a list could go on and on, but I think you get the point. Such incredible achievements are simply a reminder that the greatest danger in trying to create high performance may be setting your sights too low. So why not aim for the stars and create your own Daimlers, Benzs, Krocs, Hillbloms, and Rodriguezs across your workforce? If you even come close, you will simply be unstoppable.

• Save Your Best For Customers And Products

To really drive home this point, let's briefly revisit a company that can only be described as obsessive in its focus on customers and products. Of course we're talking about the company Walt Disney founded, and specifically their theme parks in Anaheim, Orlando, Tokyo, and outside Paris. I reviewed the Disney training manual for hosts and hostesses working in the theme parks. The section titled *The Disney Look* is fascinating. There are separate sections for hosts and hostesses with instructions on everything from costumes and hair styling to deodorants and fingernails. The paragraph on deodorants for hosts sets the tone and pulls no punches: "Due to close contact with guests and fellow cast members, the use of a deodorant or antiperspirant is required. The use of heavy colognes is discouraged. A light aftershave or cologne is acceptable." *The Disney Look* guideline for a hostess' fingernails seems to cover everything that could ever possibly happen to your nails, "Fingernails should be kept clean and if polish is used, it should be clear or in flesh tones in cream enamels. Polishes that are dark red, frosted, gold or silver toned are not considered part of the 'Disney Look.' Fingernails should not exceed one fourth of an inch beyond the fingertip." The introduction to *The Disney Look* says that strict adherence to these guidelines is a condition of employment whether you're a ticket taker, a street sweeper, performing as Captain Hook, or strolling down Main Street as Sleeping Beauty. At first glance, some of Disney's rules and expectations of employees may appear strict and even unrealistic in today's world. But creating the best products in the world and the best customer service in the world doesn't come easy. Disney's attention to detail is, of course, legendary. Extremely high performance standards are set and expected of all employees. Every inch of the park has to be picture perfect. Not just the streets and the attractions, but right down to the details of every cast member's appearance.

In contrast to Disney hosts and hostesses delivering their best performances around customers and products, some employees in other organizations, and not just giant ones, seem to save their best shots for internal turf wars and impressing the brass. Enormous effort and expense can go into these side issues. Of course this kind of behavior can only happen if the brass (you in this case!) allows it to happen. If employees believe that making a great board presentation will get them more kudos than coming in on Saturday to make sure the right product was shipped to their customer, you've already got a huge performance problem as well as a dangerous lack of focus on what's important to your enterprise. To an entrepreneur fighting for survival, devoting resources to such nonsense would be akin to having a corporate death-wish. If you really want to transform your employees into high performers, you simply must keep them focused on customers and products. There is no better way to do that than being focused yourself—which takes us to the final practice, leading by example.

• Lead By Example, Never Compromise

Above all, entrepreneurs are high performers. They have to personally set their company's standard of performance. Corporate entrepreneurs have to do the same. Of course you don't have to be a better performer than anyone who works for you. But you have to be the first in line to pitch in and get a job done, and the last to leave after it's finished. In plain-spoken English, you've got to set the standard on effort and hard work. What you don't need is another seminar on the meaning of leadership. Leading your people to higher levels of performance is pretty simple really. As John Johnson believed when he was building Jet and Ebony into the world's leading black magazines, you can't achieve anything in life without hard work. This may mean different things in different settings, but getting out of the office and doing real, frontline work every so often would be a terrific way to start. You can get away with a lot of things as an up and coming entrepreneurial manager, but being lazy isn't one of them.

The best example I've ever seen of doing just that is my old friend Po Chung, the very first entrepreneur/partner signed up by Dalsey, Hillblom, and Lynn, the three young law students who founded DHL. Today Po is Chairman Emeritus of the company. He earned his entrepreneurial stripes in Hong Kong, that beehive of energetic entrepreneurship which has to be the hardest working and fastest moving business environment in the world. Po founded DHL Hong Kong way back in 1972. At that early stage, no one had ever heard of DHL. There were no manuals to read or training classes to attend to learn how to run the world's first international courier business. He learned it by doing it all himself. His five step program provides a powerful, personal prescription for leading by example:

- Personally feel the need for the product.
- Personally deliver the product to customers.

- Stick to the basics and don't get side-tracked by management theories.
- Personally demonstrate belief in, and commitment to, the company mission.
- Continuously pass steps one through four on to your people.

INSPIRING OTHERS:
CREATING MINI- ENTREPRENEURS

> *"The genius of the Honda Motor Company*
> *is in the average worker."*

> —Soichiro Honda, Founder
> Honda Motor Company

Most of us can figure out how to inspire ourselves. But can we inspire others? The successful entrepreneur as well as the successful manager has to be able to do it. But it's a lot easier said than done. Both entrepreneurs and managers have a spotty track record on fostering high commitment and high performance in others.

The entrepreneur's excuse rings a familiar bell. Like great, natural athletes who make lousy coaches, entrepreneurs are often unaware of what they do. They don't think about it much and thus have a hard time passing on their "natural" ability as self-inspired enterprisers. For company managers it can be even more of a challenge. Not only do they have to *learn* entrepreneurial behavior to model it for subordinates, they usually have to also fend off a whole world of professional personnel people, in and out of the company, giving them a lot of really bad advice. Even today, fostering mini-entrepreneurs in big companies can easily get overrun by a lot of loony HR programs and theories.

But it's far from hopeless. We can't *force* employees to be more entrepreneurial, but *self-inspired* commitment and performance can be fostered in 99% of all people. As with everything else in this book, the best answers for getting people to "love what they do and be good at doing it," come from knowing how entrepreneurs behave—or more precisely, knowing the circumstances and environment that inspires their behavior in the first place. To a large degree, this environment can be duplicated in any job in any company. So the best way—maybe the only way—to "inspire others" is to get them to inspire themselves. The single most important thing you can do is to show the way through personal example. And for showing the way, you'll never find a better example than Soichiro Honda.

Soichiro Honda was, hands down, the most interesting Japanese entrepreneur of the 20th century. His death in 1991 was greeted with the greatest outpouring of grief and respect by employees ever accorded a Japanese corporate leader. Honda was an outsider to Japan's industrial establishment. He was the son of a blacksmith, who at 16 began his working career as a mechanic. He moved on to auto racing but after a near fatal accident, decided to try producing scooters and eventually cars. With only a third grade education, he was the original blue collar automobile man's man.

He was also a master of the carrot and stick, and never hesitated to use them. He understood that inspiring others fundamentally boiled down to answering the "what's in it for me" question. Honda answered by showering attention on good performers, always promoting fairly (Honda's relatives were not even allowed to work in the company), and putting his money behind his compassion (such as building entire factories just for handicapped workers). He also carried a big stick. He demanded top performance from Honda's engineers as well as from the engines they made. His temper flared when they missed. In one crushing outburst he could devastate a mis-performing engineer or production team. The next morning however, he was back, sleeves rolled up, working together until they solved the problem.

"The workers just idolized him." This is Tetsuo Chino (again) remembering Soichiro Honda. He grew up with him in the car business and knew him well. Chino was President of Honda USA from its startup in Marysville, Ohio in the late seventies all the way through their record breaking decade of the eighties. He was in fact the first man to produce

Japanese cars with American workers. And he was also the man who pushed the Accord to become the number one selling car in the U.S.. I met with Chino at Honda Headquarters in Tokyo. He had recently entered semi-retirement, a phase in Honda known as "soft running." He had enthusiastically agreed to meet me to tell the *inside story* of the real genius of Soichiro Honda.

"The Honda Company is probably most famous for its attention to customers. It also has a reputation of being the automobile company run by real automobile lovers. But maybe the untold story of Honda is how the founder inspired his people—even those American auto workers who everyone said couldn't make a competitive car anymore. Everyone, that is, except Mr. Honda."

So what kind of man was he? "On the one hand Soichiro Honda was tough. He was a self-made man and he didn't like to be guided by somebody else. You know our MITI (the powerful Ministry of International Trade and Industry) which is full of Japanese bureaucrats? When Mr. Honda tried to enter the auto business from motorcycles, MITI said no! They told him: 'Japan has enough auto makers already. You keep making scooters.' So Soichiro Honda fought the government. He told them: 'MITI is not our shareholder. You cannot decide my destiny. I want to make automobiles and certainly you cannot make that decision for me.' This was a famous fight in Tokyo. So he entered the auto business in spite of MITI. This was not done in Japan. But Soichiro Honda was a very unique Japanese.

"On the other hand, he was a humanistic person. He always said the technology is just a means to make people happy. The company was founded as a people oriented company. And even though he was the founder, he didn't allow his heirs in the company and none of the top executives were allowed to have their heirs in the company either. This was appreciated by the employees and is very unusual in famous Japanese companies. He was interested in the people in the community also, like the handicapped. Do you know he founded three plants in Japan specially designed to employ only handicapped people? Anyway he was very people oriented himself. Very easy to talk to. He was kind of an entertainer actually. He played music for people and entertained them. When you met him, he tried to have you enjoy the time. He tried to make everybody happy. When he was inducted into the American Automotive Hall Of Fame, all the dealers came. They said they appreciated his efforts and his products. But Mr. Honda said: 'It's not me, all the merit has to go to you, the dealers.' Then he disappeared from the head-table. He asked for a wine waiter's uniform. He dressed in the uniform and reappeared. He served wine to every dealer. He was saying to each: 'Thank you, thank you. It is only because of you I'm even in this Hall Of Fame.' I know that no other Japanese CEO would behave this way. And I doubt that any of the American CEOs in Detroit would either. But that was the type of man Soichiro Honda was.

"Mr. Honda truly thought the genius of the company was in the workers. He always liked the engineering shops and the assembly line plants best. He went there a lot himself and discussed things with the workers and the technicians and the engineers. He discussed things in detail. He would make his comments and he listened to their ideas. He strongly inspired employees about the product. Of course when he was young, he raced cars. He had a very bad accident and quit, but he was always keen to develop race cars. This is an important thing at Honda. It's not just for promotion purposes. It's very good for the engineers in developing new ideas and new technologies. Working on racing engines is very serious and is very good for timing, for faster learning. He always said: 'Beating the clock is the most important factor to becoming number one.' That kind of spirit about high performance cars was very inspiring to the engineers and even the production workers. You can foster a good spirit in the automobile business through racing. Honda people in Japan, in the States, everywhere, are very proud of our *Formula One* championships. You see, Mr. Honda believed technology has no end. You can always improve it. For example that's why we produced the all aluminum body car and we're now testing the 100 mpg engine. It's also why Honda was the first company to meet the tough USA emission standards. There are many difficulties in doing these things but our engineers are always encouraged to challenge limits. Automobile employees are very motivated by making machines no one else can make!

"Of course I must also say he was a very serious minded person. If you made any mistake in the business, he could get so mad. His anger was not just emotional. He used it as a kind of teacher too. He really wanted all of us to learn to do better. The next day he would recover and come back to us and ask how we could all improve the situation. He always did this. He was aggressive about the business but he would always try to help us. He did this especially with the young people. They knew he was serious but also there to help them. As I said, he was a very unique Japanese."

One can argue that Soichiro-san wasn't out to create "mini-entrepreneurs." Surely he wouldn't have put it that way himself. But the facts are, he inspired Honda employees to extraordinary levels of commitment and performance. Extraordinary commitment to the business of making the best motorcycles and cars in the world. And extraordinary performance in product innovation and customer service. At the end of the day, call it what you want, but this is what entrepreneurial leaders are supposed to be able to do—whether it's a factory in Japan or in Marysville, Ohio.

Honda clearly understood the power of positive and negative consequences. He knew that employee commitment and performance ultimately comes down to answering one question: "What are the consequences to employees for good performance and what are the consequences for poor performance?" This is the question you'll have to answer too—if you hope to inspire your employees to become mini-entrepreneurs in your organization. It's all about understanding the— *power of consequences.*

THE POWER OF CONSEQUENCES

There really is no mystery to why people behave the way they do. The platinum rule of human behavior is, people behave in their own self-interest. They avoid doing things where they perceive the personal consequences will be negative. They do other things where they perceive the positive consequences will outweigh the negatives. This applies to everything we do, including work. It applies in spades to the entrepreneur. The performance of entrepreneurs is dominated by the "life and death" consequences of meeting or not meeting customer demands—pure and simple!

The reality is, entrepreneurs are self inspired by the immediate, often severe and always personal consequences of their actions. There is no place to hide. There are no six month probation periods. Your kid's next meal is on the line. On the upside, there's no supervisor stealing your glory—or otherwise deciding whether you did well or not. If you do well, you'll get immediate and powerful feedback from the folks who really count—your customers. Entrepreneurs exist in an environment where their performance really matters and the consequences—positive or negative—are razor sharp.

Bureaucrats just don't live in this world. Big, modern bureaucracies are notorious for their ability to insulate employees from both the positive and negative results of their work. This is probably bad psychology—it's certainly bad business. Too many companies, with too many personnel theories, are hopelessly stuck in neutral—no personal positives, no personal negatives, just the clear signal that individual commitment and performance really don't matter much. Managing employee consequences would seem a reasonable thing for bosses to do. Everyone knows that just giving a little personal feedback can be powerful—and it doesn't cost a cent. For any lackluster bureaucracy, instilling powerful employee consequences for everyone is the fastest, surest, and cheapest way to transform themselves. The great mystery is why so many can't seem to figure this out.

Not managing consequences—or mis-managing them—can produce some really awful results. Some company managements operate in total denial. They behave as if everyone's doing their best—nobody's performing poorly—even if the company is on a collision course with bankruptcy. The cruelest and dumbest scenario comes with the inevitable layoffs—when every single employee says, "Gee, why me? I got a great performance evaluation just last year!" At the other extreme, somewhere along the line we've convinced ourselves that sales people like special recognition but no one else really needs it. Elaborate sales commission schemes and trips to Hawaii are devised to recognize the sales force, while the factory workers and clerks get to read about it in the company magazine. The biggest travesty in the management of consequences is the wacky and wonderful world of executive compensation and privilege—compared to the reward system of the rank and file. In the USA at least, many CEOs and their top lieutenants seem to work in a performance system with only three levels of consequences: high financial reward, higher financial reward, and highest financial reward! To illustrate, CEO compensation as a factor of average employee pay has been sky-rocketing for decades. In 1950 CEOs were paid about 25 times the average worker's pay. By 1980 it had risen to 100 times. And today, even in the worst recession since the 1930s, it's a staggering 350 times.

But there is hope—for those companies at least who really want to inspire their people. Any organization can start giving its employees straight, meaningful answers to the eternal question: "What happens to me if I do, and what happens to me if I don't?" For some companies, this may only require some fine-tuning. For others it will require a major overhaul in their performance systems from top to bottom. What it requires is re-creating the real-life environment of entrepreneurs. This means creating in all jobs and departments, rewards and penalties that are connected to real results. A more entrepreneurial performance environment sends a very direct message. Both good fortune and misfortune are felt by everyone, starting with top management. The bureaucratic notion that no one is responsible has to go. When a client or market is lost, no one can just stand around and just shrug their shoulders. And when a client or market is won, everyone wins. Not just the salesman, but the factory worker and the processing clerk too. And top management, just like entrepreneurs, will live and die on how well the company satisfies customers! This is the *power of consequences* at work.

Finally we get to the crux of the matter—the missing link in this business of inspiring others and creating mini-entrepreneurs. Transforming bureaucrats to entrepreneurs is a tall order. What if they just don't want to be transformed? What do I do then? Is there some fail-safe button to push? Believe it or not, there is a button to push. In fact there are three. They're each covered in the next section, so read on!

THREE PROVEN WAYS TO INSTILL CONSEQUENCES

"Our folks don't expect something for nothing . . .
they want to win so badly, they just go out there and do it!"

—Sam Walton, Founder
Wal-Mart Stores

Even a charismatic, entrepreneurial leader like Sam Walton, arriving at each store in his old Chevy pick-up and leading the troops in the Wal-Mart fight song, found that hoopla can only take you so far in the business of inspiring employees. Walton got more mileage out of company hoopla than most, probably because he was so darn good at doing it. But even Wal-Mart, the fastest growing, and now biggest, company in the history of the world uses carefully thought out policies to help answer the "what's in it for me" question. Their most prominent effort is an across the board employee stock ownership program for their 2.1 million employees.

Of course the one-two punch of having a leader like Perot, Lever, Johnson, Honda, or Sam Walton—combined with solid, on-going policies that foster a spirit of enterprise in workers, is a tough combo to beat. But companies don't get to have their founders around forever. Since Mr. Walton's death several years ago, those same policies and programs he installed have probably become even more essential to keeping that spirit alive. And certainly in giant companies like Wal-Mart, with more employees than any private company in the world, it really would be impossible for any single leader to "lay hands" on every employee.

The fact is, most of the efforts around the world to foster corporate entrepreneurship are being driven by managers in large companies, not entrepreneurs. Which brings us face to face with the challenge of developing entrepreneurial employees without the help of a Sam

Walton or a Ross Perot. In our experience, the only way to do that is to figure out how to instill entrepreneurial style consequences throughout the organization.

Fortunately, there are at least three proven ways to inspire more entrepreneurial behavior in company managers and workers. They can become owners or shareholders of the company. They can create a new, little company within the company as an "intrapreneur." Or they can be the entrepreneur of their own job or department—by working under an "entrepreneurial performance system." All three ways will help you answer that first big question on everyone's mind: "What's in it for me?" Here's a brief description of each.

• Workers As Owners

Miracles do happen! Many companies in recent years have become completely employee owned, with incredible results. There are examples every year of workers buying their company and miraculously saving it from bankruptcy! They do it with the same products, the same customers, and the same people. How can it be? It's not because they get smarter or more skilled. It's because they have, for the first time, a personal stake in the success and failure of their company. It does seem a bit like a miracle, doesn't it?

There is no question that the older, more common "partnership" form of organization has always produced incredible levels of commitment and performance. Regardless of what one thinks about lawyers, auditors, and consultants, we have to admit that the senior partners, the junior partners, and the wana-be partners usually work circles around their own clients—which are mostly large, public corporations.

Less radical forms of employee ownership have been around for years. These would include all the various types of employee stock ownership programs. Even these efforts, where employees may only own a small number of shares, have a positive impact on results. All the studies in the U.S. clearly show that companies with employee shareholders out-perform competitors with no such employee involvement. The example of Wal-Mart is a good one. They believe so strongly that employees should be shareholders; they've made the level of participation by workers a part of every manager's annual performance review and bonus. Considering all the flack Wal-Mart has taken over the years about how it treats its "associates," this massive employee ownership program stands out as the major "inconvenient truth" to critics.

Whether it's Wal-Mart, W. L. Gore, and Anderson Consulting in North America, or Thomson/RCA and John Lewis in Europe, or some of the newly privatized state industries in China, the result is the same. It's just common sense that any form of employee ownership simply has to have some positive effect on the behavior of employees. There's no mystery to it. The only mystery is why 85% of companies around the world still don't do it.

And beyond the realm of *workers becoming owners* in private stock companies, as those mentioned above, we can also look at the 150 year old Credit Union movement and other types of cooperatives. Credit Unions are perhaps the best known of all cooperatives and they take the process to a whole new level in that both employees and customers own the business! I've had the good fortune of working with a lot of credit unions, and their national association, and I must say they are fascinating organizations. Management serves at the pleasure of both employees and customers—all of which stands corporate conventional wisdom on its head. This may well be the new "third wave" of capitalism—and the ultimate model for creating entrepreneurial organizations!

• Intrapreneurship
This is an old idea with a new name. Give a small group of highly committed, top performing managers a little seed money, a lot of autonomy, participation in the financial results, and ask them to create a new business for the corporation—but outside the corporation. For some big companies such as Xerox and Levi Strauss, this method has provided the chance to create new entrepreneurial businesses and not lose the entrepreneurs. The only down-side of intrapreneuring is that only a few can play. The other 99% of your people will not be involved.

Even so, it's a terrific way to get some entrepreneurial excitement—and growth—back into your business. Below are the major steps commonly followed in implementing an *intrapreneurship project*.

- Everyone in the company is invited to participate. Nobody is left out at this stage. Small team submissions are usually encouraged.

- A customer/product vision or plan is submitted by any employee or team that wants to be considered. The plan goes to a panel of respected company executives/board members. At least some panel members must have had direct experience in starting up new products or businesses.

- A full evaluation of the proposed venture is conducted by the panel and an initial go/no go decision is rendered.

- For those plans receiving an initial go-ahead, a *contract* is agreed to by the corporation and the intrapreneur team. The *intrapreneurial contract* covers key elements such as start-up capital needs and an equity/compensation arrangement.

- Other corporate resources and assistance that may be required is also agreed to by the corporation and the intrapreneur team.

- Start-up phase begins with agreed deadlines for the development of product/service prototypes and the securing of prospect/customer commitments. Actual, or even trial, usage of the product/service prototype by prospective clients is strongly encouraged.

- The start-up phase is evaluated by the panel and the venture is either killed, significantly modified, or approved for full-scale start-up.

- **The Entrepreneurial Performance System (EPS)**
If making workers the owners isn't for you, and if intrapreneurship affects too few people, what can you do? How can you get thousands of employees to behave more entrepreneurially right now, in their current jobs? Here's the answer! We call it the "Entrepreneurial Performance

System," the third proven way to foster the spirit of enterprise in your people. In my experience this is the practical step any manager, in any company, could take tomorrow. To help get you started, a full description follows.

CREATING AN ENTREPRENEURIAL PERFORMANCE SYSTEM

Remember Lincoln Electric? Produce a lot of good welding equipment and you'll be the highest paid workers in the world. Produce poor quality or no welding equipment at all and you'll get nothing. That's the deal at Lincoln. And that is how an *Entrepreneurial Performance System (EPS)* is supposed to work. It's certainly working for Lincoln Electric in Cleveland, Ohio, and it can work for you.

Our Entrepreneurial Performance System covers all causes of sub-par performance, but relies most heavily on consequences as the primary people management tool. In so doing, the EPS focuses on the most critical factor in the real-world performance environment of entrepreneurs. In fact, when creating entrepreneurial people is the goal, managing the consequences can be more important than managing the people per se. To implement the Entrepreneurial Performance System in your company, a few basic ideas have to be in place. The four most important are:

• Consequences Determine Behavior
Every employee has to know the answer to the "what's in it for me?" question. Positive and negative consequences are the most powerful influencers of behavior. The key is to make sure every employee feels them.

• Everyone Has A Business To Run
Every employee has a business within the business to run. They all have products or services to offer, and customers or users to serve. Like entrepreneurs, the final test of their performance has to be based on how well their products satisfy their customers.

• **Customers Give Consequences—Bosses Give Feedback**
The important consequences always come from customers. The boss' job
is to feedback to workers the positive or negative consequences from
their performance and make sure that something happens because of
them.

• **The Company And The Workers Have A Shared Destiny**
The consequences to workers and the company must be in sync. What's
good for the company should be good for the workers—and vice versa.

The Entrepreneurial Performance System diagram below expands on
the simple *Power Of Consequences* model illustrated back in Chapter 5.
The point is to duplicate for your employees, to the extent possible, the
real-world performance environment of entrepreneurs. The diagram
depicts the complete performance system in which we all work. The
underlying principles never change and they apply to entrepreneurs,
bureaucrats, and everyone in between.

THE COMPLETE ENTREPRENEURIAL
PERFORMANCE SYSTEM

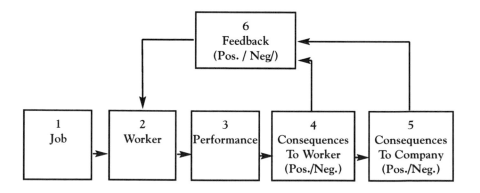

The EPS's first fundamental assumption is that 99% of all human behavior can be explained in two words: *stimulus* and *response*. The sales clerk sees a customer enter the store and responds with courteous service—for example. Or the shipping clerk gets a customer order and responds by shipping the product the same afternoon. The simple definitions of the various components of the performance system are:

1. The job or task at hand—this is the stimulus or "input" to the worker. It could be anything from the key points in a job description, to the every changing daily requirement of the job, to meeting a department's annual plan and budget.

2. The worker—whether a self-inspired entrepreneur or an entrenched bureaucrat, a senior manager or a lowly shipping clerk, the worker acts as the central processing unit of the human performance system.

3. Performance of the worker—this is the response or "output" of the worker. Whether measuring hard items like annual sales achieved, or soft areas such as customer courtesy, the worker's output is the key thing we are trying to improve.

4. Consequences to the worker—the effect of the performance back on the worker. Important consequences for workers ultimately come from customers—they are not made up results from a supervisor. And for good performance, you want to make sure there is a positive consequence back to the worker. Likewise, for poor performance, you want to make equally certain there is a negative consequence to the worker. When this doesn't happen, we say the consequences are *out of balance* with performance.

5. Consequences to the company—the effect of the performance on the company. These are the bottom line, profit and loss results as recorded by the company. There can be little debate or negotiating about consequences to the company. Again, you want to ensure

that the consequences to the company are in sync with the consequences delivered back to workers—positive or negative.

6. Feedback—the job of the manager is to make sure those consequences are fed back to the worker in an accurate, timely, and impactful way. Whether it's a sincere thank you for a job well done, a $1,000 award for a good suggestion, or when necessary, the delivery of a negative performance review, the feedback loop has to be completed by the manager.

While the components and principles of the system never change, individual responses (performance) to a particular stimulus (job or task at hand), can be quite different. Some sales clerks are courteous to customers, and others aren't. One warehouse worker may ship the product the same day he gets the order while another will ship it three days later. Why the different responses? The following chart illustrates the possible causes and the frequency of their occurrence.

Component	Cause	Frequency %
Job	Job not clear.	10
Worker	Lack of knowledge.	15
Performance	Lack of resources.	10
Consequences	Out of balance	65
Feedback	Poor / Non-existent	included in above 65

The fact is, the most common cause of a breakdown in the EPS, that is people not doing what they "should," is that the consequences are totally out of whack. They are either non-existent or even the reverse of what they should be. The shipping clerk in the example above, perceives it's easier to ship products out the door at a more leisurely pace—and he knows nobody will call him on it because he also perceives that no one in management gives a damn. So to his way of thinking, he's getting a positive consequence—for doing something that's about to give the company a negative consequence—a late shipment resulting in a disgruntled customer. The related, second greatest cause is that the boss indeed never gets around to feeding back the information to the worker regarding the negative company consequences he's created. These are breakdowns that occur over and over and over again in most organizations. But as we've stated before, practically by definition, this never happen to entrepreneurs. The biggest study in the USA on the causes of employee performance problems concluded that bad, or non-existent, management of consequences represents an amazing two-thirds of all poor performance!

This of course leads to the EPS' second fundamental assumption: The greatest influencer of behavior is the workers' perception of the consequences, positive or negative, to his performance. That's why we call it "the almighty power of consequences." As the chart illustrates, *Consequences* are number one by a wide margin. And it makes sense. Think about it; how many jobs have you had where the consequences were totally out of whack? They were either nonexistent, or the reverse of what they should have been, and/or your boss never got around to feeding back those consequences, in any meaningful way, to you. The other possible causes—the job is not clear or well defined, the worker doesn't know how to do the job, or there is a lack of resources to do the job—are all breakdowns that occur less frequently—and frankly are easy to fix. The small causal percentages in these categories makes sense if you think about it. Most workers know *what* their job is, and most workers know *how* to do their job, and most workers have adequate resources to do the job they're assigned. End of story!

This is why we say consequences represent the biggest single difference between entrepreneurial and bureaucratic behavior. Entrepreneurs live and die on the direct feedback of market consequences. The consequences are powerful and personal and the feedback is immediate. In bureaucracies it's exactly the opposite. The consequences are out of balance, they rarely come from customers, and the feedback only comes once a year at your annual performance review.

So if you're looking for the place to start, to entrepreneurially inspire your employees, you've found it. The key to creating entrepreneurial performance is to set in place, strong positive/negatives consequences—and make absolutely certain those consequences are fed back to all performers. It's the sure-fire way to get employees to *want* to change their own behavior on the job—and awaken the spirit of enterprise in your company. (*The EPS is a slightly modified version of the original work of my good friend and mentor on human performance, Dr. Geary A. Rummler. His landmark work on "Human Performance Systems" was begun many years ago at the University of Michigan. Rummler refined and greatly expanded his research over the years while founding three separate consulting and training firms. We have adapted his early, and admittedly simple, view of human behavior to our "EPS" for one reason only—it so clearly illustrates why entrepreneurs do what they do. I highly recommend Geary Rummler's own books and advisory services on the broad subject of human performance.*)

GOD HELP YOU AND YOUR EMPLOYEES

At the end of the day, why should people care about being self-inspired? What does it really matter if they love what they do and are good at doing it? I used to think, in my Harvard Business School days, that the reason employees should be self-inspired was because it made them better workers. It was good for the company. But today, I realize that's not the most important reason at all. Of course having employees who love what they do *is* a big plus for the company. But the really important reason you should be self-inspired about what you do—is you! The good news in all this is, if you do indeed love your job, it's good for you—*and coincidentally*—it's also good for your company. It's the ultimate win/win situation for all of us who aren't born rich and really do have to spend our lives laboring somewhere.

Chapter 12

What's Really Required To Create The Entrepreneurial Organization

TURNING AROUND A (FRENCH/AMERICAN) SLEEPING GIANT

"Developing better managers is not the answer to turning around a company. You have to get beyond managing. Every employee has to learn to behave as if the company is his own—as a true entrepreneur."

—Hervé Hannebicque
    Sr. Vice President, Entrepreneurship
    Thomson/RCA

How many 120 year old companies do you know of that could show this level of growth? This is the kind of explosive rise we've only seen with a few internet start-ups. Do the math. It's pretty staggering.

Total Market Value In French Francs

1996: FFr 1 (Government's "symbolic" asking price.)
1997: FFr 10 million
1998: FFr 6 billion
1999: FFr 13 billion
2000: FFr 100 billion (Actual market value on NYSE.)

This is the story of Thomson/RCA S. A., the giant French electronics company, with revenues today of $8 billion. It is actually a marriage of two old and great companies—Thomson Electric and RCA—which had both been kicked around and mis-managed for years. The comeback seems almost a miracle. *(This interview focuses on the five year period from 1996 to 2001, when one of the greatest European/American corporate turnarounds in history occurred. As of mid 2010, the turnaround has surpassed all the goals set for it back in 1996—when the post-Mitterrand French government began divesting its large portfolio of nationalized companies. The CEO was Thierry Breton, hand-picked by President Chirac to oversee the turn-around. Breton's right-hand man and architect of the transformation was my good friend Hervé Hannebicque, who carried the title of Senior Vice President— Entrepreneurship. The company name today is Technicolor S. A., is still listed on the NY Stock Exchange, and continues to thrive. But our interest here is on the amazing policies and activities, taken under the Breton/Hannebicque era, which created the amazing turn-around. Thierry Breton went on to be France's Minister of Economy, Finance and Industry. My French pal, Hervé, has become—you guessed it—France's top consultant on corporate turn-arounds.)*

From year-end '96 to year-end '99 net income rose from a FFr 3 billion loss to a FF1 billion profit. The new shareholders, including over 17,000 employees, saw their stock value sky-rocket from the IPO price of 21 Euros in October, 1999 to 130 Euros by March 2000. Not bad for a company that, for years, had been the laughing stock of French industry. That is until 1997 when Jacques Chirac, the President of France, hand-picked a new, entrepreneurial management team to turn this national embarrassment into the pride of French industry!

But first, a word on the interesting and intertwined history of Thomson and RCA: Elihu Thomson was born in Manchester, England in 1853 and moved to Philadelphia as a young man. He began his working life as a high school chemistry and mechanics teacher. He teamed up with Edward Houston in 1882 to form Thomson-Houston Company in Connecticut. Ten years later Thomson-Houston merged with Thomas Edison's company, Edison General Electric, to form General Electric Company, the same GE that is going strong today. Thomson smartly kept his international rights and re-located to Paris and "re-founded" Thomson where it is still headquartered today. Elihu Thomson was also a prolific inventor, eventually holding over 700 patents. The fate of the company in France was not rosy however. After surviving two world wars and the Great Depression, the socialist policies of the Mitterrand government finally did it in. As a nationalized French company, things went from bad to worse. Finally, in 1997, the pro-enterprise Chirac government determined to privatize Thomson along with many other famous French companies struggling under government control.

Radio Corporation of America (RCA) was originally set up, prior to WW1, as a subsidiary of the British Marconi Company. The man often called the founder of RCA was long time CEO, David Sarnoff. Actually he started out as a junior employee but rose through the ranks to lead the company to its greatest triumphs over nearly five decades. His first brush with fame involved the radio way back in 1912. Sarnoff was the operator of Marconi's transmission station on the roof of Wanamaker's department store in New York City. On the fateful evening of April 14, and for 3 horrible days afterwards, his was the only radio in America receiving transmissions from the SS Olympic, the first ship that reached the sinking Titanic and provided the names of the 750 passengers rescued from the icy water. After World War I, the U.S. Government became alarmed that the fast-growing radio industry in America was owned by a foreign company. At that time radio was viewed not only as a potentially huge commercial activity, but also as a strategic defense asset. In 1919, under U.S. Government pressure, RCA became an American company with the General Electric Company (yes, the same GE) initially holding the major ownership and dominant control. Eventually, of course, RCA became a fully independent, *Fortune 100* company. It led the worldwide growth of television and created famous subsidiaries like NBC. By the 1970s however RCA was losing ground to its Japanese competitors and seemed to be losing its focus. It then tried being a conglomerate which made things worse, and ultimately fell on very tough times. Ironically, the company that came in and picked up the pieces was none other than General Electric. GE stepped in and purchased the core businesses and sold off unrelated activities such as the Hertz auto rental business.

By the early nineties the fortunes of these two companies with common roots going back a hundred years, had been connected once again. Thomson, now owned by the French government, realized it had to obtain entree to both American technology and American markets if it ever hoped to compete with the likes of GE, Matsushita, Sony and Philips. So where did it look for help? That's right. The General Electric Company with all those RCA assets. After much negotiating, Thomson bought most of the RCA patents, products, and manufacturing plants it wanted from GE. It also got a respected American brand name, thousands of good RCA people, and perhaps most important, a presence in America.

Let's pick up the story here from Hervé Hannebicque, an original member of that new team assembled in Paris. I asked him what he and the privatization team found when they took over Thomson/RCA— which they renamed Thomson Multimedia (TMM). In his very French, French accent Hervé didn't mince words: "At Thomson, when we came in March or April of 1997, we had inherited a company in large trouble. Large trouble in terms of results. The operating results showed a loss of FFr 640 million. It was even worse for the net results—a loss of FFr 3 billion for 1996. So there was no time to do anything but to engage in actions which could affect the profitability. It was a survival situation. We needed to do something, because if we didn't, we were against the wall. It was difficult to progress and move forward. So we needed to take decisions quickly in order to put this company on another track."

I then asked him how in the world Thomson had gotten into such a mess? He seemed to be choosing his words carefully: "I think, and it's only my feeling, that it came from the previous management. I don't want to blame them or their program really. Because we know at any given time in a company, there's always a specific team with specific answers for specific problems. But at Thomson I think the major problem was much more the aim of the process, rather than specific tactics. I mean, the former chairman came from the "right schools" in France, such as ENA (the prestigious National School of Administration), and so on and so forth. He was a clever guy, but he had organized this company in an overly functional way worldwide.

"It was Marketing & Sales America, Marketing & Sales Europe, and Marketing & Sales Asia, but with no links between the product managers and the factories. No links between the factories and the sales people. So one thing was a functional, dis-connected worldwide organization. And there were three headquarters following the organization of Marketing & Sales. There was one headquarters in Boulogne near Paris, one in Indianapolis, and one in Singapore. There was really no global P&L of products and services or lines of products. So organization was the first part of the problem we saw.

"The second part, I think, was the style of management. As I heard it, the former Chairman was very authoritarian and nobody could give the headquarters an idea. There was a kind of corporate terrorism, frankly speaking. This was the feeling we got when we joined the company. The people just said: 'Ok, I need to do my job in my corner, and I don't want to show my head or give an idea.' This style completely cuts the origin or the source of imagination and innovation, right?"

I interrupted Hervé at this point to ask him the obvious: Since Thomson had been a government owned company for so many years, wasn't that part of the problem too? This part of the saga, as Hervé began to unfold it, was worse than I had imagined: "In fact, before we arrived on the scene, the government had tried to privatize Thomson. But the solution the Prime Minister of France, Mr. (Alain) Juppé, wanted to implement, became another part of the problem we inherited. I mean, to propose all of Thomson/RCA—even with its debt—to the Korean Daewoo Company, and to ask Daewoo to pay just one symbolic French franc—that was a scandal within the company. And especially for the Americans. Remember: The Americans *are* RCA! They had just been acquired by Thomson and were representing more than 65% of our global sales. So to hear from France, from the Prime Minister of France, that the value of their company was only one French Franc—it was an insult, of course, to the RCA people! And for the Thomson Asian employees, to be told that the Koreans would be the masters, the owners of their company, for a single French Franc, well that was a problem also. And in Paris, if I remember the stories, the Korean managers were already coming to the Thomson headquarters and deciding, 'This will be my office' and 'That will be your office' and so on. You can't imagine the turmoil that we inherited. We faced a very real risk of an LMBO (leveraged management buyout) by the Americans saying: 'OK. Good-bye, our French friends, we're leaving.' And Thomson, at the beginning, without the Americans, was nothing. You can't imagine the situation.

"Next, there were a lot of demonstrations in Paris by labor unions and so on. What I heard later inside Thomson, was that the former Chairman even asked the management to demonstrate in the streets against the government solution of selling to Daewoo. And when the managers refused to demonstrate, he fired them. It was quite dramatic. But the last straw was that the French Privatization Commission thwarted the whole plan. They are in charge of proposing to the government, the value of companies to be offered on the stock exchange or sold outright. It is an independent commission and they decided to not follow the French Government plan about Daewoo. This Commission told the government no—we are refusing to support the Daewoo sale. So for Thomson/RCA there was no clear future. The company was supposed to be privatized. The Privatization Commission is saying no. There are demonstrations in the streets of Paris. The Asians aren't trusting anything we say in Paris. The Americans are talking about an LMBO. And remember, this wasn't even the socialists. This was the right wing government! It was in 1995 or '96 and Alain Juppé was the first Prime Minister of President Chirac. What could possibly happen next?"

I was almost sorry I had asked. Just recounting this earlier fiasco seemed to insult Hervé's common sense and possibly his national pride. But I really wanted to hear the end of the story so I asked what *did* happen next? "What did happen?" repeated Hervé, pausing it seemed, to recollect the sequence of events: "Well, I'll tell you. President Chirac finally had to step in personally and the French government ended up taking the right approach. First, the former Chairman, Mr. Prestat, was fired. The government, which was still the 100% shareholder, then came up with a new plan. They would bring in the strongest management team they could find to completely re-energize and improve Thomson, make it as profitable as possible—and then take it public. This was very different from the previous strategy which more or less was to just give up and get rid of it for a Franc. So President Chirac appointed Thierry Breton as the new Chairman of Thomson in March 1997. I knew Breton from Bull of course. (*The giant French computer company which had been privatized earlier by a specially appointed management team that included Breton who was in charge of Mergers and Acquisitions and Hannebicque who was Sr. VP of Human Resources. All these recent privatizations of nationalized companies are part of post-Mitterrand (some would say post-socialist) France coming to terms with putting French business back on the global commercial map.*) We were both there for the successful privatization of Bull and the merging of Bull with Motorola, NEC and France Telecom. Thierry is a very good guy for mergers and acquisitions. He's very gifted at organizing this kind of marriage, or alchemy, between a three pronged alliance of Americans, Asians, and Europeans. He has a worldwide vision. I was Senior Vice President of HR at Bull so Thierry and I became friends. At Bull, we had implemented a complete turn-around of the company, which had about the same financial figures as Thomson, by the way. We privatized the company, and organized an internal shareholding process, and so on and so forth. That had been done and was very successful.

THE THREE REQUIREMENTS

With this colorful background of Thomson/RCA out of the way, the rest of the interview with Hervé was devoted to the "how to's" of actually transforming a struggling bureaucracy into a thriving entrepreneurial organization. It's not a coincidence that Hannebicque's ideas fall nicely into the three areas we call *The Three Requirements*. We had worked closely together over the past several years so a few good ideas were bound to rub off in either direction. And of course there is always the possibility that there really *are* three critical requirements and anyone who digs deep enough into the subject will figure them out! In any event, the added value that Hervé brings to the table is that he has been on the front-line, actually *doing* what we're talking about.

The three requirements to create an entrepreneurial organization are: *A Bit Of Money*, *A Bit Of Knowledge*, and an *Entrepreneur-Friendly Culture*. In discussing the three, Hannebicque starts off with *culture* which makes a lot of sense given that existing, large companies, as opposed to start-up ventures, have typically developed a deeply embedded culture over the years. So the first requirement here really has to be changing that existing organization culture.

• An Entrepreneur-Friendly Culture

This is Hervé Hannebicque on creating an entrepreneurial culture at Thomson/RCA: "So Thierry asked me to join him at Thomson. The first decision was we needed to completely change the mind-set, the habits, the behaviors, and the processes of this company. We analyzed what we did with Bull. The good things and the bad things. Because we had shared the same experience at Bull, we did not need to spend a lot of time just talking about what to do.

"My first proposal to Thierry was that we needed to split the HR function away from my entrepreneurship role. At Bull I was in charge of the classical HR function and at the same time promoting an entrepreneurial program for employees. But it's very difficult. How can you be credible and tell your worldwide management network: 'I will help you become entrepreneurs at the same time I'm organizing your area's downsizing.' So we decided to create a specific function of entrepreneurship to make it a much more a focused mission. Basically I'm in charge of Thomson's "Managing To Entrepreneuring Process." To do this you do need some power. You can only do this as an ambassador of the Chairman and a member of the executive committee. Anyway the first thing we did was to split the classical HR function away from this idea of creating an entrepreneurial organization.

"Secondly—as I said before, when we arrived the need for urgency was very clear. Thierry told me: 'Hervé we have ninety days to change the organization of this company. So you go where you want, you meet who you want, you are free. But in 90 days I want a blueprint for changing this crazy organization we have inherited. So for the first three months I was travelling everywhere in the world, meeting the people, knowing little about the company really. My conclusion after ninety days was very simple. We needed to immediately organize the company as a series of autonomous businesses. As you Americans call it, SBU's (Strategic Business Units). So we re-structured around this idea of the global P&L. It's common sense isn't it? We looked at our products, our distribution channels, and we decided to reconcile the product manager with product development. To reconnect the salespeople with the factory. It's what we needed. We were never going to be able to do that as long as we were functionally organized across the world. We needed businesses with product people and customer people all on the same team. So we organized our business into six SBUs. Three worldwide SBUs, each with a global P&L. These are businesses where the value is in core competence on a worldwide basis. In these SBUs, the sales people, product managers, product development and factory personnel, are all dedicated to the specific global business, with a common accountability. And we also have three local SBUs: one in Europe, one in America, and one in Asia. Each of these SBUs is responsible for our CTV and VCR business, which are much more local market businesses.

"Third, to support this new structure, we needed to maximize decentralization. We must be much nearer our customers. This has been a revolution at Thomson. A lot of people, especially at HQ, are shouting about it, but we did not care. We simply had to organize ourselves better around the customer, so the priority became to maximize decentralization. But at the same time our corporate functions have to promote a maximum of consistency. We need consistency inside the company and also in the marketplace—like Sony for example with one name, one brand and one image. So starting in July of 1997, the task was to maximize decentralization to be closer to customers and at the same time maximize the consistency of our corporate identity and culture. I think you call this the *loose/tight* organization. The important thing is to know what to centralize and what to decentralize. Our program is to decentralize the field to get close to customers while centralizing the consistency of Thomson's name and image in the market.

"At this same time we were working on these big organization changes, my next task was to create worldwide management networks. If we hoped to promote a new entrepreneurial culture, it could best be done through networks, not through traditional hierarchies. If we wanted to be close to our customers, we needed networks completely outside the hierarchy. If we want to compete in the digital age, and move quickly on a global basis, we can do it best through networks. So I designed and proposed the three worldwide management networks we now have:

First, we have a new Executive Committee of thirteen top people who meet every Monday via worldwide video conference, and every six months at a two to three day session to deduce the lessons of the former period and prepare for the next period. The Monday meetings, which cannot be missed by anyone, continue to give us the feeling of "crisis management," which is exactly what we want. We want no complacency at the top.

Next, we organized a second worldwide management network, the Operations Committee, with sixty people. It's made up of major project managers and the P&L managers. We meet quarterly for two days. I believe the Operations Committee is the secret of our success. To avoid the LMBO danger after Daewoo, we needed to re-build the corporate culture at this level. At these quarterly meetings, the words have been very clear: 'You are receiving the same level of information as the Executive Committee, we are all promoting transparency, you are the engines of this company, you are changing and the company is changing with you.' The specific messages have also been very clear. First it was about turnaround. Next it was partnership. Today it's entrepreneurship and innovation. The difference in the organization is dramatic. Today when we announce a new product or project, it will be done. That is a very clear change in Thomson. When we announced the employee shareholding program, people were very skeptical at first. Well, it is done. As for the promised new partnerships with Microsoft and so on, they are done. The successful public offering of Thomson shares on the

New York Stock Exchange. It is done. It's these actions, not our words, which are really changing the culture of Thomson/RCA.

"And finally we launched a third world-wide network, the Network of Entrepreneurs. For this we decided to break away from old-fashioned methods of ranking jobs. We did not want to meet only the managers of the company. We wanted to meet every six months, with the top performing people from everywhere in the world. So the invitation to be in this network of three hundred people, which we call the "Entrepreneurs Network," is based completely on performance, not on hierarchy or management level. So we have tried to break this bloody concept of hierarchy and the company entrepreneurs' role is to demonstrate and spread the new Thomson culture and entrepreneurial spirit, into every corner of the company. We do not depend on management alone to pass these messages down. They are too important. So the task is clear: To change the structure, the practices, the hierarchy, and the beliefs of the old culture. And replace that culture with a spirit of entrepreneurship across the company."

• A Bit Of Money

This requirement doesn't necessarily mean the company has to spend more money. It most likely will mean, however, dividing the pie in a new way. So let's move on to how Thomson/RCA handles the "bit of money" requirement. This is Hannebicque again: "We learned from Bull that we need to have a culture of progress, not a culture of budgets. A culture of budgets means nothing. The budget is just the train. What does it mean to organize a beautiful budget? It's only dreams. So promoting a future of progress is very, very important for us. Even if it is only a little progress. So today we say to our people in these three worldwide networks, please show us that you are making progress versus last year. And we don't mean just internally. We must also have a culture of comparative progress against the best of our competitors. It's a kind of benchmarking. There is no progress if we are unable to compare ourselves vis-a-vis our best competitors. We don't compare against the average, but against the best, because we need to be the best in class. This culture of comparative progress has been a beautiful concept for us.

"So we designed a new incentive compensation plan for all of the 6,500 managers in the company. It's called a *Contract of Progress*. All managers have a Contract of Progress which is designed and negotiated with their boss. We also decided to manage the company by semester periods— every six months—to keep the Contract of Progress very timely. In the survival situation we faced, a full year was too long. There are three short term, operating goals for the half year which are always comparative goals, to promote our culture of progress. They must be very concrete, based on facts and numbers, and they must promote the changes we want in terms of results. Another goal is in terms of behavior. And, finally there is one long term goal. Even when we were in a survival mode we couldn't afford to not think about the future. These Contracts Of Progress are now the basis of our incentive compensation plan, which is given every six months. We know this has changed a lot of things. It's a kind of backbone for our culture change. We know that our 6,500 people, who are managing the other 50,000 employees, have been very consistent in trying to meet the three short term goals. So this has been a good tool for us. It has certainly been a dramatic change from the days of nationalization, when all the employees were treated like government bureaucrats."

If the incentive compensation plan was a dramatic change, the Thomson/RCA employee ownership initiative delivered the *coup de grâce* to the old bureaucratic days. I can personally attest to the intense interest the employees have in the company's stock price. It's the first thing they ask about at meetings and seminars. And I can guarantee that in Indianapolis, Thomson/RCA's North American headquarters, there are a whole lot of people who know the daily exchange rate of the euro to the dollar. So, once again we see, in terms of creating an entrepreneurial organization it's hard to beat the impact of employee stock ownership.

Hervé, who was responsible for installing Thomson's worldwide stock ownership program, certainly agrees: "Yes. Of course. Thierry Breton got it started by getting the French government to agree to open our stock to our four industrial partners—well before the Thomson IPO on the New York and Paris stock exchanges. As you know, we have created a global alliance with four prestigious, high tech partners—Microsoft, Direct TV, Alcatel, and NEC. The deal with our partners was that each of them bought a 7.5% share of Thomson equity. That means the four companies, collectively, bought 30% of the company. As part of the original deal Breton worked out with them, each of the partners agreed to sell back a part their Thomson shares to the 373 members of the management networks. This was important as we had no stock options while we were nationalized and we needed to keep these people to grow the business and create value. The arrangement was also to ensure we were all sharing the same goals and, for sure, to convince the partners that we would, and could, successfully privatize, implement the IPO, and create value for them. So they agreed to sell back collectively, 2%, or 1/2% each, to the three worldwide management networks. This was a lot of stock being reserved for just 373 managers. You can imagine the infusion of lawyers and bankers between the USA and France and Japan to get all this done quickly but it was worth it. The name of the shareholder program for the 373 members of the networks is the Contract for Value Creation. 90% of the members are today shareholders. So the stock became a very key tool almost from the beginning.

"We were also deeply convinced that we needed a full internal shareholding process in tandem with our IPO. So we designed an employee shareholding program for 3.25% of our equity. Today 30,000 employees all across the world are eligible to become shareholders. And only a few months into the program, more than 17,000 have signed up. But you cannot imagine the difficulty of implementing a worldwide shareholding program. I spent most of 1999 on this one task from France where it was a shock—to the USA where it was straight forward—to China where it was unheard of. Only in February of 2000, did we get government approval for our China managers to join through a Hong Kong vehicle—which completed the coverage for Thomson/RCA's global operations. What a job but what a joy at the end of the day. We have Polish, Mexican, American, French, and Chinese employee owners today. And as you have seen Larry, they are all talking about the stock. They are excited. And why not? Look at the price. The stock has gone from 21 Euros to 80 Euros in just the four months since the IPO. That's why they're excited!

With the 2% coming from Microsoft, Direct TV, Alcatel, and NEC, plus the 3.25% reserved in the employee stock ownership program, plus more shares reserved for stock bonuses as part of our incentive compensation, we have a total of 6.12% of Thomson/RCA equity for employees. And the value has quadrupled. Not too bad for a company that was 100% owned by the French government two years ago. And not bad at all for a company that the government wanted to sell to the Koreans for one bloody French Franc!"

• A Bit Of Knowledge

Hervé prefers to label all training and education activities as "communication programs." I think this is because he desperately wants to keep his entrepreneurship mandate as far away as possible from the long shadow and iffy reputation of most Human Resource Departments. However he labels it, he's a big believer in disseminating new, useful knowledge. Here is how he describes that part of the *managing to entrepreneuring* process at Thomson/RCA: "We have pushed at least two major knowledge activities in the company. The first is to just learn about entrepreneurship. That means to teach what entrepreneurship is and really push the Thomson/RCA entrepreneurial concept down through the company. My job was to instill entrepreneurial behavior in the company, but a lot of people were saying to me: 'OK Hervé, but what do you mean by entrepreneurship?' Well Larry, I'm not going to give you a lesson on that in this interview, since you're our teacher! But the point is, it's time to stop speaking about managers and the techniques of management. We very much need real entrepreneurs in Thomson/RCA. As you know very well Larry, we have started the communications program on this which we simply call *Managing to Entrepreneuring.*

"The second knowledge activity is to learn *Value Based Managing* which means managing the P&L versus managing this or that. It is also a re-enforcement of the shareholding program. In the old company, the focus seemed to be more on administrative management. Now we are pushing

P&L management, which means our focus has to be much more dedicated to the customer. At the same time, because most of us are now shareholders, it's very much in our self-interest to promote value based management. So the question is how can we forget the old administrative management ways, the old theories and techniques, and become P&L managers? Well, one thing we can do is teach all our managers about value based managing. This training can at least make it faster and easier for our managers to move from being political and administrative managers to real businessmen and value creators.

"There are, of course, other areas where new knowledge or ideas were needed. They were quite specific things. We implemented several global education programs on such things to increase the company value. The first one was to communicate the need to drastically cut our costs. We called it the *Stop The Bleeding* program. The idea was to eliminate anything not useful to the customer. This was one of our early successes. Another program was directed at using re-engineering ideas to specifically boost productivity. Another was a very concrete program on protecting and leveraging the GE/RCA patent portfolio Thomson inherited. We launched all these big corporate programs in the first two years. Training and communication programs to improve specific operational areas can be a very strong way to improve company performance. To move from "managing to entrepreneuring," this kind of targeted knowledge is so much more important than the typical courses on leadership and general management principles."

I imagine all prospective corporate entrepreneurs will buy into the need of acquiring relevant new knowledge. Of course, the key word is relevant. How do you sort out the pap from the good stuff that you really need to know to grow your business? Hannebicque's story parallels our own general suggestion on this. To instill entrepreneurship in your company, two kinds of knowledge are certainly needed: First, your people have to have a solid understanding of what entrepreneurial behavior actually is—and how it can be applied in a corporate setting. Second, your people must have state-of-the-art knowledge on their products, their markets, and the key operating processes used by the company. In short they have to be trained "experts" in the basics of growing their business. Most other training, as intellectually stimulating and entertaining as it might be, should be deferred to another time and place.

ARE YOU READY TO CREATE THE ENTREPRENEURIAL ORGANIZATION?

The last question I put to Hervé was: "What are the lessons? If some other big company team came to you and said: 'We see you've been through this a couple of time. We're thinking about it for our company. You know, creating an entrepreneurial style company and trying to get the kind of financial results you've gotten. What are the three or four most important things we need to be thinking about to make this happen?' So, Monsieur Hannebicque, what would you tell them?'" Never at a loss for words, here are the final, summarizing lessons on what's really required to create *the entrepreneurial organization*—from the master who has actually done it:

• "I tell you frankly, the first thing you have to check is their own behavior. This tells you their seriousness to change. For example, all during this time, everyone in Thomson/RCA, from the Chairman on down, is flying coach to save money. Believe me, it's true. So I would want to check if they are just status guys. If they are, I would say: 'Please, if you want to change your company, are you ready to change yourself first? Are you coming here on first class tickets while your company is losing money?' And just to check deeper into their personal practices: 'Are you coming with the usual big company ways? Are you creating a bureaucracy? Are you pushing a lot of reporting? Do you have the mind-set yourself? You must check all this in yourself. Because, you know, you will have to set the first example in this process.'

• "Second, I would ask: 'Do you have the courage to do this? Because it is very difficult and you will be struggling against the tide for several years.'

- "Third, you must find out somehow if they are innovative people, willing to try new things and abandon old habits.

- "And finally I would have to say: 'Do you have the ethics for this?' In this process you cannot lie. You must be completely transparent. For example, if you are speaking about shareholding, it's vital. This is not business as usual, paying employees at the end of the month. During just two weeks we had more than 17,000 people investing their own money in the company. Try to imagine that you are working in a RCA factory in Mexico. The share price can represent more than half your monthly salary. So if you don't have ethics, if people are suspecting that you are lying, or that you are organizing a coup—then creating an entrepreneurial company is not for you . . . "

Are you *still* ready to create *the entrepreneurial organization?* Assuming you are—here's a summary check list of Hervé Hannebicque's recommended actions, all distilled from the long interview above, to get you started:

• Summary Of Recommended Actions To Create An *Entrepreneur-Friendly Culture*:

- CEO and senior management commitment is critical. A focused and rapid-fire implementation, perhaps guided by a trusted executive outside the hierarchy, is the process of choice.

- Do away with the old hierarchical, functional organization structure. Replace it with customer/product driven business units—both global and local.

- Reinforce the new structure with a flexible loose/tight organizational approach. Maximize decentralization to be closer to customers while maximizing the consistency of corporate identity and culture.

- Learn to communicate and implement through "flexible networks of employees" versus the bureaucracy of a multi-layered management hierarchy.

- **Summary Of Recommended Actions Around A *Bit Of Money*:**

- Kill your "culture of budgets" and replace it with a "culture of progress." Compare progress against yourself and your best competitors. Innovative actions, such as managing by quarters or half-years can be useful in achieving short-term progress.

- Institute incentive compensation or "pay for performance" for everyone—yesterday! Any program, no matter how rudimentary, is better than operating with no consequences at all.

- Institute employee ownership—yesterday! Again, any form you can come up with is better than nothing. Cover all managers and as many workers as legally possible. At minimum, aim for a critical mass of your workers.

- **Summary Of Recommended Actions About A *Bit Of Knowledge*:**

- Provide communication and training on why you want the company to become more "entrepreneurial," what entrepreneurial behavior really is, and how every employee can use it in their job, day in and day out.

- Provide communication and training programs to improve specific, high impact operational activities. Most product and customer training would qualify. *Value Based Managing* and the *Stop The Bleeding* programs at Thomson/RCA are excellent examples also.

ONE MORE TIME:
LESSONS FROM THE AMERICAN RUST BELT

"People are amazed when I tell them that some Lincoln factory workers earn in excess of $100,000 a year. Well, why shouldn't they? They are, in fact, dedicated entrepreneurs and they earn every dime of their money."

—Don Hastings, CEO (Retired)
Lincoln Electric

Let's go back to Lincoln Electric—"the most entrepreneurial big company in the world"—for a final thought on *creating the entrepreneurial organization*. Lincoln is that truly amazing business with the most entrepreneurial work environment I've ever seen in a big company. Remember, this is the company with no paid holidays or sick leave, or even coffee breaks, and where very demanding productivity standards are the order of the day. In the face of all this, the workers are extraordinarily committed to perform. They defer vacations to meet big client orders. They come to work early and stay late. They never go on strike. They never slack off. How can this be—in Cleveland, Ohio, ground-zero of America's industrial rust belt?

I recently talked to retired CEO Don Hastings, an incredibly nice guy, and I asked the same question. His answer: "It's not very complicated, Larry. People are amazed when I tell them that some Lincoln factory workers earn in excess of $100,000 a year. Well, why shouldn't they? They are, in fact, dedicated entrepreneurs and they earn every dime of their money. The key issue is, if you are going to encourage entrepreneurship in any organization, you must drive home the point that in order to get a commitment *out of people*, management must first make a commitment *to those people*." And what a commitment Lincoln makes to its employees! For starters they are the highest paid factory workers in the world. And Lincoln has lived up to its guarantee of continuous employment for over 50 years. Perhaps even more to the point, Lincoln's CEO earns just 5 to 6 times the average employee's salary, far below Germany or Japan's ratios, and absolutely miniscule compared to the 350 to 1 ratio American CEOs demand and get at other *Fortune 1000* companies!

Hastings summed up the Lincoln experience with a challenge all company leaders should think about: "Most companies talk about people as their most important asset. They always say it and you see it in their mission statements. But they don't really walk the talk. They say people are the most important, then the next day they lay off a thousand of them. At Lincoln, the customers and the employees always come before the shareholders. Of course by doing this we've made our shareholders wealthy in the long term. Today Lincoln has a hundred year long tradition of doing this: of valuing customers and employees ahead of the shareholder. It's so deeply embedded I don't think it will ever change. So that's the answer Larry—and it's pretty simple." In that spirit, here's your own simple list of the key points of Lincoln Electric's amazing approach to creating *the most entrepreneurial big company in the world!*

- **Summary Of Lincoln's Approach To Creating An Entrepreneurial Organization:**

- Customers and employees always come before shareholders—which has made their shareholders wealthy in the long term.
- Lincoln has the highest paid industrial workforce in the world which turns out to be very good for their bottom line.
- Like entrepreneurs, the more good product employees produce, the more money they make.
- Like entrepreneurs, employees don't get paid for downtime (vacations, holidays, sick days, coffee breaks, etc.) or for making poor quality product which can't be sold.
- Employees are self-managing so the company needs no supervisory staff. The savings allow Lincoln to pay best-in-the-world salaries to its workers.
- Lincoln offers guaranteed continuous employment. There have been temporary reductions in work up to 25% but there's never been a layoff.

• The Lincoln CEO earns only 5 to 6 times the average worker's pay. Compare this to the outrageous 350+ times at other *Fortune 1000* companies.

The best part of the Lincoln Electric story is that you could do most, if not all, of the same things they do. There's nothing holding you back. As Don Hastings says: "It's not very complicated . . . . ."

ONE MORE TIME—AGAIN:
LESSONS FROM THE SCOTTISH HIGHLANDS

Remember Fraser Morrison in Edinburgh, Scotland. His five suggestions directly attack the bone-deep differences between high-growth entrepreneurial organizations and oversized, over-managed bureaucracies. But Morrison's example was about a small to mid-sized family business. Here are those same principles, as practiced by some wonderful *Fortune 500* type companies—proving once again that "it's not how big you get, but how you get big"—that really matters over the long haul:

• **Keep It Small**
Welcome to the $62 billion company famous for the slogan, "Growing big by staying small." At Johnson & Johnson, 128 years old and still maintaining a robust 12 percent growth rate, employees are promised a "small-company environment with big-company impact." And J&J delivers on that promise. It is the most decentralized big company in the world. Its 114,000 employees are divided into 250 separate, highly autonomous units, each with its own board—resulting in an average size of just 456 people per company!

• **Keep It Personal**
Ed Penhoet—scientist, entrepreneur, and founder of Chiron, the world's No. 3 biotech company—explains how he got employees passionately committed to winning the race to discover the hepatitis B vaccine: "If you reduce it all down to one thing, it's how to make it personal. So it's their soul that's involved and they personally feel the heat of the

competition." Feeling personal consequences from your work is still the most powerful way to get people committed to the cause.

• Keep It Honest

No company can survive the test of time without internal and external integrity. Whether it's CEOs quietly paying themselves 350 times the average salary of their employees or Enron screwing its employees out of their life savings, or the banking/mortgage industry screwing all of us, the truth ultimately comes out. And when it does, the employees, the customers, and the shareholders won't believe a thing the company says for the next twenty years.

• Keep It Simple

The "KISS" principle was put to the acid test by Jack Welch when he took over a moribund, ninety-year-old General Electric Company. "Neutron Jack," the man who said he wanted to run GE like a small, entrepreneurial business, flattened the company's nine levels of management, reduced the number of pay levels from twenty-nine to five, obliterated the corporate staff, got rid of the outside consultants as well as most of the company's management training courses, and in the span of twenty years brought it from death's door to be the most valuable company in the world. Fortunately, Welch wasn't burdened with any MBA theories—he was just an engineer.

• Start Over With The Basics.

Great entrepreneurs have a sense of mission about their work, an absolute focus on customers and products, a lot of innovative action, and a ton of self-inspiration. Walt Disney beautifully described these entrepreneurial basics fifty years ago when he said:

> *"The inclination of my life—has been to do things and make things which will give pleasure to people in new and amazing ways. By doing that I please and satisfy myself"*

Start over with these commonsense lessons and you'll be well on your way to **becoming the next great corporate entrepreneur**—and—**creating the next great entrepreneurial organization!**

APPLICATIONS

Entrepreneurial Companies

From The Farrell Company's Spirit Of Enterprise Seminar

Editor's note: The following Applications are used in The Farrell Company's corporate entrepreneurship seminars. They are included here with the hope they may be of interest and practical value to executives and managers of companies and other types of organizations— as well as training directors and teachers of entrepreneurship.

APPLICATION 1

YOU'RE AN ENTREPRENEUR—WHAT NEXT?

You've just started your own business. It's the first day in your new role as an entrepreneur. You want to be successful and grow. You sure don't want to go bankrupt. You've mortgaged your family house to raise the money to get started. Everything you have is on the line, including the welfare of your children.

You have in mind a product and market that excites you. You think it has potential. But with your limited financial resources, you have to get started fast! What will you concentrate on? How should you spend your time? What are your priorities as an entrepreneur?

There are no "right" or "wrong" answers for this first Application. It's simply intended to get your "entrepreneurial juices" flowing—by seriously thinking through what you would really have to focus on as a start-up entrepreneur.

MY ENTREPRENEURIAL PRIORITIES—IN ORDER

1.

2.

3.

4.

5.

APPLICATION 2

RATING YOUR COMPANY'S ENTREPRENEURIAL SPIRIT

What's really important at your company? What worries people most? Keeps them awake nights? What excites them most? Makes them really happy and really proud? You may call them personal goals, business objectives, or company values. For this exercise, we'll just call them "priorities." Whatever they are, you can be sure they are determining the "mission" of the business. Let's look at the "mission" of your company—and the priorities that are driving it today. Base your answers on how people actually behave day in and day out—deeds always speak louder than words! Listed are samples of common business priorities.

Owner's Return	New Products	New Markets
Costs/Efficiency	Customer Satisfaction	Company Image
Job Security	Revenue Growth	Safety
Profit	Employee Performance	Employee Commitment
Product Quality	Personal Advancement	Cash Flow
Innovation	Fast Action	Integrity

When you're finished, consider how your current priorities compare to the four basics of enterprise and what changes (if any) you should try to make in your own behavior as well as across the entire company.

TOP MANAGEMENT	OTHER EMPLOYEES	YOURSELF
1.	1.	1.
2.	2.	2.
3.	3.	3.
4.	4.	4.
5.	5.	5.

APPLICATION 3—A
CREATING AN ENTREPRENEURIAL STRATEGY

The central strategic questions for any company are: what products/services will we provide and what customers/markets will we pursue. Get this right and you survive to compete another day. Get it wrong and your history! So picking the right products and markets is "entrepreneurial job one!" Identify your important current, and new, market/product businesses—and rate them in terms of *market need* and *competitive position*. Review the *What's In What* and *Creating An Entrepreneurial Strategy* sections for more background.

1. List Current And New Market/Product Combinations

2. Assess The "Market Need" (10 High to 1 Low Scale)

3. Assess Your "Competitive Position" (10 High to 1 Low Scale)

4. Plot Your Answers Accordingly On The Next Page

CURRENT MARKET/PRODUCT COMBINATIONS	MKT. NEED	COMP. POS.
1.		
2.		
3.		
4.		
5.		

NEW MARKET/PRODUCT COMBINATIONS	MKT. NEED	COMP. POS.
6.		
7.		
8.		
9.		
10.		

APPLICATION 3—B
THE CRITERIA THAT COUNT

Plot the ratings of your market/product winners from 3A on the matrix. For example a "9 market need" with a "9 competitive position" rating would be very near the upper right hand corner. A "3/7" would be near the center of the upper left hand quadrant, and so on.

This matrix will give you an overview of the combined market need and competitive position for each of your current and new market/product ideas. Based on this analysis, list below the actions you should take. The actions needed to grow will be different for each quadrant: In quadrant 1 you'll need strong marketing and sales capabilities to grow. In quadrant 3, on the other hand, you'll need strong product development capabilities. Review the *Criteria That Count* section for more ideas before you start this critical Application..

1. **Small Market/High Competitive Position:** Good possibility of success in this Rolls Royce type business. Work to find more markets for your excellent product.

2. **Big Market/High Competitive Position:** High possibility of success, but once successful, you will likely attract a high level of competition. Be prepared for strong competitors.

3. **Big Market/Low Competitive Position:** Good possibility of success, but you may have to compete on price at the low end of the market. Work to raise your competitive position.

4. **Small Market/Low Competitive Position:** Poor chance of success. Avoid this business like the plague.

Continued on the next page. . . . .

APPLICATION 3—B (continued)

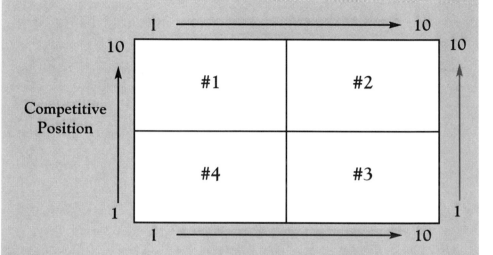

THE CRITERIA THAT COUNT

ACTION   WHO   WHEN

1.

2.

3.

4.

5.

APPLICATION 4—A

CREATING AN ENTREPRENEURIAL CULTURE

Values set the culture of any organization. An entrepreneurial culture must provide competitive advantage in products and markets and have the commitment of senior management and the bulk of the employees. So the real purpose of creating and maintaining business values is to identify and focus on those things (values) that will ensure you achieve your market/product plan. Of course no company can be the best at everything. The key to success is to figure out which two or three values will give you the greatest competitive advantage over your competition.

What values will best support your strategy? How will they give you competitive advantage? And how will you get everyone committed? You might review the section on *Creating An Entrepreneurial Culture* for more background.

WHAT VALUES DO WE NEED TO ACHIEVE THE PLAN?	WHAT'S THE COMPETITIVE ADVANTAGE?	HOW WILL I GET EVERYONE COMMITTED?
1.		
2.		
3.		
4.		

APPLICATION 4-B
KEEPING IT ALIVE

How strongly does our organizational behavior support our values? The three greatest influences on keeping values alive are below. Rate how each of these factors supports each of your values:

- High: Perfectly consistent, no improvement needed.
- Medium: Not always consistent. Improvement needed.
- Low: Rarely supports values. Complete change required.

In any area where your rating is medium or low, devise actions to correct that situation immediately. Only by maintaining your organization's values over time, can you truly become a powerful and dominant force in your chosen products and markets. This is exactly what Application 4-B is all about—so go for it!

VALUES	MANAGEMENT BEHAVIOR	RITUALS & PRACTICES	+/- FEEDBACK TO EMPLOYEES
1.			
2.			
3.			
4.			

ACTION	WHO	WHEN
1.		
2.		
3.		
4.		

APPLICATION 5
MY ENTREPRENEURIAL JOB DESCRIPTION

Walt Disney believed that everyone in The Disney Company had a definite role to play in the delivery of the product or service to the ultimate, paying customer. It is in this spirit that you should use this application—inspired by the Disney new employee orientation program. And why not start your employees out with the three questions entrepreneurs live and die by? Who are my customers, what are my products, and what do I have to do to satisfy my customers? The message is very clear and very entrepreneurial: Everyone has a product or service to provide and customers or internal users to serve. This simple addition to everyone's job description won't solve all your personnel challenges, but it may be the single most powerful tool you have to instill an entrepreneurial customer/product vision in your people and throughout your company.

	INTERNAL USERS	EXTERNAL CUSTOMERS
WHO ARE MY CUSTOMERS OR USERS?		
WHAT ARE MY PRODUCTS OR SERVICES?		
WHAT ARE MY CUSTOMERS' OR USERS' EXACT REQUIREMENTS? • Quality • Quantity • Timelines • Other		

APPLICATION 6A
CREATING AN OBSESSION FOR CUSTOMERS AND PRODUCTS

Application 6A will focus you and your employees on the two most important words in business: Customers and Products. Use the following questions to get your entrepreneurial juices flowing:

- Are you over functionalized or in danger of becoming that way? What can you do to prevent this from happening?
- How clear are your employees on who their customers are, what their products are, and what it takes to satisfy those customers?
- How can you use the four key practices for Loving the Customer in this chapter?
- How can you use the four key practices for Loving the Product in this chapter?

A final suggestion: Hold monthly brainstorming sessions using Application 6-A to maintain focus on customers and products. One hour a month to maintain your obsession for customers and products could be the most valuable hour you spend.

GREAT IDEAS FOR "LOVING" THE CUSTOMER	WHO	WHEN
1.		
2.		
3.		
4.		

GREAT IDEAS FOR "LOVING" THE PRODUCT	WHO	WHEN
1.		
2.		
3.		
4.		

APPLICATION 6B
GROWING THE OLD-FASHIONED WAY

Entrepreneurs grow their business the old-fashioned way, by making more products and selling more customers. There are only four possible ways to grow or expand any business—and they're all on the chart below. Use this Application every time you want to examine growth opportunities in the business. Identify those opportunities and the actions required to achieve them. Review *Growing The Old-Fashioned Way* in this section for more ideas.

	Current	New	
New	New Products To Current Customers	New Products To New Customers	**New**
Products			
Current	Current Products To Current Customers	Current Products To New Customers	**Current**
	Current	New	

Customers

ACTION	WHO	WHEN
1.		
2.		
3.		
4.		

374   Larry C. Farrell

APPLICATION 7
FOSTERING HIGH SPEED INNOVATION

What would you do "if your life depended on it?" That's the question you need to ask of your managers and your employees. This is the sure-fire way to gain competitive advantage for the company. So what can you do today to encourage more innovation, speed up action, and wipe out bureaucracy? Review *The Necessity To Invent* and *The Freedom To Act* sections for more examples. Remember, this is the entrepreneur's secret weapon—so use it!

TO ENCOURAGE INNOVATION:
Improve something, anything, every day.   WHO   WHEN

1.

2.

3.

TO SPEED UP ACTION:
Create a sense of urgency.   WHO   WHEN

1.

2.

3.

TO WIPE OUT BUREAUCRACY:
Growing big by staying small.   WHO   WHEN

1.

2.

3.

APPLICATION 8
SELF-INSPIRED BEHAVIOR
RAISING COMMITMENT AND PERFORMANCE

What are the most important actions you can take to raise employee commitment and performance in the company? Before you start, review the *Creating Entrepreneurial Commitment* and *Creating Entrepreneurial Performance* sections in this chapter. And what about consequences? Are they in place for everyone? Take another look at *The Power Of Consequences* to make sure you include this critical factor.

CREATING HIGH COMMITMENT	WHO	WHEN
1.		
2.		
3.		
4.		

CREATING HIGH PERFORMANCE	WHO	WHEN
1.		
2.		
3.		
4.		

APPLICATION 9

CREATING AN ENTREPRENEURIAL PERFORMANCE SYSTEM

Becoming an entrepreneurial organization depends most of all on transforming your corporate bureaucrats into corporate entrepreneurs. This will never happen if you don't start installing an Entrepreneurial Performance System in the company. The EPS chart below illustrates the basic components required for doing just that. Pay special attention to the point that positive/negative consequences are the backbone of the system.

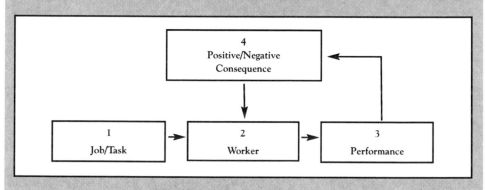

COMPONENT	QUESTION TO ASK	SOLUTION
1. Job/Task	Does the worker know *what* to do?	Set clear job standards.
2. Worker	Does the worker know *how* to do the job?	Provide training.
3. Performance	Does the worker have the resources to do the job?	Provide tools, people, time to do the job.
4. Consequences	Are the positive and negative consequences to the worker in balance?	Reset the positive & negative consequences.
	Is the worker aware of the consequence?	Give accurate, timely and powerful feedback.

Continued on the next page. . . . .

APPLICATION 9 (continued)

You can use the EPS above as your own personal troubleshooting guide to solve performance problems and/or raise the commitment and performance of your own employees. By tracking through the components of the system, you should discover which of the EPS components needs to be adjusted to change the behavior of your employee or employees. You should find the EPS Guide a valuable, on-going performance management tool.

To take this to the next level, and implement the EPS across the entire company, you should first re-read the full section of this chapter titled *Inspiring Others: Creating Mini-Entrepreneurs*. Then determine what company-wide actions are required to begin creating a more entrepreneurial environment across the entire organization. Remember, you'll never revive the enterprise if you can't revise the enterprisers—and this is where it all has to start!

ACTION	WHO	WHEN
1.		
2.		
3.		
4.		
5.		
6.		

APPLICATION 10

MY 'CORPORATE ENTREPRENEUR' ACTION PLAN

Of all the ideas and suggestions discussed in this book, which ones will have the greatest impact on raising the entrepreneurial spirit across your company—and/or for you personally?

First go back and refresh yourself on the four entrepreneurial basics: *Sense of Mission, Customer/Product Vision, High-Speed Innovation and Self-Inspired Behavior*. Then review Chapter 12 on *What's Really Required To Create The Entrepreneurial Organization: An Entrepreneur-Friendly Culture, A Bit Of Money, and A Bit Of Knowledge*.

Finally, decide which actions absolutely, positively must be implemented, who will be responsible, and when will the action be taken? And congratulations—you are now entering the exciting world of *Corporate Entrepreneurship!*

ACTION	WHO	WHEN
1.		
2.		
3.		
4.		
5.		
6.		

PART THREE

Entrepreneurial Countries

Creating An Entrepreneurial Economy To Win The 21st Century Global Economic War

Chapter 13

The Great Unanswered Mystery Of Economics

". . . *the most important question in economics: why are some countries richer than others?*"

—*The Economist*

In its classic cover feature, "The Mystery Of Economic Growth," *The Economist* said: "Understanding growth is surely the most urgent task in economics. Across the world, poverty remains the single greatest cause of misery; and the surest remedy for poverty is economic growth." But then to underscore the crisis that has plagued a majority of the world's population for a thousand years, the article sadly concluded that: "To its shame, economics neglected the study of growth for many years...with a few exceptions, the best brains in economics preferred not to focus on the most vital issue of all."

The Economist optimistically suggests this may be changing: "Citizens of the world who sensibly keep an eye on what economists are up to can at least take pleasure in this: the profession has chosen for once to have one of its most vigorous debates about the right subject." If so it's not a minute too soon as the economic evidence is crystal clear that the gap between the richest countries and the poorest is wider now than at any time in history. But will a "vigorous debate" on economic growth by economists at Oxford, Harvard, and the IMF actually lighten the load of the world's poverty stricken masses—or shed any light on what you can do to ensure rising prosperity for your kids, or even create a single job anywhere in the world? Don't hold your breath.

If economists haven't spent much time over the past several hundred years pondering why some people are rich and others are poor, has anybody? How about elected government leaders? Surely they think about it. Well, think again. On a recent flight from Washington, D. C. to Los Angeles, I found myself sitting next to a well-known Congresswoman from California, a widely respected foreign-policy expert. It's not every day one gets to chat with a political rising star. My initial reaction, I admit, was to silently wonder how many U.S. citizens realize our elected representatives (Ross Perot called them "our employees") routinely fly first class. Fortunately that awkward thought quickly passed and after a bit of conversation, the point came up that I was on my way to Singapore to give a speech on creating entrepreneurial economies. She expressed polite interest so I asked her my favorite interview question on economics: "If you could be the absolute economic czar of the United States, or any country for that matter, and you could implement any policies or programs you wanted, what are the first three things you would do to ensure that country's economic prosperity in the 21st century?" There was a very long pause, then: "That's really a good question . . . I'll have to think about it."

She seemed truly surprised by such a question as if no one had ever brought it up before. I was a little taken aback. I had naively figured our leaders in Washington were thinking about things like this all the time. It can make you wonder what politicians are spending their time on in Washington or other capitals of the world. Now I imagine she is a hard-working representative for her constituents in California, and she certainly doesn't owe an airline seat companion an answer to anything. But in an odd sort of way, I think she was probably being quite truthful. Perhaps she really hadn't thought about it. Perhaps *no one* in Washington really thinks about it much. Maybe *The Economist* is more right than they know. Could it be that nobody is thinking about it? The mind totters . . . .

But hold on. If you look long enough and hard enough, there may be some light at the end of the economic growth tunnel. I actually did find someone who has thought about it. In fact he spent most of the 20th century thinking about it. His name is K. T. Li.

THE GOVERNMENT'S MOST IMPORTANT JOB

*"The greatest advantage I had as economic affairs minister
was I never had a course in economics."*

—K. T. Li (father of the Taiwan economic miracle)
Minister of Economic Affairs, Minister of Finance,
Republic Of China On Taiwan

K. T. Li, the "father" of Taiwan's economic miracle, was simply the world's most successful economics minister over the past hundred years. The only Chinese to hold honorary *Chairs in Economics* at both Cambridge and Harvard, he is widely regarded as the chief architect of the 20th Century's greatest economic success story. I had the honor and delight of interviewing him for three hours in Taiwan, which was something akin to taking a crash course on the history of the modern world. (*Dr. Li Kwoh-Ting, born in mainland China in 1909, arrived in Taiwan with Chiang Kai-shek in 1950, directed Taiwan's economy for the next half century, passed away in 2001. He was a giant figure on the world economic stage for much of the 20th century, and is sorely missed.*)

The venerable, Cambridge educated physicist arrived on the former Japanese colony of Taiwan in 1950. He came with Chiang Kai-shek and

1.6 million mainland Chinese following their bitter defeat at the hands of Mao's freedom marchers. His role in the Taiwan economic miracle began as the President of the Taiwan Shipbuilding Corporation. He soon became Minister of Economic Affairs and in 1969, added the title of Minister of Finance, the only man to hold both jobs simultaneously. He retired from the cabinet as Minister of State in 1988 at the ripe young age of 78, and until his death carried the honorary title, Senior Advisor to the President—Republic of China. From the many honors framed on his wall, I learned he's the only Chinese ever admitted as an Honorary Fellow of Emmanuel College, Cambridge University. And in 1990, Harvard University instituted the K. T. Li Lectureship at their Center for International Affairs.

Nearing 90 when I interviewed him, he still liked to shock foreign visitors with down-to-earth quips such as: "The government's most important job is to make people rich." or "The best economic policy ever invented is common sense which you'll never find in an economics department." and "The best policy is to keep the smart people out of government...and in the private sector where they can do some good." As the architect of the 20th century's most amazing economic success story, Li was particularly proud of the fact that he never studied economics. He seemed to relish emphasizing that point: "The greatest advantage I had as economic affairs minister was I never had a course in economics. Of course the Economic and Finance Minister has many economists as advisors and they all thought I should be helped. I took their ideas with due respect. But in the end, it only requires someone with common sense to make the judgments." That common sense produced some staggering economic results.

The particular reason we want to study him here, is that his most important economic principle just happened to be: "Create and honor the entrepreneurs." He told me with absolute certainty in his voice: "They are the backbone of any growing economy. We knew they would create the jobs. Therefore our primary economic tactic in Taiwan has always been to create entrepreneurs." If you really want to know how to create a high-growth entrepreneurial economy, you've obviously come to the right place. . .

This small island in the South China Sea has the fifth largest foreign reserves in the world—after China, Japan, Russia (guns and oil!) and Saudi Arabia (all oil!)—a stunning feat when you consider Taiwan has zero natural resources to sell and its population is only 23 million. It also has the highest GNP growth (9% per annum) of any country over the past 60 years, producing a seventy times increase in per capita GNP. And defying all economic theory, it has achieved these record-beating results with practically zero inflation and one of the most even distributions of income in the industrialized world.

If your country is facing financial meltdown, as many are today, or if you just want to know what actually works in economic development, learning K. T. Li's secrets for creating economic miracles may be a lot more useful than asking the World Bank, Nobel prize winning economists—or your own duly elected government leaders. Since Li believes common sense, not arcane economic theories, will get the job done, not repeating the same mistakes over and over is a good place to start: "First, we determined that runaway inflation and rural poverty were the main reasons for the rise of Communism on the mainland. We were determined to avoid that in Taiwan. So our policy was to do the opposite." His overall philosophy for creating national prosperity is distilled below, as five broad principles. Here in K. T. Li's own words, are the ideas that created the economic miracle in Taiwan:

• The Starting Point Has To Be Population Control
"This is more important than any economic theory. When you have such a large number of young people, you have to create jobs for them. So you have to be practical. People growth and economic growth have to be together. I think this is the most important thing. By the 1960s, our population birth rate reached 38 per thousand. We could not sustain such a high rate. Now birth control is definitely against the Chinese philosophy. Confucius says that if you do not have descendants, then you are a failure. Well we did it without laws. We talked quietly to the people. They know really. They know that at the third or fourth child the situation is bad. Their house is bad. Not enough food. Today we are at 15 births per thousand. Below 2%. Look around. Whether it's

Catholic, Muslim, Buddhist, where you find too many people, you find poor countries. No work, no opportunity, no hope."

• Never Print Money You Don't Have

"Fighting inflation all the way was also a big part of the policy. And we never took the easy way on money. We even had to sell our gold but we never printed money we didn't have—never. We thought this was the way to avoid what happened on the mainland. We've gone from $130 to nearly $10,000 in per capita GNP and controlled inflation to the point that the wholesale price index in Taiwan has actually fallen six out of the last ten years. Taiwan's domestic inflation rate has been just 2.2% over the past 50 years. That's what happens if you never print money you don't have."

• Government's Job Is To Make The People Rich

"The policy has been that all the individuals: the farmers, the domestic businessmen, the exporters, should all become prosperous. As the government, our job was to do everything in our power to help them. Farmers for example, were the largest part of the labor force. Increasing the earnings of the farmers would be the best thing to keep the economy stable—that's very important. We wanted to make sure if farmers worked harder they made more money. So land was sold at only 2 and 1/2 times the fixed value of the yield. As their yield went up, it became easier and easier for the farmer to pay off the land. This we wanted. We wanted owner farmers, not tenant farmers with great, rich landlords. Another thing about agriculture—countries have to be able to feed themselves. Especially poor countries. They go broke if they have to import food. So everything we did in the early days was to help the farmers prosper. If they increased output, they prospered. Farmers will do that if you let them. It worked very, very well. We are now of course big exporters of food like rice and sugar."

• Timing Is More Important Than Ideology

"We believed that everything we did should foster private initiative, be highly pragmatic and be implemented in some logical order. This last point—the right policy at the right time—is very important to development. The country's life cycle, or stage of development, should determine economic policy, not a particular ideology. To us timing was everything. First we had to concentrate on agriculture, with strong government intervention in land reform to create owner farmers. Next we focused on domestic business. We actually implemented a policy of import substitution with high tariffs—admittedly an anti free-market policy—to help our local entrepreneurs get up and running. But, unlike socialist countries, we understood that protecting local businesses should not be a permanent policy and we got rid of it as quickly as we could. Then we understood that Taiwan had to export to grow so we opened the borders, and embraced free trade to the fullest. In this phase, which continues until today, we have done everything we can to facilitate exports by both local and international companies producing products in Taiwan. So doing things in some logical order, in phases, is more important than following the dogma of a particular economic theory. Of course in all these phases, we wanted the individuals: the farmers, the domestic businessmen, the exporters, to become prosperous. This was our most important goal—not pushing one economic idea or another as many politicians and economists seem to do. Anyway we thought that was the best way to avoid what happened on the mainland."

• Create And Honor The Entrepreneurs

"From the beginning, we believed that entrepreneurs are the backbone of any growing economy and the government should do everything in its power to help them succeed. We knew that if we helped create one entrepreneur, he could create fifty more jobs. In the beginning, we inherited from the Japanese a lot of state owned enterprises. We decided to break these up and sell them as smaller businesses to our people. All these could be handled by the private sector better so we sold them at very reasonable prices. We encouraged a lot of the former landlords to become investors for the first time in small enterprises. We wanted to create entrepreneurs. Y. C. Wang, the "famous plastics king" of the world, started this way, as did many others. The government sold the plants cheaply, helped find the private investors, did everything we could to create domestic entrepreneurs."

What does all this have to do with *The Economist's* unsolved mystery: "Why Are Some Countries Richer Than Others?" For one thing, you might be getting the idea that *The Economist* is asking the wrong people for the answer. It turns out that the world of economics isn't so different from some other "expert" professions—where having to produce practical results often seems just beneath their level of dignity, but just above their level of competence. It's hard to avoid the sinking feeling that in economics, common sense can easily get lost in the theoretical shuffle. So this is the connection: it's important to get a reality check from someone who has actually done it—such as K. T. Li.

The economic results clearly show that Li and the Taiwanese know a lot about avoiding poverty and inflation, the two big lessons they learned in losing the Chinese mainland to the communists. At its heart, the Taiwan miracle is a story of unadulterated, uncomplicated, all out enterprise. The one absolutely clear fact about this tiny speck of land in the South China Sea is that it didn't get rich by browbeating its entrepreneurs. On that happy note, the rest of this book will further explore K. T. Li's final point: "Creating and honoring the entrepreneurs." Learning just what it takes to create entrepreneurs and build an entrepreneurial economy, is the first step in creating your own economic miracle for the 21st century.

THE PROSPERITY CYCLE OF NATIONS

"For Japanese young people, factory work and blue collar work are out. Our fathers did those jobs but we want something better like planning or public relations."

—Koji Shima
Assistant to the CEO
Uni-Charm Corporation

The prosperity of individuals and companies has always been dependent on the larger, national spirit of enterprise around them. In the post-cold war world, this reality has moved center stage in government policy-making. Country competition to win the global economic wars of the 21st century has become the number one political and diplomatic issue of our time. Countries may have turned their swords into plowshares but a new kind of Armageddon awaits us. From the economic tragedy of Africa, to the capitalistic chaos still threatening Russia and much of its former empire, to the uncertain staying power of an old North America and an older Europe, to the global angst over the new, tough, and very competitive double threat of India and China (where 40% of the world's population lives!), the globe is facing an economic slugfest the likes of which we've never seen. For the foreseeable future, economic power is the name of the game. There are about 220 national players, some very powerful, some dangerously weak, all bound together by a single ambition: to end up in the winners' column in the battle for prosperity. Of course the question is how to do that.

The history of prosperity is easy enough to recount—it shows a continual coming and going of winners and losers. The ever-shifting positions in the relative prosperity of Europe, North America and Asia illustrate the point. The 19th century belonged to the Europeans, spear-headed by the Victorian Liberals of Great Britain. The 20th century winner is clearly North America, with the USA emerging as the richest nation in the history of the world. The 21st century is up for grabs, but the smart money and the trends are on the side of Asia, led by 1.3 billion hard working Chinese and another billion, equally hard working, Indians. South America could be this century's sleeping giant. If its growth trends hold and Brazil provides the economic horsepower, South America could match European levels of prosperity by 2050. In this global race, Africa lags far behind all the other areas. It holds the awful distinction of being the only continent actually growing poorer.

Within these broad regions, individual countries can experience enormous ups and downs, often in a very short space of time. For example, what really caused the dizzying decline of Great Britain, the world's wealthiest and most powerful nation at the end of the 19th century? By 1970, not a long time in Britain's thousand year history, it had to go hat in hand to the IMF for emergency loans to pay its debts! (*For most of the past thirty years, the UK has been back on a strong, highly entrepreneurial growth track. Much of the credit goes to Margaret Thatcher's take-no-prisoners style of leadership in reviving the country's entrepreneurial spirit. To many economists and pundits howevers, the amazing rebound seemed to be as big a mystery as the steep decline!)* Or what really created the economic miracle of Taiwan? Poorer than Albania in 1950, today it has the highest per capita foreign reserves of any industrial country in the world! There is no economic, political, or management theory to explain either case.

And of course it's very unclear, as of this writing, what the ultimate fall-out will be from our current, self-imposed, economic mess. Who will be the new winners and losers as we all grope through the world's worst recession in 80 years? Can a debt-ridden U.S. really rebound to lead us all back to the economic Promised Land? Will China continue on its rapacious path to be the export factory for the whole world—and in the process strangle its own "goose with two golden eggs"—the markets of North America and Europe? Will India and Japan just stand by and watch? What about the severely damaged smaller players—how many decades will it take the likes of Greece, Romania, Ireland, Portugal and Iceland to see economic growth again? And sadly, in such an environment, who can even think about aiding or bailing out the poorest, most desperate countries of the world? Against this gloomy backdrop, the UN Millennium Project goal of abating poverty by 2015 seems further out of reach today than when it was announced with such fanfare, by the United Nations, just ten years ago. Even Jeffrey Sachs, the charismatic architect of the project's *Millennium Development Goals*, and bestselling author of *The End Of Poverty*, must be scratching his head a bit these days.

One of JFK's famous economic slogans was: "A rising tide lifts all boats." That's true but we know that the tide comes in and the tide goes out. The point to ponder, in all of this, is what really causes the rise and fall of a peoples' prosperity? Is there an immutable law of the universe that says it has to be this way? Can we really do anything to change the course of history? It's worth considering.

THE PROSPERITY CYCLE OF NATIONS

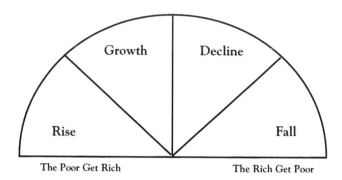

Nations, like companies, and people for that matter, have a definite life cycle. The names are a little different, but you'll recognize the four phases from *The Life Cycle Of All Organizations* described in the Introduction. The similarities are most obvious when comparing countries' long-term economic cycles, and not just their current day situations. That's why we've labeled it *The Prosperity Cycle Of Nations*. There are obvious differences in the pure life cycles of companies and countries. The time frames are very different, the stakes are very different, and in one of the most obvious of differences, countries don't just go out of business if they can't satisfy their customers—or citizens. They probably should but they don't! Even with these important differences, most countries, or societies, will ultimately pass through most of the phases in the prosperity cycle. When you think carefully about the prosperity cycle of countries, history shows that only three things can possibly happen: The poor get rich, the rich get poor, and some poor stay poor forever. Staying rich forever is potentially a fourth possibility, but it's never yet happened in all of recorded history! We'll come back to that point later of course. For right now, let's explain the three possibilities that we know every country faces:

• The Poor Get Rich

"First, we determined that runaway inflation and rural poverty were the main reasons for the rise of Communism on the mainland. We were determined to avoid that in Taiwan. So our policy was to do the opposite." This is the Taiwan story. It's actually the normal story of all prosperous nations, on the assumption that no rich country or society was rich from the day it was created. It's interesting to note that in recent memory, say the second half the 20th century, most country examples in this category have been small countries. Minister K. T. Li's warning: " . . . where you find too many people, you find poor countries . . . " looks like good advice. With the notable exceptions of Japan and Germany over the last fifty years, and at least in certain areas of China today, *small* seems to be *beautiful* for creating high growth countries, exactly the same as it has been for high growth companies. (It's worth noting also that Japan, Germany and China have all had extremely low birth rates.) These are early signals that entrepreneurial characteristics are very much at work in high growth economies. In fact the evidence strongly supports this belief. *Bloomberg Business Week's* 2010 ranking of countries on "global competitiveness" is instructive. In rank order the ten most competitive countries in their report are:

1. Singapore	6. Sweden
2. Hong Kong	7. Canada
3. United States	8. Taiwan
4. Switzerland	9. Norway
5. Australia	10. Malaysia

Actually, even I was astonished when I looked at this list. Nine out of ten of the world's most competitive economies are small countries! Even if Canada, with its 30 million people, is labeled mid-sized the list is still amazing. *Bloomberg Business Week's* working definition of global competitiveness is: ". . . the ability of a country to achieve sustained high rates of GDP growth per head." In deference to our Latino colleagues, Chile makes the top twenty on the list, proving that world class competitiveness can and does exist in South America too—albeit in a small country again!

• The Rich Get Poor
No country has ever stayed rich forever. Check your high school world history book if you don't believe me. We call it the disease of the rich— or national complacency. Japan may be at the early stages of that downward cycle now. According to Koji Shima, a typical, well educated, 21st century staffer in Tokyo, the country seems hell-bent on destroying

its primary strength, which has been the extraordinary commitment of Japanese workers to do whatever it takes to push their company (and country) ahead. The full quote of Mr. Shima, the bright, young assistant to the CEO of Uni-Charm (Japan's Procter & Gamble) was: "For Japanese young people, factory work and blue collar work are out. All young Japanese call it KKK work. Kitanai means dirty, kike means dangerous and kitsui means hard. Our fathers did those jobs but we want something better like planning or public relations." Good-bye prosperity—hello industrial decline!

Countries in the "rich get poor" category have an old familiar ring—one we've heard from the fall of Rome to the decline of Britain. It's that same old inward looking complacency. The muddying of the national sense of mission. It's the loss of urgency with too many people waiting for someone else to do the work. And it's the ring of a people beginning to see prosperity as more of a right than a reward. In short, it's an entire nation watching its spirit of entrepreneurship and enterprise slip through its fingers.

• Some Poor Stay Poor Forever

Like start-up companies that don't make it, some countries just never rise up economically. They don't even get into the cycle. Bangladesh for example, has been poor for a thousand years, and nobody seems to think its situation will ever change. Other unfortunate examples of countries stuck in this terrible no-man's land would be: Haiti, Albania, Yemen, Mozambique, and Cambodia. One thing they all do have in common is that they violate the "job/baby ratio." Regardless of one's position on birth control, when a country creates more babies than it does jobs, it's bound to get—and stay poor! The only good news here is these countries absolutely do not have to accept their fate.

You really don't have to just play with the hand you've been dealt by "the gods." Other places with few resources and very inhospitable environments have become extremely prosperous. Examples abound: We could obviously rest our case just on Taiwan, but numerous other examples exist around the world. Take tiny, frozen Iceland as a fairly dramatic European example. While they've been hit hard by "our" banking and mortgage crisis (who hasn't!) look at the following interview with Iceland's President Grimsson. I can tell you from personal experience, there is no more inhospitable environment in the world, than Iceland, for about 10 months of the year! Or go to tiny Uruguay, stuck between two very big and very tough neighbors, Brazil and Argentina. You'll see why this highly prosperous country, with 100% literacy, is called the "Switzerland" of South America. Further, in today's global economy, there's no reason why the next Microsoft or Genentech can't come from one of these "poor forever" countries. The current *Financial Times Global 500*, which ranks companies by market value, shows many such examples, Nokia in Finland, Samsung in South Korea, Teva in Israel, Koç Holdings in Turkey, Taiwan Semiconducter and Reliance Industries in India. Of course in another big sign of the times, Petro China has just leap-frogged Exxon-Mobil, Royal Dutch Shell, Apple, Microsoft and Wal-Mart to become the most valuable company in the world. I'm sure you get the point. Anything is possible—almost anywhere—in the world these days!

As mentioned earlier, while nations can and do remain poor forever, the even more compelling point for us is that no nation has ever stayed rich forever. Not the grandest of China's dynasties. Not the Romans, the Persians, the Ottomans, the Spanish nor the British. It's never happened. Today Japan is on a very slippery slope. And The United States, the 20th century's economic powerhouse, and still going strong, nonetheless has experienced a 30% decline in its relative share of world markets since 1960. So don't think for a minute that the U.S. is immune to the prosperity cycle of nations!

Does it have to be this way? Of course not. There is no law of nature or rule of behavior that says rich nations can't stay rich; that they must lose their spirit of enterprise and become poor. Anyway, you don't even have to worry about "staying rich forever." All you have to do, all any generation can do, is make absolutely certain you leave your country in better shape than you found it. If this is worth doing, just what do we do? Are there any lessons to learn, or rules to follow, in the noble effort to create and maintain national prosperity?

As noted earlier, those lessons will never be found be found in the stuff of trickle-down economics or in endless debates over the perfect capital gains tax. You won't find the fundamental principles of enterprise in an IMF report, at the London School of Economics or the Harvard Business School. In fact, governments, business schools, and the science of economics may be the worst places to look for answers. Certainly a textbook economic analysis would show that Zambia, rich in natural resources, should be more prosperous than Taiwan, with zero natural resources. Or that frozen Iceland must be an economic basket case compared to richly endowed Paraguay. Or for that matter, "east" German workers should have been as productive as "west" German workers. And that today's young generation of working Americans, like every generation before them, will retire more economically secure than their parents and grandparents. Since none of these text book conclusions are true, maybe it's time to look elsewhere for answers—to discover what really causes the rise and fall of a peoples' prosperity— and what if anything, we can do about it.

It's hardly a theoretical issue. The stakes are high and time is running out for many countries. In Africa, things are getting so bad that the only alternatives may be a complete bailout by the world's rich nations (which ain't going to happen soon brother!) or seeing a whole continent go bankrupt—both unthinkable results. And what about the "sleeper" continent? With the highest birth rates in the world, what can South America (especially Brazil) really do about its 220 million poverty stricken citizens who live side by side 110 million prosperous citizens? And can the new and enlarged European Community really just sit by and watch Greece and much of Eastern Europe slip into the third world? In Asia, the battle of economic supremacy between China, India, and Japan is in full gear. But what will be the economic role of the smaller, prosperous countries like Singapore, Taiwan, and even Australia? Who will lead and who will follow in Asia is a very old question. In the past, life could be tough for the followers. Will history repeat itself?

And lastly, in North America, what is it going to take to transform Mexico into a first world economy? Since I'm writing this book in

Arizona, where just across the border some 26,000 Mexicans have been killed in the drug wars, and our federal government, Democrats and Republicans alike, seems frozen in time when it comes to actually fixing our broken immigration system—which in fact could benefit both countries economically—the picture looks damn grim. And, of course, will super-prosperous Canada and the U.S. ever solve our deep problems of regional and inner-city poverty—or will we just have to accept that 10% to 15% of our people are going to be poor, uneducated, living on welfare, and committing most of the crimes? Can that really be an acceptable outcome amid such national riches? The 21st century and "the *new* entrepreneurial age" would seem like a perfect time to answer, finally, the long-standing question: What can be done, in fact, to create that rising tide which will truly raise all boats?

A few things seem certain at the outset. First, at the dawn of the 21st century, the ups and downs of national prosperity are coming at a faster and faster clip. The rise and fall of the wealth of nations is being measured in decades, not centuries. Second, this economic slug-fest is truly world-wide, and countries must be prepared to compete globally at a world-class level to survive. And finally, there's one very old lesson that just won't go away. It really does come from us! The prosperity of countries, like the profits of companies, still depends on the enterprise of people. You can be sure that when this goes, decline and fall can't be far behind.

The thesis here is the same underlying basics that propel growth and decline in business, are very much at work in the rise and fall of economic states: Pursuing a purposeful mission, producing goods and services a little better than your neighbor, feeling some urgency about it all and being supremely self-inspired are in fact the characteristics of all entrepreneurial and enterprising people. They are the day-in and day-out behaviors that produce prosperity for individuals, for companies—and we believe for countries.

What's always been interesting to me, and I think appealing to others, is that these principles are so simple and obvious. But what's so puzzling, is that the obvious doesn't seem to be obvious at all to so many "experts" around the globe: Not to most of our political leaders, not to the education establishment, and certainly not to the economists of the world. The experts' notion of creating national prosperity seems to be that things are terribly complicated and we need PhDs, computer models and more congressional hearings to figure out what to do.

Well, things haven't been quite that complicated, at least up to now, in the small and (still) prosperous country of Iceland. And we even got the President of the country to tell us why.

COUNTRIES: HERE COME THE VIKINGS!

"I would argue that Iceland. . . . .offers an inspiring example of what can be done if the potential that is in everybody for progress, for work, for initiative, for creativity—for entrepreneurship, is allowed to grow."

—Olafur Ragnar Grimsson
President, Republic of Iceland

"I think if you look at the history of the Icelanders, from a 21st century perspective, it's a remarkable story. At the beginning of last century, we were less than 100,000 mainly poor farmers. But everybody could write and read and everybody was culturally trained in the spirit that there were no limits to what you could do. You could go on a boat and fish and earn a living, you could start a farm, buy a few sheep and grow them. If you were energetic, prepared to work, you had a great chance at life. But it was also a society where people relied on each other in a positive way. If an accident happened, they helped each other. If a farming family lost the sheep, the neighbors would help. So it was a combination of what we would call today an entrepreneurial spirit in each and everyone as well as a cooperative culture where everyone saw it to his advantage to benefit from the progress of others."

This is President Grimsson of Iceland,* We were meeting at his official residence outside Rejyavik, thanks to the indomitable entrepreneurial spirit of my partner in Iceland, Arni Sigurdsson.** The President continued: "So when technology came in the beginning of the century, this cultural root of entrepreneurship and self-awareness and the belief in one-self and the possibility that one could do things—started to create a remarkable progress which by the end of the century, made Iceland one of the richest countries in the world with the highest standard of living, a high-tech economy, and an extensive system of education and health services available for everybody. And in addition to that we have a remarkable culture.

In terms of publishing books we have the highest rate of book publishing per capita in the world. We have a world class symphony orchestra, and every week twenty to thirty theatrical productions and art exhibitions in the capital area."

The President wasn't making up those claims. The numbers are impressive. Iceland ranks 11th worldwide in GDP per capita, ahead of such economic powerhouses as Canada, Great Britain, Sweden, Italy,

---

* *Editor's note: Iceland's economy was hit particularly hard by the current worldwide recession—thanks to their banks' over-dependence on U.S. and British backed mortgage investments that have all gone south. I first interviewed President Grimsson a few years earlier—and have chosen to not change the thrust of his comments as I have no doubt that the Viking entrepreneurial spirit, going strong for over a thousand years, will bounce back soon. So bear in mind the statistics quoted above are 'pre-recession.' Recalculating them in the trough of Iceland's very tough recession seems off the historical mark. And, the World Bank still shows Iceland's 2010 GDP per capita as 19th in the world and its income per capita as 5th in the world. And the UN Human Development Index ranks it number 3 in the world. Not bad for a country going through tough times. In any event I believe the President's comments are valuable and worth repeating. Apparently Icelanders agree—in 2008 they re-elected him to another four year term.*

** *Sigurdsson is tall and imposing like most Viking entrepreneurs. I had asked him to arrange an interview with someone in Iceland who could talk about the nation's entrepreneurial style. I suggested it could be a respected economist, someone working in the government, or even possibly the Minister of Finance if he would agree. A day later Arni said to me: "I called the Minister of Finance for your interview, but he's out of the country. So I called the President and he's agreed to see you at 5 o'clock today." This is why I love Iceland!*

Singapore, Hong Kong, and even our showcase example, Taiwan. It's number 8 on *The Economist's* Quality Of Life Index. It ranks 2nd in the world behind Japan in highest life expectancy and lowest infant mortality. The only reason it's not in the top ten or twenty in Global Competitiveness (see the listing earlier in this Chapter) can be found on any map. Iceland borders the Arctic Circle in the middle of the north Atlantic. Even with this huge logistical challenge, it still ranks 38th out of some 220 countries.

The President again: "When you look at all of that and you bear in mind that we are only 270,000 people, then you can see the potential for other parts of the world. Wherever you take an assembly of 270,000 people, whether it is in New York, Los Angeles, Tokyo, Delhi, London, or wherever, and if you challenge those people by showing what 270,000 Icelanders have done, you're entitled to ask them, 'why can't you? Why can't you?' I know that some of my countrymen have this theory that we are very special. That we are almost unique. And we have great discussions today about genetic science and capabilities based on genes. But I fundamentally believe that we are not that different from anybody else—or that this could only happen in Iceland. So I would argue that, in terms of the potential for other people in the rest of the world, Iceland offers an inspiring example of what can be done—even if you're small, isolated and living in a difficult environment. Countries can create miracles if the potential that is in everybody for progress, for work, for initiative, for creativity—for entrepreneurship, is allowed to grow.

"If you analyze Icelandic history and go back to the old Viking Sagas which recount the history of the country from the 10th century up to modern times, you will see there is a great belief in the capability of the individual. It's a belief in one's own worth and one's own capabilities—not necessarily in a negative competition, but in cooperation. I sometimes think that modern marketing theories and theories of competition have put it wrongly. They emphasize the condition for advancement is somehow a negative competition between people where you try to destroy the competitor—instead of seeing entrepreneurship and competition and growth and progress as a result of one's own drive in a positive relationship with others. So Icelanders have, at the same time, a strong sense of individuality and a deep rooted sense of community."

Bear in mind, these are very deep roots President Grimsson is talking about. If you recall the earlier interview with Kari Stefansson, the bio-tech entrepreneur, Icelanders measure their family trees in millenniums, not centuries. Iceland is also, as Dr. Stefansson made clear, one of the most homogeneous societies in the world. All this makes having a *shared national sense of mission* practically a given—as the President's words clearly show. The rest of us may have to work at it a little more. We can't put our national mission on auto-pilot and just assume it will stay on course for a hundred years—or even a decade it seems. Given this, I asked President Grimsson how he sees the role of a President or a government in fostering individual entrepreneurship and creating a more entrepreneurial society. Is it something the President of a country should be involved in or is it just something that either happens or doesn't happen in a national economy?

The President leaned forward and I detected just a slight shift from Chief Executive to Chief Politician, as he obviously relished this kind of question: "No, no—I think you can certainly create the conditions in many ways:

- "First of all, education is essential. An open, innovative, creative educational system is essential.

- "I think secondly it is important to emphasize, both by the leaders of the country and by the educational system, that everybody has the potential within himself or herself to achieve great progress and to make a difference. It's just a question of training yourself and developing your skills.

- "And third, I strongly believe that both the laws of the land as well as the ways in which corporations work, must be based on the principle that as many people as possible should be given the chance to start their own company, do their own thing, or make their own contribution.

"Also it's important for all of us to realize that we are now in such a different setting that nobody has a formula of how the future is going to be. There are lots of people who are prepared to tell you, whether they're in government or elsewhere, but the fact of the matter is nobody has a formula. Nobody knows where the initiatives are going to come from that will change our technology or our way of life. They may come from somebody in a garage in Seattle like Bill Gates or an Icelandic scientist like Kari Stefansson doing important things in biotech. It means that anybody can influence the world in a fundamental way. And the role of the government is to make sure that we allow this big potential to have the impact it can have. If this means changing the operations of the corporations and the laws of the land to make it possible, so be it!"

Since about three quarters of the world's countries have never had a successful and prosperous economy like Iceland has, I asked the President what specific advice he could offer other nations: "As you travel the world and meet other heads of state, let's say from some desperately poor country, what advice would you give these poor countries? It just seems some of them stay poor forever. How do they break their cycle of poverty and suffering?" Grimsson responded: "The advice I have given to some of them, such as Kofi Annan at the UN when he came here is: 'When you come to Iceland, instead of talking to me or meeting the ministers, or listening to experts, I will take you to one of the small towns or villages here in Iceland. I will show you the standard of living in the private houses, the excellence of the schools, the excellence of the sports forum and the swimming facilities, the health care center, the football ground, the harbor, the ships, the companies, the workplaces, and then I will show you a picture of that poor village fifty years ago, or even thirty years ago. After doing that I would tell them, 'none of this was created by the government or by the President. This was created by the people who live in this town. It was through their own initiative, entrepreneurship, energy and dedication. And you can do exactly the same in your own country.

"I think this is very, very important. When leaders of countries travel, they usually go to the capitals. They go to Washington or New York, they go to London, Paris, Berlin, which are marvelous cities—I like them all. But if they really want to understand the potential of growth, of what can be done, I would take them into the small Icelandic villages and townships and see how the people create a uniquely high standard of living, and try to inspire them by example of what they could do in their own country."

I thought we were coming to a good place to conclude the interview, and I knew that President Grimsson had other activities scheduled, so I said: "Thank you very much Mr. President. I know you have a busy schedule but is there anything else you would like to say on anything we've discussed?" He surprised me—very pleasantly—by wanting to talk on a bit longer. I got the sense that he was enjoying this and was really warming up to the subject at hand: "Yes indeed. It's a very interesting subject. I think it's a fascinating subject. Because what you call entrepreneurship, and I would call entrepreneurial creativity, is the key element to progress in the 21st century. I have come to the conclusion from my own thinking and my discussions with corporate leaders and leaders of other nations, that it doesn't really matter how much financial strength you have, or industrial base, or high technology, or big bureaucracies in your government ministries. If you lack the vibrant element of, shall I say, entrepreneurial creativity among your people, your staff, and your workforce, you're going to lose out. Only those that encourage creativity, whether it's a nation, a corporation or an individual entrepreneur, are going to be successful in the 21st century economy. And in that notion of individual creativity, is the inherent sense that everybody's capable of making a difference, of being an entrepreneur, of driving progress. I also believe that encouraging creativity and entrepreneurial opportunities throughout society is the best way to promote democracy and create a more peaceful and secure world."

There was one last question I just had to ask: "Thank you again Mr. President, and now I have a last question. Isn't this the thousand year celebration of Leif Eriksson?" Well, if the entrepreneurial spirit is a fascinating subject to President Grimsson, you can only imagine how fascinating the story of Leif Ericksson is to any Icelander. Here's President Grimsson's own wonderful and entertaining Icelandic Saga:

"It is indeed. We will soon celebrate, together with America and Canada, the one thousandth anniversary of Leifur Eriksson's discovery of America. I'm very pleased about that because I brought the proposal to your President that we should all commemorate these events. It's not just because they are interesting historical events, but also because by looking at these stories, which are described in detail in the Icelandic Sagas from the 13th century, we can gain an understanding about ourselves. We can use the history of Leif Eriksson, and the other discoverers, to challenge ourselves. It must have taken a great spirit of discovery or entrepreneurship, to sail across the unknown ocean and be willing to go into unexpected lands and discover new continents. I believe we need that sense of discovery and exploration in the 21st century. We need this cultural root of daring to go into the unknown. Whether it is science, the genetic essence of man, space travel, or whatever else the future may offer us, we need some roots and heritage to gain and maintain our balance. Therefore we are celebrating these big events with the United States and Canada to draw a lesson from the Vikings' journeys and prepare ourselves for what is ahead in the new millennium.

"I think we should also realize that Leif Eriksson, and the other Viking discoverers, came from the only democratic commonwealth that existed in Europe at that time. It was the Icelandic Commonwealth—founded by the establishment of the Icelandic Althing (Parliament) in 930—the oldest Parliament in the world. So they came from a democratic community and they were also Christians, which many people are not aware of. So these Icelandic discoverers of America, one thousand years ago, were influenced by the two greatest cultural strands of the western world—democracy and Christianity. "

So, does President Grimsson convey a *national sense of mission* for Iceland? Do the country's modern economic results indicate they are successful at *making products and selling customers?* Are the people *innovative and action taking?* Do they appear to be *self-inspired?* Anyone who has spent more than thirty minutes in Iceland knows the answer to all these questions is yes—in spades. And you will certainly recall these four points as the same simple, basics of enterprise that entrepreneurs and their companies live by.

Abandoning those simple basics hasn't worked for companies—and it won't work for countries. It doesn't pass the test of history or of common sense. Nations need to learn, and start practicing, these old truths, not new theories, about fostering and maintaining prosperity. We call it *creating an entrepreneurial economy.*

Chapter 14

The Entrepreneurial Economy

"We were charged with promoting entrepreneurship throughout the country. But neither I nor my senior staff had any idea what entrepreneurship was."

—Mustapa Mohamed
Minister of Entrepreneurial Development
Government of Malaysia

Go back to K. T. Li's common sense principles: Population control, fight inflation, make people rich, don't get hung up on ideology, and create an entrepreneurial economy. Of special interest to us is the final, underpinning principle—which K. T. Li carefully labeled "Create And Honor The Entrepreneurs."

That was exactly the mandate given to Mustapa Mohamed in Malaysia, the only Minister of Entrepreneurial Development in the world. There's something else about Minister Mustapa that is even more unusual than his title. He's that rarest of rare "experts" who will actually admit to what he doesn't know. After acknowledging that no one at the Ministry had the foggiest idea what entrepreneurship was all about, a rather serious glitch given his Ministry's mission, he went about educating himself and his senior staff—with a tiny assist from us. This is how I met him. Of course this is one of the small, useful lessons that most government leaders never learn: If you openly admit you don't know everything, it makes it smart, not embarrassing, to go back to school and learn what you need to learn. Anyway, Minister Mustapa went on to develop valuable policy initiatives and support programs to keep entrepreneurs and small business high on the priority list of the Malaysian government—where it remains today. This focus on entrepreneurial development has often been cited as one of the reasons Malaysia has re-bounded so well from the various Asian economic ups and downs of the recent past. As the Minister liked to say: "When you're competing with the likes of Taiwan, Hong Kong, and Singapore, you'd better know what you don't know—because you won't be getting any second chances against those Asian tigers!"

So how does someone like the minister of entrepreneurial development foster a high growth, entrepreneurial economy? What exactly does it take to "create and honor the entrepreneurs"? Hopefully we can do more than engage in a "vigorous debate" as economists are doing today. Certainly we need a more promising response than the politician's: "That's really a good question . . . I'll have to think about it." Well, the good news is that we actually do know a lot about how to go about this. Let's return for a minute to the basic entrepreneurial practices of entrepreneurs and see how they work for a city, a state, or the economy of an entire country.

THE ENTREPRENUERIAL BASICS: APPLIED TO THE ECONOMY

Instilling the entrepreneurial spirit across an entire economy may sound complicated, but the fundamental questions to ask aren't. You'll recognize them all. Let's examine them one by one:

• Creating A National Sense Of Mission

Let's return to those simplest of words—with such profound impact. *What* is your country's mission for the 21st century? And *how* are you going to achieve it? Is your economic *strategy* smart—or stupid? Is your *culture* supporting your national strategy or blocking it? Are your *values* maximizing your *competitive position* or eroding it? If you can't answer these fundamental questions, or worse, if your answers are all in the negative, you're probably living in a country headed for tough times. The good news is that it doesn't have to be this way. Any country can develop, over time, a competitive strategy and a powerful culture. For sure, all nations will need these qualities in spades, to successfully compete in the global economic wars facing all of us! So whatever you can do to invigorate your national, regional, or even local sense of mission, will be well worth the investment. You owe it to yourself, and your children's children, to at least give it a try!

• Creating Customer/Product Competitiveness

Does your country produce superior goods and services at lower prices than your best foreign competitors? Do you have the competence to produce the highest quality products in the world? Do you provide better service than your best competitors in every field? Do you have the smartest and hardest working labor force in the world? Making and selling products and services the world needs, whether they be automobiles or internet portals—is still what matters most. These are the qualities that will continue to determine the competitive position of your country and your future national prosperity!

• Creating A National Urgency To Improve

Do you have a national sense of urgency about solving old problems and exploring new frontiers? Do you encourage innovation and action in all facets of national life? Do you hate bureaucracy? What are you doing to wipe it out? If you're stuck in a poor country, does every single person understand that "improving something—anything—everyday" is the fastest and surest path to national prosperity? If you were lucky enough to have been born in a rich country, what are you doing to avoid complacency? Will yours be the first rich society in history to conquer complacency? This is what it's going to take. Entrepreneurial countries, like companies and individual people, are fast moving and innovative— always.

• Creating A Nation Of Self-Inspired People
What is your country, or state, or city really inspired about? Are you and yours focused on the day-in-and-day-out high performance and high commitment it takes to be the best in the world? Are you working smarter and harder than your best competitors? Are the consequences in place to make all this happen? If your people, especially the young, do the right thing, what happens to them? If they do the wrong thing, what happens? If the positive and negative consequences are not timely and powerful, do you have the social and political will to change them?

Let's take a more in-depth look at how just one of these Entrepreneurial Basics applies to an entire economy. We've selected *Sense Of Mission*, but note how this over-arching principle also impacts customer/product competitiveness, the urgency to improve things, and fostering self-inspired people.

CREATING A NATIONAL SENSE OF MISSION

Does your country know *what* to do and *how* to do it? Do you have a strategy of high purpose and a supporting culture of high standards? A few countries around the world certainly do. Unfortunately, most people and their governments do not have a winning, national sense of mission. They fall short on one or both of the two fundamental variables: The *what* and the *how* of the national mission. The *what*, or the economic strategy, to the extent there is one, may be neither smart nor focused. Instead it typically promises something for everyone and is represented with a lot of feel-good political rhetoric. The *how*, or the popular culture and values being propagated across the country, are coming from God knows where, and they will most often have absolutely nothing to do with achieving the nation's economic strategy. If this sounds even vaguely familiar, you'd better hope your country gets this message soon. Creating a powerful and competitive sense of mission is exactly what it's going to take to reach the winners circle in the 21st century. To illustrate, here once again is the "What / How" matrix, adapted to countries, and highlighting two of my favorites—Brazil and Taiwan.

NATIONAL SENSE OF MISSION

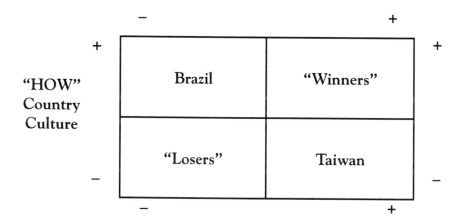

"WHAT" Country Strategy

To get a grip on this seemingly simple, but profound analysis of a nation's well-being, it may be helpful to look at extremes. Brazil, that beautiful country with beautiful people and an amazing national appetite for having a good time, spent most of the 20th century re-defining economic chaos. It was, until very recently, the classic example of a country with a great and colorful culture, along-side a truly unfathomable economic strategy. At the opposite extreme, Taiwan is the country with the most successful economic strategy of the 20th century, but would be dead last on anyone's list of places to go to have fun. It's the archetypical example of a country with a great enterprise strategy but existing within a grim, nose-to-the-grindstone culture.

BRAZIL: WE'RE GOING TO HELL, BUT WE'RE GOING FIRST CLASS

Several years ago a Brazilian executive who was attending my seminar, delivered one of the great quotes on "national sense of mission." When he first saw the "What / How" matrix above, he said: "I've found Brazil's spot, upper left-hand corner! Our sense of mission seems to be, 'So what if we have a crazy economic strategy? We've got this great culture and we're having such a good time, who cares?' It's like we're going to hell but we're going first class!" Only a Brazilian could show such loving tolerance of his country's split personality.

Up until the early 21st century at least, that Brazilian's humor was the perfect definition for this bigger-than-life country. I fell in love with Brazil 30 years ago and ever since have been over-awed by its people, its culture, its enormous potential, its unbelievable poverty, and its absolutely loony economic history. Brazil's global image has always been that it's a country full of talented people—pursuing a grand but unfulfilled national mission. It is true that Brazil has embarked on a heroic effort to implement a more sane economic strategy over the past decade—particularly with regard to reducing its foreign debt (it had the highest in the world a decade ago—the spot now occupied by the USA!) and increasing its foreign reserves. But looking into its lop-sided sense of mission over the past hundred years is an economic and social lesson worth remembering. It has been, after all, the world's premier example of how a nation can have a good time while going broke.

To illustrate this in as benign a way as possible, I will go back to the lunch discussion I had with Olavo Setubal, former Foreign Minister of Brazil, Mayor of Sao Paulo, and elder statesman of Brazil's ruling elite. When I met him, he was Chairman of Bank Itau, Brazil's second largest bank, which just happens to be owned by his family. I had thought this gregarious power-broker, with his vast experience in government and business, would be a good person to ask about Brazil's national mission. I even hoped with his high profile political days behind him, he might provide an inside view of Brazil's economic strategy. Over lunch at the

bank's private dining room, with his body guards planted at each door—
a sober reminder of the country's Wild West crime rates, I asked the
most obvious question that comes to mind when visiting Brazil: "With
your tremendous economic potential, what's the plan to eradicate
Brazil's poverty? What's going to happen to the 95 million poor people?"
There was a long silence while we were served a delicious Brazilian hors
d'oeuvre—and finally the answer: "Nothing is going to happen to them.
There is no plan. The world has always had, and always will have, poor
people." Well, that seemed clear enough: nothing good is going to
happen to Brazil's 95 million poor people—ever! Then I asked a more
general question—about the country's very low ranking on most per
capita   socio/economic measures—such as being ranked 75th on the
UN's Human Development Index—and sitting just below the likes of
Libya and Albania and just above Bosnia and Iran. It was the same sort
of answer: "No one in Brazil seriously worries about 'per capita'
statistics—that's something only you Americans like to analyze." It was
on to the main course and a long, pleasant conversation that somehow
never returned to the more awkward topics of poverty and the per capita
quality of life.

Mr. Setubal certainly didn't make these rather shocking comments with
any hint of malice or even cynicism. They seemed, rather, to be self-
evident truths to him. And who knows? Perhaps they are and he was
just stating the obvious. After all, eradicating poverty would be a tall
order for most of the world. But it just sounded so—how to put it—so
"missionless." And so different from the upbeat, determination in
Taiwan, for example, where they did exactly that: eradicating poverty
in one generation.

Maybe none of this would matter, except happy-go-lucky Brazil has the
fifth largest population (195 million in 2010) and the seventh largest
economy (just over $2.4 trillion GDP) in the world—and, as noted
earlier, is expected to be the economic engine that pulls all of South
America into the developed world in the 21st century. And it turns out
that whether it's self-fulfilling prophecy, coincidence, or just plain bad
luck, having a great culture and a lousy economic strategy has left Brazil
with some pretty nightmarish socio-economic results like these:

- Ranks 75th in the world on the United Nation's Human Development Index—putting it squarely in the China / India camp—the only other economic giants with such enormous, unsolved social and distribution of wealth problems.

- On the 2010 World Bank's "Ease of Doing Business" survey, the country ranks 129th out of the 183 countries surveyed. In the same neighborhood you'll find such other shining examples of the free enterprise system as Nigeria, Morocco, and Bhutan. Good luck to Brazil's future entrepreneur wanabees!

- While boasting the world's 7th largest economy in total GDP, it ranks 105th in per capital GDP—at $10,200—just four spots above communist Cuba!

- 50% of the population—about 95 million people—live below the poverty line. 33% of the people have incomes of less than $250 a month. The Government benignly calls it "living on marginal activities."

- Brazil suffers one of the highest infant mortality rates (51/1000) in the world outside of Africa.

- At 1.6%, the annual investment in education ranks 7th lowest in the world as a percentage of GDP. 92% of Brazilian children don't finish lower school, while only 1% go to university.

- Brazil has 400 scientists per million population, while the USA has 8,000 per million.

The real problem may simply be that this is the country that ranks first in the world in wanting to have a good time—that is, holding the world's greatest party every year during Carnival, dancing the samba, going crazy over their beloved fútbal, making babies, and going to Disneyworld—where Brazilians rank number three in foreign visitors after Canadians and Brits. Unfortunately this obsession with having a good time hasn't done much for the national prosperity index.

One is always left to wonder if things are getting better or worse in Brazil. Is national prosperity just around the corner? Are they closing the income gap? Or will they just throw in the towel and declare national bankruptcy? Happily there are some very encouraging signs today. First among the recent encouraging signs was that Brazil's best Finance Minister of the last hundred years, was elected, and re-elected, President. Fernando Henrique Cardoso did what everyone said was impossible. He broke the back of inflation. *The Economist* put it bluntly: "Before Cardoso, to outsiders, Brazil—to be frank—was a joke. Since he arrived on the scene, Brazil and its 195 million people have gone through a headlong economic revolution. And whatever its faults or problems, no outsider today sees Brazil as a joke." And the current government of President Luiz Inácio Lula da Silva, just plain "Lula" to his followers, has continued those economic improvements in spite of his strong, left-of-center, political instincts. He has dramatically reduced the nation's foreign debt—and for an avowed laborite has been a prudent conservator of the nation's all-important foreign reserves. His term expires in 2011—and he can't run again—so we can all just hope that the long, painful road to recovery will continue under the next regime. There is obviously much work yet to be done.

The truth is, Brazil is actually two economies in one country. The working half of the economy would look like any European country. The other half lives in abject poverty with little hope for improvement. And the working half, no matter how industrious they are, cannot produce enough to lift the other half out of poverty. This has to mean it's time to look for completely new solutions. Of course, one that comes to mind here would be to unleash Brazil's entrepreneurial spirit, squarely within that half of the country with little means and little hope. Given half a chance, several million new Brazilian micro-entrepreneurs could stand all past economic history on its head. And today there are many strengths for Brazil's future entrepreneurs to build on:

- Brazil should, and will, soon become the first permanent South American member of the UN Security Council, as well as the elite *Group of Seven*, that powerful club of the major industrialized nations. These steps would give Brazil a huge voice in world affairs and global economic councils—boosting its diplomatic reputation and increasing its trade and investment profile.

- Brazil has clearly learned how to cut inflation. It's currently running at 5.5%, a far cry from the 1000% to 2000% range of the past.

- The country ranks first in the world in self-sufficiency, importing only 6% of its GDP.

- They can feed themselves! It ranks 7th in agricultural production and 10th in agriculture exports.

- The country has vast quantities of natural resources just waiting to be sold globally.

- And perhaps, because they are such great, fair-minded, and fun loving people to work with—they have no external political or military enemies. And that's pretty important in today's world.

But, of course, nothing fundamental and lasting will ever change if the country's national sense of mission becomes hostage again to the economic values and beliefs espoused over lunch. The current leaders who set the nation's economic strategy have to stay the course and bring to Brazil what JFK was promising to America in the 1960s, "a rising tide that lifts all boats." That tide is just beginning to hit the shores of Brazil today. Let's hope it continues—and that all those talented Brazilians finally fulfill their grand, national mission.

TAIWAN: WE'RE GOING TO HEAVEN, BUT IT'S HELL GETTING THERE

If you don't believe in economic miracles, then you haven't been to the Republic of China on Taiwan—the reigning champion of national enterprise. If nothing else, Taiwan is a country with an overpowering national mission—to create prosperity for its citizens. Here are a few of its record breaking achievements that are virtually guaranteed to not resemble anything going on in your homeland:

• Average 9% GNP growth for sixty years—number one in the world.

• A 70 fold increase in per capita GNP since 1950—tops in the world.

• The richest industrial country in the world—per capita. With $372 billion in foreign reserves, it's number 5 in the world after China, Japan, Russia and Saudi Arabia. However, since every penny of Saudi's reserves come from oil, I'd say Taiwan deserves the top spot—per capita. An awesome achievement for a country of 23 million people and no natural resources!

• Average domestic inflation rate of only 2.2 % for six decades.

• Near 100% re-valuation of its currency over the past two decades while still increasing exports each year. Now that's hard to do!

• Infant mortality rate of 6/1000 is better than Germany, Japan and the USA.

• Distribution of income ratio remains one of the most equitable in the world—confounding its socialist and communist adversaries.

There's sixty years of hard work, personal sacrifice, military intimidation from China, and political ostracism from the rest of the world in those numbers. Yes, Taiwan may be going to *heaven*, but they've truly gone through *hell* getting there.

Turning conventional economic theory on its head, Taiwan has long mystified international economists. Strapped with a huge twin surplus in foreign trade and dollar reserves, it should be suffering from what economists call *Dutch Disease*—industrial stagnation due to earning more money than you can re-invest. You're certainly not supposed to maintain the same record-setting 9% GNP growth you've had for over half a century. Exactly the opposite has happened. Of course Dutch Disease is a hard theory to prove since Taiwan is about the only country that actually has the disease!

Taiwan not only mystifies but infuriates the world's left-of-center social engineers. They keep asking when the politically incorrect Taiwanese are going to fall into the famous *Kuznet* trap, that old socio-economic chestnut that says rapidly developing economies always produce a widening of the gap between rich and poor. Again, exactly the opposite has happened in Taiwan. The average income of the top 20% of Taiwanese, over the average income of the bottom 20%, has dropped from being 15 times greater to less than 5 times today. This gives Taiwan one of the most equitable distributions of income in the world . . . so much for modern economic theory!

As a point of interest and comparison to Brazil, our other *sense of mission* example, Taiwan has a near zero rate of poverty, and no foreign debt. In fact it is one of only two countries in the world (Finland being the other) that has repaid in full, every penny of economic aid it received from the U.S. The final portion of that debt was paid off amid great fanfare in the early 1960s.

Outsiders have to remember the mainland Nationalists had been ravaged by war with Japan since 1931 and were then driven out of their homeland in a bloody civil war with Mao's communist hordes. They ended up on a mountainous island, one tenth the size of California, with few assets and virtually no natural resources. How then, did this small group of people, beaten and broke in 1950, accumulate a $372 billion surplus in foreign reserves by 2010? And just to drive the point home, how can this occur in a country with almost no diplomatic recognition around the globe? To most observers, it all sounds impossible. However it sounds, the causes of Taiwan's sky-rocketing prosperity since 1950, turn out to be pretty basic things—starting with the economic beliefs and strategy of the ruling elite in the government. In the following discussion, see if you detect any similarities with the ruling elite of Brazil. I kind of doubt you will.

The top academic economist in Taiwan is Dr. Chi Hsieh. K. T. Li told me Hsieh was "a very practical man for an economist" so I figured that was a pretty strong recommendation and went to see him. As the Chairman of the Economics Department at National Taiwan University, Hsieh gets a lot of questions from foreign countries on what they should do to create their own economic miracle. His polite but blunt answer says it comes down to a matter of will more than brains: "Knowing what to do and having the will to do it are separate universes. Go back to the late forties, early fifties. Taiwan faced a very tough situation in the domestic economy, as well as a dangerous international political situation. Taiwan's economy was dominated by state enterprises inherited from the Japanese: Maybe 70% of the economic output. But the government restrained itself to reverse the expanding of the public sector. The government privatized most of the public enterprises. To a great extent, the government encouraged the private entrepreneur. Also the government picked a very tough way to deal with inflation. Most countries take the easy way, printing the money and behaving like really big government is really good government. Taiwan has always been very conservative financially. Even though the popular thing was to spend, the government did not spend. They had strong will. And up to today, they still stick to this policy.

"My theory is I don't believe anyone in the government could forecast what was going to happen from these policies. For example, no one believed Taiwan would become a big exporter. Well maybe someone like K. T. Li believed. But most didn't. But the leaders were ready to give many things a try. And when something worked, they really pushed it. For example when exporting began to work, the government moved in with all means to promote exports. I mean they did everything possible. Here is the key point for policy makers. You don't have to be so intelligent—a genius. You just have to be smart enough to see changes. You don't have to be brilliant, or a great man to do this. But you have to remain alert. If your policy is working, push it 100%. This is my theory of what our government really did.

"Of course this requires hard work by the people. But I believe this is also economic, not just a cultural thing. It's a famous debate in the textbooks. Any country has to decide where to keep its best people. In some countries, especially in the developing world and the socialist countries, the best people went to the government. That is where they could do the most good, become famous, and so on. In Taiwan, the government never expanded the public sector. All the opportunity was in the private sector. So for the young people, the people who have the very strong desire of achievement, what you call the entrepreneurs, then they will say I will not join the government. I will go to the private sector. This is just common sense.

"So the important point for all countries is you have to find a way to let the people taste the development. Participate in it. That means if they do certain things, they and their family will be better off. Government's job is to stand by and watch and try to create a lot of these kinds of opportunities for the people. It's all common sense. But as I said, the hardest part is sticking to the common sense. Maybe this has been the most important capability of Taiwan's government for fifty years—not deviating from common sense principles."

So doggedly keeping your eye on the enterprise ball does require some trade-offs, or at least some patience. The original trade-off that Chiang Kai-shek and his defeated government made was economic freedom for political freedom. The wide open national elections in Taiwan, which recently (and peacefully) brought the opposition party to power for the first time, is a rather clear sign that those days are now over. The other trade-off was in the "quality of life" area. This is a country that tops the world in foreign reserves, but isn't even listed on the The Economist's annual rankings of the top eighty countries in the world on Quality of Life. The most persistent criticism of Taiwan's government is that they haven't paid enough attention to infrastructure, social issues and quality of life issues. Anyone who's suffered through a traffic jam or a typhoon in Taipei would agree I'm sure. For these critics, it should be welcome news that the Taiwan government is in the midst of the largest public works program ever undertaken by a country. They budgeted an incredible $300 billion across 779 separate projects to improve services throughout the country. Few countries in the world could afford this, but of course Taiwan can. Perhaps Taiwan's current robust democracy and its belated attention to quality of life issues are just more examples of K. T. Li's belief in: "The right policy at the right time!"

Taiwan and Brazil are both great countries, but for very different reasons. I'm sure you get the picture even from these brief illustrations. Such enormous differences really come from the differences in the *national sense of mission* being promoted by each country's leadership. This reveals itself in both the country's economic strategy and its underlying culture. In the examples of Brazil and Taiwan, it is clear that both countries are trying hard to improve the area of their national mission they have neglected in the past. This is good news for their people.

And what about the people of your state or region? What will it take to create an entrepreneurial economy in your own backyard? We'll end with a close-up view of one man's mission of creating an entrepreneurial economy—in the beautiful, bluegrass state of Kentucky. This is the story of Kris Kimel, good friend and amazing guy who has been mining this field for fifteen years—and just hit the mother-lode. Read on!

STATES: KENTUCKY'S ENTREPRENEURIAL CONSCIENCE

"We're pleased and proud of the fact that creating an entrepreneurial economy has become . . . . a part of public policy in Kentucky."

—Kris Kimel, Founder and President
Kentucky Science & Technology Corporation

"Basically in our work at the Kentucky Science and Technology Corporation (KSTC), it became evident that the key for development for communities and states and regions in today's world, was really contingent upon their ability to grow and expand new knowledge driven companies. That came, certainly from looking at the literature and the research, as well as our own experience and the work that we had accomplished. It was in a sense an emerging thing that came out of ten to fifteen years of work within KSTC.

"It was based on what we saw happening globally. And specifically in Kentucky, despite progress over the prior decade or so, we found ourselves still lagging behind many states in such critical areas as new firm creation, research and development, availability of risk capital, and so on. And given our belief that the key to developing this region was contingent upon creating what we termed the *entrepreneurial economy*, having weaknesses in those critical areas—at least in our minds—created a greater sense of urgency to do something."

This is Kris Kimel, or as we like to call him, the state of Kentucky's "entrepreneurial conscience." How does one get into this line of work anyway? What's the prerequisite for leading a campaign to create an entrepreneurial economy in a state? In Kimel's case it began with a couple of senior level government appointments when he was quite young: Here's Kimel again: "Well, first I was the Executive Assistant to the Kentucky Attorney General for eight years But it really started when I became the Chief of Staff for the Lieutenant Governor of Kentucky starting way back in 1983. It was in that capacity that I became very interested in the whole issue of technology policy, entrepreneurship, and the innovation of those things in creating economic growth. So I started the Kentucky Science & Technology Corporation in late 1987. So you could say I've been at it, seriously at it, since 1983. Over 25 years."

From my own experience, there is no more knowledgeable person on this subject than Kris Kimel. A few years back, when I first met him, he was already several years into his crusade which he called: "Kentucky, Inc.—Creating An Entrepreneurial Economy." And he's at his entrepreneurial best when he delivers his compelling argument for doing just that in the bluegrass state. According to KSTC's original research, Kentucky had (and still has in some areas) severe shortcomings in key entrepreneurial indices. For example, among all fifty states of the United States, Kentucky's rank in a few key indices was very low:

Key Indices	Rank
• World Wide Web hosts per capita.	#50
• % of adults with a high school degree.	#50
• % of adults with university degree.	#46
• Start-up "incubators" per capita.	#43
• New firm creation.	#42
• Equity capital available.	# 40
• Industrial R&D investment	# 40

Given these dismal entrepreneurial indicators, I asked Kimel to say a word or two on the general economic strategy and culture of Kentucky. What would creating an entrepreneurial economy do that general, run of the mill economic development might not do? I think he had been asked this question a thousand times. His finely tuned answer: "Well, historically Kentucky's economy has been, like a lot of states, based on plentiful and fairly inexpensive natural resources and labor. In our case it was agriculture and tobacco. Over the past several decades we've seen a profound shift away from those types of things. Kentucky then developed reliance on larger industries and outside industries. As a consequence, there has been a lack of emphasis on entrepreneurship and creating companies. Of course one could argue that farmers are one of the earliest entrepreneurial groups. But by and large there has been an over dependence on larger and outside companies as opposed to creating knowledge and wealth within the state. That has made the challenge a bit more difficult. Kentucky has certainly benefitted from the relocation of some very good manufacturing plants into the state. The big Toyota plant, for example, is a very nice thing to have, but it's not a long term solution to economic development in Kentucky. They could be gone tomorrow. So what we have to do in Kentucky, as do all states, is to focus more on creating our own knowledge and our own expertise and our own value, because that's where the real payoff comes from—those kinds of companies and those kinds of long-term, well paying jobs."

I asked Kimel what kinds of specific activities KSTC has undertaken to create an entrepreneurial economy? His response: "We've focused our attention in a fairly systemic way. We focused both in the areas of education and also economic development and competitive economy issues. We've done a number of specific things. We produce and issue an *Entrepreneurial Capacity Report*. We've also developed and implemented initiatives to help companies develop and grow. We hold an annual Entrepreneurship and Commercialization Institute in Kentucky, again geared toward the start-up and growing of knowledge and technology-based companies. We've also created a program aimed at college and university students. It's basically a web-driven program to provide information and advice to students who have an interest in starting companies. We run a monthly competition with those students—in which we hold a business idea competition and award $1,000 every month to students who win based on their business idea and plans. The winner can be one student or a group of students. We're also involved in helping to expand the research and development capacity of the state. We believe that a lot of the energy for creating these new companies is going to come from universities. So we have a variety of things that we're currently involved in: both helping to educate people about entrepreneurship as well as helping people to actually start and grow companies."

Kris Kimel knows the political and governmental landscape in Kentucky very well. That's surely been a factor in KSTC's success, and probably a lesson for others trying to re-focus a state-wide economy. Anyway, I wanted to ask him his views on the proper role of government in this whole process. His answer: "Well, the government has an important role. I think the government's role is to help create the conditions under which this type of economy can thrive and grow. I don't think it's necessarily in managing programs, or those types of things. It's more in terms of creating conditions. For example, looking at different kinds of incentives that the public sector might offer to encourage high growth technology companies. Or possibly making some capital available in the pre-competitive phase of entrepreneurial development—like in the early R&D areas which some governments do now. Perhaps some very, very early stage, pre-seed capital that might be made available to help stimulate start-ups. But again, it's primarily in helping to create the conditions and structures for these companies to succeed and grow. To help create the environment in which this can happen as opposed to directly involving themselves in trying to manage actual programs. You have to be very careful in having public organizations getting too involved—because they respond to a very different set of conditions. We just don't want or need government getting involved in making business decisions. On the other hand, making public officials aware of the real meaning of entrepreneurship, what it really represents, and that it goes beyond just someone starting a company, all these are terribly important."

Touché! And to cap it off, I wanted to hear specifically what advice Kris Kimel might give others who wanted to create a more entrepreneurial economy in their own states. So I asked him if an economic development team came to see him from Maine, or Oregon, or Puerto Rico, and said: "Look, we've heard you've been doing this for two decade or so in Kentucky. We're ready to do the same in our own state. What advice can you give us to raise our chances of being successful?" Kris thought for a moment, shifting a bit perhaps into more of an official "advisory mode" and responded with several important points:

- "First, we've learned that creating an entrepreneurial economy is as much about changing the culture as it is about influencing some of the economic institutions and factors in a state. Changing that culture is somewhat of a slow process but it doesn't have to take forever. We tried to walk-the-walk in the sense that we tried ourselves to be entrepreneurial in creating the type of programs and initiatives that we thought could jump-start this. I've also talked again and again to everybody in the state about the three or four things that characterize an entrepreneurial economy. One is knowledge. Entrepreneurial organizations recognize the value of knowledge and are driven by knowledge. The second is to be highly innovative. And third, is to be fast. To understand the importance of velocity, and speed, and moving quickly. Certainly coming from your books, I know you agree that relentless innovation and fast action are big parts of it.

- "Second, as we recognized that these things are vital in an entrepreneurial company or economy, we certainly tried to behave that way ourselves. So we were, I think, somewhat aggressive. We worked with people where we could, but certainly we were fairly aggressive in trying to stimulate and work with other partners to get as many things going as we possibly could. We recognized that this isn't going to happen in a linear way and that's why we tried to get as many things going as we could, knowing that some would succeed and some would fail and that we wouldn't know where the successes were going to come from at the beginning. It was always very important to us to get as many things going as we could and that has been our driving philosophy.

- "In addition, I think another key strategy for any state or region wanting to foster this kind of economy is addressing the issue of risk capital. And I mean at all stages -- in everything from research and development, to pre-seed, through early stage venture, and mezzanine financing. And this requires some working together between the public and private sector. The public sector has a role in the very, very early stage of development, where the commercial marketplace probably isn't going to be particularly interested because of the risk involved. And then as you move down the entrepreneurial pipeline, the private sector has to step up to create angel networks, venture funds, early stage funds, etc., that are going to provide the different stages of capital that new and growing companies need. This has certainly has been one of the bigger problems historically in states like Kentucky, where we have not had that kind of strong, indigenous risk capital industry. And while it is now starting to emerge, we have found ourselves in many respects playing catch-up because we haven't had a venture capital industry. In a sense, that's the thing, not the only thing, but risk capital is certainly a major part of the fuel that drives the development of these kinds of companies."

- "At the Kentucky Science and Technology Corporation, we crafted our own definition of entrepreneurship to try to illustrate it to public officials. Our working definition is 'the unrestrained pursuit of new ideas resulting in an innovative creation.' From that definition, there are several key points. One is that while entrepreneurs are certainly cognizant of the barriers and the problems that exist, they aren't constrained by them. They're not letting those things discourage them at the beginning. Another key point is that an entrepreneur or an entrepreneurial organization is not only searching for new ideas, but they are also creating something. It could be adding value to an existing process or the creation of a whole new company. The important part of the definition is they're actually *creating something*! You know, you can be creative and still not actually create anything. But we stress to everyone, especially in the public sector, that the definition doesn't only apply to people creating new companies. Creating an entrepreneurial economy, is about all of the institutions and all of the companies in an economy, coming together and striving to become entrepreneurial in their operations."

- "Also I think you have to bring people together—and you've all got to be relentless in coming up with ideas and ways of implementing strategies that can lead toward the creation of this kind of economy. Perhaps the key thing is, as part of the definition, is that you've got to move fast. We have found that there's not much time to think about these things. You kind of have to act and be prepared to adjust as you go along. As someone once said, you have to be willing to jump off the building and grow your wings on the way down. Obviously it's not about having everything figured out up front at the beginning. So I think really it's certainly being clear in what you're trying to accomplish, being very strategic, acting quickly, and doing as many things as you can and recognizing this is not a linear process. This is not A plus B equals C. And if you move along in a very linear process, you're still going to be doing it thirty years from now, while everybody's kind of passed you by."

- "A final important point is that, as you know, KSTC is an independent, non-profit company. We work very closely with government, but we're not part of government. I think that's been an advantage. It gives us a lot more flexibility not only to do things, but it gives us more flexibility to make mistakes. And we've certainly made our share of mistakes. But learning from those mistakes, and not being afraid of making mistakes, I think has aided us a great deal in helping to accomplish what we set out to do."

As a kind of summarizing question, I asked Kris: "What's the payoff at the end of the day. Has this kind of effort had a real effect on Kentucky over the 25 years? Is it worth all the effort or not?" He didn't hesitate a second: "The payoff, at least from our perspective, has been in seeing people begin to appreciate the value of ideas, begin to appreciate the value of relentless innovation, and appreciate the integration of those factors and how they interact to create an entrepreneurial environment and culture. In Kentucky we're seeing a real spurt in activity in terms of the start-up of new companies. We're also seeing a lot of very dynamic entrepreneurs beginning to take root. We see the school systems begin to look at it, understand the value of entrepreneurship not only in the education of kids, but also in terms of how they themselves operate. Of course, it hasn't happened overnight.

"One of the things that we worked hardest at, and we are really pleased with, is that the Kentucky Legislature, during its last session, passed the first comprehensive Science and Technology package in the state's history. That package includes funds to help stimulate and invest in pre-competitive research and development, both at universities and among private companies. Quite honestly, I think one of the big outcomes we've seen was the passing of that bill, House Bill 572. That came out of, in large part, the Kentucky Science and Technology Strategy that

KSTC developed and released way back in the fall of 1999. Governor
Patton asked us to put together a science and technology strategy for
the state, which we did and it was heavily based on the whole issue of
creating an entrepreneurial economy. In fact the legislation actually
makes reference to the importance of creating an entrepreneurial
economy right in the preamble. We were very proud of that because
what that signifies, in addition to the specific measures that are in the
bill, is a statement of public policy: 'It's in the state's interest to create
an entrepreneurial economy'—and that was something we had been
working on for some time. We're pleased and proud of the fact that
creating an entrepreneurial economy has become, with the passage of
this bill, a part of public policy in Kentucky."

Chapter 15

What's Really Required To Create An Entrepreneurial Economy

"We spent 51 years under Soviet communism. All the theories from western economists and management experts confuse us. But when Larry Farrell describes it, even former communists can understand what it takes to actually create enterprise."

—Tomas Sildmae
Minister of Economy
Republic of Estonia

I'm not tooting my own horn—well, maybe just a bit. But Minister Sildmae's comment was actually aimed at a very serious problem. The very young Tomas Sildmae, Minister of Economy for the newly independent Republic of Estonia, was using our simple definition of entrepreneurship to promote his economic development program. His dream was to foster a full-blown entrepreneurial economy in post-Soviet Estonia. But along the way, he was getting a lot of free, and confusing, advice from western "experts." It seems that in the euphoria of the collapse of communism, New York and London bankers, Harvard and Cambridge economists, and legions of IMF bureaucrats were crawling all over eastern Europe offering their "help" in the restructuring of the economies. Sildmae told me he appreciated the attention but the expert advice was mostly unusable: "Our problems are very, very basic—like getting old KGB agents out of the state owned monopolies and encouraging young entrepreneurs to start new enterprises to compete with them. But the advice I'm getting is about global banking systems, forecasting models and hedge funds. I don't understand those things and I can't use them."

No one is arguing that all challenges have simple solutions. But creating an entrepreneurial economy is one that does. For several years we've been urging our government clients to "dumb down" their notions of what it takes to create entrepreneurs—and an entrepreneurial economy. Our message is, forget all the psychological testing nonsense, seminars on how to write a perfect business plan, and most assuredly don't have people waste two years getting an MBA.

This straight-forward message seems to be resonating with many, very smart governments around the world. Over the past ten to fifteen years, we've seen a tremendous awakening of interest in the notion that government should employ *entrepreneur and small business development projects* as a major component of its overall economic development strategy. A sampling of governments around the world, who have used our entrepreneur development consulting and training, is the best illustration I can give of how widespread this phenomenon has become.

- Asia: China / Malaysia / Singapore

- Europe: Estonia / United Kingdom / Ireland

- North America: Kentucky/New York City/Yavapai-Apache Nation

- South America: Brazil / Uruguay

- Africa: South Africa

- United Nations: Secretariat for Enterprise Development

From advising government Ministers and their staffs on developing an entrepreneurial economy at one end of the spectrum, to training unemployed welfare recipients to become micro-entrepreneurs at the other, this approach certainly appears to be an idea which the world is ready to use. And what we've seen first-hand has to be just the tip of the iceberg.

The bottom line is governments everywhere are using entrepreneurship as an economic development tool. They see creating a more entrepreneurial economy as the surest (and cheapest) way to create new jobs, raise prosperity, and ultimately win their fair share of the global, economic pie. As Tomas Sildmae, the young Minister of Economy in Estonia, also told me: "After 52 years of communist rule, we had to learn how to create real companies and real jobs. We discovered that if we could help create one entrepreneur, he would create another 50 jobs. Estonia will never get a better return on investment than that."

THE THREE REQUIREMENTS

We've learned that what's really required is putting in place just a few key fundamentals—and then let human nature take its course. Here's what's really required for countries, states and cities to create a more entrepreneurial economy.

• A Bit Of Money

> *"We created a venture capital fund which is almost unheard of for a city."*
>
> —Charles Millard, President
> Economic Development Corporation
> New York City

First, underscore the word 'bit.' The average business start-up cost in the U.S. is only about $14,000. Many great companies have been started for a lot less: Apple Computer $1,350, Nike $1,000, Domino's Pizza $900, and literally zero for DHL, Virgin, and biotech superstar, deCODE Genetics. Second, government economic development officials have become true believers that fostering entrepreneurship is a political and economic winner. As Charles Millard, the President of New York City's Economic Development Corporation under Mayor Giuliani, and the 'Godfather' of Silicon Alley, told me: "It's a great investment, especially when compared to other social costs of government. That's why we started the world's first city financed Venture Capital fund—to help make Silicon Alley competitive with Silicon Valley." When you think about it, it's really a no-brainer that investing $14,000 to help a citizen start a job-creating business is a better bet than dead-end expenses like keeping a family on welfare at $25,000 a year or putting another young person in jail at $45,000 a year!

If your government leaders don't realize that funding entrepreneurship is a bargain compared to funding welfare, you might want to find out what planet they've been on for the past fifty years—or at least get them to read this page. Governments are embracing this new use of taxpayers' money for one very simple reason: they like the numbers. When they see that the average cost of starting a business is a lot less than a year of welfare, or a year at Harvard (or two years at their own state universities,) or a year in prison, most government officials get very interested. You'll recall the numbers:

- Average start-up cost: $14,000
- A year on welfare: $25,000
- A year at Harvard: $35,000
- A year in prison: $45,000

So the first possibility of providing that "bit of money" the entrepreneurs need could be in the form of funding new solutions for some old social problems. Becoming self-employed entrepreneurs is the best hope for unemployed welfare recipients, down-sized skilled workers, refugees and immigrants, and even some young criminals. Starting micro-companies is the best bet to get all these people off the public dole and enable them to become positive, tax-paying contributors to the economy. Micro-credits or micro-grants to such people are ideas whose time has come in public policy circles. The financial assistance should probably be labeled a "long-term investment," given the enormous economic advantages of creating a business, even a very small one, over welfare and prison. Do the numbers and I think you'll agree. There really is no comparison in terms of job creation, tax revenue generated, and the general prosperity of the neighborhood where the new business is located. For politicians, there's an added plus. This is an ideology-free idea—at least so far. The idea that it's better to help people start their own small business than give them food stamps forever, is so compelling it has attracted political leaders from both the right and the left.

Secondly, more mainline entrepreneurial financing could and should be available from the government. As all first-time entrepreneurs know, you don't have to be on welfare or a convicted felon to have problems getting start-up financing. That's why the U.S. Small Business Administration, established in 1953, is today one of the most important economic tools of the American government. It provides financial, technical and management assistance to help Americans start, run, and grow their businesses. With a portfolio of business loans and loan guarantees worth more than $45 billion, the SBA is by far the nation's largest financial backer of small businesses. Last year, the SBA also offered management and technical assistance to more than one million small business owners. These are big, impressive numbers, and every country should have a well funded SBA equivalent.

And as you'll see in the upcoming interview with Charles Millard on New York City's Silicon Alley, some governments are beginning to provide *venture capital* to fledgling entrepreneurs. Millard actually initiated the concept of government backed venture capital with the Discovery Fund in New York—and helped create an economic renaissance for the city. If your country, state, or city is trying to develop a more entrepreneurial economy, but offers no help in start-up financing: loans, venture capital, tax-friendly enterprise zones, or whatever, you're fighting this battle with one arm tied behind your back.

And finally, do the entrepreneurs in your area have access to the private venture capital industry? If not, your economic development team isn't doing its job. This is absolutely essential—and easy to do. Creating strong links to centers of venture capital should be a top priority for every economic development agency in the world. And your would-be entrepreneurs need to know how to promote themselves to the venture capital community and successfully navigate the tough application process all VC firms will put them through. Remember, venture capitalists are most interested in ventures with exceptionally high growth potential—which means a lot of jobs and a lot of tax revenue. Which also means that VC goals are actually well aligned with government economic development goals! To jump-start your own thinking on the possibilities, here, straight from the VC *handbook* are the six classic stages of financing offered by VC firms—which roughly correspond to the stages of a company's development:

- Seed Money: Low level financing needed to prove a new idea—often provided by wealthy angel investors.

- Start-up: Early stage money for companies that need funding of expenses associated with product development and marketing.

- First Round: Funding for early manufacturing and sales.

- Second Round: Working capital for early stage companies that are selling product, but are not yet turning a profit.

- Mezzanine Financing: Also called scale-up funding, this is expansion money for a newly profitable company.

- Bridge Financing: Money intended to finance the "going public" process.

In the larger scheme of things, why should government be putting tax dollars into fostering a more entrepreneurial economy? This was virtually unheard of when K. T. Li arrived on Taiwan in 1949 and started it all. But today, government leaders, from Singapore to Northern Ireland to New York City to the Yavapai-Apache Nation are doing just that. Why the surging interest in entrepreneurship as an economic development tool? What are these governments hoping to achieve? It's pretty simple really. As Nora Wang told me, when she was still New York City's Commissioner of Employment—and used my firm to provide entrepreneur development training to people coming off welfare: "Let's face it—if we can move one citizen off welfare to becoming a small business owner, who will create five or ten more jobs, and start paying taxes—well, the City will never get a better return on the dollar than that."

Speaking of returns, no example better illustrates the power of providing "a bit of money" to entrepreneurs than Silicon Valley. The venture capital industry started there forty years ago—but really took off during America's "entrepreneurial revolution" in the mid 1980s—and then just exploded around the "internet bubble" of the 1990s. It initially consisted of a small group of individuals, or angel investors, who were investing in companies that would become household names such as Intel, Apple, and Sun Microsystems. Since those early days, hundreds of billions in equity capital has been raised by venture capitalists around the world. The industry has become a permanent fixture in global capital markets, from India and China to Europe to North America— where it all started. Silicon Valley still leads that world. An amazing $25 billion plus is being raised each year, covering some 2,500 deals, by more than 300 venture capital firms in and around Silicon Valley!

There is no question however that this phenomenon was supported, if not created, by the great research universities in the area. Stanford, Berkeley, UC San Francisco (for biotech), Cal Tech, etc., all provided the talent and breakthrough ideas the VC people were looking for. Which leads us to the next requirement—a bit of knowledge.

• A Bit Of Knowledge

"We believe that a lot of the energy for creating these new companies is going to come from universities."

—Kris Kimel, Founder and President
Kentucky Science & Technology Corporation

While most entrepreneurial start-ups don't need a lot of money, they do all have one need that is absolutely essential: a product or service that customers are willing to pay money for. In fact the number one reason for start-up failures in the world is not lack of money or lack of management know-how. It's simply that the business couldn't come up with a product or service that the world wanted to buy—or buy in enough quantity to make it profitable. It's called building a better mousetrap and it's the single most important requirement every entrepreneur faces. And where can you learn this most essential, entrepreneurial knowledge? In university engineering schools, biology departments, and computer science classes. Or at a vocational trade school or even working a few years at a big company. The one place you *cannot* learn this essential entrepreneurial knowledge is in a business school . . . . . more on this point later.

So are your schools producing the highest skilled, most competitive workers in the world? Are your citizens, and especially your young people, receiving the very best in academic and technical education? Are you providing post graduate research and education opportunities targeted to the high growth markets of the 21st century? And finally are your students actually learning to make or serve something the world wants to buy?

Believe it or not, your answers to these questions will define your place in the world for the next fifty to one hundred years. This is not about who's going to be homecoming queen, or which fraternity to join, or who's bringing the beer for the big college football game this weekend. We're talking about the single, most strategic thing you and your country can do right now, to insure that your grandchildren will live in a "healthy, wealthy and wise" society. Our bias is that the best road to travel to reach that best-of-all-possible places, is one that makes plenty of room for a creative, competitive, and entrepreneurially driven economy.

There are two classes of knowledge essential to the creation of an entrepreneurial economy:

- The first, and frankly the most important, is knowing how to create and make things the world needs. On this score, you can be sure that Kris Kimel is not talking about the business schools of the world when he says universities will have a huge impact on the creation of new companies. He's talking about the commercialization of breakthrough research and fresh ideas that will come out of all manner of university laboratories and disciplines. He means the creation of new technologies and new products that will enhance and re-shape the way we work and live.

This class of knowledge, in fact, will determine a country's or region's place in the *new* entrepreneurial age. It can't be the other way around. This means (hopefully) no more "National Industrial Plans" that produced such colossal losers as steel mills in Saudi Arabia, automobiles in the former Yugoslavia and today's Malaysia, and computers in Brazil. Creating businesses based upon the interests and knowledge of a country's entrepreneurs, not its politicians, has always been the best way to create national competitive advantage. This down-home method of establishing your *country strategy* surely flies in the face of careful analysis ala the "experts" (Harvard's Michael Porter and MIT's Lester Thurow come to mind) but let's look at the facts. Why has Finland been number one in mobile phones, or India so important in software development, or to take a really off-beat example, why is Nashville, Tennessee the number one city in the world for writing and producing music? None of these success stories are due to sophisticated economic development studies by consultants or government planners. They were all, of course, based on the interests, skills, and knowledge of the people there.

• The second class of knowledge is knowing the basics of creating, growing, and maintaining the entrepreneurial companies that have to bring those new technologies and new products to the marketplaces of the world. In this class of knowledge, we've presented in this book what we believe are the time-tested fundamentals: Having a powerful sense of mission, maintaining absolute focus on customers and products, practicing high-speed innovation, and fostering self-inspired managers and workers. Of course there is a lot of other very useful business knowledge you can obtain, but neglecting these basics is a recipe for disaster—in our view!

So, what are your answers to the earlier question? Do you have a country or region strategy to provide those "bits of knowledge" your entrepreneurs will need? However you answer, the following summary points should help you devise an *entrepreneurial knowledge strategy* for the 21st century:

- The essential idea is that to be a successful entrepreneur, you must "get very good at something." We are talking about producing students who are real *experts* at something, not graduates who can maybe add a column of figures, sort of write a coherent sentence and download someone else's research for their history essay. To prepare future entrepreneurs, the education establishment, from vocational high schools to graduate universities, should be absolutely focused on enabling students to make products and provide services that the rest of the world wants and will pay for.

- Learning how to be a successful entrepreneur does not require a business school degree, period! In most cases it will just slow the process down. There's nothing wrong with having a few business schools around to educate managers, but that has nothing to do with creating entrepreneurs and entrepreneurial economies.

- The competitive differences among countries, which are enormous, are being largely driven by shocking disparities in basic knowledge around the world. They range from a medieval 13% adult literacy rate in the central African country of Niger, to the United States where an amazing 81% of high school graduates are involved in some form of higher education. And the so-called "digital divide" is making it worse. While countries like the U.S., Singapore and Finland now have "two and three computer families," in war-torn Afghanistan only one of every four children will ever see the inside of a schoolroom. These disparities don't make for minor differences in a country's competitiveness. The acquisition of knowledge is the first line of battle in the global economic war. If you can't survive that battle, you've already lost the war.

- It's one thing to create the best workers in the world. It's quite another to keep them in your own country, or even community. It's called brain drain and it's a malady you can't afford. According to *The Economist*, the top five countries for retention of highly educated people are the USA, Netherlands, Chile (South America's bright star again!), Germany and Japan. The bottom of the barrel: Russia, South Africa, India, Philippines, and Sweden—the only "rich" country in the bottom rankings. Of course Sweden also has the highest rate of income taxes in the world. Talk about the hidden costs of over-taxing your most valuable asset—your educated people and your future entrepreneurs!

Two of the most innovative and ambitious education programs in the world to foster entrepreneurship, which we are intimately familiar with and were briefly noted in the Introduction, deserve further mention here:

First is the Republic of Ireland's landmark legislation which mandates that every Irish university student must take at least an introductory course on entrepreneurship. Through the good offices of Terri Scott, the innovative President of the Institute of Technology in Sligo, (and our former client at a large project up in Belfast, UK) we've been appointed as the outside advisors on this exciting program. The national goal is to get, and keep, Ireland on an entrepreneurial track as the best way to insure the nation's future prosperity. The best news is that the lead universities in the "Accelerating Campus Entrepreneurship" initiative are not the country's more academic institutions, rather its network of Institutes of Technology, which are spread across the country. Obviously these are the educational institutions which are the potential hotbeds of future entrepreneurs. These are students who are indeed learning how to make and deliver products and services the world will buy. The entrepreneurial course will simply awaken them to the possibilities of commercializing their knowledge and turning it into their own business! This large scale Irish effort is being undertaken at exactly the right time and in the right setting. It should be a model for other universities and even entire countries to follow!

What makes the Irish "ACE" initiative all the more remarkable is that this new investment is being undertaken during the country's worst recession in a hundred years. If nothing else the timing dramatically underscores the depth of the Irish government's belief in the future value of creating a more entrepreneurial economy!

Second is the enormous global effort of Junior Achievement Worldwide . . . . . the largest educational institution in the world which today reaches over 10 million kids a year. Entrepreneurship is one of JA Worldwide's three focus areas, along with teaching kids Financial Literacy and Work Readiness. We were brought in by Darrell Luzzo, at the time JA's visionary Sr. VP of Program Development, to create entrepreneur development courses for middle and high school level students. The two programs, JA It's My Business for middle school, and JA Be Entrepreneurial for high school, will both teach the same core message as described above; that the most important knowledge entrepreneurs must acquire is the ability to make something the world needs and will buy! This is a massive undertaking which will teach entrepreneurial skills to more students, in more countries, than any other school or university program in history! If you need further evidence that the education industry is now doing its part to support "the *new* entrepreneurial age," this is it. (Today Luzzo is working his magic at Laureate Education, where as noted earlier, we have created an on-line course in 'social entrepreneurship.")

• An Entrepreneur-Friendly Culture

"In the early years, believe it or not, it was government entrepreneurship that built this country."

—Koh Boon Hwee, Chairman
Singapore Telecom

There is no God-given reason why the next Sam Walton or Bill Gates couldn't or shouldn't come from your town. But are there factors that could stack the deck in favor of some places or people over others? There sure seem to be. They can range from macro political conditions (don't try this in North Korea) to family considerations (keep your day job as you start up.) If you're setting out to foster entrepreneurship in your country, state, or city, you at least need to know that differences do exist, and depending upon where you call home, what you might be up against.

To illustrate, a recent Kaufman Foundation study found, there are vast differences in entrepreneurial activity and inclination between countries. The range can be astonishing even among the highly industrialized nations. At the high end, one in every 12 persons in the USA is involved in a business start-up, while only one in every 63 persons is similarly involved in Japan. The Kaufman study covers the G-7 countries. It measures the number of company start-ups per 100 population. The current rankings of the G7 countries are:

Country	Start-up Rate	Country	Start-up Rate
USA	8.4	Italy	3.4
Canada	6.8	UK	3.3
Germany	4.1	France	1.8
		Japan	1.6

Even within the same country, there can be huge differences. In the U.S. for example, The Small Business Survival Committee (SBSC) ranks all fifty states and the District of Columbia on an entrepreneurial scale. The SBSC is a public policy advocacy group, whose listings are admittedly heavily weighted by public policy factors such as taxes, crime rates and labor laws. Their current listing ranks South Dakota at the very top and Washington, D.C., dead last. Of course, the cultural differences between the Coyote State and the nation's capital, America's ground-zero of government bureaucracy, could fill several Ph.D. dissertations. If you're interested in packing up and moving to an entrepreneur-friendly state, the top 15 states on the list are:

1. South Dakota
2. Wyoming
3. Nevada
4. New Hampshire
5. Texas
6. Washington
7. Florida
8. Alabama
9. Tennessee
10. Mississippi
11. Alaska
12. North Dakota
13. Colorado
14. Pennsylvania
15. Missouri

And finally, moving down to a micro-economic level, business magazines love to rank even the Best Cities for Business. Last year, *Inc.* magazine ranked American cities by the number of business start-ups per population. The top twenty-five were:

1. Las Vegas, NV
2. Boise, ID
3. Anchorage, AK
4. Ann Arbor, MI
5. Austin, TX
6. Boulder, CO
7. Houston, TX
8. Denver, CO
9. Dallas, TX
10. Fort Collins, CO
11. Colorado Springs, CO
12. Albuquerque, NM
13. Kalamazoo, MI
14. Fort Worth, TX
15. Provo, UT
16. Portland, OR
17. Salt Lake City, UT
18. Orlando, FL
19. San Francisco, CA
20. Salem, OR
21. Santa Rosa, CA
22. San Antonio, TX
23. Anaheim, CA
24. Seattle, WA
25. Eugene, OR

Do you notice anything odd about this list of America's most entrepreneurial cities? Twenty-two of the twenty-five are in the West and about two-thirds of the twenty-five are small to medium sized cities. Only four of these twenty-five entrepreneurial hot spots are also in the top twenty-five cities in population. Those four are: Houston (#8), Dallas (#12), Anaheim (#16), and Seattle (#22). Is there a message in here somewhere?

You're entitled to ask, what do all these surveys mean? Probably not too much. Be sure, your aspiring entrepreneurs won't really have to move to South Dakota or Las Vegas to start a company! The practical point to keep in mind is that there may be political, legal, educational, or cultural factors negatively influencing the level of entrepreneurship in a country, a community, or even a family. The good news is such negative factors are almost always man-made, which means they can be changed and replaced by more entrepreneur-friendly conditions. Also most entrepreneurs can find creative ways to go around the barriers they encounter. Even so governments should try to make the path as entrepreneur-friendly as possible. It's very important to be pro-active in removing as many barriers as possible. So to help you do that, here are some of the most important entrepreneur-friendly factors to examine and hopefully improve:

• Are our government laws and policies as pro-entrepreneur as possible—across the board?

• Do our education systems—from trade schools to Ph. D. programs— honor entrepreneurship and actually teach students how to make things the world needs?

• Is government and private start-up money available to local entrepreneurs?

• And perhaps most important of all, are our entrepreneurs honored and celebrated as 'cultural and economic heroes' of the community?

To see all this in action, let's examine one of the most prosperous and entrepreneurial countries in the world. Over the past 35 years I've been to and worked in Singapore more than any other city (country) in the world. I've not counted the exact number of visits, but it has to be over a hundred. So I know Singapore, and its business community, fairly well. But of course, everyone knows *some* things about Singapore: It's the cleanest, most efficient and most modern capital city in Asia—if not the entire world. And you can't chew gum, you can't spit in public, you can't write graffiti on walls and you can't throw paper in the street. And if you bring an ounce of drugs into the country—you're a goner, no questions asked. And I suppose that most everyone still remembers that this amazing little country was built on the dreams and shoulders of one great man—Lee Kuan Yew. Lee guided Singapore for 30 years, and transformed it from an undeveloped colonial outpost with no natural resources into a first world "Asian Tiger."

But what do we really know about how three million Singaporeans became the model in Asia for clean government, a clean environment, low crime rates, outstanding academics and a booming economy capable of reinventing itself over and over again? How did Singapore's economy get started—and what has kept it in the top 5 or top 10 ranking of every (per capita) economic study in the world—including the one's shown in this book. From an outsider's perspective the place looks like the 20th century's most successful example of cooperation between an intelligent *and* disciplined government and a nation of free-wheeling enterprisers.

To get the real story I went to the one person I knew who I thought could give us the inside story of how the government of Singapore goes about maintaining an entrepreneur-friendly environment. Koh Boon Hwee has done it all. Following his engineering degree at the University of London and his MBA at Harvard, he's been a manager (MD of HP Singapore,) an entrepreneur (founded the successful Omni Corporation,) a senior overseer of big government assets (Chairman of Singapore Telecom, Singapore Airlines and the Development Bank of Singapore,) and all around wunderkind of Southeast Asia.

I started the interview by asking Koh the bottom-line question for Singapore, or any country trying to raise its national prosperity on the wings of the entrepreneurial spirit: "What should the role of the government be in fostering a high growth, highly entrepreneurial economy? He came right back with a little history lesson on *Singapore, Inc.*: "The Singapore government has played a unique role in the development of our country. In the early years, believe it or not, it was government entrepreneurship that built this country. They took all the entrepreneurial risk with Neptune Shipping Lines, Singapore Airlines, and they even built the shipyards that have become a very important industry in Singapore. Government was *the entrepreneur* in the mid 1960s when we became independent. At that point, the country was relatively poor and there just wasn't enough private sector capital to embark on these kinds of projects. But it has always been the government's policy, at Lee Kuan Yew's insistence by the way, that the boards of these government enterprises should be a combination of government civil servants and private sector people, and the Chairman, CEO and President should all come from the private sector. So for example, in 1986, when I was still the Managing Director of Hewlett-Packard Singapore, the government asked me to become the Chairman of the Board of Singapore Telecom, the country's largest company—which I did of course. In Singapore, such companies, with big government shareholding, which are still quite common, are called 'government-linked companies. I've worked in several of these actually—and it seems to work out well for everyone.'"

Fast-forwarding, I wanted to get to the current situation where today the government is saying that Singapore has become too rich and too comfortable—and is losing the entrepreneurial spirit that made it successful in the first place. To fight this, the government has embarked on a big, typical Singaporean government campaign, well financed and well thought out, called *Century 21*. The stated goal is to remove the barriers that inhibit local entrepreneurs and 're-create' a more entrepreneur-friendly environment. I know for certain that 'Singapore, Inc.' has gotten the message. We've worked with many of Singapore's most famous companies, training their management teams to be more entrepreneurial: Singapore Airlines—arguably the best airline in the world, Singapore Telecom—the country's number one company in market value, Singapore Technologies, Television Corporation of Singapore, and many others. All of them are trying, at the government's urging, to equip their managers with "corporate entrepreneurship" type skills to compete in the tough 21st century global economy.

So I asked Koh for his take on the government's Century 21 campaign. His reply was very direct: "I think the government's recognition that more entrepreneurship is needed for the continued development of the economy is a good, and necessary, thing. I firmly believe that the time has come for this. I also think the spirit of entrepreneurship in the U.S., and especially your willingness to dump old systems that don't work in favor of new ones that do, should be a very strong model for us. Those kinds of attitudes and skills are very important, especially for a small country like Singapore. Small countries can't use their domestic markets as levers. For economic development then, your relevance depends on whether you are more creative and more innovative. That means in terms of products, or processes, or systems, you always have to be a step ahead. And I think that is where the entrepreneurs will play the biggest role for Singapore—keeping us one step ahead of our competitors.

"The government is also doing more today to help local entrepreneurs and enterprises to regionalize their activities, and this requires some level of risk taking. It also requires willingness in Singaporeans to go live and work in other places whose environments are not like Singapore, so for the first time the government is urging us to leave our comfortable life in Singapore and work elsewhere for the good of the country long term.

"Singapore will also be more open to foreigners and foreign companies in the future. Of course you might ask, 'Why not always favor your own local companies?' The reason is you have to be exposed to the outside world in terms of technology. These companies bring superior levels of technology, new ideas in how things are managed, and impose a level of competition that enhances the overall capabilities in the country over time. If you have a closed market where competition from the outside world is restricted, you will not be better off in the long run. The level of local competition will be less intense, and that doesn't really spur your domestic entrepreneurs to achieve what they really need to do to be competitive worldwide. And of course because our domestic market is so small, we absolutely have to have entrepreneurs with a global vision and world-class products.

"Further, what the government, and many business leaders see in our future is a very different scenario from the past. The government is favoring small companies today, not just the giants they supported in the past. We are looking at the overwhelming trend toward a service economy, or an information intensive economy. In the future, size and economies of scale and scope will not be so important. Look for example at the new industries, like the internet or whatever. They don't take humongous capital to start up. Frankly the principal assets are the human beings that walk in and out of the offices every day and the value of an idea is much more important than the value of fixed assets. Therefore we can have an economy of small companies that can be successful. It is possible. Of course our manufacturing industries aren't going to go away entirely and in those, scale and scope are still going to be important. But our real future, and what we are planning on, is to base Singapore's economy on smaller, highly entrepreneurial knowledge and information type industries—where we believe we can compete with the best in the world."

The remarkable thing about Singapore has always been that it is willing to buck the popular tide to secure the peaceful and prosperous future of its three million people. The Singapore Government has been harangued for forty years by the West, that it lays much too heavy a hand on the economy. Interestingly, over the same time frame, the economic results in Singapore have been far superior to the home economies of its critics. Singapore's government is re-embracing the entrepreneurial spirit and the need for a major effort across the country to re-create a more entrepreneurial economy. But the exact approach may not please pure free-market economists or conservative pundits across the globe. I think—no, I'm absolutely certain; the government will be in the thick of this effort up to its eyeballs. This is simply the Singapore way to create a more entrepreneur-friendly culture—and it's hard to argue with all their past successes. In fact maybe some of us in the West could learn a thing or two about government/private sector cooperation from the Singaporeans!

EVEN *THE NEW YORK TIMES* GETS IT!

It's an odd feeling when something you've been preaching for years shows up as a revolutionary insight on the editorial pages of *The New York Times*. I didn't know whether to feel proud, vindicated, or robbed of my original concepts. So I settled for putting it in this book as a form of blue-chip endorsement.

Several years ago, an op-ed piece by *Times* columnist Flora Lewis was headlined: "For Europe's Jobless, Self-Employment Might Work." Now this is the same *New York Times* that editorially, has never seen a social welfare program it didn't like. So when even they start pushing entrepreneurship as the way to solve chronic unemployment, we have to believe we're on to something anyone could agree with. Lewis was writing about Europe, where the seemingly permanent unemployment rate hovers in the 10% to 15% range. She hit the nail on the head with the assertion that Europe's answer to unemployment has been generous benefits, followed by a lot of hoping and praying that someday more jobs will be created. She argued: "The new economic revolution re-opens the question. Big factories and offices are laying off workers, but the possibilities for self-employment have been little explored. The assumption is that someone must hire you." Bravo!

Now here's where it gets interesting. The column goes on to suggest there are three requirements to transform Europe's unemployed welfare recipients into self-employed entrepreneurs. The requirements are:

- Micro Credit: ". . . the magic breakthrough tool is credit—microcredit—at commercial rates but without the commercial requirements of collateral or existing earnings."

- Advice On How To Do Business: ". . . the provision of advice on how to do business, set prices and so on."

- Reform The Regulatory Environment: ". . . an important reform of the huge jumble of regulations, licenses, permits and so on that countries impose on new small businesses."

There you have it—*The New York Times* on "a bit of money, a bit of knowledge, and an entrepreneur-friendly culture." It all sounds rather familiar, doesn't it?

And the *Times* continues to beat the entrepreneurial drum—right up to the current recession. In June of 2010, Thomas Friedman, perhaps the most influential op-ed writer at the paper today, wrote a terrific piece titled, "A Gift For Grads: Start-Ups." Lamenting the still gloomy job prospects for college graduates, and Washington's seeming lack of interest in fostering a more entrepreneurial approach to fixing the economy, Friedman says: "We owe our young people something better—and the solution is not that complicated, although it is amazing how little it is discussed in the Washington policy debates. We need three things: start-ups, start-ups and more start-ups. Good jobs—in bulk—don't come from government. They come from risk-takers starting businesses . . ." Bravo!

With even *The New York Times* on board with the **new** entrepreneurial age, I'm sure we're destined to see more government and public policy leaders like K. T. Li, the architect of Taiwan's economic miracle, Fernando Cardoso, the great Finance Minister (and later President) of Brazil, President Grimsson of Iceland, Kris Kimel in Kentucky, Koh Boon Hwee in Singapore, and Charles Millard (whom you will meet next) from New York City's Silicon Alley. They may come from different parts of the world and different political camps, but they all recognize that the **new** entrepreneurial age offers unparalleled challenges and opportunities. Creating prosperity at home and competitiveness abroad is the name of this game—and developing a more entrepreneurial nation, state, or city, may be the most important job any public leader will have in the 21st century!

Next, straight from the Big Apple, is the right man with the right message to do just that: The New Yorker with enough chutzpah to try making Silicon Alley" hotter" than Silicon Valley!

CITIES: THE GODFATHER OF SILICON ALLEY

"The first thing government should do is—no harm."

—Charles Millard, President
Economic Development Corporation
New York City

Having already interviewed several Silicon Valley entrepreneurs for earlier books, I became intrigued with the emergence of *Silicon Alley* in New York City. It's no secret that for a couple of decades, New York wasn't even in the digital age race. That, of course, had been dominated by California's Silicon Valley, with little satellites popping up in Seattle (thanks to Bill Gates) Boston, Austin, and even Northern Virginia. Then I read in *The New York Times* that the number of new Silicon Alley internet companies going public had actually surpassed the number of Silicon Valley IPOs for the year! I decided to find out what was going on. During my search for the history of Silicon Alley, a reporter at the *Times* mentioned the name Charles Millard and then referred me to the trade magazine, *Silicon Alley Reporter*. I asked the first person I talked to there: "Is it right that this fellow, Millard, knows something about Silicon Alley?" The immediate and very New York answer: "He knows everything. He's the Godfather of Silicon Alley." Bingo! So I called him and arranged an interview at The Harvard Club, my favorite spot in New York City.

It turns out that Charles Millard, social liberal and fiscal conservative, has a very impressive, if occasionally controversial, history: Phi Beta Kappa at Holy Cross College, JD with Honors from Columbia Law School, VISTA Volunteer in Brooklyn, Human Rights organizer in Pinochet's Chile, U.S. Congresswoman Millicent Fenwick's legislative assistant, five years at Davis Polk and Wardwell, a blue chip, Wall Street law firm, two terms as a New York City Councilman—the first Republican in a quarter-century to be elected from Manhattan, Mayor Giuliani's hand-picked President of NYC's Economic Development Corporation and President Bush's Director of the $50 billion Pension Benefit Guaranty Corporation—from 2007 to 2009. "PBGC" is that much-in-the-news agency which insures the pension funds of large, bankrupt American companies—like Lehman Brothers, Chrysler, Circuit City, etc. During his term, he reduced the agency's overall deficit from $18 billion to $11 billion—but was vilified and investigated by Congress for implementing a new, very aggressive investment strategy of the agency's assets—and for being too cozy with big Wall Street firms in the process. A year later, in May of 2010, the investigation was closed and all charges were dropped by the Obama administration with the statement: "The Inspector General did not identify a single rule or law that was violated during Millard's tenure at the agency or at any other time." Hmmmm . . . Sounds to me like one more good public servant caught in the political cross-fire. In any event, our interest here is centered on his five years of heading New York's EDC—where he was one of Mayor Giuliani's key advisors for fostering the city's amazing economic renaissance—and moving the Big Apple headlong into the digital age.

Millard showed up at the Harvard Club with no tie, which the octogenarian afternoon nappers there would have seen as a new-age assault on the Club's centuries-old dress code—if any of them had been awake. Anyway, his casual attire was the first, refreshing tip-off that I was meeting a new breed of New York City mover and shaker! By the time I met him, Charles Millard had indeed been on a varied, and fast, track: "Well, I left the law firm to run for the City Council, basically asking the voters of the east side of Manhattan to please give me a two-thirds pay cut! They did, so I was a City Councilman, representing the upper east side of Manhattan, about 140,000 people. I was elected in 1991. I was the first Republican elected from Manhattan to the City Council in 25 years. I was re-elected in 1993. Then Mayor Giuliani appointed me to be President of the Economic Development Corporation (EDC) in late '95. I stayed there for almost five years—a very exciting time in New York—economically speaking."

Millard became Rudy Giuliani's point man for economic development—and the creation of the City's burgeoning cyberspace economy. Giuliani had come to office in January of 1994, so Millard's tenure covered most of the period which is now being called New York City's renaissance.—leading up to the city becoming the pride of America for its heroic performance during the tragedy of 9/11. In any event, the turn of the century had clearly been a time of entrepreneurial and economic re-birth in the city. So what was going on that catapulted New York City into the internet world? How did this government do what governments almost never do—that is to lead the way and set the stage for profound and long lasting economic development? It turns out that Millard, the "Godfather," does know everything about it.

Here's the inside story: "At the Economic Development Corporation (EDC) there were many, many things that we did. I'll mention a few before I focus on Silicon Alley. I was responsible for the city's negotiations and the revitalization of 42nd Street, which everyone knows has been a fantastic success for the city. I also did all the negotiations on the tax incentive packages to keep large corporations in New York: Bear Stearns, Merrill-Lynch. McGraw-Hill and many others. I also was the Chairman of the Industrial Development Agency which does get a little closer to your interest. The IDA issues triple tax-exempt bonds on behalf of small companies and that way their debt is tax exempt which is obviously a tremendous benefit to them. Those bonds are used for all kinds of small companies around the city. I was involved in the negotiations on the New York Stock Exchange and the NASDAQ staying New York, the stadium finance issues on the Yankees and the Mets, and so on.

"So, on to my role with Silicon Alley, and here's where we'll get into some interesting things that we did. We created a venture capital fund which is almost unheard of for a city. We put ten million dollars into a fund called the New York City Discovery Fund. We leveraged that by raising additional money from other people who care about economic development: New York Power Authority, Con Edison, Brooklyn Union Gas, and so on. We also went to the Small Business Administration and got them to put quite a bit of money in. They're a very, very interesting partner because—they're impatient, but they're not hogs. In other words, if they give you $40 million, all they want is an 8% return. So it's very attractive to entrepreneurs. The SBA is trying to foster economic development in the best way that they can.

"Anyway, the venture capital fund was very successful. We hired a group called Prospect Street to run it. Prospect Street were venture capitalists so we weren't the actual decision makers. And I think this is one of the important things; people recognized the guys in government are not actually venture capitalists. They don't really know how to do this and too often people in government think they do. They say "that's a great idea and we should do that." There's no reason to think just because you got elected you know how to negotiate a venture capital deal. And I think it was very insightful for the Mayor to say: 'Yeah, we're not going to try to make these decisions ourselves. We'll have some veto power. We'll be able to control it in some ways. We'll set up some rules up front like you have to invest in companies in New York or in companies moving to New York. But we're going to hire somebody else to run it like a private sector venture capital fund.

"I also created a Business Recruitment Division within EDC. New York City had never had a business recruitment team. Lots of other cities do, but not New York. I think it was out of arrogance really. You know, we thought that we didn't need to. So it was great when we started sending our team on the road. People said: 'Wow, that's so great that New York really wants my business, that's fantastic.' And that became our tag line: 'New York City—We Want Your Business.' It's not all that original, but so what? We ran some ads, and we had a team out on the road. We would mail ahead, and then send a team into a city. Maybe we'd be going to a conference so we'd mail saying: 'We're going to be in town anyway, would you like to meet while we're in town?' We'd send it to 250 companies, pre-selected because of their size or their industry or their growth rate and then maybe ten of them would want to meet while our guys were there anyway for a conference. In the time I was President of the EDC, we brought about forty new companies in the information technology world into New York City. So that was great. Now these things were simultaneous to the Silicon Alley development, so people also wanted to come to New York when they learned how hot Silicon Alley was.

"We also created two venture capital shows. One of the biggest problems is that entrepreneurs need access to capital, but nobody wants to lend it to them. Nobody wants to take the risk. And in New York you didn't really have an infrastructure of venture capital five years ago. You just didn't. Not that there was nobody, but if they were here, they would go to California to look for technology companies to invest in. And so if you were a New York company and you went to a conference where you'd meet some venture capital people, you'd fly to California to meet the guy whose office was ten blocks away from your office in Manhattan. At a minimum we thought we ought to be able to save everybody the air fare! The *New York City Venture Capital Conference* is now in its fifth year, and it's become a very big deal. We also created, in conjunction with a publication called Alley Cat News, a Venture Capital Conference which does happen in California. It's called *Alley To The*

Valley, and we take New York companies out there to try to talk to California VCs. Obviously we hope they'll get funding. We also want the California VCs generally to be aware of how hot New York is, so that even if they don't make those investments, they'll be more attentive to New York opportunities in the future. The Alley To The Valley conference is in its third year this year.

"We had to create, along with the Downtown Alliance, which is the downtown business improvement district, a program called *Plug N Go*. Plug N Go provides small chunks of pre-wired, internet ready space, priced below the market. So if you're an entrepreneur, the idea of getting into an office in New York isn't insurmountable. If you have an internet business, you can't take the seven days to three week it takes to get Verizon to wire your office or whatever else might be needed. So before you, as the landlord, can rent this as a Plug N Go location, it's got to be pre-wired and you have agreed that you will charge a rent below the market rate. More important than even the price, you, as the entrepreneur, don't have to be credit-worthy. And you don't have to take five or ten thousand square feet—you can take two or three thousand square feet. And you don't have to sign a five or ten year lease; you can sign a two year lease. Why would you sign a five or ten year lease? You don't know where you're going to be in five or ten years when you're a start-up. So you just "plug in and you go!" Over two hundred Plug N Go leases were signed while I was at the EDC.

"There's one other important thing. I told you that we negotiated tax incentive packages that traditionally have been with very large employers, like a McGraw-Hill or a Merrill-Lynch. Basically when you get a tax incentive package, you get it based on the sales tax. You only get the sales tax relief if you spend. If you have 10,000 employees, you're probably spending a lot. If you only have 100, you might not be spending so much so fast. So I found a way to create a new program focused on these fast growing companies, that maybe have only have a hundred employees today. If you believe they're going to have 500 employees in four or five years, well, give them the incentives now to grow and whenever they have to add new employees, they have an incentive to add them in New York. We did that with Double Click,

Theglobe.Com, Star Media, and a number of others. The point is we took this old program and tweaked it so that it would apply better to Silicon Alley companies. And the Mayor was fully behind these customized tax incentives."

As Millard paused and took a sip of coffee, I commented: "That's a lot of new activity Charles. Was any of this kind of entrepreneurial economic development going on before Mayor Giuliani—and you—arrived on the scene? As I recall, there was always a lot of so-called community based social programs in New York City, but not much in the way of start-up business development. Isn't that right? "Well, that's exactly what I want to get to—the philosophy here. I just want to make sure we get it all out first. We discussed the Discovery Fund, the New York City Venture Conference, Alley To The Valley, Plug N Go, the Recruitment Team, the small business tax packages. . . . . there may be a couple of other things, but I think those are the main activities regarding Silicon Alley. Anyway, for me it was all a great experience."

"Now philosophically, which I think is obviously part of what you're getting at, what should governments do? One of the most important things, I think, is that the Mayor has stayed out of the way. You'll notice there are no regulations here—from any of the EDC activities. It's just like doctors. The first thing government should do is—*no harm*. You really have to stop and think about that for a second. This goes beyond just entrepreneurs. So before bureaucrats and politicians start talking about 'things to do,' it's always really important to stop and say, is this the kind of thing that might be doing harm that I can't anticipate. The City Council, to use a good example, created a second, smaller fund. It's $25 million. It's not leveraged. It's all city money, which I think was a mistake. Early on that money was proposed by the City Council to be a loan fund for emerging industries—basically for Silicon Alley. Well, these entrepreneurs don't have the cash flow to pay the loans. So what you had was all these people saying: 'Hooray, the city wants to put more money aside for us.' Of course putting money aside isn't what we should be doing anyhow. You know, investing it is different from putting it aside. The people on City Council, I can tell you from experience, had no clue about the distinction between bonds and equity. I don't mean *no one* on the Council understood that, but the actual business-like decision of what's an intelligent program was lost on them. So we had to go back and say: 'Look, if you're going to do this, it really should be equity because nobody will be able to repay the loans. And the great thing about the Discovery Fund is we've had a return. Do you want your grandiose new fund to be one with no return because people can't pay the debt and then you basically have to forgive the debt? Or do you want to make it equity so that if they do hit it, you get a return?' They went: 'Oh yeah, I guess that makes sense.'

"The second point is that you have to understand the needs of the businesses. And you have to listen to them because people in government, especially elected officials, don't really understand business. They really don't like business. I mean they all say: 'Oh I like small business.' Well, even though the new jobs tend to be created by small businesses, an awful lot of jobs still exist in larger companies. Politicians, especially left of center, and especially in New York, really don't believe in the profit motive. It's not something they value very highly. They view businesses as a necessary evil. Yes, they create jobs, thank goodness for that, but this whole profit thing to the average elected official in New York—they just don't care. They view profit primarily as something they can tax. And they completely fail—your entrepreneurs will really agree with me I think—they completely fail to understand that a young business is always at risk of going out of business. The people who you're writing for, if they're really early stage entrepreneurs, understand this for sure. They're people who are mortgaging their house, are factoring their receivables because they've just got to get some cash flow, and are spending on their personal credit card because their business credit isn't even good enough to get a business credit card. But they love their business and they are getting somewhere, but it's a very tough hand-to-mouth existence. They could go out of business any day. And then let's say you've had two good years, you could still go out of business. Politicians sort of seem to think that once you're in business, it's a static thing. That you will always be in business—and the only issue now is how much do I tax you? And if you don't understand how a business works, you run into taxes that are just outrageous. And people don't grasp that, because they think, well, you're guaranteed a profit. You're a businessman, you make a profit, and so and so. They never think that this tax or this regulation might cause you to not make a profit."

As Millard was serving up this robust condemnation of politicians, I was thinking of some of the government officials I had met around the world who were as pro-entrepreneur and pro-business as Milliard himself. So I asked him: "Isn't the political landscape changing across the world and in the country? It certainly seems to be changing in New York City. Aren't we in fact on the right track now?' I think my description was a bit too optimistic for someone who had just spent five years battling all those "left of center" City Councilmen in New York. His response: "Changing, yes. But look—the New York City Council has fifty-one members—if you take out the twelve, let's say, who are the most business friendly—the remaining thirty-nine would think that it's a privilege for you to do business in the City of New York and you should pay for it." As I laughed at what I instantly knew was going to be a great line in the book, even Charles Millard chuckled a little at his own deft turn of phrase.

I thanked Millard for all the great information and insights, and asked him the type of closing question I try to ask everyone: "If the mayor or a team came to you from Phoenix, or Detroit, or Miami, or Timbuktu, and they said: "Look, we want to get something like this going, so what do we do? What are the two or three most important things we absolutely must do to be successful?" Millard took a deep breath and seemed to almost physically lean into this question: "We've got to spend another minute or two on that one." Here's his thoughtful reply:

• "Just like the 'do no harm' point, government can't really create this. Nobody at City Hall sat around and said: 'I know, let's get a bunch of young guys in black turtlenecks, give 'em some European cigarettes, make sure they have pony-tails, stuff 'em in some lofts, get em some pizza boxes, and we'll call it Silicon Alley.' That's not what happened. First, I think you need to follow the market. When you see something bubbling in your environment, then you've got to go help it. The government shouldn't try to figure out what industries are going to succeed. This was not an old style industrial policy that New York City adopted. The city saw something growing and went all out to help it. That's number one.

- "Number two, whatever you do you can't get suckered into helping losing propositions. People in government always want to be able to say yes to anybody who's asking. Sometimes the most caring thing is to say no. Small, failing businesses are always asking for government help. Philosophically, in a capitalist system, you have to have failure as a real option. You can't have government bailing out everybody from failure. Because it's that failure that makes the entrepreneur work really hard, right? Also, I don't want my tax dollars going to somebody who's already failed, right? So the second point is it's not government's role to make them successful, but to create an environment where they can succeed. If you see something growing, and you want to water it, that's fine. But the government can't be sitting there trying to plant a seed and say that it doesn't really know if that seed will grow in that soil.

- "Any city should also look at ideas like Enterprise Zones. But there are two very different concepts in Enterprise Zones. One is, here's a hundred million dollars from the city, to give or invest in this area. The other is, here's X amount of tax credits or write-offs that we're going to give to people who make their own investments in this area. So if I just give you money, I'm subsidizing hope. If I give you tax write-offs, you've got to have generated income and profits in order to get that benefit, so I'm subsidizing success. I'm giving you an incentive to succeed in that neighborhood, because that's the only place where you're going to get that tax incentive. But, and this is important, you don't have to apply to me for the tax benefit. So, do you want $100 million invested and administered by the city, and all the politics that goes behind that—meaning you have to ask the politicians to get your piece of the action. Or do you want, if you've invested X amount of money, and you have X number of employees, in X area, to get the tax benefit—and you never have to talk to Charlie Millard, or the mayor, or your congressman, or anyone else. You get it because it's in the tax code. And that's the way it ought to be."

- "And finally—You have to be ready to refute your skeptics. We had a lot of critics and skeptics. For example one of the points a lot of our skeptics made was, 'where are your academic institutions in all this.' So we engaged the Center For Assisted Technology from NYU, and others, to help us and go with us to all the conferences and important road shows to indicate that New York has plenty of academic horsepower—and they're committed to supporting Silicon Alley and the city's economic development goals in any way they can. You have to stand up and refute the skeptics in these efforts or they will bury you."

There's the word from the *Godfather*—a few years ago. So let's fast-forward for an up-to-the-minute status report on *Silicon Alley*—as we're all still trying to crawl out of this awful recession. Clearly, Millard's efforts are continuing to pay off for New York City. To wit:

In a story titled "Silicon Alley High," *The New York Observer* reported in February of 2010: "In the past few years, as Wall Street and publishing have imploded, the city's tech community has quietly flowered. These days, it is a scene unto itself, fronted by a bevy of young entrepreneurs and promising the kind of optimism and guts now absent from most of the city's other glossy industries. Silicon Alley is probably better off today than at any time in its short life. Innovation has shifted from chips and hardware to software and design and social networking, where New York thrives. And the city is awash in venture cash—which always helps!"

The Economist followed up in June of 2010 with this upbeat report: "'It's true, this is where it's happening,' proclaimed Michael Bloomberg, New York's billionaire mayor, in a speech on May 25th. The city indeed has some real internet winners today. These successes are helping to attract venture capital to New York—enough at least for Mr. Bloomberg to be able to boast that 'during the first quarter of this year, venture-capital funding increased in New York by 19% even while it went down in

Silicon Valley and the rest of the nation.' Of course Bloomberg is something of an expert on the subject himself, since his founding of Bloomberg News several years ago is still the biggest internet-media success story ever in New York City."

Whatever the future may hold, one thing is clear from the story of Silicon Alley. Government has a big role to play in fostering entrepreneurship and economic development, and can be very successful at it—as Charles Millard's story makes abundantly clear. It does require however, that those same three fundamentals are in place: An Entrepreneur-Friendly Culture, A Bit of Money and A Bit of Knowledge.

The best news in the Silicon Alley story is not in the specific actions Charles Millard took to respond to the skeptics—as innovative and impressive as those actions were—but rather that such success stories are actually possible. That economic development can really and truly be accomplished. That something so important and so valuable can be created in a short period of time. So take heart everyone—an entrepreneurial economy can be created in your country, or your state, or your city. Trust me, if it can be done in the rough and tough political trenches of the Big Apple, doing it in your hometown should be a cinch!

Chapter 16

Entrepreneur Development At American Indian Tribes

"Entrepreneurship is the opposite of being a victim."

—Chad Smith, Principal Chief
The Cherokee Nation

"Entrepreneurship is the opposite of being a victim." These were the first words from Chad Smith, Principal Chief of the Cherokee Nation, the second largest tribe in America, after I finished my presentation to him on creating a more entrepreneurial economy across the tribe. He continued: "This is the kind of development our young people need to participate in the American dream. Indian culture says our most important obligation is to help our tribe, but we've learned you can't help your tribe if you're living in poverty yourself. So I have a short answer and a long answer to what you've been saying. The short answer is *we're in*—and the long answer begins with the Cherokee's 'Trail Of Tears' back in 1838." Thereupon, the Chief of this fabled tribe gave me and the others in the room, a history lesson of economic oppression and broken promises that I'll never forget.

The next day, Governor William Anoatubby, the elected leader of the Chickasaw Nation, and the chief architect of what is arguably the most successful tribe in the country at creating tribal owned businesses, echoed those sentiments with: "This is exactly what we need—we've done well with creating tribal businesses, but now we need to create individually owned businesses. So let's get started!"

And at the end of the week I heard a similar response: "This is the best economic development idea I've seen in the five years that I've been Chairman of the Yavapai-Apache Nation." The speaker was Jamie Fullmer, the young leader of the famous Arizona tribe that created and has managed the top rated gambling casino in the state for eight years running. They are so good at starting up and running their own gaming businesses that they now have a consulting arm that advises other tribes on how to do the same.

So, in just one week back in March of 2007, I had the unforgettable experience of meeting with three visionary Native American chiefs, two in Oklahoma and one in Arizona—to overview and get their blessing for—the entrepreneur development projects we were planning to implement across their respective tribes. What is common about the three elected leaders—and their brilliant economic advisory teams with whom we had been working—is that they all have an abiding commitment to the long-term economic development and prosperity of their people. They also share a profound determination to not squander the wealth currently being generated by their hugely successful gaming businesses. They all understand that the casino business is not, and should not, be the long term answer to their nations' economic well-being. What was most interesting to me, even surprising, was their extreme enthusiasm for the notion of developing entrepreneurs within their tribes—despite their historic communal culture—and extending that entrepreneurial spirit well beyond their own world to compete head-on with tough, seasoned competitors around the U.S. and even globally.

At least part of their optimistic attitudes came from, I think, their recognition that for the first time, the best tool ever invented for creating individual and family prosperity was going to be instilled in their young people. Certainly these three chiefs have the will—and their tribes have the financial resources—to kick-start a new entrepreneurial age that can change many of their peoples' lives forever. And to put it more bluntly, they are simply sick and tired of seeing Native Americans at the bottom of the heap on most of the key socio-economic indicators of the country.

Living in a highly entrepreneurial economy would be a very different proposition from the paternalistic welfare state America's native population has suffered at the hands of the infamous Bureau of Indian Affairs (founded almost 200 years ago in 1824) and other government institutions set up to "help" the American Indian. The BIA's bureaucratic paternalism, a grim reminder of its original purpose of relocating and controlling the tribes, has done next to nothing over the years to inspire young Native Americans to participate in the wealth creating, free enterprise system that most of us take for granted.* As Neil McCaleb, the top economic advisor to the Governor of the Chickasaws and a former Presidential appointee to head The Bureau of Indian Affairs told me about his time in Washington: "It was the worst three years of my life. It was a struggle; even for the Native American staff there. They seemed very committed to the free enterprise system,

---

*To be fair giant strides have been taken at the BIA in recent years to shed their long and painful legacy—and to become a force for American Indian self-development and self-determination. However it's a long road to redemption. The very fact that we still have this agency, with so much mandated authority over these "sovereign nations" within the U.S., attests to its often contradictory role. Alas the BIA remains a double-edged sword over the heads of Native Americans.

but the minute they walked through the doors at BIA they became like everyone else—total government bureaucrats engulfed in a sea of policy driven paternalism."

ENTREPRENEUR DEVELOPMENT PROJECTS—THE KEY COMPONENTS

Needless to say, the upside potential in creating a more entrepreneurial economy in any area of high unemployment—whether inner cities, or rural regions, or 'Indian lands'—is enormous. But in all such efforts, it has to be done carefully and it has to cover all the bases from A to Z. We learned this critical point in our very first large-scale development project, appropriately titled "Go For It," which was located in Belfast, Northern Ireland. We've followed what we learned there in all our projects since—including our projects with Native Americans. Here's a synopsis of all those projects:

• The Goal
Since the driving force of every successful economy in the world is entrepreneurship, the project goal is to develop and instill a more entrepreneurial economy across an entire economy (country, state, city or region) by encouraging, training, and supporting large numbers of new entrepreneurs each year. Their start-up ventures will create new local jobs, produce new tax revenues and permanently enrich the region's economy. The good news is that such a project does not require new committees, more bureaucracy, another consultants' study, or even a large financial investment. The project approach we use is based on our 30 years experience of researching and teaching entrepreneurship. And the core 'technology' of our projects consists of the practical, four phase process described a few paragraphs below.

• The Target Population
With such a project, we believe each client has the opportunity to turn an economic problem into a great economic success. The "problem" is too many adult citizens in the region are not in control of their and their family's prosperity and economic well-being. They are unemployed, under-employed, or working in non-satisfying, dead-end jobs. Further,

too many young, school-age youth are facing the same prospects as they enter the work-force. This is an enormous waste of the region's most precious asset—educated young people. However this economic problem can be turned into a great economic success. The way to achieve such an economic 'miracle' is to re-direct and train this large group of citizens—young and old—to become self-employed entrepreneurs. Entrepreneurship has become the preferred 'career choice' of millions of young and old people around the world each year—and it could/should be the same within all regions.

One interesting point we've learned is that many citizens may already be in a class of high potential, future entrepreneurs. This is because many of them may already have the essential knowledge required to become a successful entrepreneur. That knowledge is not business or management knowledge, rather it is the knowledge of knowing how to make products or provide services that the world needs. Whether that knowledge and experience is in hi-tech services, manufacturing, maintenance and repair, personal services, business services, health care, retail or even arts and crafts, such participants in the program can be shown how to transform their acquired knowledge into an entrepreneurial venture. For others in the program, who may not yet have such commercially viable knowledge, they will be able to acquire that necessary product and service knowledge within the program—as part of the on-going services provided by the project.

In the process, both classes of participants will ultimately not only create jobs for themselves; they may also create jobs for hundreds of future employees and make a large, permanent contribution to the growth of the regional economy.

• The Four Phases Of The Projects
Based on our own experience, here are the critical phases, in sequence, which must be part and parcel of all entrepreneur development projects:

Phase One—Involve The Local Leadership: The objective here is to both inform and inspire the key influencers of the community—specifically the government, business, financial, legal and educational (academic *and* vocational) leadership. Through a series of 'Executive

Overviews' we want to introduce that regional leadership to the project's goals as well as gain their commitment to support the project generally and the program participants specifically. In this regard, we seek to gain specific kinds of local, on-going support, mentoring and professional advice for the entrepreneur hopefuls graduating from the program. The 'Executive Overviews,' which can be re-scheduled periodically as needed, should conclude with a strong reminder of the enormous, positive impact entrepreneurship has on national and regional economies.

Phase Two—Inspire The Potential Entrepreneurs: This Phase— inspiring and recruiting participants to enroll in the program—is typically the most challenging segment in any entrepreneur development project. It is also the key factor determining the size of the entire project and therefore the overall impact on the local economy. For these reasons, we recommend that significant effort and time be put into this phase. A variety of promotional and educational approaches can be used. For example, a high-profile series of entrepreneur expos or traveling road shows can be launched to cast a very wide net and reach the largest possible audience of potential entrepreneurs. There is no charge to attend these events and everyone is invited: currently employed managers, professionals and workers in all fields, university students, high school juniors and seniors, and even unemployed people from all walks of life. While all potential entrepreneurs are welcomed, special efforts are made to encourage applicants with interest in high growth and high job creating businesses. The region-wide promotion campaigns can be re-scheduled periodically to insure a steady stream of applicants for the program.

Phase Three—Develop The Entrepreneurs: All aspiring entrepreneurs are enrolled in our *Getting Entrepreneurial!* training program to learn the entrepreneurial basics. The goal is to give each participant both the confidence and the fundamental skills to become a successful business owner. Special attention is paid during the training to help participants pick products and markets that will carry the highest chance of success based on their individual interests, skills and of course the market needs. The end result is that they all leave the training phase with their own *Start-up Action Plan*. Typically, the action plan steps include gaining further product and market knowledge for their best business ideas as well as seeking out potential sources of start-up financing. Of course financing has been a real strength in the American Indian projects as the tribes themselves provide the start-up loans. The development phase also includes follow-up sessions at 30 and 90 day intervals to refresh their entrepreneurial skills, review the *Start-up Action Plans*, and deal with any obstacles the participants may have encountered, whether they be product issues, marketing issues, financial problems, legal questions and so on.

Phase Four—Provide On-going Support Services: On-going services are critical to the graduates who have made it through the training phase. This is where we can draw on the community leadership, enlisted earlier to provide such help—often as a combination of pro-bono advice and purchased services. The goal is to create a network of public and private sector advisors to help the new entrepreneurs resolve specific enterprise issues whether they be in the areas of technology, product, market, management, legal, financial, intellectual property, government regulations, etc. The kind of support most programs require ranges from a fully functional 'incubator' site, to acquiring additional financing, to gaining further product and market knowledge. On-going mentoring support by experienced entrepreneurs in the region is also highly desirable.

All four of the phases are required. At the Yavapai-Apache Nation project in Arizona for example, Chairman Fullmer's hand-picked head of the tribe's small business initiative, Donna Nightpipe, said it best: "Up to now, the tribe would give seed money to members who asked for it and their businesses would fail. There was no leadership support, no education or training, no product or market expertise, and no follow-up. We just gave them the money and watched them fail." Chairman Fullmer, with three university degrees and part of the new generation of progressive, development-oriented tribal leaders concurred: "In the past we'd send up these businesses all on their own and they all came back down. That's not going to happen anymore."

• A Word About Project Fees

Projects for developing human resources are among the lowest cost of all economic development investments made by governments around the world. The really good news with this type of economic development project is that—just one or two successful business start-ups out of every ten participants will more than return the government's total financial investment in that group. In terms of jobs created, tax revenue generated and general economic activity, using tax dollars to help create entrepreneurial small businesses is a no-brainer . . . . .

Some critics may say these American Indian home-grown economic development projects are doomed to failure. But knowledgeable supporters say the Native American community is at a tipping point. The number one challenge facing forward-thinking Chiefs like Chad Smith, Bill Anoatubby and Jamie Fullmer, is how best to invest their enormous, new found gaming profits for the long haul. Bill Largent, who runs the Office Of Native American Affairs at the Small Business Administration in Washington D.C., is a fierce advocate of these entrepreneur development projects and has a blunt answer to any nay-sayers: "Of course it will be challenging. If it were easy, it would have been done a long time ago. But being challenging cannot be a reason for not trying an idea with such great promise!" And I might add, being challenged is nothing new to American Indians. If you want to learn about surviving tough challenges just go back and read up on the Cherokee's 'Trail Of Tears.'

RESULTS IN APACHE LAND—A CASE STUDY

> "This is the best economic development idea I've seen
> in the five years I've been Chairman of the Tribe."

> —Jamie Fullmer, Chairman
> Yavapai-Apache Nation

We all know and read about the rich and famous entrepreneurs of the world like Bill Gates, Oprah Winfrey and Richard Branson. But these celebrity entrepreneurs represent only the tiniest fraction of the millions of people starting businesses around the world every year. The overwhelming bulk of entrepreneurs is not particularly interested in becoming celebrities and will never grace the covers of *Fortune* or *Business Week*. They are simply trying to make a living by their own wits. Most of the thousands I've met over the years don't even call themselves entrepreneurs—or think of themselves as being part of the latest, hottest genre of business. Rather, they see themselves as putting food on the table, albeit by doing something they like to do and are pretty good at doing.

This nuts-and-bolts nature of the run-of-the-mill entrepreneur has been vividly reinforced to me through our economic development projects with American Indian tribes. For example, at the Yavapai-Apache Nation in Arizona, the types of businesses being started by the program graduates are about as basic as it gets. Here's a sampling:

• **Travel Agency.** The business idea this clever first time entrepreneur came up with was a no-brainer. She currently works for the tribe and knew that the husband-wife team running the off-reservation, non-tribal travel agency that handled all the tribe's travel for years (business travel as well as large tours every year for tribal elders) had just retired and closed the business. She partnered with her niece, who just happened to be a certified travel agent and got the Tribe's agreement to give her a chance to handle all tribal travel. Her future vision includes promoting tours beyond tribal members, to the more upscale markets of Sedona and Prescott Valley, Arizona, for visits to the Holy Land. This second phase strategy comes from her personal passion for religious history, which was enriched by getting her master's degree in religion from an Israeli University. Yes, it's a no-brainer because it's a virtual start-up monopoly—but it's also a win-win for the entire tribal economy to buy services from members versus using outside suppliers.

• **Large Vehicle Customization.** The closest competitors to this business start-up are in Phoenix, two hours to the south. This means all of the mid and northern Arizona owners of over-sized vehicles—of which there are tens of thousands in these largely rural areas of the

Larry C. Farrell

state—are potential customers. The stroke of native genius by this father–son entrepreneurial team was to seek out and become the exclusive, local distributor of a large, experienced shop in Phoenix. While the son is currently employed as a master auto body repairman, the Phoenix based firm will further train the owners and their future employees in the specialized area of customizing large, desert terrain vehicles. Even more importantly, because the firm in Phoenix is an exclusive distributor of a large Japanese maker of wheel and body products for over-sized vehicles, the start-up business on the reservation will become a sub-supplier of the same world-class product line.

• **Wood Cutting:** A young, experienced forester is setting up a wood cutting business to supply both the tribe and the surrounding region with fire wood. All he needs is a good truck and good saws and he will be in business—doing exactly what he currently does as an employee for another company. The Tribal loan has been made, he has his truck and equipment, and he's up and running. His competitive advantage will be two-fold: First, he will be, on day one, the lowest cost supplier in the area, and second the tribe will be a guaranteed customer of approximately half his output. Another entrepreneurial no-brainer!

• **Pawn Shop:** There happens to be, for better or worse, an active market within Indian Nations for pawn shops. However it can be a rough and tumble business, handling firearms and often being presented with stolen goods. Fortunately, the entrepreneur hopeful who came up with this idea is amply equipped to handle it. At his day job, he's a bailiff of the Tribal courts and therefore has experience dealing with weapons as well as some pretty ornery people. Interestingly, he had been thinking about this business idea for five years, ever since he had to pawn some jewelry himself and saw the high profit margins possible in the pawn shop business. He also discovered that the closest pawn shop to the reservation was an hour away in Prescott—and he made it his business to become friends with the proprietors. As part of his start-up plan, he even established a working relationship with them wherein they will teach him the business, especially the critical art of valuing pawned items, for a small percentage commission on his first three years sales.

• **Indian Arts & Crafts:** The young woman starting this business comes from a family with a long history of making Indian arts and crafts—jewelry, dolls, baskets, and so on. Her 21st century idea is to use her wide-spread family of artisans as suppliers and establish both a retail tourist store on the reservation (right in front of the Tribe's large and thriving Casino) as well as an internet site selling her authentic Yavapai-Apache arts and crafts—direct from the reservation to the whole world.

• **Bail Bondsman:** The correct name of this business should be "Bail Bondswoman." The tribal woman starting this venture up has been a long-time employee of the Tribal judicial system, and in that capacity she has seen firsthand how difficult it is for arrested Yavapai-Apaches to make bail. It's even difficult for the families to visit them while they await trial since all tribal members are held 240 miles away in Gallup, New Mexico—because no jail around the reservation has room for them. The closest competitors are in Flagstaff to the north and Prescott to the south—and neither of these bail businesses is keen to get involved with the legally sovereign court systems of the American Indian. This will likely remain a small business—but once again it's a win-win for the tribal economy to keep as much economic activity as possible within the family.

• **TV Documentary Production:** The start-up enterpriser is a high energy, creative Apache with years of experience working for others as a cameraman and editor of videos and films. He recognized there are no TV shows in Arizona on the history and current activities of Arizona Indians. He wrangled a letter of intent, from a large and respected Phoenix based cable channel, for a 30 minute weekly TV show. I accompanied him on his first sales calls to gain advertisers—and he immediately signed up Arizona's dominant electric utility and a state-wide grocery chain which has stores on or near many reservations. He's on fire with enthusiasm about this business, and if successful within the state, hopes to expand the model across the country.

• **Sporting-Goods Store:** The proprietor of this venture is a well-known athlete in the region, having played high-school and college basketball and football and staying active in the regional sports scene as a coach. What he and his business-partner wife realized over the years is that to buy a pair of sneakers, or a football, or a set of quality golf clubs, residents and tourists have to drive to Flagstaff or Prescott. In the entire Verde Valley of Arizona, a booming growth market of 100,000 residents with another 100,000 tourists each year, there's not a single sporting-goods store. The business plan is to open a retail store in the region's residential center, extend and support it with sports clinics for young, local athletes and their coaches, and finally open a more upscale store in Sedona for tourist fishers, golfers, hikers, and hunters. This clever start-up has three great advantages going for it: First, there's not a competitor in sight. Second, the athlete-entrepreneur has instant access to, and credibility with, every school athletic department across the region, which is crucial to creating highly profitable ongoing commercial accounts. And third, his wife is prepared to follow my standard advice of not giving up her (highly paid) day job as a dealer at the tribe's casino—at least not until the first store is up and running.

The fact of the matter is none of these product/market choices are surprising. These American Indian entrepreneur hopefuls, who have diligently gone through the entrepreneur development process, are simply using the criteria they were taught to use in picking their start-up products and markets. They were told, over and over again, that whatever business they chose to start it absolutely had to effectively answer three critical questions:

• What do you love to do?

• What are you good at doing?

• What unmet needs do you see in the marketplace?

These are the three most important questions *any* entrepreneur wanabe has to answer to be successful. The participants going through the project were told that their success as a first-time entrepreneur would be enhanced ten times over if they could come up with a business idea that satisfactorily answered all three questions—and that's exactly what they did.

When working out on the Yavapai-Apache reservation, reviewing such start-up plans, and meeting face to face with the future entrepreneurs involved, I realize I'm a million miles away from the famous entrepreneurs I've interviewed and written about over the past thirty years. It's a good feeling, actually, because it brings me back down to earth as to what entrepreneurship is really all about.

Which leads to a closing thought on *Creating An Entrepreneurial Economy*. The most misunderstood point about the world's entrepreneurial boom is in fact, it's the people living at the lowest rungs of society that can benefit the most from becoming entrepreneurs. Most of us come from decent families, have had reasonably good educations, and don't live in grinding poverty. In short we have had choices in our life. Certainly we've had some choices about our careers—to work for a company, or a government agency, or to teach school—or to even start a small business. Poor and uneducated folks living at the bottom of the ladder, who are worried about getting enough to eat each day, rarely have such an array of good choices! But entrepreneurship can give them a way out. Anyone can do it—regardless of their station in life, the color of their skin, who their family is, their gender or even their formal education. If you've got a good idea (that meets the three criteria!) and you're willing to work hard, *you cannot be stopped!* This is why making entrepreneurship an option for less advantaged people is so important. It's their best, and maybe only, chance to do something important, fulfilling, and financially rewarding with their life. Entrepreneurship is truly the ultimate meritocracy for us all.

APPLICATIONS

Entrepreneurial Countries

From The Farrell Company's Creating An Entrepreneurial Economy Seminar

Editor's note: The following Applications are used in conjunction with The Farrell Company's economic and entrepreneur development projects for governments. They are included here with the hope they may be of interest and practical value to government officials, economic development specialists and teachers of entrepreneurship.

APPLICATION 1
RATING YOUR REGION'S OR COUNTRY'S ENTREPRENEURIAL SPIRIT

How does your country or region stack up against the very best in the world, in terms of the four fundamental entrepreneurial practices—as applied to an entire economy? A "1" is like Taiwan under K. T. Li. A "10" is East Germany during the iron grip of Communism. And what actions are needed to raise your country's entrepreneurial spirit?

NATIONAL SENSE OF MISSION
Does your country have a shared national mission? Is your economic strategy 'smart or stupid'? Is everyone committed? Does your culture support your strategy or block it? Are your national values maximizing your global competitive position? How do you rate on this characteristic?

| 1 | 2 | 3 | 4 | 5 | 6 | 7 | 8 | 9 | 10 |

CUSTOMER/PRODUCT COMPETITIVENESS
Does your country produce superior goods/services at lower costs than your best competitors? Do you have the highest skilled and hardest working labor force in the world? These qualities are determining the competitive position of your country! What is your global rating here?

| 1 | 2 | 3 | 4 | 5 | 6 | 7 | 8 | 9 | 10 |

NATIONAL URGENCY TO IMPROVE
Do you have a national sense of urgency about solving old problems and exploring new frontiers? Is there an attitude across the work force of 'what can I do today better than yesterday?' Do you encourage and reward innovative action across the country? What are you doing to avoid complacency and bureaucracy? Where do you rank globally on this?

| 1 | 2 | 3 | 4 | 5 | 6 | 7 | 8 | 9 | 10 |

A NATION OF SELF-INSPIRED PEOPLE
What are you, as a society, inspired about? Are your people demonstrating both higher performance and higher commitment than competitor nations? Are the positive and negative consequences in place to make all this happen? How do you compare globally on this point?

| 1 | 2 | 3 | 4 | 5 | 6 | 7 | 8 | 9 | 10 |

ACTIONS NEEDED TO RAISE THE NATION'S ENTREPRENEURIAL SPIRIT?

-
-
-

APPLICATION 2
RATING YOUR REGION'S OR COUNTRY'S CAPABILITIES TO CREATE AN ENTREPRENEURIAL ECONOMY

How does your country or region stack up against the very best in the world in terms of the three critical components required to create an entrepreneurial economy? (1 High/10 Low scale.) And what actions are needed to create a more entrepreneurial economy in your country?

ENTREPRENEUR-FRIENDLY CULTURE
Does the behavior of the nation's leaders and heroes support entrepreneurship? Does government policy show that creating an entrepreneurial economy is a high priority? Are entrepreneurs viewed as heroes or villains by average citizens, and especially young people? Where do you rank globally in having a country culture that recognizes entrepreneurship as a national value?

1   2   3   4   5   6   7   8   9   10

A BIT OF MONEY
Is individual seed money available for micro and small business start-ups: family savings, second mortgages, personal loans, even credit cards? Does the government provide any start-up financing? Is venture capital available—for first and second level financing? Do you have an active IPO market? Where do you rank globally on all forms of entrepreneur funding?

1   2   3   4   5   6   7   8   9   10

A BIT OF KNOWLEDGE
Are your citizens, and especially your young people, receiving the very best in academic and technical education? Are they learning to do things and make things the world wants to buy? Does the academic/technical establishment teach the value of entrepreneurship and innovation? Do business schools focus on managing or entrepreneuring? How do you rank, as a society, in research grants received, patents obtained and copyrights owned? Where do you rank globally in 'owning' world-class knowledge?

1   2   3   4   5   6   7   8   9   10

ACTIONS REQUIRED TO CREATE A MORE ENTREPRENEURIAL ECONOMY?

-
-
-

APPLICATION 3
ACTION PLAN FOR INVOLVING THE REGIONAL / NATIONAL LEADERSHIP

This is the first step in creating a more entrepreneurial economy. What actions should you be taking to both inform and inspire the key influencers of the community? What can you do to introduce them to the enormous positive impact entrepreneurship has on national and regional economies and the importance of obtaining their commitment to the effort. Possibilities abound: A series of 'Executive Overviews' to local and regional leaders, a large-scale PR and advertising campaign, one-on-one meetings with key influencers, testifying at government hearings, etc. Remember, the target audience should be government, business, labor, financial, educational and social leaders.

WHAT ARE THE MOST IMPORTANT ACTIONS TO TAKE?　　WHEN

1.

2.

3.

4.

5.

APPLICATION 4

ACTION PLAN FOR INSPIRING THE FUTURE ENTREPRENEURS

This Phase—inspiring and recruiting participants to come forward—is typically the most challenging segment in entrepreneur development projects. It's also the key factor determining the size and cost of the effort—and therefore the ultimate results. For these reasons we recommend significant effort be put into this phase. There are a variety of promotional and educational approaches which can used to attract the largest possible number of future entrepreneurs: Advertising and promotion campaigns are often very useful. Some countries have also found success by creating an "Entrepreneur Exposition" where everyone is invited to come learn about entrepreneur development programs and opportunities. To reach rural areas, nation-wide "road-shows" of the exposition could be considered. Finally, a series of promotional or educational outreach programs to academic and vocational high schools could be very helpful in reaching young people. Target populations include employed managers, professionals and skilled workers in all fields, university students, graduating high school students—especially from vocational schools, plus any skilled, but unemployed, persons. While potential entrepreneurs from all product/service sectors might be welcomed, special efforts should be made to encourage applicants in high growth and high job creation type businesses.

WHAT ARE THE MOST IMPORTANT ACTIONS TO TAKE?   WHEN

1.

2.

3.

4.

5.

APPLICATION 5

ACTION PLAN FOR DEVELOPING THE ENTREPRENEURS

Two kinds of training are required in any entrepreneur development project: First, and most important, would be required product and market training each applicant may need for his chosen business. This is critical. You should seriously consider creating a network of product and service training resources to be made available to the potential entrepreneurs. This critical requirement can also be reinforced in the entrepreneurship and business training. Of course solid, "non-academic" resources also have to be available for the entrepreneurship and business training. The end-result of the entrepreneur development phase should be that each new entrepreneur will have his own "Entrepreneurial Action Plan" for starting and/or growing his own business. This plan often includes additional product and market type training. Also valuable are refresher and Action Plan status sessions 30 and 90 days after initial training—as well as 6 and 12 month reviews. The 30 day refresher session can be crucial to keeping the momentum alive and solving any early problems individual entrepreneurs may have in implementing their start-up plans.

WHAT ARE THE MOST IMPORTANT ACTIONS TO TAKE   WHEN

1.

2.

3.

4.

5.

APPLICATION 6

ACTION PLAN FOR ON-GOING
SUPPORT TO THE ENTREPRENEURS

On-going support services will be critical to all the future entrepreneurs who have made it through the selection and training phases. This is where the community leadership—enlisted earlier to provide such help—can become so important. The goal is usually to create a network of public and private sector advisors/mentors to help the new entrepreneurs resolve specific enterprise issues whether they be in the areas of technology, product, market, management, legal, financial, intellectual property, government regulations, etc. The types of support most entrepreneur development programs require ranges from on-going mentoring and business advice, to help securing financing, to gaining further product and market knowledge. A network of expert, local resources should be created and made available to advise and support the new entrepreneurs in the three critical areas described in Chapter 15 of the book:

• Creating an Entrepreneur-Friendly Environment
• Securing Start-up Money
• Acquiring Additional Knowledge

WHAT ARE THE MOST IMPORTANT ACTIONS TO TAKE?   WHEN

1.

2.

3.

4.

5.

Conclusion

Getting Entrepreneurial!

DO SOMETHING GREAT!

"The managers knew how to manage but they couldn't do anything. Anyway, managing is the easy part. What's hard is inventing the world's next great product."

—Steve Jobs, Founder
Apple Computer, NeXT Inc., Pixar

Doing something at the original Apple Computer meant making a better computer, not devising a better planning system or organization chart. But then Steve Jobs never attended a management seminar. And I doubt he spends much time now boning up on the latest theories from business schools and consultants. After all he's been pretty busy creating three great companies over the past thirty years. And that's the point isn't it? Thinking about getting entrepreneurial won't mean a thing unless you first learn to make something the world needs—and figure out how to sell it. We call it *doing something great.*

DOING IT JUST FOR THE MONEY
—A RECIPE FOR DISASTER

*"People who just want to start a company because it's a good
way to become wealthy—well, they almost always fail."*

—Ed Penhoet, Co-Founder
Chiron Corporation

Our second short, concluding thought is: For God's sake, don't become
an entrepreneur just because you think it's your best shot at getting rich!

To expand on that, here's Ed Penhoet (again,) co-founder of Chiron and
mega-star of the biotech industry: "You see, you have never heard me
say that I did any of this to make money. It wasn't a motivating factor
for me. I can't say I don't enjoy the financial rewards that come with
building a successful enterprise. That would be foolish. On the other
hand, I know very few people who have been successful in any
environment who simply went at it as a way of making money. It's
almost a truism that people who are successful want to accomplish
something; and they may become wealthy as a result of what they have
contributed to society, but not the other way around. People who just
think, oh gee, it says in the paper that Herb Boyer just made $100
million starting Genentech. Well, gee, maybe I'll start a biotechnology
company too. You know, that's almost a certain recipe for disaster.
People who just want to start a company because it's a good way to
become wealthy—well, they almost always fail."

Or how about Ron Doggett, the entrepreneur who went "back-to-the-
future" with his famous Slim Jim brand? You will recall Doggett started
as a manager with giant General Mills, became a fabulously successful
entrepreneur with GoodMark Foods, and exited by selling out to
another giant, ConAgra. On the point of "doing it just for the money"
Doggett says: "If you're going after this to become rich, you're facing a
very high failure probability. I think I'm probably like everyone else
who considers themselves to be an entrepreneur. I never thought about
getting rich or the "richness" of it. I really never thought about it. I was

always in it for the next achievement, the next accomplishment, the next growth goal."

And finally, for the "take no prisoners" version, listen to Ben Tregoe. You will remember him as the articulate co-founder of Kepner-Tregoe, the firm that has taught over five million people around the world how to make rational business decisions: "If somebody starts a business, they've got to be willing to be absolutely nuts about what they're doing, and be totally dedicated to it and work a hundred hours a week, or whatever it takes—and in my experience you just don't do that unless there's something more fundamental than just saying, well, let's do this because we're going to make a few bucks at this thing."

We're not saying there's something wrong or immoral about getting rich, or even wanting to get rich. To the contrary, if you do the kind of things that the great entrepreneurs in this book have done, you deserve to get rich! Just don't get the cart before the horse. The evidence says that if getting rich is your driving force, it's tantamount to an entrepreneurial death wish. Don't take my word for it. You've just heard the same from Ed Penhoet, Ron Doggett, and Ben Tregoe. And you'll hear the same from ninety-nine of the next hundred entrepreneurs you meet. That's just about the average I've found after meeting several thousand of them over the past thirty years.

WELCOME TO THE *NEW ENTREPRENEURIAL AGE:* ONE LAST TIME

> *"The inclination of my life—has been to do things and make things which will give pleasure to people in new and amazing ways. By doing that I please and satisfy myself."*

> —Walt Disney, Founder
> The Walt Disney Company

We're now brought full circle to where we began this book, with Walt Disney's eloquent description of the entrepreneurial basics. Throughout the book we've labeled them: *Sense Of Mission*, *Customer/Product Vision*, *High-speed Innovation*, and *Self-inspired Behavior*. Most people simply call it—*the entrepreneurial spirit*.

I think there's no better way to finish this book than to repeat the short, final paragraph of the Introduction: "Achieving Disney-like appreciation for, and familiarity with, these proven, common sense practices is what I hope you will take away from this book. The goal is simple, yet profound: to learn and apply the entrepreneurial basics to create growing prosperity for yourself, your company and your country—in our downsized and uncertain 21st Century global economy."

Thanks for joining us, one more time, in **The New Entrepreneurial Age!**

INDEX

GlaxoSmithKline, 58
global economy, 15, 30-32, 34,
	95, 110, 118, 393, 443, 482

Google

	company/corporation, 78, 157,
		159, 162, 171
	Brin, Sergey, 78, 159
	Page, Larry, 78, 159
GoodMark Foods
	company/corporation, 183,
		185, 188-90, 480
	Doggett, Ron, 183-86, 189-90,
		480-81
Gratzon, Fred, 168, 172
Great Depression, the, 37, 110,
	172, 212, 239, 343
Grid Systems, 250
Grimsson, Olafur Ragnar. *See*
	Iceland
Grove, Andy. *See* Intel

	Hamper, Ben, 123, 216
Hannebicque, Hervé. *See*
	Thomson/RCA
Hastings, Don. *See* Lincoln
	Electric
Harvard University, 13, 50, 55,
	65, 76, 78, 97, 104-05, 112-
	13, 115, 134, 136, 161, 167-
	68, 177, 182, 212, 214, 295,
	317, 320, 340, 381-83, 394,
	428, 430, 435, 442, 448-49
Hertz, 288-90, 344

Hewlett-Packard
	company/corporation, 171,
		251, 443
	Hewlett, Bill, 175
	Packard, David, 175
Hewlett, Bill. *See* Hewlett
	Packard
high-speed innovation. *See*
	innovation
Hillblom, Larry. *See* DHL
Hilton, Conrad, 76
Holy Cross College, 99, 104, 448
Honda
	company/corporation, 28,
		87, 252-53, 265, 274, 297-
		98, 324, 326-28
	Honda, Soichiro, 23, 43,
		74, 87, 122, 139, 177, 297-
		98, 324-28, 331
	Chino, Tetsuo, 297
	Kume, Tadashi, 297-98, 325-26
Hong Kong, 16-17, 148, 210, 212,
	287, 292, 323, 353, 391, 398,
	405
	Horn Group, 171, 299-301
Horn, Sabrina. *See* Horn Group
Hour Glass, The 148-56, 167
Hsieh, Chi, 416
Human Genome Project, 110-12,
	118, 284
Hwee, Koh Boon. *See* Singapore
	Telecom

For sales, editorial information, subsidiary rights information
or a catalog, please write or phone or e-mail
Brick Tower Press
1230 Park Avenue, 9a
New York, NY 10128, US
Sales: 1-800-68-BRICK
Tel: 212-427-7139
www.BrickTowerPress.com
email: bricktower@aol.com.

For sales in the UK and Europe please contact our distributor,
Gazelle Book Services
Falcon House, Queens Square
Lancaster, LA1 1RN, UK
Tel: (01524) 68765 Fax: (01524) 63232
email: gazelle4go@aol.com.

For Australian and New Zealand sales please contact
Bookwise International
174 Cormack Road, Wingfield, 5013, South Australia
Tel: 61 (0) 419 340056 Fax: 61 (0)8 8268 1010
email: karen.emmerson@bookwise.com.au

CPSIA information can be obtained at www.ICGtesting.com
Printed in the USA
BVOW08s0914240114

342918BV00001B/12/P